The Changing Fortunes of Central Banking

Understanding the changing role of central banks and the novel policies they have pursued recently is absolutely essential for analysing many economic, financial and political issues, ranging from financial regulation and crisis, to exchange rate dynamics and regime changes, and QE and prolonged low interest rates. This book features contributions by many of the world's leading experts on central banking, providing in accessible essays a fascinating review of today's key policy and research issues for central banks. Luminaries including Stephen Cecchetti, Takatoshi Ito, Anil Kashyap, Mervyn King, Donald Kohn, Otmar Issing, Hyun Shin and William White are joined by Charles Goodhart of the London School of Economics, whose many achievements in the field of central banking are honoured as the inspiration for this book. *The Changing Fortunes of Central Banking* discusses the developing role of central banks and the policies they pursue in seeking monetary and financial stabilisation, while also giving suggestions for model strategies. This comprehensive review will appeal to central bankers, financial supervisors, academics and economists working in think tanks.

PHILIPP HARTMANN is Deputy Director General of the research department at the European Central Bank (ECB), which he helped to build from its beginning. He also coordinates the ECB's work on financial integration and is a Fellow of the Centre for Economic Policy Research. He has published research on financial, monetary and international issues in several books and numerous journal articles and he serves as an associate editor of the *Journal of Financial Stability*. His policy work has been published in many official reports and discussed in fora including the ECOFIN Council, the ECB Governing Council and the Basel Committee on Banking Supervision.

HAIZHOU HUANG is Managing Director at the China International Capital Corporation. He is Vice President of the China Society of World Economics and a member of the China Finance 40 Group (CF40).

He has published in leading academic and policy journals, including *American Economic Review*, *European Economic Review Journal of International Economics*, and *Journal of Monetary Economics*. He is also a special-term professor of finance at both the PBC School of Finance and Shanghai Advanced Institute of Finance.

DIRK SCHOENMAKER is Professor of Banking and Finance at Rotterdam School of Management, Erasmus University, and Senior Fellow at the Brussels-based think tank Bruegel. He is also a member of the Advisory Scientific Committee of the European Systemic Risk Board at the ECB and a Research Fellow at the Centre for European Policy Research. He has published in the areas of central banking, financial supervision and stability, European financial integration and sustainable finance.

The Changing Fortunes of Central Banking

Edited by

PHILIPP HARTMANN
European Central Bank

HAIZHOU HUANG
China International Capital Corporation

DIRK SCHOENMAKER
Erasmus University Rotterdam

CAMBRIDGE
UNIVERSITY PRESS

CAMBRIDGE
UNIVERSITY PRESS

University Printing House, Cambridge CB2 8BS, United Kingdom

One Liberty Plaza, 20th Floor, New York, NY 10006, USA

477 Williamstown Road, Port Melbourne, VIC 3207, Australia

314–321, 3rd Floor, Plot 3, Splendor Forum, Jasola District Centre, New Delhi – 110025, India

79 Anson Road, #06-04/06, Singapore 079906

Cambridge University Press is part of the University of Cambridge.

It furthers the University's mission by disseminating knowledge in the pursuit of education, learning, and research at the highest international levels of excellence.

www.cambridge.org
Information on this title: www.cambridge.org/9781108423847
DOI: 10.1017/9781108529549

First published 2018

Printed in the United Kingdom by TJ International Ltd. Padstow Cornwall

A catalogue record for this publication is available from the British Library.

ISBN 978-1-108-42384-7 Hardback

Contents

Figures

Tables

Contributors

Robert Z. Aliber, University of Chicago

Richard Berner, Stern School of Business, New York University, formerly Office of Financial Research, US Department of the Treasury

Forrest Capie, Cass Business School, City University, London

Stephen Cecchetti, Brandeis International Business School

Raphael Espinoza, International Monetary Fund

Charles Goodhart, London School of Economics

Philipp Hartmann, European Central Bank

Haizhou Huang, China International Capital Corporation

Otmar Issing, Center for Financial Studies, formerly European Central Bank

Takatoshi Ito, Columbia University

Anil Kashyap, Booth School of Business, University of Chicago

Mervyn King, London School of Economics and New York University, formerly Bank of England

Donald Kohn, Brookings Institution

Tommaso Mancini-Griffoli, International Monetary Fund

Marcus Miller, University of Warwick

Erlend Nier, International Monetary Fund

Udara Peiris, Higher School of Economics, Russia

Dirk Schoenmaker, Rotterdam School of Management, Erasmus University Rotterdam

Miguel Segoviano, International Monetary Fund

Andrew Sheng, Asia Global Institute, University of Hong Kong

Hyun Song Shin, Bank for International Settlements

Dimitrios Tsomocos, University of Oxford

Paul Tucker, Harvard Kennedy School

Alexandros Vardoulakis, Federal Reserve Board

José Viñals, International Monetary Fund

William White, Organisation for Economic Co-operation and Development, formerly Bank for International Settlements

Geoffrey Wood, Cass Business School, City University, London

Charles Wyplosz, Graduate Institute of International and Development Studies

Acknowledgement

This collection of essays celebrates the life of a great central banker, Professor Charles Goodhart. For over half a century, he has dedicated his professional life to the research and practice of central banks, shaping policy, establishing influential analysis and laying the intellectual foundations of many students.

1 | Introduction and Overview

PHILIPP HARTMANN, HAIZHOU HUANG
AND DIRK SCHOENMAKER

1.1 Introduction

This volume tells the story of the changing fortunes of central banks from powerful, narrowly targeted, monetary institutions to expanded institutions with multiple tasks and uncertain outcomes. During this journey, the central banks gained hard-fought independence in the 1990s, which they are about to lose, at least partly, under a broader monetary and financial stability mandate. When governments must provide a fiscal backstop to the financial system, they also want to have a say. The script starts with twelve key contributions from the life of a central banker, Charles Goodhart.

The first contributions concern, fittingly, monetary history. Examining the 1907 collapse of the US economy, Goodhart (1969) established in his Harvard PhD thesis, *The New York Money Market and the Finance of Trade, 1900–1913*, that part of the explanation was found in fluctuations in the banking system, which operated at the time without a central bank. The interaction between money and banking has been at the heart of central banking until today. Goodhart (1972) repeated the historical 'banking' exercise for the UK in *The Business of Banking, 1892–1914*. Another key paper on monetary history by Goodhart (2018) is 'The Bank of England, 1694–2017', which will be published shortly by the world's oldest central bank, the Sveriges Riksbank. This history examines *inter alia* the relationship between the government and the Bank of England. Goodhart identifies a general pattern that the more severe the crisis is, and the less successful the central bank is in defusing that, the more likely will it be that the government will (re)take control. Independence is not an absolute concept.

The authors would like to thank Forrest Capie, Jagjit Chadha, Charles Goodhart and Geoffrey Wood for suggestions for the Introduction.

The second set of contributions is in the area of monetary policy with Goodhart's move to the Bank of England. This period – covering the late 1960s until the early 1980s – reflects the rise and subsequent collapse of monetary aggregates. At the time, the monetarist debate in the USA (Friedman and Schwartz, 1963) was crossing the Atlantic. In a key paper, 'The Importance of Money', Goodhart and Crockett (1970) investigated whether money was a leading indicator for moves in output and prices. While initial results suggested quite a stable relationship, Goodhart (1984) discovered 'The Problems of Monetary Management: The UK Experience'. This led to the famous Goodhart's Law that 'whenever a government seeks to rely on previously observed statistical regularity for control purposes that regularity will collapse' (Goodhart, 1984, p. 96). This Law also appears to be applicable to financial regulation, as discussed below. Finally, Goodhart's (1989a) *Economic Journal* paper, 'The Conduct of Monetary Policy', makes the point that state-of-the-art macroeconomic models have a much greater tendency to revert to a (unique) equilibrium than the economy in practice. The many imperfections behind this behaviour justify more intervention and more discretion than contemporaneous theory would suggest.

A third set of papers is on the determination of the money supply. In Chapter VI of his textbook, *Money, Information and Uncertainty*, Goodhart (1989b) argues that the multiplier approach – to go from base money to broad monetary aggregates – obscures the behavioural process whereby people and institutions choose to apportion their wealth and income (see also Goodhart, 2009). More recently, Goodhart (2017) argues that is has become impossible to continue with the fiction that the central bank sets the money stock by varying the monetary base within a system in which there was a predictably stable money multiplier. As banking is a services industry, it is more relevant to find the optimal balance between the control of monetary expansion and flexibility in allowing client access to money, via borrowing from banks. This conflict between 'control' and 'flexibility' mirrors the long-running debate between the 'Currency' and 'Banking' Schools, whereby the former puts greater weight on control and the latter on flexibility. In the aftermath of a financial crisis, there is a tendency for control, even at some expense in efficiency, growth and flexibility. In contrast, the greater the prior experience of stability, and the greater the ingenuity of the bankers, the more the banking system is allowed to generate flexibility and (apparent) efficiency.

A fourth set of contributions covers the heyday of central banks, as powerful institutions with narrowly defined monetary mandates. Mainstream academics stressed time inconsistency as the principal reason for central bank dependence. Politicians will reduce interest rates just ahead of elections to stimulate employment. This argument assumes short (or no) lags in monetary policy. But Goodhart and Huang (1998) argued that there are long lags in monetary policy. Politicians are then liable to vary interest rates 'too little, too late', but not in a desire to fool people into working harder. Given the time lags, the aim of monetary policy must be to control the future forecast of inflation, i.e. inflation targeting (the next topic below). This academically inspired move to central bank independence can be remembered as a period with high spirits and expectations. Charles Goodhart was a member of the Roll Committee (1993), a committee of the great and the good from the City that paved the way for the independence of the Bank of England, and was also among the first group of external members of the Bank's Monetary Policy Committee. On the academic side, Goodhart (1994) wrote a tongue-in-cheek paper, 'Game Theory for Central Bankers: A Report to the Governor of the Bank of England', making fun of the time-inconsistency literature. On a more serious note, Capie, Goodhart and Schnadt (1994) did a major review, 'The Development of Central Banking', covering thirty-two central banks, including their rise to independence.

As the newly independent central banks started a quest for a new compass for monetary policy in the late 1980s/early 1990s, Goodhart provided supporting evidence to the parliament in Wellington for the Reserve Bank of New Zealand as the first mover towards inflation targeting in 1989. In a fifth set of papers, which include 'Strategy and Tactics of Monetary Policy: Examples from Europe and the Antipodes' (Goodhart and Viñals, 1994) and 'The Political Economy of Inflation Targets: New Zealand and the UK' (Goodhart, 2010), Goodhart made the case for inflation targeting, whereby the government sets the objective and provides the central bank autonomy to vary interest rates so as to reach the target. Next, Goodhart, Osorio and Tsomocos (2010) discuss the ongoing debate whether monetary policy should target inflation (i.e. consumer prices) or asset prices. Their results suggest that the interest rate is preferable to the money supply instrument because in times of financial distress the central bank automatically satisfies the increased demand for money (note the earlier argument of the Banking School about flexibility). While monetary policy aimed at stabilising consumer inflation, but not asset price inflation, can produce financial instability, they show that central banks' financial stability objective should be primarily achieved by regulatory measures, a topic to which we return below.

Moving on to the monetary architecture on the international scene, the sixth set of contributions covers the currency board of Hong Kong, which Charles Goodhart helped to establish in 1983. In his 'Hong Kong Financial Crisis (1983)' paper, Goodhart (1997) exposes the usual pattern of the political origins (faltering negotiations between Chairman Deng Xiaoping and Prime Minister Margaret Thatcher on the future of Hong Kong) of the subsequent monetary crisis. As the Hong Kong dollar had no anchor, the exchange rate fell and in turn so did property prices. The answer was to establish such an anchor through the Hong Kong currency board, which is one of the longest, and still existing, arrangements of its kind. In a fascinating study, Goodhart and Dai (2003) describe how the Hong Kong Monetary Authority (HKMA) coped with the speculative attack in 1998. Speculators had developed an ingenious 'double-play', simultaneously selling both the foreign exchange market and the Hang Seng equity market short; whether the authorities used an interest rate defence, or abandoned the 'link', the speculators would gain either way. Therefore, the authorities decided on a bold, unexpected and unconventional response. HKMA undertook a massive counter-intervention, again both in the equity and in the foreign exchange markets, amounting to buying up around 5 per cent of the total capitalisation of the Hang Seng equity market.

Foreign exchange markets and high-frequency data analysis, the seventh area of contributions, are important for the international financial system. In his inaugural lecture at the London School of Economics (LSE), 'The Foreign Exchange Market: A Random Walk with a Dragging Anchor', Goodhart (1988a) investigates what determines exchange rate movements. He found it hard to find evidence of either short-term overshooting or longer-term reversion to equilibrium, as predicted by theory. The interplay between those basing their views on fundamentals and those who use a random walk approach influences the market outcome. In his research, Goodhart sought to watch actual behaviour of exchange rates and to talk to practitioners, culminating in a raft of studies based on high-frequency exchange rate data. This way, he – together with a group of PhD students at the LSE – became one of the pioneers of high-frequency data analysis. For example, in *The Foreign Exchange Market*, Goodhart and Payne (2000) explain the regular patterns in intra-day foreign exchange rate activity and the effects of macroeconomic news of rates and analyse the profitability of technical trading rules in these markets. Goodhart and O'Hara (1997) review the huge spectrum of applications and the new insights that can be gained from high-frequency data analysis in financial markets in general.

The eighth set of contributions covers monetary union. While academics tend to make the economic argument for the Economic and Monetary Union (EMU) applying the theory on optimal currency areas, Goodhart (1995) recognised from the start that it was a political project, with a paper aptly titled 'The Political Economy of Monetary Union'. In a stimulating paper titled 'The Two Concepts of Money: Implications for the Analysis of Optimal Currency Areas', Goodhart (1998) draws on monetary history to examine the concept of money. The Metallists assert that the value of money lies in its ready adoption by the market as an efficient way of carrying out transactions in an 'optimal currency area'. However, the Cartalists consider instead that the value of money comes from an act of government that coerces people to use its money, in particular to pay taxes, by declaring it the sole legal tender. The Cartalists stress that a state is needed behind the currency. It is no surprise that Goodhart sides with them.

Moving to broad central banking, the ninth area covers the functions of monetary policy and financial stability and their interaction. In his epic volume *The Evolution of Central Banks*, Goodhart (1988b) examines the rationale for having central banks. In response to the Free Banking School, Goodhart argues that a *not for profit* central bank plays a necessary, stabilising role in the banking system. He thus stresses its financial stability role, including being the lender of last resort to the banking system, in the early days of central banks. In Goodhart (1987), he adds that banks are special (compared to other financial intermediaries) in requiring particular regulation, supervision and being a lender of last resort, because they combine non-marketed loans, whose true value is uncertain, with fixed-value deposits. The question of the interaction between money and banking came back at the planning for EMU in the 1990s: Should the

European Central Bank (ECB) get a narrow monetary mandate or should it be a broad central bank combining the monetary and financial stability mandates? In a paper titled 'Should the Functions of Monetary Policy and Banking Supervision Be Separated?', Goodhart and Schoenmaker (1995) seek to address that question. While there could be conflicts of interest between the two mandates, they argue that any central bank, narrow or broad, has to take into account the health of the banking system when implementing monetary policy, as banks are at the heart of the monetary transmission mechanism. With hindsight it is interesting to note that the ECB started on the narrow (Bundesbank) model and after the global financial crisis (2007–8) and the subsequent euro sovereign debt crisis (2010) has ended up on the broad (Bank of England) model combining monetary policy and banking supervision.

While central banks as well as separate supervisory agencies started to regulate and supervise banks and other financial institutions, it was not clear exactly which market failures and externalities supervisors were addressing. The tenth set of contributions starts with an influential book, *Financial Regulation: Why, How and Where Now?*, in which Goodhart, Hartmann, Llewellyn, Rojas-Suarez and Weisbrod (1998) examine the rationale. They highlight three main reasons for government intervention in the financial sector: (1) asymmetric information between customers and financial firms justifying prudential and conduct of business supervision of individual financial firms; (2) externalities in the financial system justifying the financial stability or macro-prudential role of central banks; and (3) market power of financial institutions and/or infrastructures justifying competition policy. It appears that supervisors are mainly concerned with the first, depositor protection, and wider investor/policyholder protection, partly because their political masters are mostly concerned with the protection of consumers, who are also voters. That means that externalities, or endogenous feedback loops in the financial system, get less attention. Ahead of the global financial crisis, Danielsson, Embrechts, Goodhart, Muennich, Keating, Renault and Shin (2001) warned in 'An Academic Response to Basel II' that the newly designed Basel II rules to safeguard individual banks would make the overall banking system more procyclical and fragile with self-reinforcing dynamics. They stressed the endogeneity of risk in the financial system, while the Basel II regulations assumed that risk is exogenous. Looking at the early years, in *The Basel Committee on Banking Supervision* Goodhart (2011a) argues that the Basel Committee suffered from the fallacy of composition, which concerns the idea that to safeguard the system it suffices to safeguard the components. But in trying to make themselves safer, financial firms can (be made to) behave in a way that collectively undermines the system. The Basel Committee thus failed to strengthen the stability of the financial system as a whole.

The eleventh set of contributions contains courageous endeavours to model financial stability. The great success of monetary policy in the 1990s and early 2000s was supported by models designed to forecast inflation in the medium term. If only such models were available for financial stability, central banks could also improve their track record in this domain. Back at the financial stability wing of the Bank of England, Goodhart, Sunirand and Tsomocos (2004, 2006) made a theoretical step in this direction by developing 'A Model to Analyse Financial Fragility'. This clarifies a number of issues, from problems relating to individual bank behaviour and risk-taking, to possible contagious interrelationships between banks, and the appropriate design of prudential requirements and incentives to limit 'excessive' risk-taking. Importantly, the authors use heterogeneous commercial banks, allowing them to study the interaction between banks. By doing so, they deviate from the representative agent approach, which is dominant in academic macroeconomics.

The twelfth and final contribution covers the new challenges for central banks after the global financial crisis. Taking a long-term view, Goodhart (2011b) identifies four periods in 'The Changing Role of Central Banks'. The first (Victorian) and third (1980–2007) epochs of central banking were characterised by highly successful monetary regimes (gold standard and inflation targeting, respectively), reliance on market mechanisms and independent central banks. Post World War I, the first epoch came to a crashing halt in the Great Depression (the second epoch), and deflation then led to a period of government domination, direct controls and subservient central banks. Goodhart (2011b) argues that there is a good chance we will have a repeat of the second epoch, with more intrusive regulation and greater government involvement (e.g. in bank resolution and with a bank tax). The old Scottish saying that 'he who pays the piper calls the tune' is still applicable. Goodhart predicts that the idea of the central bank as an independent institution will be put aside in these areas, while the operational independence in setting the official short-term rate may stay.

1.2 Overview of the Book

The above contributions provide an excellent introduction to the chapters in this volume. They cover the same topics, as most authors have been colleagues and/or co-authors of Charles Goodhart.

Part I contains contributions relating to monetary economics and policy. Chapter 2 in this volume is by the former Governor of the Bank of England, Mervyn King, with the title 'Money: How Could Economists Do without It?' King argues that monetary economics has given up the idea of money, by focusing on the real interest rate in a simple model of a single commodity and a single inter-temporal price (i.e. the real interest rate). This simple model cannot tackle questions about the consequences of the massive expansion of central bank balance sheets and base money (i.e. quantitative easing), and of the impact of negative interest rates on private sector behaviour. King highlights that a more sophisticated understanding of the monetary and financial sectors of our economies is needed.

Chapter 3, by Forrest Capie and Geoffrey Wood, both of Cass Business School, is titled 'Monetary Control in the UK: The Impossible Dream?' They discuss the difficulties of monetary control under different exchange rate regimes following World War II. After attempts to control the money supply domestically (e.g. under the 'Competition and Credit Control' approach) had foundered, resort was made to an external constraint. When the sterling–Deutschmark link subsequently collapsed, the UK adopted an inflation-targeting regime, with no mention of money or monetary control. The authors, like Mervyn King, discern signs of a return of money in monetary policy discussions.

In Chapter 4, Paul Tucker, former Deputy Governor of the Bank of England, discusses central bank independence in his chapter titled 'Pristine and Parsimonious Policy: Can Central Banks Ever Get Back to It and Why They Should Try'. Tucker begins by noting that central banks are more powerful now than they have been for almost a century, which has contributed to discomfort and criticism. He argues that central bank mandates need to comply with general criteria for the legitimacy of unelected power. He finally develops general principles for constraining central bank balance sheet management, with the aim of achieving an appropriate demarcation between monetary policy and fiscal territory.

Chapter 5, by Donald Kohn, Brookings Institution, carries the title 'Central Bank Talk about Future Monetary Policy: Lessons from the Crisis and Beyond'. Forward guidance about future policy actions (or pledge of lack of action) has come into much wider and more intensive use since policy interest rates approached zero in the fall of 2008. But time-based guidance is not compatible with the considerable uncertainties that surround our knowledge of how the economy works. Kohn argues such guidance should be exited as policy rates lift off.

Chapter 6, by Hyun Song Shin, Economic Adviser and Head of Research at the Bank for International Settlements (BIS), is titled 'Bank Capital and Monetary Policy Transmission'. Shin notes that standard macroeconomic models make little explicit mention of banks. But how banks manage their balance sheets has implications for monetary policy and financial stability. Shin provides two examples. First, while research supports the notion that soundly capitalised banks enjoy lower funding costs and lend more, banks still pay substantial dividends instead of improving their capital base through retained earnings. Second, the usual relationship that lower interest rates engender more lending may break down when market rates turn negative. Negative interest rates may weaken bank profitability, given that deposit rates rarely follow policy rates below zero. Shin concludes that a better understanding of banks' funding methods is important to assess the macroeconomic outcomes of monetary policy.

The monetary economics and policy part concludes with Chapter 7, 'When are Central Banks More Likely to Target Asset Prices?', in which Haizhou Huang, Managing Director at China International Capital Corporation, examines central banks' monetary policy operations. Focusing on the working of the transmission channels and their interaction with the balance sheets of banks, firms and households, Huang finds that central banks are more likely to implement a monetary policy that targets asset prices during times of crisis. He also obtains empirically that developing and banking-based economies intend to target asset prices more directly, even during non-crisis times.

Part II contains contributions relating to financial stability and regulatory policy. In Chapter 8, 'The Macroprudential Toolkit', Richard Berner, former Director of the Office of Financial Research at the US

Treasury, stresses the need for a policy framework for financial stability. Key ingredients are: an ongoing assessment of potential threats; high-quality data to inform that assessment; a comprehensive policy toolkit; criteria to assess the effectiveness of the tools; and clear governance, and roles and responsibilities to assure implementation. Although there are significant improvements in financial system resilience and the tools to promote it, Berner makes suggestions to enhance the macroprudential toolkit and the institutional framework to implement it.

Chapter 9, by José Viñals, Tommaso Mancini-Griffoli and Erlend Nier at the International Monetary Fund (IMF), is titled 'Three Cooks or Three Wise Men? The Interplay between Monetary, Macroprudential and Microprudential Policies in Supporting Financial Stability'. The authors note that monetary, macroprudential and microprudential policies all affect financial stability. Moreover, the policies are not independent of one another. They find that a clear allocation of objectives and instruments is best able to achieve a safer financial system, and that appropriate institutional arrangements are needed to harness complementarities and reduce conflicts. The three policies can reinforce and complement each other like 'three wise men'.

Chapter 10, 'Liquidity, Default and the Interaction of Financial Stability and Monetary Policy', is authored by Dimitrios Tsomocos at the University of Oxford, together with Udara Peiris at the Higher School of Economics, Russia and Alexandros Vardoulakis at the Federal Reserve Board. The authors argue that the assessment of both liquidity and default within a framework of missing financial markets, multiple currencies, heterogeneous economic actors and multiple externalities is needed for analysing the interplay of financial and price stability. The complementarity and substitutability of regulatory and monetary policies can be examined. The optimal policy mix may be subsequently determined given the objectives of the fiscal and monetary authorities.

Chapter 11, 'Systemic Risk Quantification for Macroprudential Stress Testing', is by Miguel Segoviano and Raphael Espinoza at the IMF. While the devastating effects of systemic risk are well known, the quantification of losses due to systemic risk amplification mechanisms between banks and non-banks within the financial system, and their incorporation into macroprudential stress-testing frameworks remains challenging. The authors develop a novel framework for estimating systemic risk amplification losses based on readily available supervisory and market information. The framework enables policymakers to quantify the likelihood and intensity of contagion events.

In Chapter 12, 'What Binds? Interactions between Bank Capital and Liquidity Regulations', Stephen Cecchetti of the Brandeis International Business School and Anil Kashyap of the Booth School of Business examine the working of supervisory rules. The authors present a simplified framework in which the risk-weighted capital ratio, the leverage ratio, the liquidity coverage ratio and the net stable funding ratio are all related to a small set of fundamental bank balance sheet characteristics. Next, they examine the interactions among the requirements to understand which are likely to bind. Cecchetti and Kashyap conclude that the two liquidity requirements will almost never bind at the same time and that stress tests can change which of the two capital requirements binds.

In Chapter 13, which concludes the financial stability and regulatory policy part, Dirk Schoenmaker of Erasmus University Rotterdam poses the question 'Is Burden Sharing Needed for international Financial Stability?' Schoenmaker begins by noting that a credible fiscal backstop is needed to underpin banking stability. But is such a backstop feasible in an international banking system? First, the fiscal capacity of the home country can be limited. Small and medium-sized countries have therefore started a process of downsizing their banks. Next, the home country only cares about the domestic externalities of its banks in crisis times. Schoenmaker argues that countries can only address this issue through some form of burden sharing, if we want to maintain international banking as well as financial stability.

Part III moves on to the topic of foreign exchanges and international architecture. Chapter 14, by Charles Wyplosz of the Graduate Institute Geneva is titled 'The Case for (and Requirements of) Monetary Unions'. The founding fathers were focused on the essentials: central bank independence backed by fiscal discipline. The sceptics correctly observed that a central bank must be ready to lend in last resort, which creates liabilities that fiscally independent countries may refuse to accept. To enhance monetary union, Wyplosz argues that: the central bank must be concerned with financial stability (including having to lend as lender of last resort); collective supervision and backstops are needed for banks; central bank management must be shielded from political pressure; fiscal discipline must be constitutionally guaranteed at the proper level.

In Chapter 15, Takatoshi Ito of Columbia University discusses the market microstructure of foreign exchange markets with the intriguing title 'Machines versus Humans: Will Human Forex Dealers Become Extinct?' By the early 2000s, the interbank human brokers were almost all replaced by electronic broking systems, which centralised interbank forex trading. While bank computers made the market more efficient and more liquid, high-frequency trading strategies turned away human dealers. Many microstructure changes in the 2010s, such as minimum quote life and retreating from decimalisation to half pip price unit, were designed to protect human dealers. Human dealers may provide heterogeneity among market participants that may prevent a potential flash crash.

Chapter 16 is by Robert Z. Aliber of the University of Chicago and critically examines flexible exchange rates with the title 'The Case for Flexible Exchange Rates Revisited'. The positive claims of the advantages of a floating currency arrangement (notably monetary policy independence) depend on an implicit assumption that investor demand for foreign securities would be constant despite various money market shocks. Yet, the banking crises over the last forty years resulted from an increase in cross border investment inflows to a country, which led to an increase in the price of its currency and an increase in the demand for (and price of) its securities and an economic boom. Aliber argues that the case for flexible exchange rates is flawed as a guide to policy.

Chapter 17, by Marcus Miller of the University of Warwick, is titled 'Cross-Border Banking and Monetary Independence: Difficult Partners'. First, he examines how, with cross-border banking, financial crisis can spread internationally irrespective of the exchange rate regime. Second, he looks at why appropriate regulation must take account of 'externalities', particularly those operating through asset prices. With Value-at-Risk rules and mark-to-market pricing alone, the financial system can exhibit 'catastrophic' behaviour. Miller concludes that with cross-border banking, a floating exchange rate cannot ensure monetary independence. Prudential regulation is a more relevant policy option.

Chapter 18, 'International Liquidity', is the final chapter in Part III. Here Philipp Hartmann of the ECB discusses how international liquidity has evolved before, during and after the financial crisis. Based on a framework that is broader than the ones recently used by the BIS, the IMF or academic scholars, he does not find a general shortage of liquidity across the five dimensions considered. The reasons behind diverse developments point to a number of important policy considerations. For example, financial regulation has to preserve incentives for market making, spillovers of extreme unconventional monetary policies cannot be ignored, soaring corporate cash hoarding needs to be brought back into real investment, and large public debt overhangs suggest that fiscal consolidation would be a sustainable avenue for re-increasing the availability of liquid and safe international assets.

Finally, Part IV covers the millennium challenges of central banks. In Chapter 19, Otmar Issing, former Chief Economist of the ECB, discusses central bank independence with the title 'Overburdened Central Banks: Can Independence Survive?' Issing argues that expectations have been exaggerated regarding the role of central banks, not only in crisis management but beyond, in controlling the macroeconomic situation. Central banks are overburdened with new responsibilities and competences. It will be hard, if not impossible, to meet those heightened expectations. As a consequence, the status of their independence will come under heavy pressure.

Chapter 20, by Andrew Sheng of the Asia Global Institute, analyses central bank balance sheets under the title 'Central Banks, National Balance Sheets and Global Balance'. Central banks manipulate their balance sheets to achieve their monetary policy and financial stability goals. Given the rising size of their balance sheets, central bank balance sheets are no longer independent of national and even global balance sheets. Using recently available net international investment positions, Sheng examines how reserve currency countries can run up large deficits in trade and capital accounts, so long as these are financed by the surplus countries. He also shows that monetary policy by the reserve currency countries can facilitate capital account flows larger than trade flows, so that global imbalances could become exacerbated by central bank balance sheets.

William White, former Economic Advisor of the Bank for International Settlements, discusses the shortcomings of modern macroeconomics in Chapter 21, titled 'Recognising the Economy as a Complex, Adaptive System: Implications for Central Banks'. While monetary policy has been conducted for decades on the basis of a simple, understandable and stable model, White argues that the economy is a complex adaptive system like many others found in both nature and society. Monetary policy could thus draw lessons from other disciplines. While taking steps to 'lean against' rapid credit growth to reduce the likelihood of financial crises, steps must also be taken to deal with crises when they do occur. Central banks should also adapt to the associated need to cooperate more actively with other arms of government. White concludes that there are limits to central bank independence.

In the final chapter, Chapter 22, Charles Goodhart of the London School of Economics provides a lucid tale: 'The Changing Fortunes of Central Banking'. During the last fifty years there have been some dramatic changes in the powers, role and functions of central banks, with more independent power to vary interest rates in pursuit of price stability, and more powers to regulate and supervise key financial institutions in pursuit of financial stability. Goodhart discusses the underlying causes of such trends. He concludes with a brief 'wish-list' about what differing characteristics he would like to see in such a braver new world. The first item on this wish list is to stop anthropomorphising banks. Strategy is set, and decisions are taken, by individuals – mainly senior bank managers, especially the chief executive officer (CEO) – not by an institution. The second item is the reform of housing finance. The typical financial boom/bust cycle has involved the interaction of a property price cycle with a bank lending cycle. The worst mix which we had was the finance of long-term mortgages, with a small equity buffer, on the basis of short-term, wholesale, runnable bank funding. What is needed, since property finance is, by nature, long term, is some combination of a much larger equity buffer with finance provided by much longer-term funding, e.g. covered bonds. The third item is to remove the fiscal advantages for debt finance. There is a need to shift the balance of advantage more towards equity and away from debt finance. The fourth item is that central bank economists need to combine macroeconomics and finance/financial expertise, and the recruitment needs of central banks require university curricula that combine the two.

1.3 Conclusion

The main conclusion of this volume on the changing fortunes of central banking is that a 'full' central bank is responsible for both monetary and financial stability, which are inextricably linked. These central banking functions form two sides of the same coin. Studying the one without the other is at one's peril. On the monetary side, several authors in this volume argue for the return of money in our models. On the financial side, the design and use of macro-models without financial frictions (or financial intermediaries) should be something of the past. The common denominator of the two sides is the overlap between money and banks. Next, financial stability models with only exogenous shocks and no endogenous feedback loops should also be mistrusted. The chapters in this volume contribute to the challenging research agenda in these areas.

Another important conclusion is that central banks cannot work in isolation. The cross-border linkages in the international monetary and financial system create important interdependencies. While central bank governors have had a long-standing practice of monthly meetings in Basel, the Financial Stability Board has become a focal point for finance ministries, central bankers and financial supervisors to discuss the international agenda for regulatory reform in the aftermath of the global financial crisis. The expanding tasks of central banks both in monetary policy with quantitative easing and in financial stability with macroprudential policy take them closer to the fiscal authority (i.e. the government) and threaten the cherished independence of government. The room for independent manoeuvre of central banks has thus decreased, both internationally and nationally.

A final conclusion of this volume is that incentives matter for behaviour. An important distorting incentive is that the cost of debt is deductible for corporate tax, while that of equity is not. This leads to excessive debt financing, which makes the financial system extra fragile. The IMF (2016) has dubbed this the Great Distortion. Academics and policymakers are united in their call for an equivalent treatment of the cost of debt and equity for tax purposes.

While central banks' fortunes are changing, a much deeper understanding of the importance of central banks and their role in, and interactions with, monetary policy and financial stability, as well as economic growth and society at large, is needed. The collection of chapters in this volume not only celebrates the life of a great central banker in our time, but also opens new avenues for policy making and academic research in central banking in a challenging world.

References

Capie, F., C. Goodhart and N. Schnadt (1994), 'The Development of Central Banking', in F. Capie, C. Goodhart, S. Fischer and N. Schnadt (eds.), *The Future of Central Banking*, Cambridge: Cambridge University Press, pp. 1–252.

Danielsson, J., P. Embrechts, C. Goodhart et al. (2001), 'An Academic Response to Basel II', *Financial Markets Group*, Special Paper, 130, LSE.

Friedman, M. and Anna J. Schwartz (1963), *A Monetary History of the United States, 1867–1960*, Princeton, NJ: Princeton University Press.

Goodhart, C. (1969), *The New York Money Market and the Finance of Trade, 1900–1913*, Cambridge, MA: Harvard University Press.

    (1972), *The Business of Banking, 1892–1914*, London: Weidenfeld and Nicolson.

    (1984), 'The Problems of Monetary Management: The UK Experience', in C. Goodhart, Chapter III, *Monetary Theory and Practice*, London: Macmillan.

    (1987), 'Why Do Banks Need a Central Bank?', *Oxford Economic Papers*, 39(1), pp. 75–89.

    (1988a), 'The Foreign Exchange Market: A Random Walk with a Dragging Anchor', *Economica*, 55(220), pp. 437–60.

    (1988b), *The Evolution of Central Banks*, Cambridge, MA: MIT Press.

    (1989a), 'The Conduct of Monetary Policy', *Economic Journal*, 99(396), pp. 293–346.

    (1989b), *Money, Information and Uncertainty*, 2nd edition, London: Macmillan Education UK.

    (1994), 'Game Theory for Central Bankers: A Report to the Governor of the Bank of England', *Journal of Economic Literature*, 32(1), pp. 101–14.

    (1995), 'The Political Economy of Monetary Union', in P. Kenen (ed.), *Understanding Interdependence: The Macroeconomics of the Open Economy*, Princeton, NJ: Princeton University Press.

    (1997), 'Hong Kong Financial Crisis (1983)', in D. Glasner (ed.), *Business Cycles and Depressions: An Encyclopedia*, New York, NY: Garland Publishing Inc.

    (1998), 'The Two Concepts of Money: Implications for the Analysis of Optimal Currency Areas', *European Journal of Political Economy*, 14, pp. 407–32.

    (2009), 'The Continuing Muddles of Monetary Theory: A Steadfast Refusal to Face Facts', *Economica*, 76(s1), pp. 821–30.

    (2010), 'The Political Economy of Inflation Targets: New Zealand and the UK', in R. Leeson (ed.), *Canadian Policy Debates and Case Studies in Honour of David Laidler*, London: Palgrave Macmillan, pp. 171–208.

(2011a), *The Basel Committee on Banking Supervision*, Cambridge: Cambridge University Press.

(2011b), 'The Changing Role of Central Banks', *Financial History Review*, 18(2), pp. 135–54.

(2017), 'The Determination of the Money Supply: Flexibility versus Control', *The Manchester School*, 85(s1), pp. 33–56.

(2018), 'The Bank of England, 1694–2017', in *Central Banks*, Sveriges Riksbank, forthcoming.

Goodhart, C. and A. Crockett (1970), The Importance of Money, *Bank of England Quarterly Bulletin*, 10(2), pp. 159–98.

Goodhart, C. and L. Dai (2003), *Intervention to Save Hong Kong*, Oxford: Oxford University Press.

Goodhart, C., P. Hartmann, D. Llewellyn, L. Rojas-Suarez and S. Weisbrod (1998), *Financial Regulation: Why, How and Where Now?*, London: Routledge.

Goodhart, C. and H. Huang (1998), 'Time Inconsistency in a Model with Lags, Persistence, and Overlapping Wage Contracts', *Oxford Economic Papers*, 50(3), 378–96.

Goodhart, C. and M. O'Hara (1997), 'High Frequency Analysis in Financial Markets: Issues and Applications', *Journal of Empirical Finance*, 4(2–3), pp. 73–114.

Goodhart, C., C. Osorio and D. Tsomocos (2010), 'The Optimal Monetary Policy Instrument: Inflation versus Asset Price Targeting, and Financial Stability', in D. Cobham, Ø. Eitrheim, S. Gerlach and J. Qvigstad (eds.), *Twenty Years of Inflation Targeting: Lessons Learned and Future Prospects*, Cambridge: Cambridge University Press.

Goodhart, C. and R. Payne (2000), *The Foreign Exchange Market*, London: Macmillan.

Goodhart, C. and D. Schoenmaker (1995), 'Should the Functions of Monetary Policy and Banking Supervision Be Separated?', *Oxford Economic Papers*, 47(4), 539–60.

Goodhart, C., P. Sunirand and D. Tsomocos (2004), 'A Model to Analyse Financial Fragility: Applications', *Journal of Financial Stability*, 1(1), pp. 1–30.

(2006), 'A Model to Analyse Financial Fragility', *Economic Theory*, 27(1), pp. 107–42.

Goodhart, C. and J. Viñals (1994), 'Strategy and Tactics of Monetary Policy: Examples from Europe and the Antipodes', in J. Fuhrer (ed.), *Goals, Guidelines, and Constraints Facing Monetary Policymakers*, Boston, MA: Federal Reserve Bank of Boston, pp. 139–87.

International Monetary Fund (2016), 'Tax Policy, Leverage And Macroeconomic Stability', *IMF Policy Paper*, 7 October.

Roll, E., Chairman of an Independent Panel's Report (1993), *Independent and Accountable: A New Mandate for the Bank of England*, London: Centre for Economic Policy Research.

PART I

Monetary Economics and Policy

2 | *Money*

How Could Economists Do without It?

MERVYN KING

It was said of one British economist that if you read his work in the reverse order to that in which it had been written, you could see that the subject made some progress. The same might be said today about the subject of monetary economics. All of the richness of the analysis of a wide variety of financial instruments, and their role as part of an optimal portfolio, inherent in the writings on monetary economics in the 1950s and 1960s, as well as the insights of Hayek, Keynes, Robertson and Simons during the interwar period, has been lost as the profession has converged on a simple model of a single commodity and a single inter-temporal price, the real interest rate. Money has disappeared from the picture altogether. Earlier generations of monetary economists would be baffled.

One man who has stood out against these developments is Charles Goodhart, whom I regard as Mr Monetary Economics of the United Kingdom. As an academic and senior economist at the Bank of England, Goodhart always accepted that it was important to understand the demand for, and supply of, money to appreciate the impact of central bank policy. It was not enough to think in terms of 'the' interest rate. Of course, all models make simplifying assumptions; that is why they are models. But models which assume a representative household, so ruling out internal debt, and ignore the role of banks and the structure of financial instruments do not offer much help when trying to understand the causes and consequences of a major financial crisis. New Keynesian models, and their translation into mathematical form as dynamic stochastic general equilibrium (DSGE) models, omit money and banks altogether. Even in his eightieth year, Goodhart (2016) raised some pertinent questions about the consequences of the massive expansion of central bank balance sheets and base money, and of the impact of negative interest rates on private sector behaviour. None of these questions can be tackled seriously without a more sophisticated understanding of the monetary and financial sectors of our economies than is present in the models taught to graduate students and incorporated into the forecasting models in most central banks.

Charles Goodhart was the progenitor of studies on the demand for money in the Bank of England (the key paper is that by Goodhart and Crockett of 1970). On the one hand, this research supported the view that monetary aggregates not only were important determinants of spending and inflation, but could also be controlled by prices, in large part interest rates, set by the central bank. This view was in contrast to the weight placed on broader measures of liquidity by the Radcliffe Committee (1959). On the other hand, Goodhart and other economists at the Bank of England were only too well aware that changes in the institutional arrangements for the financial sector could lead to shifts in the demand for money. The introduction in 1971 of *Competition and Credit Control*, which abolished the cartel among UK clearing banks that had fixed spreads between deposit and loan rates, was such a change, and led to a surge in broad money as banks offered higher interest rates, so boosting the demand for bank deposits (see Capie and Wood in Chapter 3 of this volume for more on Competition and Credit Control). Strikingly, throughout this period there was no system of formal regulation of banks. The informal approach to bank supervision adopted after the wave of greater competition in the 1970s was superseded by the Banking Act of 1979 which for the first time provided a legal basis for bank supervision in the UK.

One of the great virtues of the approach which Charles Goodhart fostered in the Bank might be described as 'pragmatic monetarism'. Both words matter. In an attempt to bring down inflation from its peak of 27 per cent in 1975, the UK government, Labour and Conservative administrations, turned to monetary targets as a way of introducing discipline into macroeconomic policy. Decisions on both monetary and fiscal policy were taken by the government, with the Bank of England left to implement rather than initiate policy. After many attempts to devise an appropriate monetary target, the results for the ultimate objectives of policy were better than those for the intermediate target variables. Inflation did fall, despite a deep recession in the early 1980s, but the monetary aggregates seemed not to behave in a predictable manner. As a result, the UK then first informally pegged sterling against the Deutschmark and then formally joined the Exchange Rate Mechanism in 1990, only to be ejected in September 1992.

Goodhart's contribution was both to be pragmatic and to care about money. In the period of the 1970s through 1990s, the pragmatic approach led Goodhart (1984) to be sceptical of a rigid adherence to a particular monetary aggregate. But it never prevented him from thinking that money was important, a trait that has infected much of the modelling of monetary policy subsequently. Looking back on this period, it is striking that monetarists exaggerated the predictability and stability of the demand for money, whereas later generations of economists forgot about the significance of money and its special role in a capitalist economy. As I wrote in *The End of Alchemy*, 'it is ironic that economists who believe that money matters ... argue that the demand for money is highly stable, whereas Keynesian economists argue that money does not matter because its demand is unstable. Both groups are wrong – money really matters when there are large and unpredictable jumps in the demand for it' (King, 2016, p. 182).

There is a paradox in the role of money in the analysis of economic policy today. It is that as price stability has become recognised as the central objective of central banks, the attention actually paid by central banks to money has declined. It is no accident that during the 'Great Inflation' of the post-war period money was ignored by much of the economic establishment in the UK as a causal factor for inflation. In the late 1970s, the counter-revolution in economics – the idea that in the long run money affected the price level and not the level of output – returned money to centre stage in economic policy. As Milton Friedman (1963) put it, 'inflation is always and everywhere a monetary phenomenon'. If inflation was a monetary phenomenon, then controlling the supply of money was the route to low inflation. Monetary aggregates became central to the conduct of monetary policy. But the passage to low inflation proved painful. Nor, as mentioned above in the UK context, did the monetary aggregates respond kindly to the attempts by central banks to impose control.

Therefore, as central banks became more and more focused on achieving price stability, defined in terms of an explicit target for the rate of inflation, less and less attention was paid to movements in money. Indeed, the decline of interest in money appeared to go hand-in-hand with success in maintaining low and stable inflation. How do we explain the apparent contradiction that the acceptance of the idea that inflation is a monetary phenomenon has been accompanied by the lack of any reference to money in the conduct of monetary policy during its most successful period?

Of course, some central banks, especially the Bundesbank and the Swiss National Bank, always paid a good deal of attention to monetary aggregates.[1] When the European Central Bank acquired responsibility for monetary policy in 1999, it adopted a reference value for money growth as one of its two pillars of monetary policy, with an assessment of the outlook for inflation as the other. Elsewhere, the Federal Reserve, at its own request, was relieved of the statutory requirement, imposed in 1978, to report twice a year on its target ranges for the growth of money and credit.

The conventional resolution of the paradox to which I have referred is that, in the modern world, monetary policy is determined by the short-term interest rate set by central banks and not by changes in money supply. Although correlated with the price level in the long run, the supply of money is determined as a residual and is not itself an independent explanatory variable determining either inflation in the long run or output in the short run. In short, interest rates are a sufficient statistic of the stance of monetary policy.

The view that money does not matter has been encouraged by those who point to regressions of inflation and output on monetary growth, and find that the influence of money is either insignificant or unstable. A well-known example is the paper by Estrella and Mishkin (1997), which regressed inflation in the USA on lagged values of output, money growth and inflation itself, and found that the influence of money, while varying with the sample period, was not significant over the period 1979–5. But these results, although seemingly striking, tell us little about the significance of money in the transmission mechanism of monetary policy. They are based on what economists call reduced-form equations, the coefficients of which will be complex functions of the true structural parameters of the economy, as well as expectations of future policy responses by the monetary authorities. There is no reason to expect a simple relationship between inflation and output and money growth in reduced-form estimates. This last

---

[1] The Swiss National Bank later replaced its target for the monetary aggregates with one for inflation.

point was clearly grasped by Friedman and Schwartz (1963) in their classic study of money in the USA. They took great care to identify periods in which there was an exogenous shock to the money supply, such as moves onto and off the gold standard, and changes in reserve requirements imposed on banks. Hence the interpretation of time-series data for money and inflation is not straightforward.

In the short run, an increase in money is divided between a rise in prices and a rise in output, as has been clearly understood since the essay on money by David Hume (1752). Yet the transmission mechanism between a change in the supply of money and its effects, first, on demand and output and, second, on prices remains contentious. In modelling the transmission mechanism, economists have tended to rely on two types of 'rigidities' which introduce time lags into the process by which changes in money lead to changes in prices. These are lags in the adjustment of prices and wages to changes in demand – so-called 'nominal rigidities' – and lags in the adjustment of expectations to changes in the monetary policy regime – so-called 'expectational rigidities'. These rigidities mean that money affects real variables in the short run and prices in the long run. Although the existence of a short-run trade-off between inflation and output, and the long-run neutrality of money, are both well founded empirically, the theoretical underpinnings of both nominal and expectational rigidities are weak.

The theoretical difficulties in the modelling of monetary policy are well captured by Friedman's dictum that there are 'long and variable' time lags between changes in policy and their impact on inflation (Friedman, 1961, p. 464). To understand these theoretical shortcomings, it is helpful to consider an abbreviated history of the models used by economists to analyse the impact of money. For much of the post-war period, the standard or consensus model used for macroeconomic analysis comprised four basic equations. Of course, econometricians disaggregated these into models of greater size and with a varying degree of success. But the basics are included in these four equations. First, there was an equation for aggregate demand which related total demand (or output) to either money or interest rates and to expected inflation. The aggregate demand function is sometimes known as the 'IS' curve. Second, there was an equation describing the supply side of the economy in which total output was related to differences between expected and actual inflation; this is the

'Phillips–Lucas supply curve'. Third, there was an equation for the demand for money relating broad money holdings to total expenditures and the interest rate: the 'LM' curve. Fourth, there was an equation describing monetary policy in which the supply of broad money was determined by the actions of the central bank in controlling base money (bank reserves plus notes and coins in circulation), which in turn influenced broad money provided by the banking system through the 'money multiplier'. This equation represented the monetary policy reaction function of the central bank. The model determined the values of output, inflation, the interest rate and money growth.

Most models used to analyse monetary policy were based on a variant of this four-equation system, with increasing importance given to the role of expectations in the Phillips curve as thinking developed. In this framework, an unexpected increase in the money supply reduces the nominal interest rate in order to persuade households to hold larger money balances. If inflation expectations are slow to adjust to the increase in the money supply – because of expectational rigidities – then the fall in the nominal interest rate also implies a fall in the real rate of interest. This raises expenditures on items such as investment and consumer durables which are sensitive to interest rates. If prices and wages are slow to adjust to higher demand, because of nominal rigidities – then in the short run firms are induced to supply more output. As the pressure on capacity in the economy rises, employees demand higher wages to reflect increased demand and both wages and prices rise. In the long run output is determined solely by real factors, and the increase in money supply is reflected in a rise in the price level.

More recently, the analysis of monetary policy has been conducted within a model that is similar in many respects to the traditional model, but where the equation for money supply is replaced by an explicit feedback rule for interest rates. The money demand equation plays no explicit role in determining output, inflation and interest rates. Money, it would appear, has been eased out of the picture. In these models, a loosening of monetary policy – characterised by an unexpected reduction in the nominal interest rate – raises demand, output and, ultimately, inflation. In the long run the inflation rate is determined by monetary policy, in the sense that the monetary policy reaction function determining interest rates contains an explicit inflation target.

Most central-bank forecasting models are based on this conceptual framework. In practice, two problems have arisen with such models.

First, as both Charles Goodhart and I experienced during our time as members of the Monetary Policy Committee, the assumption of a policy reaction function means that whatever policy is followed in the short run inflation always comes back to the target in the medium term. In other words, the credibility of the inflation target is taken as given. But over the past twenty years, there were several instances when the experience of prolonged shocks to inflation – either above or below target – raised the question of whether the target still had complete credibility. The model was uninformative on that. And in Japan today, the belief that simply announcing a higher target for inflation, having missed a lower target for a considerable period, will result in its achievement begs the question of the credibility of the central bank. Simply to assume that misses the main challenge facing the Bank of Japan.

The second problem is that official short-term interest rates have fallen effectively to zero in recent years. Therefore, the policy rule has had to be replaced by a judgement on measures to affect directly the supply of money. But the 'money multiplier' between base money which the central bank can control and broader measures of the money supply has collapsed. The link between base and broad money is weak. Central banks have had to generate substantial increases in base money in order to bring about relatively small changes in broad money growth. The increase in base money is not generating inflation because of a substantial jump in private-sector demand for liquidity in the wake of the financial crisis.

The question of whether monetary policy is impotent when interest rates are at, or close to, zero has remained open since the possibility of a 'liquidity trap' was suggested by Keynes (1936) in *The General Theory*. Broadly speaking, there are two answers to this question. The first is that monetary policy is indeed impotent when interest rates are zero. At this point, households and firms have an infinitely elastic demand for money balances, and so any increase in money supply is absorbed passively in higher balances. An increase in money supply has no implications for spending or output. In such circumstances, the only way to affect the economy is by an expansionary fiscal policy. The second answer is that, at some point, households and firms become satiated with money balances, and any attempt to increase further the money supply leads them to adjust portfolios in order to limit their holding of money balances. These changes in household portfolios lead to changes in relative yields on different financial and real assets, and hence on asset prices and so spending. Despite interest rates remaining at zero, monetary policy, in this world, can influence nominal spending. The sheer scale of base money creation by central banks in the industrialised world during recent years has shown that money creation can indeed affect spending, although there are limits as to how effective it can be.

The channel by which money must influence behaviour is through changes in risk premia. This is consistent with the observation that if interest rates are held constant, then the pure expectations theory of the term structure of interest rates, and the uncovered interest parity arbitrage theory of exchange rates, offer no way out for monetary policy to affect economic behaviour. If future interest rates are incorporated into optimal consumption behaviour, then the only channel by which monetary policy can operate – other than via interest rates – is through changes in risk premia. A rigorous model of the monetary transmission mechanism will, therefore, require a more rigorous and fully articulated theory of risk premia than is currently available.

Where might we look to find a rigorous theory of the impact of money on risk premia? Little help will come from traditional finance theory. The reason is extremely simple. Most finance theory is based on the assumption that equilibrium yields on assets, including risk premia, are independent of the quantities of the supplies of different assets. Hence the search for a better model of the monetary transmission mechanism is, in part, a search for evidence of supply effect on financial asset yields. That is why the view that money matters, over and above interest rates, is intimately bound up with a question of whether the supplies of different assets affect yields, and hence whether the composition of government debt affects both money and real economic behaviour.

What does this debate about the transmission mechanism of monetary policy mean for the analysis of monetary policy today? The role of money in determining the price level, and its embodiment in the quantity theory of money, evolved over several hundred years. The broad shape of this theory was accepted by most economists. It is certainly evident in the writings of both John Maynard Keynes (e.g. 1930a, b, 1936) and Irving Fisher (e.g. 1911, 1930, 1933). Interestingly, the argument that monetary policy should be thought of in terms of interest rates rather than the money supply was present in

Keynes's own writing. In modern analysis, the behaviour of central banks is expressed in terms of a 'policy reaction function', which describes how interest rates are set in response to developments in the economy in order to achieve a target for inflation.

The challenge thrown up by the consequences of the financial crisis is that interest rates set by central banks have been constrained to zero for some time. Yet central banks believe that the use of their balance sheet can influence spending and the outlook for inflation. It is hard to analyse such a situation clearly without thinking in terms of the demand for, and supply of, money. Charles Goodhart (1989, 1995 and 2016) has done more than anyone to elucidate the factors that determine the supply of money. In essence, his answer is that the private sector is the principal driver of the supply of money through its changing demand for borrowing from the banking system, which in turn responds to the requirements of its customers. Central banks can influence that by changing interest rates, and when interest rates fall to their effective lower bound, direct creation of base money can have some effect on the overall money supply independently of the behaviour of private borrowers.

I return to the paradox with which I began. Most people believe that economics is about money. Yet most economists hold conversations in which the word 'money' appears hardly at all. Surprisingly, that appears true even of central bankers. The resolution of this apparent puzzle is, I believe, the following: There has been no change in the underlying theory of inflation. Indeed, after the great inflation of the post-war period, improvements in monetary policy led to low and stable inflation and went hand in hand with a rediscovery of the old virtues of sound money and the quantity theory of money. Prices rise when the supply of money exceeds its demand. Economists and central bankers understand this link but conduct their conversations in terms of interest rates, not the quantity of money. In large part, this is because the model of monetary policy that has worked well for some considerable time is one in which central banks set interest rates and the public then determines the quantity of money which is supplied elastically at the set interest rate. Shifts in the demand for money are sufficiently unpredictable that, in their month-by-month decisions, central banks allow demand to determine quantities given the interest rate set by the monetary authority.

There are real dangers in relegating money to this behind-the-scenes role. Three dangers seem to me particularly relevant to present circumstances. First, there is a danger of neglecting parts of the monetary transmission mechanism that operate through the impact of quantities on risk premia of various kinds. The current debate about the appropriate monetary policy when interest rates are at their effective lower bound illustrates the point. Second, by denying an explicit role for money there is the danger of misleading the people into thinking that there is a permanent trade-off between inflation, on the one hand, and output and employment, on the other. Third, by discussing monetary policy in terms of real rather than monetary variables, there is the danger of giving the impression that monetary policy can be used to fine tune short-run movements in output and employment, and to offset each and every shock to the economy. The experience of the recent financial crisis should have disabused us of this notion. These dangers all derive from the habit of discussing monetary policy in terms of a conceptual model in which money plays only a hidden role.

References

Estrella, Arturo and Frederic S. Mishkin (1997), 'Is There a Role for Monetary Aggregates in the Conduct of Monetary Policy?', *Journal of Monetary Economics*, 40(2), pp. 279–304.

Fisher, Irving (1911), *The Purchasing Power of Money*, New York, NY: Macmillan.

(1930), *The Theory of Interest*, New York, NY: Macmillan.

(1933), 'The Debt-Deflation Theory of Great Depressions', *Econometrica*, 1(4), pp. 337–57.

Friedman, Milton (1961), 'The Lag in Effect of Monetary Policy', *Journal of Political Economy*, 69(5), pp. 447–66.

(1963), *Inflation: Causes and Consequences*, Bombay: Asia Publishing Rouse; reprinted in Friedman, *Dollars and Deficits*, Englewood Cliffs, NJ: Prentice-Rail, p. 39.

Friedman, Milton and Anna J. Schwartz (1963), *A Monetary History of the United States, 1867–1960*, Princeton, NJ: Princeton University Press.

Goodhart, Charles (1984), 'Problems of Monetary Management: The UK Experience', Chapter 3 in C. Goodhart (ed.), *Monetary Theory and Practice*, London: Macmillan.

(1989), *Money, Information and Uncertainty*, 2nd edition, London: Macmillan Education UK.

(1995), *The Central Bank and the Financial System*, London: Macmillan.

(2016), 'The Determination of the Money Supply: Flexibility versus Control', Paper presented at the MMF Conference, Bath University, 7 October.

Goodhart, Charles and Andrew Crockett (1970), 'The Importance of Money', *Bank of England Quarterly Bulletin*, 10(2), June, 159–98.

Hume, David (1752), *Political Discourses*, 2nd edition, Edinburgh: Kincaid and Robertson.

Keynes, John Maynard (1930a), *A Treatise on Money, Volume 1: The Pure Theory of Money*, London: Macmillan.

(1930b), *A Treatise on Money, Volume II: The Applied Theory of Money*, London: Macmillan.

(1936), *The General Theory of Employment, Interest and Money*, London: Macmillan.

King, Mervyn (2016), *The End of Alchemy: Money, Banking and the Future of the Global Economy*, London: Little Brown.

Radcliffe Report (1959), *Report on the Working of the Monetary System*, London: Her Majesty's Stationary Office.

3 Monetary Control in the UK
The Impossible Dream?

FORREST CAPIE AND GEOFFREY WOOD

3.1 Introduction

Work on monetary economics has, certainly since the 1950s, been dominated by that done in the USA. And that in turn has, since the publication of Friedman and Schwartz's (1963) great book, invariably been in that book's shadow. The full title of the book is in the context of the present chapter particularly important: *A Monetary History of the United States, 1867–1960*. It is clear that for those years the approach used by Friedman and Schwartz – of treating the USA as a closed economy – is fully justified. But the UK does not approximate to a closed economy, and it is a very long time since it has. In 1890 the UK was more open than the USA was in 1963. By the simple measure of the share of foreign trade in national income, 23 per cent of the UK's gross national product (GNP) was engaged in foreign trade in 1890, compared with 3.2 per cent of the USA's GNP in 1963.

That difference between open and closed economies matters in several areas of economic study, and in no area does it matter more than in monetary economics. Nonetheless, it is not uncommon for work on economies other than the USA's (and even there it is doubtful whether the simplification is any longer sensible) to neglect that distinction. In this chapter we start by showing the importance of economic openness for work on monetary economics in the UK, first setting out the basic theory. Then we turn to problems this theory reveals in the interpretation of so-called 'causality tests' of the relationship between money and income, showing how careless interpretation can lead to the belief that money was irrelevant in the UK. Drawing on some empirical work and on Friedman and Schwartz's (1982) other great book, *Monetary Trends in the United States and the United Kingdom: Their*

We are indebted to Alex Cukierman for his helpful comments on a draft, and to the conference participants and the editors for subsequent comments and suggestions.

Relation to Income, Prices, and Interest Rates, shows the error of that view. This leads straightforwardly to the difficulties of money control under different exchange rate regimes.

We are then able to consider various UK approaches to monetary control, and in particular the approach in which Charles Goodhart was himself closely involved, set out in a paper known as 'Competition and Credit Control', which was published in 1971.

3.2 Money and Openness

The original analysis of money and openness was set out by David Hume, in short papers of remarkable penetration and lucidity. The crucial essays are 'Of Money' and 'Of the Balance of Trade' (both 1752). The first of these sets out the quantity theory of money, and explains money neutrality as a consequence of the rationality of individuals who, no doubt because he was writing in Scotland, could be relied on to choose between goods according to how well they satisfied a want and their price *relative to* other competing and complementary goods. Prices in money terms did not matter. Money illusion, as it would now be called, was absent. In consequence, the basic model yielded one-to-one proportionality between once-for-all-changes in the quantity of money and changes in the price level.

This was not modified by 'Of the Balance of Trade', but there attention turned to the role of money in an open, as opposed to an implicitly closed, economy. In an open economy on the gold or any other metallic standard, a monetary expansion at home spills over to the rest of the world, since all countries on the same monetary standard are in effect one 'monetary country'. An increase in the quantity of money in one area would produce an increase in demand for goods and services, or a fall in interest rates, or both, and would then produce either an increase in demand for foreign goods, or an outflow of funds in search of higher yield. Some of the increase in the money stock would flow overseas; how much would depend on how large the country was relative to the rest of the world but regardless of that the money would be distributed so that, in principle and assuming absence of transport costs and so forth, it would produce an equal rise in the price level across the whole world.

This can readily, and under relatively common conditions, produce the illusion that money is irrelevant, because it follows income and is implicitly therefore assumed to be irrelevant to the path of nominal income, and merely accommodates to what has been determined by other forces; or even that it has no systematic connection whatsoever with movements in nominal income.

The point that these are confusions arising from failure to distinguish between open and closed economies was made in a short empirical paper on money–income relations under the gold standard (Mills and Wood, 1978). That paper used a Sims test to discover the temporal relationship between nominal income fluctuations and fluctuations in a measure of the money stock for the UK in the years 1870–1914. These were the years of the classical gold standard, and therefore allowed testing of the prediction that income would lead money in an open economy with a rigidly fixed exchange rate. The prediction was confirmed. Combining this result with, for example, that of Sims (1972), which found that for the USA money led nominal income, leads to the conclusion that the exchange rate regime in an open economy can change the sign of the temporal relationship, and further, that estimating a Sims relationship over a period of mixed exchange-rate regimes can lead to a finding of no temporal relationship at all.

Demonstration of the role of openness can readily suggest two conclusions: that attempting monetary control in an open economy is pointless, and of course also that it is impossible. Neither proposition is correct. The error of the former is set out very clearly in Friedman and Schwartz (1982). Two quotations make the point well:

[I]n a fixed exchange rate regime the quantity of money in one country is exogenous and cannot be determined, except for brief periods, by the monetary authorities. (p. 305, fn.14)

The 'brief periods' qualification we turn to below.

But to continue, in the same footnote they write:

[C]hanges in the quantity of money, however produced, will affect income ... the exchange rate regime does not affect the 'causal' relationship between money and income; it affects the forces determining the quantity of money.

That is very important in the UK context. Williamson and Wood (1976) considered the widespread claim that Britain's persistent, and in the 1970s very high, inflation was the result of some common external cause which had raised inflation in a large part of the world.

That was surely an uncomfortable claim to defend as Britain's inflation was sometimes markedly higher than in many other countries, but in any event Williamson and Wood (ibid.) took the claim seriously, and examined numerous channels (goods price arbitrage, for example) that could possibly push up prices in the UK. They concluded that though these channels clearly existed, many of the consequent pressures had been accommodated by money growth, and that, in addition, there had been persistent attempts to run the British economy at a very high pressure of demand. This latter point had led, as the model set out by David Hume (1752) would lead one to expect, to persistent balance of payments deficits on current account, and from time to time capital outflows insofar as these could occur in the presence of exchange controls.

It appears, then, that as is to be expected in an open economy with a pegged exchange rate, monetary pressures caused by external factors could only briefly be resisted unless the exchange rate moved, and domestic monetary stimulus faster than that elsewhere soon had to be reined in unless the exchange rate were to change. (German experience under the Bretton Woods System shows that on exactly the same grounds money growth slower than elsewhere cannot be sustained.)

But that still leaves two questions. Was there in place a workable system of monetary control in the pegged exchange rate years? And when sterling floated, were methods of monetary control then in place up to the job?

3.3 Monetary Policy after World War II

To some extent the controllability of money was irrelevant given the circumstances in post-war Britain. One important point to which we briefly return later is that money was not *seen* as being of importance. Apart from that there were two major constraints on conventional monetary policy in the post-war years. One was the scale of the national debt, and the other, related, was the inability of the clearing banks to function 'normally'. (See Goodhart [1999] for an account of the extraordinary growth of debt in the run-up to these post-war years.)

The debt built up in wartime was huge. It peaked in relation to gross domestic product (GDP) in 1947 at 250 per cent. Even after

close to twenty years of inflation and some of the best growth performance the British economy had ever experienced, the debt income
ratio was still 90 per cent at the end of the 1960s. Simply managing
this debt was seen as a problem in itself and one allowing little room
for manoeuvre.

As debt matured, it needed replacing. But selling new debt or operating to influence other variables was not easy, and particularly not
at prices that were palatable to the authorities (the Government and
the Bank of England). Selling it at all could often be difficult given
self-imposed interest rate constraints; and in view of that self-imposed
problem, selling it so as to control money could readily be a very considerable task.

The clearing banks presented an associated problem in the sense
that they had been obliged (pretty well instructed, in fact) in wartime
to hold large amounts of government debt. In the war years there
were of course fewer alternative opportunities for other lending and
they were no doubt content to play a patriotic role. But after the war
their balance sheets were badly distorted in relation to pre-war positions. Whereas before the war roughly half of a bank's balance sheet
was in loans to the private sector, after the war that share had fallen to
below 20 per cent. Nor was the position readily rectifiable. How could
the banks get rid of this – from their point of view (and indeed also
from the point of view of firms desiring bank finance) – undesirably
large amount of government debt?

It was not possible to expand their balance sheets without raising
new capital and that was not allowed. The Capital Issues Committee,
established in wartime and given further powers in 1946 for the direction of new capital issues on the stock exchange, prevented the raising
of new capital for other than specified and approved purposes.

3.3.1 Policy

Prior to World War II there were views on monetary policy that
might be called the old orthodoxy. In that regime things were relatively straightforward. In order to change monetary conditions the
Bank of England (the Bank) used Bank Rate and open-market operations. Therefore, to tighten monetary conditions the Bank raised
Bank Rate and sold Treasury bills at prices that exerted upward pressure on the short rate.

But after the war a new orthodoxy emerged, in part as a consequence of the huge scale of debt and its consequences for the banking system and beyond, and in a part as a consequence of some changing ways of thinking. Monetary tightening would involve the same initial steps – raise Bank Rate – and support with open-market operations. But the belief had developed that the whole structure of interest rates was affected.

Unfortunately, there was a clash here with the needs of financing the Exchequer. In order to keep financing costs down, the Bank would buy gilts.[1] This gilts-buying process necessarily put more cash into the system and so the attempt at tightening was defeated. Money supply expanded, inflation became persistent, and the problems spilled over into the external accounts where they were manifest in balance of payments deficits, sometimes crises, and, in the end, devaluation.

In a further attempt at avoiding pushing the structure of interest rates higher and so raising the cost of financing government debt, resort was made to placing direct controls on banks (quantity rationing) – something that had been in operation during the war. And as direct controls were relied on increasingly to hold bank advances, Bank Rate was regarded as being of use primarily for external purposes. It was believed for a long time that it should be used as a shock measure. In place for an equally long time was the Goschen Rule (named after the nineteenth-century Chancellor associated with advocating it; see Capie [2010, p. 191]) that Bank Rate should be raised sharply – usually that meant a jump of 2 per cent – when there was serious pressure on the exchanges and then reduced gradually – usually by steps of 0.5 per cent – when the pressure had eased.

It is important to bear in mind that the Bank believed that it had enormous expertise in markets, both financial and foreign exchange, and, indeed, it had. That expertise was its major defence against Treasury interference. It knew how markets worked and it should be left to operate in these markets without any interference. The Treasury accepted that position.

The position of sterling after the war, even after the devaluation of 1949, meant that pressures were frequent and much effort was put

---

[1] This was a complicated business involving 'leaning into the wind' – waiting for a buying opportunity on a market in which prices were falling and similarly, selling on a rising one and taking due account of the psychology. The Bank was addicted to psychology.

into trying to keep sterling within its agreed bands. While there had been much discussion over what the Bank could and should do, it was widely accepted that the Bank had responsibility for the exchange rate and should be left to do whatever was necessary to keep the rate on track. The Radcliffe Report (1959) had suggested that the Treasury should decide on Bank Rate changes, but that was brushed aside. What happened was that the Bank would decide, based on external considerations, what change was needed and notify the Treasury of its intentions. The Treasury would almost invariably rubber stamp the proposal. On rare occasions and for explicitly political reasons the Treasury might suggest a change in timing. But generally speaking, at least until 1970, the Bank was left to decide on Bank Rate.

With sterling frequently under pressure, and it being implicitly understood that there were levels of Bank Rate that would not be breached, other measures were employed. Again the Bank devised these measures and used them with more or less complete freedom. The central bank swaps that were in use from the early 1960s, the short-term credits that were arranged, particularly in the severe crisis of late 1964 but at several other times too, were all done without Treasury approval. More remarkable was the staggering scale of forward intervention in the foreign exchange markets between 1964 and 1967. And all the Treasury got was a note at the end of the month telling them what had been done (Capie, 2010).

In other words, from after the war until around 1970–1 the Bank had a target, the exchange rate, and was left alone to use whatever instruments it had (some might suggest 'chose to have' better captures the situation) to meet the target.

3.3.2 Money Not Important

Money played little or no role in monetary policy in the twenty-five or thirty years after the war. The money supply was not believed to be a useful concept, and in any event it could not be measured; but above all it was irrelevant in policy terms. The Radcliffe Report (1959) brought together the majority view of policymakers and British academic economists at the end of the 1950s. The central conclusion (though none was listed in the Report) was that velocity was infinitely variable and that what needed attention was the 'whole spectrum of liquidity'.

This view perhaps mattered less, given the particular circumstances of the time that there was a fixed exchange rate of a kind in place and that monetary policy was therefore essentially controlled from elsewhere; though we have also noted that there were factors that allowed some scope for policy action. But the long and the short of it is that no attention was given to money. So far as there was concern, it was over bank credit.

3.3.3 Controls on Bank Lending: Reserve/Deposit Ratios; Liquid Asset Ratios; Ceilings; Directives; Special Deposits

It followed that what passed for monetary policy came in the form of controls on bank lending. Some of these are explained or at least explicable in terms of the legacy of war, and others had their origins in arrangements from the distant past but were formalised after the war.

The latter were less intrusive, having developed out of practices that the banks had devised themselves. These were the various ratios the banks had organised their balance sheets around: cash/asset ratio; liquid assets ratio; and capital/asset ratio. The banks had found their own way to appropriate levels for these ratios in the course of the nineteenth century. They evolved according to conditions and the changing institutional environment. They began high and came down slowly to levels consistent with an acceptable level of profitability and stability. So, for example, when the Bank of England's role as lender of last resort became clear, and it became clear to the economy that the Bank would fulfil it whenever required, a little after the middle of the nineteenth century the ratios slipped further. Before World War I the cash ratio had settled at around 12 per cent and the liquid assets ratio at around 30 per cent. These broadly held across the inter-war years. After World War II the cash ratio was closer to 8 per cent and the liquid assets ratio at 30 per cent, and it was at these levels they were formalised. The fact that no attention was given to the capital/asset ratio is not surprising. The banks' assets were so full of government debt that there was little risk to consider. (Government debt then was of course 'safe' only in nominal terms, but since bank liabilities were also in nominal terms that was no source of concern.) The liquid assets ratio was seen as key to controlling the balance sheet and the authorities focused on it.

In fact, the banks tended to operate with higher ratios than were required. In the course of the 1960s there was much debate on whether it was appropriate to reduce the liquid assets ratio and some moves were made in that direction.

3.3.4 Direct Controls

There were three main means of direct control over banks in the 1950s and 1960s: ceilings on lending; specified direction of lending; and special deposits. In addition to these was the use of hire-purchase controls, which were seen as a key part of monetary policy.

The use of these kinds of controls is partly explicable in terms of wartime legacy. It is also partly a reflection of the growing confidence in management of the economy not through the use of prices or markets but by direct means, and the belief that the bureaucracy knew what mattered and could direct it. Additionally, and never forgotten, there was the desire to keep the costs of government borrowing down.

Ceilings were therefore placed on bank advances from time to time – they took the form of 'x per cent of loans outstanding' at a chosen date. When it was clear that they were not working satisfactorily in the mid-1950s, the Bank was urged to come up with a new means of control in time for the Radcliffe Committee. That was when it devised 'Special Deposits'. When the Bank wanted to restrict bank lending it would call for deposits from the clearing banks to be placed with the Bank. There was much debate about how exactly this worked but the idea was to raise the existing liquid assets ratio by 2–3 percentage points.

Supplementing these direct controls on the banks but very much seen as central in monetary policy were hire-purchase controls. These would be amended in terms of required down payments and length of times for repayment in support of the ceilings and special deposits.

The scope for using open-market operations was limited. Whenever the Bank wanted to tighten conditions in the money market and push rates up problems arose in the gilts market (see Allen, 2018). Since the Bank wanted orderly markets, it would accommodate and buy gilts thus putting money back into the system.[2]

---

[2] It never committed itself to the meaning of 'orderly' as clearly as Beryl Sprenkle did when he was US Under Secretary of Treasury. A market was disorderly, he told a Congressional questioner, when the Fed or Treasury was intervening.

Dissatisfaction with controls came from many sources. One that received a mention at the time, but perhaps insufficient investigation, was the part that overdrafts played. While overdrafts had long been recognised as a central part of British banking, when it came to the operation of controls they might have been an obstruction. If the overdraft facility had legal force (and assuming the facility was not fully used) it would have been impossible to impose a ceiling on bank lending. There are many questions still outstanding on this issue, but it does seem to deserve further investigation. The outcome would allow a better judgement to be made on the working of all manner of controls. Certainly the commonly understood and legally accepted view of overdrafts was that they were entirely, and always, at the lending bank's discretion.[3]

3.4   The Return of Money: Competition and Credit Control

There were two main influences that produced a reassessment of the role of money in Britain in the 1960s. One was the growing interest within academic economics that was taking place, initially mainly in the USA and associated with the work of Milton Friedman and colleagues at the University of Chicago. The other was the work of the International Monetary Fund (IMF) and there most closely associated with the work of Jacques Polak on the monetary approach to the balance of payments.

The first influence slowly made inroads into some parts of British academic life. The second was forced on us when we got into balance of payments difficulties sufficiently serious to require turning to the IMF for help. They in turn imposed conditions which included more careful monitoring and controlling of a monetary aggregate, their preferred one being Domestic Credit Expansion.

The latter influence gathered great force following the first need for an IMF standby in the 1960s, and then much more so following devaluation at the end of 1967. There was great resistance in Britain over the idea of any kind of conditions being imposed, but also over the idea of using any monetary aggregate. But the IMF was firm and so

---

[3] We are indebted to correspondence with Professor Philip Rawlings of London University for his most helpful guidance on this matter.

began some grudging acceptance of the need for some kind of monetary control.

The ideas from the USA began to reach a wider public through journalists such as Peter Jay and William Rees-Mogg at *The Times* in the late 1960s. The Bank began to feel obliged at least to prepare a defence against the kinds of attacks being made.

In part from such pressure the Bank came to employ more economic expertise in the 1960s. It began to recruit some graduates with economics degrees and to use academic economists on secondment. Among the former, Andrew Crockett was important; among the latter, Andrew Bain and Charles Goodhart were major contributors. Goodhart stayed and joined the permanent staff.

Bain had written a paper on money for the *Quarterly Bulletin* in the late 1960s but it did not get published since the Bank was not yet ready for it. It was then Goodhart and Crockett who carried on with the work and eventually published 'The Importance of Money' in the *Quarterly Bulletin* in 1970. That can be seen as a landmark. Policy did not immediately change but it showed that the Bank had begun to accept that more attention needed to be paid to money.[4] There was a great deal of exchange with the Treasury on these matters in different combined money study groups and a range of topics was covered. The stability of the demand for money function was seen as one of the most important of these.

A substantial amount of work was carried out on that both inside and outside the Bank. There were two possible motivations for the studies. One was the Radcliffe Report (1959), which took the view that money was close to infinitely elastically substitutable for other assets. The other can be derived from a view in Goodhart and Crockett (1970) – that Milton Friedman had turned the quantity theory of money into a theory of the demand for money, and the stability of the money demand function was therefore crucial. That Friedman had so changed the quantity theory, rather than shifting it away from a Fisherian version to a Marshallian one, is arguable. (See Eltis [1995], especially the chapters by Blaug, by Patinkin and by Wood.) But be that as it may, money demand functions were

---

[4] A careful reading of that paper also reveals prescience of future debates about the appropriate time horizon for the conduct of monetary policy.

estimated, and stability in that demand as a function of a few variables seemed, over data from comparatively modern times, to be fleeting. That was the conclusion of most Bank studies, and of many academic ones. The approach that could be derived from Radcliffe, of looking directly at elasticities of substitution, was much rarer. It was followed by Cagan and Schwartz (1975) for US data, and Mills and Wood (1977) for UK data; both found elasticities of substitution which might reasonably be described as low, and were certainly far away from the infinity implied by the Radcliffean view.

Despite the Bank's money demand function findings, and numerous academic ones, money was seen as being important, although 'monetary policy' remained difficult to conduct. The position was well stated in the conclusion of the paper by Goodhart and Crockett (1970, p. 97):

The monetary authorities are in a position to alter financial conditions decisively by their operations in certain key financial markets. These market operations can have a considerable influence upon interest rates and also upon the climate of expectations.

The effect of these operations in financial markets is to cause disequilibria in portfolios ... There are, however, reasons for believing that these studies may underestimate the strength of monetary policy. In particular, most of these studies use calculated nominal rates of return as an indicator of the impact of monetary policy.

On the other hand, attempts to measure the effects of monetary policy by correlating changes in the money stock with changes in money incomes probably greatly over estimate the strength of monetary policy. There is a two-way relationship between these variables.

Attempts to disentangle this two-way interaction by considering, for example, the lead/lag relationship, reinforce the view that monetary policy has some causal impact on money incomes, but do not allow this to be clearly isolated and quantified.

Given this careful acknowledgement of the importance of money, control of it was clearly important. In a compelling analysis (1971) Donald Hodgman (who had visited the Bank) showed very forcefully that the reluctance of Bank and Treasury to countenance any great degree of interest rate flexibility had been at the root of previous failures in monetary control, and had led inevitably to the numerous direct controls that were by that time in place. Strikingly, John Fforde of the Bank had reached the same conclusion, and in 1970 argued it

in a Bank paper (reproduced as an Appendix by Goodhart in 2015).[5]
That in turn served as the basis of a paper by Andrew Crockett which
was sent to the Treasury in 1971. (In his history of the Bank, Capie
describes Fforde's paper as 'undoubtedly the most important document he had written since joining the Bank in 1957'.) These two
papers and subsequent discussions led to the above-mentioned
Competition and Credit Control, which was examined by Hodgman
in an appendix to his paper (1971). Hodgman concluded that, subject
to certain minor caveats, it was a workable system.

3.4.1 Reservations and Implementation

The scheme was considered in detail in the Bank, and caveats made
(by Charles Goodhart). Competition and Credit Control became government policy, and was adopted in 1971 (Bank of England, 1971).
Things rapidly went wrong, with both the economy and the monetary
control. There can be no doubt that the bulk of the blame rests, and
always will remain, with the Heath Government and the massive
demand stimulus which it quaintly called a 'dash for growth'. It is unlikely that, especially given the residual reluctance to let interest rates be
fully free, any monetary control mechanism could have stood against
this. But there were inherent monetary control problems as well. The
introduction of competition led to banks bidding for market share.
They raised deposit rates while holding lending rates relatively stable.
And the mechanism of special deposits under Competition and Credit
Control made the situation worse, as it made it still more tempting for
liquidity-squeezed banks to bid for funds. Some of the resulting money
growth was undoubtedly 'artificial', and would have no effect on the
economy. (See Greenwell's Monetary Bulletins, a monthly publication
of those years, published by the Gilt-Edged Team at Greenwell's [as
W. Greenwell and Co, a firm of stockbrokers, was known]. The
Bulletins attempted from time to time to quantify that component of
the remarkable growth in the supply of money.)

Attempts were made to control money (and a device was invented
by Charles Goodhart which sought to eliminate the 'artificial' part).
But it was not long, after changes of government, before the UK went
back to the past.

---

[5] Fforde's paper had been unpublished until that time.

In brief, after the attempts to control the money supply domestically seemed to have foundered, resort was once again made to an external constraint. Sterling informally became linked to the Deutschmark.[6]

In turn, this ended through the pressure of events. Inflation had come down rapidly and substantially in the UK, and it was time to ease policy. But Germany had reunited, and the Bundesbank needed to tighten policy to restrain German inflation. British inflation did, however, need no such restraining; so after a brief period of turbulence, sterling was floated and the UK adopted an inflation-targeting regime. Responsibility for achieving the inflation target rested with the Bank, but there was no mention of money or monetary control in the new framework.

3.5 Conclusion

This vanishing of money was not a phenomenon unique to Britain. In his 2002 paper, 'No Money No Inflation', Mervyn King quotes a governor of the Bank of Canada, Gerald Bouey, as saying, 'We didn't abandon the monetary aggregates, they abandoned us'.

King then goes on to say that a most successful period of inflation control has been combined with a period where central bankers apparently paid no attention to money. Rather, official short-term interest rates have become the monetary variable. But is this entirely wise? King notes that '[t]he disappearance of money ... is more apparent than real'. But he also remarks that there are dangers which 'derive from discussing monetary policy in terms of a conceptual model in which money plays only a hidden role'.

He continues: 'My own belief is that the absence of money ... will cause problems in the future.'[7] In fact, there may be two quite distinct sorts of problem.

In August and September 2016 (the time of writing this chapter) the possibility of such problems emerging seemed quite strong. After the UK had voted to leave the European Union, the Bank of England cut its policy rate and announced further 'quantitative easing', the term by which central bank security purchases had become known.

---

[6] See Lawson (1992) for details on this episode.
[7] Whether interest rates can be a satisfactory indicator of the stance of monetary policy has been discussed before. A point that emerged as crucial, and surely will again, is how securely inflationary expectations are anchored.

At the same time, a measure of the money supply (M4x) had grown at 5.8 per cent in the year to June (the fastest such rate since 2008) and at an annualised rate of 8 per cent in the three months to June.

A second type of problem is also brought into focus when one thinks explicitly about money. The money stock comprises in large part the liabilities of the banking sector. Thinking about the first compels thinking also about the second. A sustained low interest rate policy may be inimical to banks making profits and thereby both weaken them, in conflict with the objective of financial stability, and reduce their ability to lend to customers. The very policy which seeks by low interest rates to stimulate the economy may actually prevent that stimulus being transmitted to the economy.

It seems that there is a chance that money, and its explicit control, may once again become of manifest concern. It is to be hoped that monetary control in the UK does not then remain 'the impossible dream'.

References

Allen, William (2018), *Market Microstructure and Monetary Policy: The Bank of England in the Gilt-Edged Market, 1928–1972*, Cambridge and London: Cambridge University Press.

Bank of England (1971), 'Competition and Credit Control: A consultative Document'. Bank of England Quarterly Bulletin, June.

Cagan, Phillip and Anna Schwartz (1975), 'Has the Growth of Money Subsitutes Hindered Monetary Policy?', *Journal of Money, Credit, and Banking*, 7(2), pp. 137–59.

Capie, Forrest (2010), *The Bank of England; 1950s to 1979*, Cambridge and New York, NY: Cambridge University Press.

Eltis, Walter (1995), *The Quantity Theory of Money from Locke to Keynes and Friedman*, Aldershot: Edward Elgar.

Friedman, Milton and Anna J. Schwartz (1963), *A Monetary History of the United States, 1867 – 1960*, Cambridge, MA: Princeton UP for NBER.

Friedman, Milton and Anna Schwartz (1982), *Monetary Trends in the United States and the United Kingdom: Their Relation to Income, Prices, and Interest Rates*, Chicago, IL: University of Chicago Press.

Goodhart, Charles (1999), 'Monetary Policy and Debt Management in the United Kingdom: some historical viewpoints', in K. Alec Chrystal (ed.), *Government Debt Structure and Monetary Conditions*, Becton: Park Communications Ltd.

(2015), 'Competition and Credit Control: Some Personal Reflections', *Financial History Review*, 22(2), pp. 235–46.

Goodhart, Charles and Andrew Crockett (1970) 'The Importance of Money', *Bank of England Quarterly Bulletin*, 10(2), June, pp. 159–198.

Greenwell's Monetary Bulletin: Various Issues, London: W Greenwell and Co., Stockbrokers.

Hodgman, Donald (1971), 'British Techniques of Monetary Policy', *Journal of Money, Credit, and Banking*, 3(4), pp. 760–80.

Hume, David (1752), *Political Discourses*, Kincaid and Robertson, Edinburgh. Economic essays therein reprinted 1955, *Writings on Economics*, ed. E. Rotwein, published by Nelson and Sons, London.

King, Mervyn (2002), 'No Money, No Inflation', *Bank of England Quarterly Bulletin*, Summer, pp. 162–77.

Lawson, Nigel (1992), *The View from Number 11: The Memoirs of a Tory Radical*, London: Bantam.

Mills, Terry and Geoffrey Wood (1977), 'Money Substitutes and Monetary Policy in the UK 1922–1974', *European Economic Review*, 10(1), pp. 19–36.

(1978), 'Money-Income Relationships and the Exchange Rate Regime', *FRB of St Louis Review*, August, pp. 22–7.

Report on the Working of the Monetary System (known as the Radcliffe Report) (1959), *Her Majesty's Stationary Office*, London.

Sims, Christopher (1972), 'Money, Income, and Causality', *American Economic Review*, September, pp. 540–52.

Williamson, John and Geoffrey Wood (1976), 'The British Inflation: Indigenous or Imported?', *American Economic Review*, September, pp. 520–31.

4 | *Pristine and Parsimonious Policy*

Can Central Banks Ever Get Back to It and Why They Should Try

PAUL TUCKER

This volume of essays is being compiled at a moment when the independence of central banks is being seriously questioned and challenged for the first time in many years.

My contribution starts, therefore, with a broad summary of some of the criticisms and concerns that are circulating, in varying degrees, in the main currency jurisdictions. Part of the problem is that we have discovered that society's 'contract' with its central banks is considerably more incomplete than had been recognised before the Great Financial Crisis. A full treatment of this issue would have to range very widely. Instead, I drill down to the particular question of how far a central bank should be free to deploy its balance sheet as it wishes, since many of the current concerns revolve around that in some way. In an attempt to get at the underlying issues, I will articulate some general principles for delegating powers to independent agencies in constitutional democracies, irrespective of the substance of the delegated regime. Once some special features of central banking are introduced, those general principles provide a platform for proposing some more particular precepts for central bank operations.

The big question here is about legitimacy, for which instrumental effectiveness or efficiency is just one important part. Even if central banks and independent technocratic institutions like them could do everything better than elected politicians, that does not mean that they should.[1]

---

[1] This chapter draws on broader work by the author on the legitimacy of unelected power, from the book *Unelected Power* by Paul Tucker. Copyright © 2018 Paul Tucker. Reprinted here with permission from Princeton University Press.

4.1 Four Challenges to Central Bank Independence

In the wake of the crisis and the painfully slow and uneven recovery that has followed, four broad issues have emerged to confront the current status and scope of our independent central banks:

1. that monetary policy might, after all, involve long-term trade-offs and so political management needs to be reintroduced,
2. that monetary policy is having big distributional effects, again requiring political input,
3. that the results of central bank policy are not living up to their billing and prestige as *The Only Game in Town* and
4. that central banks are *over-mighty citizens*, insufficiently constrained and too broadly empowered.

4.1.1 Non-Neutrality: Hysteresis and Trade-Offs

A central tenet of monetary economics is that money is, in the jargon, neutral and, even, super-neutral – which is to say that increasing the amount of money in the economy does not create more output and employment in the long run and that increasing the growth rate of money simply translates into a higher steady-state rate of inflation.

While that has long been contested by commentators on the Left, recently some prominent US-based mainstream academic economists have begun to argue that monetary policy could (and should) be used to combat longer-run hysteretic effects of massive shocks to the economy (Blanchard, Cerutti and Summers, 2015). In a nutshell, the proposal is to run what Janet Yellen has described as a 'high-pressure economy' in an attempt to recover lost ground and to restore the pre-crisis normality (Yellen, 2016).

Whether to do so would have to be weighed against the risks of creating an inflationary spiral or of triggering a renewed wave of financial sector improvidence. If, after all, it turned out that there happened to be little slack in the economy and that the pumped-up aggregate demand did not generate extra productive capacity, inflationary pressures would intensify in the short run. But, more importantly, longer-term inflation expectations might rise if persistent attempts to generate extra supply led markets and wage bargainers to the view that policymakers were minded to take asymmetric risks with inflation. The big question, which tends to be left hanging in the air, is who should make the decision whether to persist with a high-pressure policy. Can it be left to unelected technocrats?

It seems likely that the possibility of hysteresis persistently depleting economic capacity has little or no bearing on the familiar inflationary bias of monetary policy under day-to-day political control. That makes a case for monetary policy remaining under central bank control. But given that motivation for insulation from day-to-day politics, an independent monetary authority should have discretion to run a 'high pressure economy' only if medium-to-long term inflation expectations remain in line with the target it has been given for inflation.

Any such conclusion has to rest on a judgement that the social costs of the inflation bias are not worth inflicting upon people. While not exhausting the case for independence, that is not a judgement for central bankers themselves.[2]

4.1.2 Distributional Considerations

The second challenge to post-crisis central banking has been more overtly political, not in the sense of straightforward party politics but in the sense of particular parts of society being either systematic winners or systematic losers from monetary policy since 2009. In a number of countries, perhaps particularly Germany and the UK, it is argued that a combination of persistently low official interest rates with quantitative easing and credit easing – prosaically, buying lots of government bonds and privately issued bonds – has pushed up asset prices, enriching the rich, and pushed down returns on savings, hurting those households and pensioners who are not remotely rich but who rely on income from a lifetime of saving. Since democratic politics is the forum in which sectional interests and preferences get debated and settled, this invites the protest that central banking has found itself stranded in foreign territory, losing its legitimate moorings.

To make sense of this, we need to distinguish distributional *choices* from distributional *effects*.

There is no doubt that monetary policy can have, and has been having, distributional effects. When a central bank raises interest rates to restrain demand, there will typically be some cost to debtors and asset holders and some uplift in the running return to savers. In normal

---

[2] See *Unelected Power*, chapter 24.

circumstances, those effects are dominated for society as a whole by the benefits of maintaining sustainable growth and, separately, over time they tend to be offset by the obverse effects that kick in during periods of easy monetary policy. The distinctive thing about the current conjuncture is that super-low interest rates and asset purchases have gone on and on for years and years, so the distributional effects have been more pronounced and long-lived. Given the different tendencies to vote of the segments of society affected, it is not hugely surprising that these effects should prompt public debate and some disquiet.

Looking back, central bankers should have been active in highlighting these costs of their policy and also the risks of refuelling imprudent risk-taking in the financial system.[3] Had they done so, it would have been clearer to the public and to civil society that the political authorities had the means and responsibility to mitigate some of the distributional consequences of monetary policy. Separately, it would have helped, gently but cumulatively, to make the point that politicians have had the option of supporting the economy via structural and fiscal policies of various kinds, instead of relying almost exclusively on monetary policy. That takes us to the third challenge.

4.1.3 The Only Game in Town: Central Banking as False Hope

Over the past few years, central banks have had to get used to the refrain that they are the only game in town. That this hasn't caused a political explosion among the people would be remarkable were it not for the pre-crisis orthodoxy that monetary policy could get us through any cyclical downturn. That we find ourselves in this position even when the orthodox view loses credibility is, more worryingly, not at all surprising.

There exists a strategic tension between central banks and elected policymakers. The latter have few constraints on their powers but carry equally few legal obligations. In consequence, when short-term politics (what political scientists call 'political transaction costs') make it difficult for them to act themselves to contain a crisis or bring about economic recovery, they can sit on their hands safe in the knowledge that their central bank will be obliged by its mandate to

---

[3] The Bank of England published a paper on distributional effects during 2012.

try (within the legal limits of its powers). That can lead to a flawed policy mix, creating risks in the world economy and financial system. Central banks are, in effect, faced with choosing between a flawed policy and abandoning their mandate in order to induce others to act.

At times the Bank for International Settlements, the central bankers' bank and refuge, has got close to advocating the latter course. Its annual reports have set out at length why and how the true heavy lifting of sustainable economic recovery is unavoidably in the hands of the governments, banks, households and firms whose balance sheets needed strengthening and whose economies need to be more flexible in cushioning and adjusting to shocks. By supporting near-term demand for goods and services, the central banks can create time for those fundamental adjustments and reforms to be effected, but they can do no more than that.

Notwithstanding those likely truths, it is a mistake to stipulate or imply that central banks should sit on their hands in order to induce governments to act. To do so would be to set aside the legal mandates from democratic assemblies. It is one thing for central banks to be the only game in town, but it would be quite another to abrogate the sovereign power, taking it to themselves.

Constrained as they are to do as much as they can within their powers, they have ended up looking like something they are not: *the* macroeconomic policymakers. The upshot has been a central banking community that is liable to be held responsible for something it simply cannot deliver: prosperity.

The only answer in the short term is for central bankers to get back to repeating, over and over again, that they can buy time but cannot generate prosperity. To channel the late Eddie George, former Governor of the Bank of England, stability is what central bankers exist to deliver, and stability is a necessary condition for the good things in life but it is not remotely sufficient.

This requires central bankers to pull off a tough act of communication. The public should trust them for what they can do, but not rely upon them for what they cannot do. Under current circumstances, that entails admitting ignorance of the deep forces that might be reshaping real-economy prospects as well as advertising their limited powers.

Those challenges are compounded by the remarkable expansion in central banks' powers and responsibilities. If central banks are not omniscient, why give them even more powers?

4.1.4 Over-Mighty Citizens: Central Banks in a Democratic Society

In the decade or so before crisis broke in the summer of 2007, central banks' core objectives and functions seemed settled: price stability and monetary policy. But as Paul Volcker had warned emphatically at the end of the 1980s, no good could come of the central banking community losing interest in or influence over the financial system. Disaster duly followed when they became, by doctrine, inclination and expertise, overly detached from the need for system stability (Volcker, 1990).[4] The consequent reawakening to some of the fundamental truths of a monetary economy in which most monetary liabilities are issued by private businesses has prompted extensive regulatory reforms. They have left central banks with a range of powers and functions not seen since the 1920s, if then.[5]

But compared with a century ago, we live in societies where full-franchise democracy is mature and embedded. Those are conditions where constraints are badly needed to avoid central banks being over-mighty citizens.

4.2 Detour: Principles for Legitimate Delegation to Independent Agencies

It is nigh on impossible to make progress in identifying those constraints without addressing deeper issues about the role of unelected power in our democratic societies.

That is because problems of how to cabin unelected power run through the architecture and operation of the administrative state, with its plethora of independent agencies, semi-independent agencies and agencies under the day-to-day control of elected politicians. Independent central banks lie towards one end of that spectrum, insulated from the day-to-day politics of both the elected executive

---

[4] Volcker gave the 1990 Per Jacobsson Lecture titled, 'The Triumph of Central Banking?' The presence of the question-mark was underlined during Q&A.

[5] That stability is inextricably tied up with central banking had been clear enough from Charles Goodhart's earlier historical excavation of central banking's origins and core tenets, notably in *The Evolution of Central Banks* (Goodhart, 1988).

government and the legislature.[6] The kinds of constraint applied to independent central banks ought, at a high level, to apply to other truly independent agencies too. I call these the *Principles for Delegation*. I shall do no more than selectively summarize them here.

My broad answer to the general question of conditions for the legitimacy of independent agencies in a democratic, liberal republic comes in two broad parts: criteria for *whether* to delegate and precepts for *how* to delegate.[7]

Criteria for whether to delegate: a policy function should not be delegated to a truly independent agency unless (1) society has settled preferences; (2) the objective is capable of being framed in a reasonably clear way; (3) delegation would materially mitigate a problem of credible commitment; and (4) the policymaker would not have to make first-order distributional *choices*. Whether those conditions are satisfied in any particular field is properly a matter for public debate and for determination by elected legislators.

Precepts for how to delegate: (1) the agency's purposes, objectives and powers should be clear and set by legislators; (2) its decision-making procedures should be set largely by legislators and should accord with the values of the rule of law; (3) the agency itself should publish the operating principles that will guide its exercise of discretion within the delegated domain; (4) there should be transparency sufficient to permit accountability to the legislature for the agency's stewardship of the regime and, separately, for politicians' framing of the regime; and (5) it should be clear *ex ante* what (if anything) happens, procedurally and/or substantively, when the edges of the regime are reached but the agency could do more to avert or contain a crisis.

---

[6] Within the term 'elected executive branch' I am including the ministers of parliamentary systems since the individuals are elected to the legislature and because it is clear to the people that they are electing a party or coalition of parties to executive power.

[7] There is, in fact, a third component comprising conditions for delegating multiple missions to a single agency: only if the missions are inextricably linked, and in particular rely on seamless flows of information; and decisions are taken by separate policy committees, with overlapping membership but each with a majority of dedicated members. These constraints are highly relevant to multiple-mission central banks but are not pursued here.

At root, these Principles for Delegation require delegated responsibilities and powers to be framed as *regimes* with a monitorable objective.[8] While that might seem familiar enough in the field of monetary policy, the regimes actually in place prior to the crisis turned out to be radically incomplete, barely contemplating the nature and scale of balance-sheet operations and regulatory interventions by central banks since 2007.

4.3 Central Banking as a Co-manager of the State's Consolidated Balance Sheet

How, then, should the Principles for Delegation be applied to central banking? One obvious way into this would be objectives. A central bank's core objective might be cast as nominal stability; or intertemporal stabilisation consistent with maintaining the nominal anchor; or, as I prefer, broad monetary stability, defined to include the stability of the private banking system; or monetary stability plus some even wider conception of financial stability that includes remedying allocative inefficiencies caused by financial system pathologies. We shall come to that, but there is, in fact, a rather more elemental starting point, one that is prior to questions of independence. It is to ask what a central bank *is*.

4.3.1 *What Do Central Banks Do?*

It is useful to think of the central bank as conducting financial operations that change the liability structure and, potentially, the asset structure of the state's consolidated balance sheet.

If a central bank buys (or lends against) only government paper, the state's consolidated (or net) balance sheet's liability structure is altered, with monetary liabilities substituted for longer-term debt obligations. If it purchases (or lends against) private-sector paper, the

---

[8] A preliminary version of the Principles for Delegation was given in Tucker (2014a). A fuller explication is forthcoming in a book under contract with Princeton University Press. It draws on the work of, among many others, Alesina and Tabellini (2007, 2008) on whether to delegate to technocrats, of Milgrom and Holmstrom (1991) on the incentive problems of multiple-mission agents, and of Pettit (2004, 2012) on forging the people's purposes and on contestability.

state's consolidated balance sheet is enlarged, the asset portfolio changed and its risk exposures affected. In either case, any net losses flow
to the central treasury in the form of reduced seigniorage income,
entailing either higher taxes or lower spending in the longer run (and
conversely for net profits).

Taken in the round, the state's aggregate risks might not necessarily
increase with such operations. If purchasing private-sector assets
helped to revive spending in the economy, that might, in principle,
reduce the probability of the state making larger aggregate welfare
payments and receiving lower taxes. But the form of the risk would
change and, because the driver of the risk transformation was central
bank operations, the decision taker on the state's risk exposures would
switch from elected fiscal policymakers to unelected central bankers.

Seen in that light, the question is what degrees of freedom central
banks should be granted to change the state's consolidated balance
sheet and to what ends.

4.3.2 A Minimalist Conception

A minimalist conception, articulated some years ago by Marvin
Goodfriend among others, would restrict the proper scope of central
bank interventions to narrow open-market operations (OMOs).
These open-market operations exchange monetary liabilities for
short-term Treasury bills (in order to steer the overnight money-
market rate of interest). This model has profound implications.

The lender of last resort (LOLR) function is restricted to accommo-
dating shocks to the aggregate demand for central bank (base)
money. It plays no role in offsetting temporary problems in the distribution of reserves among banks in the private money markets: if the
money markets are disfunctional, solvent banks simply go into bankruptcy if they cannot acquire reserves via the central bank's OMOs
(Tucker, 2014b).

At the effective lower bound for nominal interest rates, the only
instrument available to the central bank would be to talk down
expectations of the future path of the policy rate ('forward guidance').
All other interventions to stimulate aggregate demand – for example,
quantitative and credit easing – would fall to the 'fiscal arm' of government. That, not a judgement on the merits of the minimal conception, is my main point: what is not within the realm of the central

bank falls to elected policymakers, with the attendant problems of credible commitment and time-inconsistency.

This model could be said to be both pristine and parsimonious.

4.3.3 A Maximalist Conception

At the other, maximalist, end of the spectrum, the central bank would be given free rein to manage the consolidated balance sheet, which in theory would even include writing state-contingent options with different groups of households and firms. That would take central banks very close to *being* the fiscal authority and cannot be squared with any mainstream ideas of central banking competencies in democracies.

4.3.4 Terms of Central Bank Independence: A Matter of Convention, Not Natural Law

So in one direction the state's overall capabilities shrivel and in the other its functions are either seized by or abandoned to unelected central bankers.

Positive economics on the effectiveness of different instruments in mitigating the effects of various kinds of shock hitting the economy cannot help us with this, because it does not speak to which arm of the state should control which tools. The underlying problem appears to be that we do not know where the welfare advantages of credible commitment (a precondition for delegation) are outweighed by the disadvantages of the loss of majoritarian control.

This looks like a trade-off between incommensurable values. But that would be a misthink. Central banks are not independent just as a matter of instrumental expedience, solely as a means to improving the effectiveness of policy, vitally important though that is to socioeconomic welfare. In a fiat-money system, independence is a corollary of the high-level separation of powers in our democracies between executive government and legislative fiscal authority. The executive branch should not control monetary policy because that would give them the power to tax without the authorisation of the legislature; and, given the imperative of re-election, they could not be trusted not to resort to that power. In other words, management of a state's consolidated balance sheet is partly delegated to its central bank in order to underpin the values of constitutional democracy itself.

As described, that does not demand more than the minimum conception of central bank operations outlined above. But in the presence of fractional-reserve banking, price stability is an incomplete specification of the economy's need for monetary stability. It also needs stability in the banking system (understood as private issuers and providers of monetary liabilities and services). As the issuer of an economy's final-settlement asset (money), this gives the central bank an unavoidable role as lender of last resort: as liquidity reinsurer to those private-sector intermediaries that provide liquidity insurance to the rest of the economy. It will lend to individual (sound) private monetary institutions even when there is no aggregate shortage of central bank money, in order to avoid the unnecessary social costs of banking collapse.

In consequence, the central bank's balance sheet can never be the pristine thing that purists purport to desire or that the minimalist conception assumes.

Nevertheless, constraints are needed on central banks deploying their power in specific markets or in specific ways if they are to stay on the 'right side' of a blurred line between monetary policy and fiscal policy. The expression 'right side' is in quotes because this is a matter of *convention*. It does not find its roots in natural law or some inalienable essence of central banking. Rather, each society has to determine where the line should be drawn, with our democratic values entailing that the convention should be open, comprehensible and enforceable.

In consequence, the political purpose of general principles on central bank balance-sheet management is to frame the options reasonably open to a polity when establishing *its* preferred convention for separating 'fiscal policy' controlled by elected politicians from 'monetary policy' controlled by an independent authority. We live in a world where, in a deep sense, there are not pure realms of 'fiscal policy' and 'monetary policy' but, rather, a clear separation between what is controlled by elected and unelected policymakers. Different jurisdictions can adopt different conventions, but only within a constrained family of options if they share the deep values of constitutional democracy.

That family of options is, therefore, constrained by the more general Principles for Delegation to independent agencies. The apparent tension or incommensurability between commitment technologies (efficiency) and majoritarian legitimacy (decency) can, therefore, be squared by each polity imposing constraints appropriate to its particular constitutional embodiment of more widely shared democratic values and norms. What follows is where the Principles seem, to me, to lead for central banking.

4.4   The Fiscal Carve-Out for Central Banking

To restate our problem, one of the challenges of central banking is how we, the people, can delegate enough without delegating too much. On the one hand, the central banks' purpose is credibly to commit to monetary stability (broadly defined), which is to be achieved by insulating them from the temptations of allowing economic and financial booms. Thus, they are to be separated from the people's political agents who control fiscal and structural policies. But, on the other hand, it turns out that some central bank operations can pose risks to the public finances and, further, can have fiscal-like characteristics if they deliberately steer the allocation of credit to particular parts of the economy. In blunt summary, there is a risk that central bank independence not only transfers to unelected technocrats the powers that the people wish to insulate from politics, but also transfers powers that we positively want to be in the hands of elected politicians.

In other words, society needs, as we have said, to decide where the boundary should be drawn between central bank and finance ministry policymakers.

Since this is creating a zone of constrained delegation to central bankers, I call it the *Fiscal Carve-Out* (FCO). The Principles for Delegation demand that the FCO be as explicit as possible if legitimacy is to be sustained.

As a matter of fact, the FCO is rarely transparent but nor is it completely invisible, and it always exists, if only *ex post*. Society needs to take steps to pin down and make transparent the FCO under which central banks *already* implicitly function. Yes, they take risks. Yes, they can suffer losses. Yes, they can in principle step in to underpin the liquidity of markets or even, *if* society wishes, to steer the price of credit to particular sectors through weight of money. Their room for manoeuvre, the boundaries of their domain, can and should be set out in advance, substantively and/or procedurally.

A jurisdiction's FCO for its central bank needs to cover: the kind of assets it can lend against; the kind of assets it can buy, in what circumstances, for which of its statutory purposes, and whether those operations are ever subject to consultation with the executive government or legislature; how losses will be covered by the fiscal authority and how they will be communicated to government and legislature. In addressing each of these issues, the FCO must be realistic about what a central bank will end up doing, within the limits of its legal mandate, in the face of adversity. In the same spirit, for the regime to be credible, central banks should not deny that they will do things that, in the event of a crisis, they will end up doing if within their legal powers.

This does not mean that either the legislature or executive government must list or approve every security that the central bank may lend against or buy outright. An FCO might reasonably be cast in terms of general criteria, leaving the detailed fleshing-out of the regime to the technical expertise of the central bank. My point is that any discretion should be constrained by a clear standard. In particular, there should be no surprises if the central bank loses money; and their role in allocative choices should be minimised.

4.5 Parsimony Given Statutory Objectives

Beyond all that, central banks should adopt and publicly articulate a principle of 'instrument parsimony', meaning that they should conduct the most vanilla set of operations consistent with achieving the objectives set for them by the legislature. The purpose here, again reflecting our Principles for Delegation, is to help the public and the legislature monitor what central banks are doing with their balance sheets. Easier, I suggest, for legislative overseers routinely to ask the central bank to explain why it has changed its short-term interest rate (and, possibly, a macro-prudential regulatory lever) than to have to make sense of why it is intervening in a whole range of financial markets to influence term premia, liquidity premia and credit-risk premia.

So I favour central banks using the fewest instruments consistent with achieving their objectives, taking into account the constraints imposed by the frictions and imperfections of the real-world economy they seek to influence.

In practice, that entails a highly parsimonious approach when short-term interest rates are above the effective lower bound. But while this principle is particularly apposite for normal circumstances ('peacetime'), it should apply all of the time.

Thus, while it was more than tolerable for central banks to become innovators during 2007–09 as the circumstances had not been foreseen and there was an imperative of shielding the public from a repeat of the Great Depression, the sequential unrolling of multiple, experimental acronymed programmes can and should be avoided if similar conditions were to arise again. Subject to where any particular jurisdiction decides that its *Fiscal Carve Out* constraints should bind, central banks ought now to know enough to use the minimum number of such programmes to meet the challenge presented by such conditions.[9]

Those contingency programmes should be articulated in advance. They will never be complete, but they broadly define the line where a central bank needs political support for going into territory that, technically, is within its legal powers but was never remotely contemplated.

4.6 Precepts for Central Bank Balance-Sheet Operations

Summing up, I am proposing the following general principles to guide debates on central bank balance-sheet regimes (not all defended here):

1. Each central bank should have clear purposes, powers and constraints for its balance-sheet operations. The constraints comprise an FCO specifying where the dividing line between independent central bankers and elected fiscal policymakers should lie.
2. The regime should be time consistent: central banks should not deny that they will do things that in fact they would do. So any constraints should be binding and incentive-compatible for lawmakers.
3. Central bank balance-sheet operations should at all times be as parsimonious as possible consistent with achieving their objectives, in order to aid comprehensibility and accountability.
4. Within the FCO constraints, central banks should minimise risk of loss consistent with achieving their statutory objectives.

---

[9] For example, the Bank of England would not need to reinvent something like the March 2008-launched Special Liquidity Scheme (SLS), because since the autumn of 2008 it has been committed to lending, against a wide range of collateral, via a Discount Window Facility and longer-term repos. The SLS was an innovation to plug a serious gap that no longer exists in the Bank of England's standard regime.

5. Central banks should not lend, even against good collateral, to borrowers that are fundamentally insolvent (Tucker, 2014b).
6. If they are permitted to operate in private-sector paper, the selection of individual instruments should be as formulaic as possible, in order to avoid the central bank making detailed choices about the allocation of credit to borrowers in the real economy.
7. Central banks should draw up and publish comprehensive contingency plans for the pursuit of their objectives, within their mandate and, in particular, FCO constraints. Those plans should pre-programme any coordination with other parts of government that control material parts of the consolidated state balance sheet (e.g. government debt managers), so that a back door is not opened up to political control of policy intended to be delegated to the central bank.

There is not space here to apply these precepts to different kinds of central banking operation, but such an audit is both feasible and desirable.[10] It would provide useful input to a debate that is next to unavoidable given a revolutionary change in central bank practice over the past decade or so.

By moving to pay interest on reserves, a step taken by the European Central Bank and the Bank of England before the crisis, and by the Federal Reserve, with the express consent of Congress, during the crisis, central banks now have three instruments of balance-sheet policy available to them: the short-term policy rate of interest, the size of the balance sheet and the composition of the asset portfolio. Clear objectives and constraints, based on clear principles, are going to be needed more than ever.

4.7 Conclusion: Parsimonious but Not Always Pristine Central Banking

I have argued that central banking cannot always be pristine, but that it can and should be as parsimonious as possible taking into account their statutory objectives and what is going on in the economy. Practically, this means that they should shrink their balance sheets

---

[10] For an examination of operations in government and private sector paper, for business cycle and 'credit cycle' objectives, see Tucker (2016).

when they can, rather than casting around for other good works they might take on.

Getting back to base is all the more important given the current four-pronged debate about the merits and risks of central bank independence. That 'base' cannot be identical to the flawed pre-crisis orthodoxy that helped lead to our current economic problems. But the new base must be recognisable, since that is itself a source of legitimacy. And it should be chosen by the people's representatives after public debate. Contrary to some suggestions, far from being off-limits, central bank independence can be debated because our societies should truly believe in and consciously choose where to accept unelected power. Of all today's great institutions, central banks do not need 'safe spaces'.

References

Alesina, Alberto and Guido Tabellini (2007), 'Bureaucrats or Politicians? Part I: A Single Policy Task', *American Economic Review*, 97(1), pp. 169–79.

(2008), 'Bureaucrats or Politicians? Part II: Multiple Policy Tasks', *Journal of Public Economics*, 92, pp. 426–47.

Blanchard, Olivier, Eugenio Cerutti and Lawrence H. Summers (2015), 'Inflation and Activity: Two Explorations and Their Monetary Policy Implications', Working Paper Series WP15-19, Peterson Institute for International Economics.

Goodhart, C. (1988), *The Evolution of Central Banks*, Cambridge, MA: MIT Press.

Milgrom, Paul and Bengt Holmstrom (1991), 'Multi-task Principal-Agent Analysis: Incentive Contracts, Asset Ownership and Job Design', *Journal of Law, Economics & Organisation*, 7 (special issue), pp. 24–52.

Pettit, Philip (2004), 'Depoliticizing Democracy', *Ratio Juris*, 17(1), pp. 52–65.

(2012), *On the People's Terms: A Republican Theory and Model of Democracy*, Cambridge: Cambridge University Press.

Tucker, Paul (2014a), 'Independent Agencies in Democracies: Legitimacy and Boundaries for the New Central Banks', the 2014 Gordon Lecture, Harvard Kennedy School, 1 May.

(2014b), 'The Lender of Last Resort and Modern Central Banking: Principles and Reconstruction', *BIS Papers No. 79*.

(2016), *The Political Economy of Central Bank Balance Sheet Management*, New York, NY: Columbia University, 5 May. www
.newyorkfed.org/newsevents/events/markets/2016/0504-2016

Volcker, Paul (1990), *The Triumph of Central Banking?*, Per Jacobsson Lecture.

Yellen, Janet L. (2016), 'Macroeconomic Research After the Crisis', delivered at 'The Elusive "Great" Recovery: Causes and Implications for Future Business Cycle Dynamics' conference, Federal Reserve Bank of Boston, 14 October.

5 Central Bank Talk about Future Monetary Policy

Lessons from the Crisis and Beyond

DONALD KOHN

Discussion of the likely evolution of the economy and monetary policy settings was an aspect of central bank communication for some time before the global financial crisis (GFC). It most often encompassed forecasts for the economy and inflation that economic agents could translate into an expected path for policy interest rates, but for a few central banks and under some circumstances it had gone further to at least give hints about the central bank's expected path for its policy. During the GFC and sluggish recovery, forward guidance about future policy settings has become more widespread and more detailed and specific. That is because with the policy rate pinned near its effective lower bound (ELB), little scope existed to alter actual policy in order to affect expectations about future policy actions, and those expectations are critical to the effectiveness of policy. Moreover, at the ELB, meeting their objectives required the monetary authorities to react differently to incoming data and changing forecasts than they had in better times. Therefore, central banks have needed to rely on language to shape expectations and communicate that their reaction functions have shifted in particular ways.

I am going to concentrate my discussion on the experience of the US Federal Reserve. I will put the discussion of the USA in the context of some general principles about forward guidance. I will look at how forward guidance about future policy rates has evolved in the USA, and whether and how it was effective in shaping expectations and boosting demand as intended, and how it might evolve further as policy rates slowly lift off the ELB. I am particularly interested in the intersection of the design of forward guidance and uncertainty. Uncertainty in the Knightian sense is far more pervasive than we economists and central bankers were aware of or admitted to in the pre-crisis great moderation period. In my view, that uncertainty, and the associated humility policymakers should feel about their ability to predict the future, should affect and be reflected in the nature of any forward guidance central banks offer on the future path of policy.

Unless the limits of knowledge are recognised and acknowledged, repeated revisions of forward guidance could undermine confidence in the central bank and its ability to affect expectations with its words.

Uncertainty would seem to be especially incompatible with date-based forward guidance, which requires some sense of not only how economic relationships will evolve but also when – the timing of such an evolution. The Federal Reserve took a number of steps towards more explicit date-based guidance when its policy rate was pinned near the ELB. It has backed off several of those as its policy rate has lifted off, but not all of them. In particular, the Federal Reserve still publishes the policy rate path each Federal Open Market Committee (FOMC) participant believes will best accomplish the Committee's objectives conditioned on his or her individual expectations for labour markets and prices. The plot of the 'dots' used to indicate each participant's expected policy rate trajectory is a form of date-based guidance and seems to have induced policymakers and their observers to spend as much or more time discussing the timing of policy moves – e.g. next meeting, before the end of the year – as the conditions under which such moves might occur. As rates rise further above the ELB, the FOMC should find ways to convey the uncertainty underlying the policy-makers' expected path, to downplay implied timing, and to emphasise economic conditions and the potential response of policy to those conditions in its communications. I will conclude with some suggestions of the steps the FOMC might take to exit more fully from the date-based aspect of unconventional monetary policy at the ELB and shift more towards guidance based on forecasts of progress towards its goals.[1,2]

---

[1] Although I have not found a direct reference to forward guidance per se in Charles Goodhart's writings, we can infer considerable scepticism about its practical value from two discussions of the interest rate conditioning assumption for central bank forecasts. In the first (Goodhart, 2009) he points out a number of drawbacks to the monetary policy committee publishing its expected path for rates as a basis for its forecast: the difficulty of finding a consensus on a large and diverse committee; the risk of the public taking the path as more of a commitment than is intended, giving insufficient weight to uncertainty; problems with market participants giving too much weight to the central bank forecast and insufficient to their own judgements; opening the central bank to criticism when actual rates didn't follow the forecast; and constraining needed flexibility. In the second reference (Goodhart and Lim, 2011), Goodhart and his co-author show that central bank forecasts (and market forecasts for that matter) are systematically biased and have no predictive value past two quarters.

[2] The analysis and suggestions of this chapter overlap to some extent with those in Feroli et al. (2016). My scepticism about the cost-benefit calculus of central banks giving specific information about expected future policy paths under most circumstances was also voiced in Kohn (2005).

5.1 Forward Guidance

Central banks have become increasingly transparent about their views and analysis of key elements of monetary policy over the past few decades. The fundamental tenet behind this has been that markets work better and are more likely to be in synch with, and reinforce the effects of, central bank policies when economic agents understand how the monetary policymakers are expecting the economy to evolve and how policy is likely to respond. The most important element has been greater transparency about the objectives of monetary policy, in particular an inflation target – either set by governments or, for European Central Bank (ECB) and the Federal Reserve, chosen by the central bank itself – to implement a legal mandate for price stability.

5.1.1 Forward Guidance at the Effective Lower Bound

Until the GFC, central banks generally concentrated on informing observers about their predictions for the economy and inflation relative to their objectives for those variables, allowing market participants to infer the likely course of policy interest rates from the pattern of past central bank behaviour. Most central banks (the Federal Reserve was an occasional exception) shied away from explicitly forecasting their own actions, fearful that such predictions would be misleadingly interpreted as commitments rather than forecasts subject to correction in response to unexpected developments, possibly constraining or complicating the exercise of needed policy flexibility. In addition, as implicit and explicit inflation targeting took hold in a period of relatively benign economic conditions, agents seemed to be able to do a good-enough job of predicting central bank actions, and when they didn't policy authorities had plenty of scope to adjust their policy stances to correct and compensate.

As noted in the introduction, in the GFC and its aftermath, with policy rates close to or at their ELBs for an extended period, more central banks started to discuss more explicitly their intentions for their policy interest rate – forward guidance.

Forward guidance is an attractive policy tool at the ELB. Monetary policy works importantly through the effects of expected policy actions on current financial conditions. Central banks have considerable experience over the years with this linkage and with the empirical evidence relating financial conditions to future spending and prices. In that regard, forward guidance about future policy rates is perhaps a more comfortable 'unconventional policy' than asset purchases, which work through term premiums and the central bank's balance sheet size and for which there is little precedent to gauge effects.

Moreover, central banks have needed to convey that their policy reaction functions were changing at the ELB, and forward guidance is a direct way of doing that. Unprecedented economic and policy conditions from 2008 onwards meant that policy reaction functions would need to adapt and past policy responses to price and activity indicators would not be good guides to likely policy choices.

For example, policy would need to compensate for a period of excessively tight conditions at the ELB when rates could not be cut substantially further and asset purchases by themselves were not enough to make up for this shortfall. Policy strategy would also need to take account of the benefits of speeding the return of output and employment to higher levels and inflation to target after the deep recession to avoid a drop in inflation expectations and to draw discouraged workers back into the labour force. Finally, policy trajectories would need to take account of asymmetric policy loss functions in which the costs of tightening more quickly than turned out to be called for were seen to be much higher and harder to correct near the ELB than the costs of being too slow, the inflation effects of which could always be corrected by a steeper trajectory of rate hikes. These policy influences argue for a reaction function that keeps interest rates lower for longer than might be implied by past responses to changing outlooks for economic activity and inflation and for tightening more gradually.

It is especially critical to achieving the central bank's objectives that at or near the ELB economic agents understand that reaction functions have indeed changed in this direction. If financial market participants start to build in a more rapid increase in policy rates than the policymakers think will be appropriate, the resulting increases in longer-term interest rates, declines in asset prices, and firming of exchange rates will tighten financial conditions and undermine the recovery in the economy and the return of inflation to its target level. Away from the ELB, policy can correct for this by easing unexpectedly, but of course this is not available at the ELB and words are the main way to correct such misperceptions.

Finally, the simultaneous use of multiple tools – asset purchases and current and expected interest rates – has suggested that explicit discussion of each might reduce confusion about how each would be deployed and unwound, as happened in the taper tantrum of mid-2013.

5.1.2 Forward Guidance Comes in Many Varieties

Broadly, the policy committee can forecast its policy rate based on its projections for the economy, with the understanding that as the economy evolves so too will the trajectory of policy rates – the policy committee will re-optimise. Alternatively, the policy committee can commit to a particular course of action, say keeping rates lower for longer than a re-optimisation process would suggest even if the economy follows its expected path. Either the forecast or the commitment can be tied to the passage of time or to evolving economic conditions.

Several economists writing about policy at the ELB have advocated a commitment strategy, in which the commitment is to be 'irresponsible' in the future by deliberately allowing inflation to overshoot its target for a time even after the economy has reached its potential (e.g. Woodford, 2012). The theory is that as agents come to expect the overrun, real interest rates are reduced further, speeding up the return to full employment and the inflation target. To be sure, some central banks have lived with, or said they will live with, a temporary overshooting of inflation targets. In the UK, inflation was temporarily high after the GFC as the price level adjusted to the fall in sterling, and the Monetary Policy Committee (MPC) is predicting another overshoot in the wake of sterling weakness after Brexit; in the USA the Federal Reserve said that it might expect to overshoot its inflation target temporarily so long as labour market slack persisted (the 'balanced approach' to its dual mandate). Furthermore, Federal Reserve policymakers have talked about running a 'high pressure' economy to repair damage to potential gross domestic product (GDP) from the GFC, which implies taking risks on the side of an inflation overshoot.

However, with the recent exception of Japan, policy committees have been reluctant to embrace a commitment to overshooting in the absence of one of these special circumstances, fearing that the short-term gains were uncertain and would be more than offset later by the costs of unanchoring inflation expectations. So almost all forms of forward guidance used have been conditioned on economic developments following their expected path and have envisioned inflation returning to its target value once the special circumstances have

passed. Still, as discussed below, the Federal Reserve's forward guidance has embodied other forms of commitment – at a minimum to a
different reaction function than had been followed in the past, and
often to the passage of time, though this last commitment has usually
been qualified.

5.1.3 Challenges for Forward Guidance

Monetary policymaking is a complex, subtle undertaking. It should
be focused on attaining its objectives as expeditiously as possible consistent with macroeconomic stability. It needs to use all available
information about likely progress towards its objectives, and that
information should be interpreted through some sense of the underlying structure of the economy and relationships among key variables
that is explained to the public. Policy explanations should include discussions of equilibrium values as well as of the forces pushing the
economy towards those equilibriums or holding it back.

But, critically, all that is subject to revision as new information
arrives in an uncertain world, and any explanations or expectations
must take account of that uncertainty. New information will give
insight on the evolving state of the economy and also on the end
points – where it might be evolving to. The past eight years have been
marked by a considerable degree of uncertainty in several dimensions.
Among them are how the interplay of financial factors, including
debt-burdened balance sheets and impaired lenders, would affect the
recovery from a very deep recession and how markets, households
and businesses would respond to unprecedented monetary policy
actions. Unusually, the past eight years have also seen a high degree
of uncertainty about the degree of labour utilisation and growth rate
of potential GDP, the relationship between the level of GDP and the
change in inflation, and the level of interest rates consistent with
the economy producing at full employment with stable inflation.
Estimates of these key variables have been subject to considerable discussion and frequent revision (Bernanke, 2016).

We have been in uncharted waters – circumstances beyond the
experience of policymakers and economic agents. And all this uncertainty and change has occurred at a time when central banks have
felt it necessary to supply more guidance about their expectations
about the future path of their policy rates.

In addition, with so little history to guide decisions, monetary policymakers have had unusually diverse views and persistent disagreements about the appropriate policy to achieve agreed objectives. Disagreement on the policy committee is constructive, even necessary, to prevent 'group think', and any forward guidance should not be allowed to impede the discussion of these disagreements, internally or in public. But disagreements can interfere with giving a clean read on the path forward.

Finally, forward guidance about future policy rates can damp market reactions to incoming data and reduce volatility. Indeed, reducing market uncertainty is one of the channels through which forward guidance can ease financial conditions more broadly at the ELB and stimulate spending. But the challenge is to allow constructive, countercyclical, market reactions to come through – i.e. allow markets to tighten a bit when outcomes exceed the central bank's expectations and ease when they fall short – and not to remove more uncertainty than is justified by the underlying understanding of the way forward. Reduced volatility can induce risk-taking in the form of higher leverage and greater maturity transformation that might have adverse implications for financial stability when market participants become overly confident they know the path of interest rates (Adrian and Shin, 2008, 2014).

In these circumstances, finding the right balance between forecast and commitment, time and economic conditions, confidence and acknowledging uncertainty, and figuring out how to preserve the benefits of committee diversity while conveying a reasonably clear message have been challenging.

5.2   Federal Reserve Forward Guidance

5.2.1 Evolution

The Federal Reserve's forward guidance has evolved in response to shifting circumstances and to a little experimentation and learning on the job. Hints about which way the FOMC might be leaning in its policy considerations were incorporated into policy announcements as early as 1999 and into the speeches and testimony of its chairman even before that. But these had very short horizons – often the very next meeting. The slow recovery from the recession of 2000–1 with both inflation and interest rates at unusually low levels presented the FOMC with policy and communication challenges very similar to those it was to face after the GFC. The Committee in 2003 was concerned that market participants were expecting policy interest rates to follow the fairly steep upward path they had typically traced after previous recessions, and it saw the resulting longer-term interest rates and asset prices as running an unacceptable risk of deflation and prolonged high unemployment. Therefore it cautioned market participants not to expect a rapid turnaround in rates after the trough of the recession and it subsequently wanted them to recognise that the Committee's view of appropriate monetary policy encompassed an unusually flat upward rate trajectory ('at a pace likely to be measured'). This guidance was conditioned on the economy following its expected path. But market participants came to have firm expectations that 'measured pace' meant a quarter of a percentage point at each meeting; also, the Committee seemed to be locked into a commitment that some members found uncomfortable because it tended to damp market reactions to new information, and they were concerned that the predictability of the path of short-term rates would foster risky behaviour in the financial sector, including the maturity transformation of the carry trade.

When its policy interest rate got to the ELB in the fall of 2008, the FOMC once again saw a need to caution economic agents that under the circumstances it expected the rate to stay there a long time – longer than some economists and market participants seemed to anticipate drawing on a historic pattern of sharp recoveries from deep recessions. The FOMC started with vague language about how long economic conditions were likely to warrant really low rates – e.g. 'some time', 'extended period'. By August 2011 it felt that its vague guidance on how long very low rates would persist wasn't getting through effectively – markets had built in an earlier increase in rates than the FOMC considered appropriate for achieving its objectives. Effective communication of its intentions and its desire to promote better growth through more accommodative policy required more specific date-based forward guidance, and it noted that it expected conditions to warrant its highly accommodative policy to be maintained at least through mid-2013. As the recovery languished, the minimum end date was extended (in January 2012) to the end of 2014, and (in September 2012) to mid-2015. In each case the date was conditioned on the Committee's expectations that economic developments would make that policy setting appropriate for that length of time. The January 2012 change in date coincided with the first publication of the dots marking each participant's view of the path of appropriate monetary policy. But the Committee felt that the explicit date in its policy announcement would be clearer and carry more weight than a scattering of dots from all participants.

In December 2012, date-based forward guidance transitioned to guidance more based on economic conditions. Specifically, the Committee said that it anticipated that the exceptionally low funds rate 'will be appropriate at least as long as the unemployment rate remains above 6.5 percent, inflation between one and two years ahead is projected to be no more than one-half percentage point above the committee's 2 percent longer term goal, and long-term inflation expectations continue to be well anchored'.[3] The use of thresholds instead of only time would be a more explicit rendition of the Committee's reaction function and should allow market prices to reflect the effect of changing economic conditions on the likely date of the first rate increase. Still, the FOMC didn't abandon time-based guidance in that it noted in December that these thresholds were consistent with its earlier time-based guidance. In this and subsequent announcements it also indicated that highly accommodative policy would remain appropriate for a 'considerable time' after asset purchases ended and the economic recovery strengthens. And it has continued to publish the dots with their explicit time dimension, reinforced in the fall of 2014 by publishing the median of the dots, and emphasising the shifting time-based pattern of participants' rate expectations in its communications.

5.2.2 Effect

A number of studies have examined the effect of Federal Reserve forward guidance in the past several years on financial markets. Those studies tend to look at the response of interest rates and asset prices in a window around announcements. Isolating the effects is complicated by the fact that in some cases new forward guidance was

[3] The threshold approach had been championed by Charles Evan, president of the Chicago Federal Reserve bank and explained in Campbell et al. (2012).

accompanied by other policy actions, such as added asset purchases. In addition, some of the changes may well have been anticipated by markets, so the effects preceded the announcement. Still, the studies show that announcements generally reduced the expected path for the federal funds rate over the next several years – they were effective in that regard, with much smaller, if any, effects on expected rates further out or on private borrowing costs (e.g. Swanson, 2016). The specific date-based guidance seems to have had the largest effects.

But expected policy rates can fall for several reasons. What forward guidance generally has been trying to convey is that policy rates will be lower relative to actual and expected economic conditions than market participants had anticipated – i.e. the reaction function and policy strategy have shifted. But expected rates can also decrease if market participants believe the central bank has an advantage in forecasting and the more accommodative forward guidance conveys information that the economy and prices will be weaker than market participants had projected. In the latter case the central bank's words can depress demand, so the effectiveness of forward guidance at the ELB depends on the dominance of the expected shift in reaction function (Woodford, 2012).

The studies that have tried to ascertain the effects of the Federal Reserve's forward guidance on economic outcomes and market perceptions of the reaction function have generally found that it has been somewhat successful. Two model-based studies have detected positive effects on output and inflation (Del Negro et al., 2012; Becker and Smith, 2015). Two other studies have used the configuration of forecasts of interest rates, activity, and prices in surveys of primary dealers and economists more generally to ascertain perceptions of the FOMC's reaction function. One found that forward guidance, along with asset purchases, has been effective at getting across the message that the Federal Reserve was putting more emphasis on economic slack than it had before the GFC (Engen et al., 2015). The other found that market economists expected lower levels of unemployment for any given level of inflation (Femia et al., 2013).

So forward guidance has worked in the sense of signalling a different reaction function than market participants had been expecting and one more in keeping with achieving the Federal Reserve's objectives. It has also tended, however, to damp volatility and market reactions to incoming data, though this could be at least partly a consequence of the constraints of the ELB, where rate risks are one-sided (Feroli et al., 2016; Williams, 2016).

Forward guidance does not appear to have materially constrained policymaking – i.e. to have reduced flexibility to make needed policy adjustments. That, however, may be partly due to the circumstances that have prevailed. In particular, the repeated downward revisions in expected growth, in the unemployment rates consistent with stable inflation, and in the likely value of the policy interest rate at equilibrium, implied a later and flatter rate trajectory; that is, the FOMC never was tempted to raise interest rates before its commitment to keep them near zero had expired.

But the persistent changes in the date-based forward guidance and then in the path for the funds rate implied by participants' rate expectations, may have damaged the Federal Reserve's reputation and confidence in its analysis (Feroli et al., 2016). Even the economic conditions-based guidance of the thresholds proved a poor guide to policy action: The unemployment rate was a full 1.5 percentage points below the threshold when rates were first raised. And casual observation would suggest that much of the discussion of monetary policy in the media centres around the dates on which policy might be tightened – the next meeting, how many times before yearend – often driven by the configuration of the dots, not the underlying forces shaping policy. Even the Chair's carefully reasoned speeches about policy strategy are examined mostly for any clues about near-term rate prospects.

It is difficult to give useful forward guidance in an uncertain economic environment. A diverse Committee is trying to shape the expectations of a market that is itself driven by diverse investors influenced by herding and other behaviour not necessarily linked to a sober assessment of monetary policy strategy considerations. Market participants want to know with more specificity and commitment what the monetary policymakers will do and when they will do it than the policymakers themselves can usefully tell them (Kohn, 2005).

5.3 Conclusions and Recommendations

Date-based forward guidance was effective at the ELB in changing expectations and assessments of the Federal Reserve's reaction function. And it has a place when interest rates and asset prices reflect market expectations greatly at odds with those of the central bank, and central bank options to deal with those expectations are limited by the ELB. But it is difficult to convey with the appropriate degree of uncertainty and can constrain needed policy flexibility. Also, it has some possible costs in damping reactions to the implications of incoming data for the outlook, promoting excessive risk-taking, and reducing confidence in the central bank when it is frequently revised. Therefore, time references should be rare and mostly vague or general, in keeping with the limit of our knowledge.

The most useful information for economic agents is a sense of the policy strategy and the policy committee's view relating that strategy to its expectations for the evolution of the economy. That reaction function is hard to convey in a few sentences or in a formula using a limited set of actual or forecasted variables. Reaction functions are best spelled out in monetary policy reports, testimonies and speeches, where conditionality or commitment can be explained along with the policymakers' understanding of the economic dynamics.

The Federal Reserve has appropriately backed off specific time-based guidance as policy rates have lifted off the ELB. But elements of time-based guidance persist in general references in its announcements ('gradual', 'some time'). And those dots keep focus in the markets and in the public statements of some FOMC participants on dates rather than conditions for rate adjustments.

I start from the presumption that the dots are here to stay; removing them would be seen as a step back in transparency and, appropriately presented, they can be aids to understanding. My recommendations to the Federal Reserve centre on reducing the remaining weight on time-based forward guidance to align it better with underlying uncertainty and on increasing the attention to helping people understand the reaction function.

1. Stop publishing the median of the dots; it is not necessarily a good representation of the Committee's centre of gravity given the small size of the FOMC, and it greatly increases attention to a narrow path for rates.
2. Find some way to indicate uncertainty around the expectations for appropriate policy. That is not easy because those dots represent as many as nineteen different forecasts, each with its own uncertainty, but it is vital to come up with some way of indicating the

broad range of possibilities in an uncertain world. The fan charts that the MPC at the Bank of England uses in its inflation report graphically illustrate the range and subjective probability of possible outcomes, albeit drawn from a very different type of forecasting exercise.

3. De-emphasise the implied path for rate increases over the next year or two in the official pronouncements of the Federal Reserve and the press conferences of the Chair. Certainly, shifts in the dots have been useful to understanding and highlighting underlying changes in FOMC participants' assessment of the economy and inflation, but more useful would be a direct discussion of those changes with reduced emphasis on the specific time path of policy.

4. Similarly, in their speeches and media appearances, FOMC participants should agree to downplay the time dimension of policy – whether rates should go up at the next meeting, or how many times they might rise this year – and instead highlight their read on the economic circumstances that should trigger rate changes and how they see the situation developing economically. They should refocus the discussion to what good forward guidance should be about – the strategy of monetary policy. The financial cable networks won't like it, but the Federal Reserve and the markets will benefit.

5. The dots are part of a broader projection exercise in which each FOMC participant gives a projection of inflation, unemployment and growth. The FOMC should identify – not by name – which dots go with which economic forecasts. This would, in effect, give observers an opportunity to infer individual participants' reaction functions; it should help economic agents to infer the Committee's reaction function more accurately than simply looking at the median of multiple forecasts.

6. Finally, the Federal Reserve should use the semi-annual monetary policy report to better explain and focus on its broad strategy. I have previously advocated that the monetary policy report include the material that has gone to the FOMC on policy rules (Kohn and Wessel, 2016). For some time, as an input to its policy process, the Committee has been shown the results of a number of policy rules based on both incoming data and economic forecasts. And this material has been accompanied by explanations of why the current and expected settings of monetary policy might deviate from the rules. I believe a Federal Reserve initiative to present this

material could reduce the impetus behind a legislative proposal to require the Federal Reserve to publish a policy rule, explain any time it deviated, and subject those deviations to review by a Congressional agency.[4] But it would also serve as a jumping-off place for a discussion of broad strategy, which might help focus more attention there and less on the date of the next policy action.

References

Adrian, T. and H.S. Shin (2008), 'Financial Intermediaries, Financial Stability and Monetary Policy'. Paper presented at the Federal Reserve Bank of Kansas City Economic Policy Symposium, Jackson Hole WY, August.

(2014), 'Procyclical Leverage and Value-at-Risk', *The Review of Financial Studies*, 27(2), pp. 373–403.

Becker, T. and A.L. Smith (2015), 'Has Forward Guidance Been Effective?' *Federal Reserve Bank of Kansas City Economic Review*, Q3, pp. 57–78.

Bernanke, B. (2016), 'The Fed's Shifting Perspective on the Economy and its Implications for Monetary Policy', *Ben Bernanke's Blog*, August. www.brookings.edu/blog/ben-bernanke/2016/08/08/the-feds-shifting-perspective-on-the-economy-and-its-implications-for-monetary-policy/.

Campbell, J.R., C.L. Evans, J.D.M. Fisher and A. Justiniano (2012), 'Macroeconomic Effects of FOMC Forward Guidance', *Brookings Papers on Economic Activity*, Spring.

Del Negro, M., M.P. Giannoni and C. Patterson (2012), 'The Forward Guidance Puzzle', *Federal Reserve Bank of New York Staff Reports*, No. 574. Revised December 2015.

Engen, E.M., T. Laubach and D. Reifschneider (2015), 'The Macroeconomic Effects of the Federal Reserve's Unconventional Monetary Policies', *Board of Governors of the Federal Reserve System Finance and Economics Discussion Series* 2015-005.

Femia, K., S. Friedman and B. Sack (2013), 'The Effects of Policy Guidance on Perceptions of the Fed's Reaction Function', *Federal Reserve Bank of New York Staff Reports*, No. 652.

Feroli, M., D. Greenlaw, P. Hooper, F.S. Mishkin and A. Sufi (2016), 'Language after Liftoff: Fed Communication Away from the Zero Lower Bound'. Paper presented at the University of Chicago US Monetary Policy Forum, New York, February.

---

[4] The Federal Reserve did this – presented the rule material – in its July 2017 monetary policy report.

Goodhart, C.A.E. (2009), 'The Interest Rate Conditioning Assumption', *International Journal of Central Banking*, 5, pp. 85–108.

Goodhart, C.A.E. and W.B. Lim (2011), 'Interest Rate Forecasts: A Pathology', *International Journal of Central Banking*, 7(2), pp. 135–71.

Kohn, D. (2005), 'Central Bank Communication'. Proceedings of the Annual Meeting of the American Economic Association, Philadelphia, January.

Kohn, D. and D. Wessel (2016), 'Eight Ways to Improve the Fed's Accountability', *Bloomberg View*, February. www.bloomberg.com/view/articles/2016-02-09/eight-ways-to-improve-the-fed-s-accountability.

Swanson, E.T. (2016), 'Measuring the Effects of Federal Reserve Guidance and Asset Purchases on Financial Markets'. www.ericswanson.us/papers/facts3.pdf.

Williams, J.C. (2016), 'Discussion of Language after Liftoff: Fed Communication Away from the Zero Lower Bound'. Proceedings of the University of Chicago US Monetary Policy Forum, New York, February.

Woodford, M. (2012), 'Methods of Policy Accommodation at the Interest-Rate Lower Bound'. Paper Presented at the Federal Reserve Bank of Kansas City Economic Policy Symposium, Jackson Hole, WY, August.

6 | Bank Capital and Monetary Policy Transmission

HYUN SONG SHIN

Banks figure very prominently in policy discussions and in popular commentary, but the macroeconomics profession still has a rather uneasy relationship with banking. Some progress has been made in incorporating banks into theoretical models, but the standard workhorse macro models have little room for banks. Introductory textbooks in macroeconomics do not say much about banks, and for that matter, more sophisticated macro models used in central banks seldom mention banks, either.[1]

For my part, I remember a long discussion over coffee with a distinguished macroeconomist in early 2008. At issue was whether bank failures can be expected to have any adverse impact on the economy. His argument was simple, and in some ways compelling. Banks are intermediaries; lenders give funds to banks who then lend on to ultimate borrowers. If banks are not there to be the middle men, lenders will surely find other ways to lend to ultimate borrowers. Market instruments could take the place of banks; new intermediaries will spring up to take their place. There may be short-term disruptions, but as long as there are willing lenders and willing borrowers, the market will find a way to match them. What was all the fuss about?

We argued about the severity of the possible feedback effects to the real economy but we did not manage to agree that morning, in spite of many cups of coffee.

The author thanks Stefan Avdjiev, Claudio Borio, Jaime Caruana, Dietrich Domanski, Ingo Fender, Leonardo Gambacorta, Krista Hughes, Catherine Koch and Philip Turner for comments on earlier drafts; and Kristina Bektyakova, Sebastian Deininger and Anamaria Illes for excellent research assistance. An earlier version of this paper was presented at the European Central Bank and its Watchers XVII conference (Shin, 2016). The views expressed here are my own, and not necessarily those of the Bank for International Settlements.
[1] There are exceptions, such as Charles Goodhart's (1989) textbook, *Money, Information and Uncertainty*.

I was reminded of this conversation recently by all the press commentary on monetary policy transmission and how it may have changed with the introduction of negative policy rates by some central banks. Many of the arguments that we hear today in the commentaries and speeches are quite reminiscent of the arguments that my distinguished interlocutor was offering in 2008. Preparing my chapter for this volume has given me a chance to mull over the arguments again. Based on these reflections, I would like to offer two main points, which follow Charles Goodhart's (1989) work closely.

The first is on the way we view banks as actors in the economy. Banks are sometimes seen as passive actors who merely enable the decisions taken by lenders and borrowers. For this reason, they are seen as background detail that can be airbrushed out of our economic models for the sake of simplicity, much as my interlocutor was doing back in 2008. However, I would argue that this is a mistake. It turns out to be important to take account of banks as actors in their own right, managing their balance sheets actively, pursing their own objectives and reacting to the constraints that other actors place on them. This will sound very abstract for now, but let me come back to this and make it more concrete when discussing the impact of negative interest rates.

My second point is about bank capital. For most central banks, discussions about bank capital crop up most often in connection with their financial stability mandate or perhaps with their financial supervision mandate, if they have a role there. But the sound capitalisation of banks turns out to be vital for the transmission of monetary policy, also. In this sense, bank capitalisation ought to be a key concern for central banks in fulfilling their *monetary policy mandate*, as well as for their financial stability mandate.

6.1 Bank Capital as the Foundation for Lending

Banks are intermediaries; they borrow from other lenders, combine the borrowed funds with their own funds, and then lend the combined total to ultimate borrowers. Bank capital refers to the bank's own funds. The more capital a bank has, the more of its own funds it has to lend out. But bank capital plays a more important role than this for overall lending. As well as lending out its own funds, a bank with plenty of its own funds is able to borrow *more* from its creditors, and on much better terms than if the bank is poorly capitalised.

Therefore, if the objective of monetary policy is to unlock bank lending to the real economy, ensuring that banks have enough capital to support their lending activity is vital.

It is also true that bank capital is a loss-absorbing buffer in the sense that the bank's own funds can absorb losses from lending activity without imposing losses on the creditors to the banks. But solvent banks can sometimes be reluctant to lend, and weakly capitalised banks may seek to improve solvency metrics such as their ratio of capital to risk-weighted assets by cutting back on lending. If a bank's solvency metric is expressed as a ratio, there may even be some apparent tension between the monetary policy objective of unlocking bank lending (which entails expanding credit) and the supervisory imperative of ensuring the soundness of individual banks (which can be achieved by cutting back credit). This is why we sometimes hear calls for the relaxation of bank capital rules.

But this tension between the monetary policy objective and the supervisory imperative is more apparent than real; both the macro objective of unlocking bank lending and the supervisory objective of sound banks are better served if banks have more capital. In general, sound banks lend more, and do so in a sustainable way over the cycle.

The bank's own funds come from several sources, but the most important source is the bank's *retained earnings*. This portion of the bank's own funds refers to the accumulated stock of all of the bank's profits since its inception that have not been paid out as dividends to shareholders. This is probably not something that many of you follow closely, and so let me show you some numbers for the retained earnings of euro area banks.

Figure 6.1 shows the total amount of retained earnings for a group of ninety euro area banks as well as the cumulative amounts paid out as dividends since 2007.[2] I chose 2007 for this illustration, as 2007 was the beginning of the global financial crisis, and policymakers could see that all was not well for the world economy. Figure 6.1a shows the total accumulated dividends for this group of banks, while Figure 6.1b gives a snapshot of the same categories broken out by country of residence at the end of 2014.

---

[2] The list of banks follows in the appendix. The banks in the sample are locally incorporated banks in the euro area, not the consolidated global banking groups.

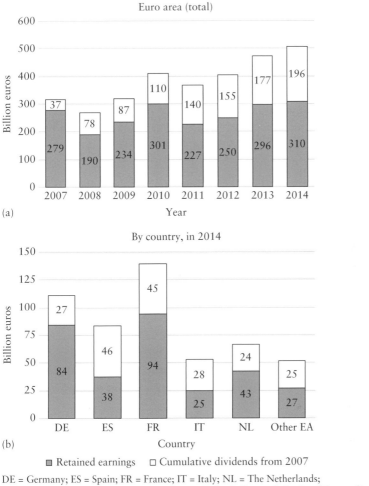

(a)

(b)

■ Retained earnings   □ Cumulative dividends from 2007

DE = Germany; ES = Spain; FR = France; IT = Italy; NL = The Netherlands;
Other EA = Other euro area (Austria, Belgium, Finland, Greece, Ireland and Portugal)

Figure 6.1 Total retained earnings and accumulated dividends of a group of ninety euro area banks
Sources: S&P Capital IQ; BIS calculations.

The grey bars indicate the total euro amount of retained earnings of the ninety banks in the sample. Notice that retained earnings can decline sometimes; this happens when the bank makes losses and has to dip into its retained earnings to make up for those losses.

By the end of 2014, the total retained earnings of this group of banks stood at 310 billion euros. Meanwhile, the accumulated dividends for this group of banks since 2007 amounted to 196 billion euros. This means that the retained earnings of these banks would have been 63 per cent higher in 2014, had the banks chosen to plough back the profits into their own funds rather than paying them out as dividends. If greater retained earnings had supported a virtuous circle of greater lending and higher profits, the hypothetical increase in retained earnings might have been larger still. In the case of some countries, the accumulated dividends exceeded the retained earnings of the banks; for the subsample of banks from Spain and Italy, retained earnings would have been more than double what it was at the end of 2014, had profits been ploughed back into the bank.

Figure 6.2 presents more detailed cross-section information on retained earnings across banks. The top panel shows the cross-section distribution of retained earnings. I have plotted the distribution at three snapshots in time: at the beginning of the crisis in 2007, during the euro area crisis in 2011 and, more recently, at the end of 2014.

We see that retained earnings can actually turn negative. This happens when accumulated losses exceed the accumulated stock of past profits ploughed back into the bank. We also see that the number of banks with negative retained earnings jumped in 2011, but the distribution shifted to the right in 2014. Yet, there remain many more banks with negative retained earnings than at the start of the crisis in 2007.

Why do banks choose to erode their capital in such large amounts? This is more than just an idle question, because banks' capital – their own funds – has important implications for bank lending in support of the real economy. I will come back to the question later but, for now, let me illustrate the role of bank capital in lending with some charts from a working paper with my Bank for International Settlements (BIS) colleague Leonardo Gambacorta (see Gambacorta and Shin, 2016). The paper studies a sample of 105 advanced economy banks to shed further light on their lending decisions. Figure 6.3 is from that working paper.

The top panel of Figure 6.3 shows a summary scatter chart that plots the relationship between the cost of the bank's borrowed funds and its overall leverage. Here, leverage is defined as the ratio of a bank's total assets to its equity. You can see that the scatter chart is quite dispersed, but the scatter chart overstates the noise in the relationship as it is just the simple scatter for the mean values for each

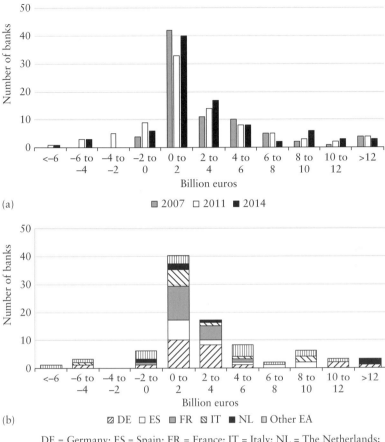

(a)

■ 2007 □ 2011 ■ 2014

(b)

▨ DE □ ES ▥ FR ◪ IT ■ NL ▥ Other EA

DE = Germany; ES = Spain; FR = France; IT = Italy; NL = The Netherlands;
Other EA = Other euro area (Austria, Belgium, Finland, Greece,
Ireland and Portugal)

Figure 6.2 Frequency distribution of retained earnings (a) in the total euro
area and (b) by country, sample of ninety euro area banks
Sources: S&P Capital IQ; BIS calculations.

bank, without controlling for bank characteristics or macro variables.
In our more detailed empirical analysis, we find that a 1 per cent
point increase in the equity-to-total-assets ratio is associated with a
four basis point reduction in the cost of borrowed funds for the bank.

This finding sets an important benchmark when considering the
benefits of higher bank capital for bank funding cost. For typical
levels of bank leverage, it would appear that banks could go a long

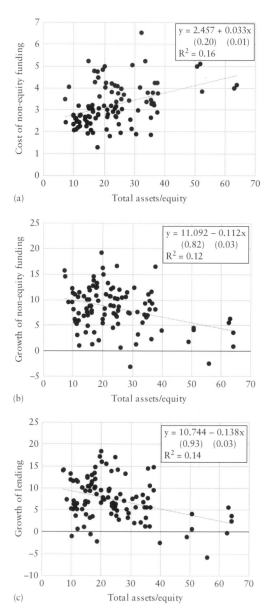

Figure 6.3 Bank capital and loan growth

Note: The panels present scatter plots between (a) the leverage of 105 advanced economy banks and cost of funding in percentage, (b) annual growth rate of debt financing in percentage and (c) annual growth rate of lending in percentage. Standard errors are in brackets.

Source: L. Gambacorta and H. S. Shin (April 2016), 'Why Bank Capital Matters for Monetary Policy', *BIS Working Papers*, No. 558.

way towards mitigating their supposedly higher cost of equity funding by keeping back more of their profits for retained earnings (and, hence, capital).[3]

The lower funding cost translates into greater intermediation activity by the bank. The centre panel of Figure 6.3 shows that banks that have more own funds, and hence lower funding costs, raise borrowed funds at a faster pace. The upshot is that banks with lower leverage expand their lending at a faster rate, too – this is the 'sound banks lend more' principle mentioned earlier. The bottom panel of Figure 6.3 shows this for the summary data. In the detailed analysis, we find that a 1 per cent point increase in the equity to total assets ratio is associated with a 0.6 per cent point uptick in the subsequent growth in lending.

To drive home the point, let me reach back to the analogy I used in 2014 at the European Central Bank (ECB) Annual Symposium (in Shin, 2014). That is, a bank's lending is to its capital as a building is to its foundations. If the bank's capital forms the foundations, its leverage corresponds to the height of the building that stands on the foundations. The size of the building is the total lending done by the bank. The bank can expand lending by using more borrowed funds and increasing its leverage. But it turns out that this kind of lending is not very resilient. It is 'fair weather lending', to coin a phrase. As soon as economic conditions turn less favourable for leverage, the bank shrinks its lending with very bad consequences for the real economy.

Figure 6.4 illustrates how the cyclical variation of lending plays out for a typical bank. It shows a scatter chart that plots the relationship between the annual change in total assets on the horizontal axis and how the assets are financed as between its own funds (in transparent circles) and in borrowed funds (in dark circles) on the vertical axis.[4]

The fitted line through the scatter plot between the change in assets and the change in borrowed funds has a slope that is essentially equal

---

[3] Consider a balance sheet of size 100, with equity of 10. If equity is raised to 11, a 4 basis point reduction in the cost of borrowed funds results in a cost saving of $0.0004 \times 89 = 0.0356$. If the cost of equity is assumed to be 10 per cent, the cost of equity funding is 1 when equity is 10 and 1.1 when equity is 11. The additional cost of equity is 0.1. The reduction in the cost of borrowed funds is 36 per cent of the supposed incremental cost of equity.

[4] The slopes of the two lines add up to 1, due to the balance sheet identity. See Adrian and Shin (2014).

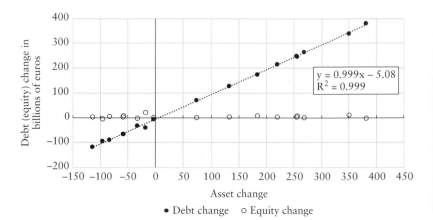

Figure 6.4 Annual changes in assets (from 1999 to 2015), equity and debt for a large European bank
Note: Scatter plot showing how much of the change in assets is accounted for by changes in debt and equity, respectively. Annual changes in billions of euros are shown for large European bank (1999–2015).
Sources: S&P Capital IQ; BIS calculations.

to 1, meaning that the change in assets in the short term, over horizons of around one year, are almost all accounted for by the change in debt. The transparent circle scatter for equity is flat, meaning that the bank's own funds do not vary much over the cycle.

This scatter chart reinforces the analogy between equity and the foundations of the building. It suggests that the foundations of the building are pretty much fixed, and what changes is the size of the building that stands on those foundations. The taller the building, the higher the leverage and the greater the amount of lending that is done by the bank. During boom times, the height of the building increases as the bank adds new floors to the existing structure. In other words, the bank increases its total assets by increasing its leverage atop the same equity base. The boom is associated with greater availability of credit and lower-risk weights for the bank's assets. The problems arrive when financial conditions turn for the worse and the bank is no longer able to secure borrowed funds. Then, the lending too grinds to a halt.

I would argue that there is an important lesson for monetary policymakers from the Sutyagin house analogy. If the aim of monetary policy is to induce banks to lend and to do so in a way that is sustainable over the cycle, securing a strong enough foundation is a vital first step. The foundation for lending is the bank's own funds – its capital. Otherwise, any additional lending may end up being fair weather lending that will vanish at the first sign of trouble.

Let me now come back to the question posed earlier as to why banks have been so reluctant to plough back their profits into their own funds. We need to better understand the reasons for this reluctance, but we may ask whether there are possible tensions between the private interests of some bank stakeholders versus the wider public interest of maintaining a soundly functioning banking system that can supply credit in support of economic activity.[5]

When the bank's share price is substantially below the book value of the bank's equity, shareholders may feel they can unlock some value from their shareholding by paying themselves a cash dividend, even at the expense of eroding the bank's lending base. As many of the shareholders are asset managers who place great weight on short-term relative performance in competition against their peers, the temptation to raid the bank's seed corn may become too strong to resist. The bank's management, for their part, may see the lower capital base as unobjectionable if it means that they can meet their return-on-equity target more easily by reducing the base for the calculation of return-on-equity.

These private motives are reasonable and readily understandable, but if the outcome is to erode capital that serves as the bank's foundation for lending for the real economy, then a gap may open up between the private interests of some bank stakeholders and the broader public interest. To the extent that undercapitalised banks perpetuate a weak economy and thereby keep bank stock prices under pressure, it may even be the case that paying out large dividends also fails to promote the collective interests of the bank's shareholders, let alone the wider public interest. One thing is clear: Banks have paid out substantial cash dividends, even in those regions where bank lending may not be sufficient to support recovery of economic activity after the crisis. This should be of concern to central bankers in pursuit of their monetary policy, as well as their financial stability mandates.

---

[5] For further development of this point, see Adamati et al. (2010) and Admati and Hellwig (2010).

6.2 Negative Interest Rates and Credit Growth

We have focused so far on bank capital as the basis for lending. What about interest rates? How does the central bank policy rate affect lending? This question has been gaining more attention recently in connection with the discussions on how negative central bank policy rates affect lending growth.

Let me start with a quick overview of what has been happening to credit growth in jurisdictions where the central bank policy rate is negative. Figure 6.5 plots the annual growth rate of bank lending to households and firms in Denmark, the euro area, Japan, Sweden and Switzerland.

The first thing to note is how diverse the experience with credit growth has been. Credit growth to firms and households turned positive in the euro area last year, and is running at around 1 per cent per year, while in Switzerland the growth rate has fallen from an annual rate of 8 per cent at the end of 2014. But the case that stands out is Sweden, where lending has been growing at close to 6 per cent annually. The contrast between Sweden and Switzerland is especially noteworthy.

How would banks fit into the picture? How would lower interest rates stimulate greater bank lending? In normal times, when interest

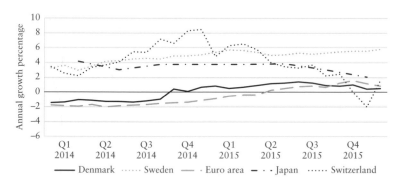

Figure 6.5 Annual growth in loans to household and non-financial firms by resident banks
Note: All outstanding loans; all maturities. Data are at a monthly frequency except for Japan, which is quarterly. The latest observation for the Japan credit series is for Q4 2015. For all other series, the latest observation is January 2016.
Sources: Bank of Japan; ECB; Datastream.

rates are positive, there is actually a lot in common between the textbook model above and how bank lending would respond to lower policy rates. Lower central bank policy rates can be expected to boost bank lending, too. In normal times, changes in the policy rate have a virtually one-for-one relationship with the change in the term spread, the difference between long-term and short-term rates. This is because the long-term rate moves by much less than the policy rate itself. Figure 6.6 illustrates this feature for the USA.

Figure 6.6a plots the ten-year and three-month US Treasury rate, with the gap in grey indicating the term spread – the difference between the ten-year rate and the three-month rate. Before the crisis, we see that the grey region widens when the short rate goes down. But after the crisis, once we hit the zero lower bound, the term spread is driven by fluctuations in the long rate.

Figure 6.6b plots the scatter chart between the twelve-month change in the ten-year rate and the twelve-month change in the three-month rate. Before the crisis, the black dots line up quite well along the diagonal line of slope minus one. But as the grey dots show, this feature breaks down after the crisis. We see that the three-month rate is immobile, and the term spread is driven entirely by the long rate.

For a bank whose funding cost is tied to the short-term rate, but whose lending rate is closer to the long-term rate, a higher term spread makes lending more profitable, which induces banks to lend more. A steeper yield curve driven by a low short rate is therefore favourable to bank lending, and this is why bank profitability tends to rise with an increase in the term spread.[6]

The introduction of negative policy rates has led to an active debate about bank profitability, but bank profitability should be discussed in connection with its impact on the real economy. If banks were to diversify into other business areas, such as asset management, but abandon lending, this might help their profitability but might do less for lending in support of the real economy. The issue is not only banks' profitability, as such, but the profitability of their lending activity.

---

[6] For more detailed evidence on this point, see Borio, Gambacorta and Hofmann (2015).

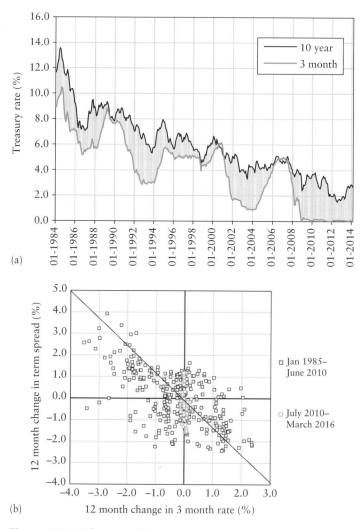

Figure 6.6 (a) Change in US ten-year and three-month treasury term spread and (b) change in three-month rate
Source: Federal Reserve.

The problem comes when you push the model beyond breaking point, and the abstraction is no longer acceptable. Then, the details start to matter, and airbrushing banks out of your macro model can lead to misleading conclusions. What if the car's wiring is now switched, and pressing the accelerator pedal actually activates the brakes?

The bank-driven credit story and the textbook story have similar predictions during normal times, but they start to diverge when the policy rate becomes negative. As we saw above, in the textbook explanation, there is nothing special about zero. However, for a bank, its overall funding cost may not fall much below zero. That is especially true if the bank is reliant on deposit funding from retail customers. It is rare for retail deposit rates to fall below zero, even when the central bank policy rates turn negative. Meanwhile, lending rates may fall nevertheless, especially if the central bank also pursues asset purchase programmes that push down long-term rates. This means that banks' lending rates will decline even if deposit rates do not, squeezing lending margins and dissuading banks from lending.

Figure 6.7 plots deposit rates in those jurisdictions where the central bank has adopted negative policy rates. The Swiss data show that wholesale deposit rates to large depositors went negative at the beginning of 2015, following the central bank policy rate into negative territory, but that household deposit rates have stayed above zero. The same is true of deposit rates in Denmark, Japan, Sweden and in the euro area.

The evidence is that banks have been reluctant to bring retail deposit interest rates down below zero, even if deposit rates to corporate and institutional clients can dip below zero. How important the zero lower bound turns out to be for retail deposit rates depends on how easily non-rate terms can be adjusted for retail clients, for instance, through fees. Another important element is how much of the banks' overall borrowed funds comes from retail depositors. In this respect, there is a wide range across different economies, as seen in Figure 6.8.

Figure 6.8 illustrates the diversity in the bank funding model across countries. Japanese banks have a high reliance on deposit funding, both as a proportion of banks' total assets and as a proportion of total loans. At the other end of the spectrum come Sweden and Denmark. In the case of Denmark, its unique system of covered bonds sets it apart from the other cases listed in Figure 6.8.

This brings us to Sweden. We saw earlier how bank credit growth has been buoyant in Sweden, in spite of negative policy rates. One possible reason for this is that Swedish banks are not so reliant on deposit funding.

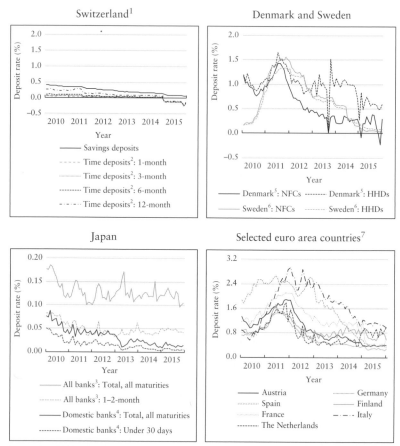

HHDs = households; NFCs = non-financial corporations.

[1] Interest rates on new deposits. [2] Median value of deposits of at least CHF 100,000. [3] New time deposits. [4] Certificates of deposit. [5] New domestic deposit rates for deposits with agreed maturity, excluding pooling scheme. [6] New domestic deposit rates of banks on all accounts. [7] Annualised agreed rate on new deposits with agreed maturity to non-financial corporations and households, all maturities.

Figure 6.7 Deposit rates of banks
Sources: Bank of Japan; Danmarks National bank; ECB; Sveriges Riks Bank; Swiss National Bank.

There is also perhaps an even more important point. Swedish banks are sensitive to monetary developments in the euro area, and especially to the slope of the euro yield curve. In recent months, Swedish banks have taken advantage of low long-term borrowing rates in euros, and have been issuing euro-denominated bonds of

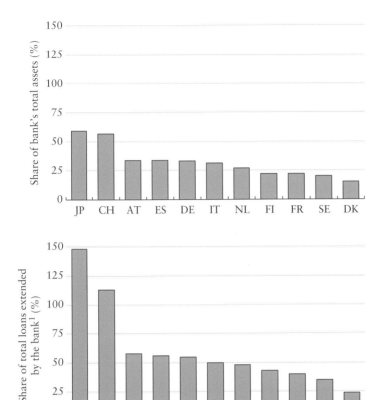

AT = Austria; CH = Switzerland; DE = Germany; DK = Denmark; ES = Spain;
FI = Finland; FR = France; IT = Italy; JP = Japan; NL = The Netherlands; SE = Sweden.

[1]For Switzerland, loans are the sum of amounts due from customers and mortgage loans.

Figure 6.8 Deposits of households and non-financial corporations up to December 2015
Note: Total outstanding deposits; for euro area MFIs excluding ESCB; for Switzerland amounts due in respect of customer deposits.
Sources: Bank of Japan; ECB; Swiss National Bank; Datastream.

longer maturity. The banks then swap the euros for Swedish krona in the capital market, meaning that they borrow Swedish krona by pledging the borrowed euro funds as collateral. Having borrowed the Swedish krona, they lend it out to domestic borrowers in Sweden (see Hilander, 2014).

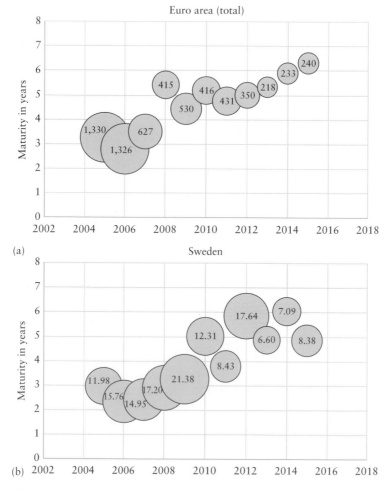

Figure 6.9 Gross issuance of euro-denominated debt securities (sum of domestic and international debt securities (in billions of euros))
Note: Size of the bubble indicates the relative gross issuance amount in billions of euros. Height of the bubble indicates weighted average maturity in years.
Sources: BIS debt securities statistics.

Figure 6.9 shows the gross issuance of euro-denominated bonds by banks. The size of the bubble indicates the relative size of gross issuance amounts over time, while the height of the bubbles indicates the average maturity of the gross issuance. Figure 6.9a shows the issuance activity of euro area banks, and Figure 6.9b shows the issuance activity of Swedish banks. Euro area banks have been issuing far less in notional amounts after the crisis than before, although the maturity is higher than before the crisis. For Swedish banks, their issuance activity is not much smaller now compared to before the crisis, and the maturity has also increased.

One indication of the banks' currency swap activity is the so-called cross-currency basis between the Swedish krona and the euro. This refers to the difference between the interest rate on the euro implied by the cross-currency swap versus what banks have to pay to borrow euros in the open market. The cross-currency basis for the Swedish krona versus the euro has been positive, meaning that the euro interest rate implied by the cross-currency swap is *lower* than the euro interbank rate. Another way of saying this is that there is an 'abundance' of euros in Sweden from sellers who wish to borrow Swedish krona by pledging euros as collateral. Only a few other currencies have this feature, and most of them are countries where the banks issue long-term bonds in international currencies to fund domestic lending. Australia is a good example, and Norway is another.

If we take in the bigger picture by zooming out and seeing the international dimension of bank lending, we get a better view of recent events. Figure 6.10 shows how the euro exchange rate affects cross-border lending to banks in Sweden. The top panel shows the relationship between the euro-denominated cross-border borrowing of banks in Sweden and the euro exchange rate. It shows that banks in Sweden tend to draw on more euro-denominated funding from outside Sweden when the euro is weak. This negative relationship between the euro exchange rate and cross-border flows is a fairly recent phenomenon, as is shown by the coefficients on the twenty-quarter rolling regressions in the bottom panel. In this sense, Sweden's buoyant credit growth may be related as much to monetary developments in the euro area as to domestic circumstances.

6.3 Concluding Remarks

I have made two arguments that very much echo Charles Goodhart's work. The first is that banks deserve attention as actors in their own right. By paying attention to essential details, we will be better equipped to recognise when the predictions of the standard textbook model

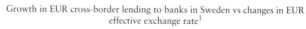

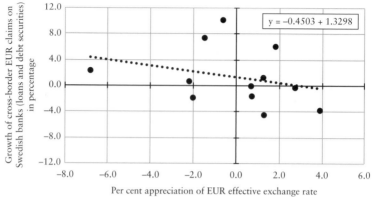

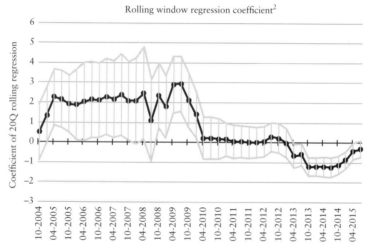

[1]The line is a fitted regression line. Positive changes in FX rate denote euro appreciation; percentage changes refer to EUR cross-border claims (loans and debt securities) on banks in Sweden.
[2]The dark circles indicate the regression coefficient from a 20-quarter rolling regression. Grey lines indicate one standard error bands.

Figure 6.10 Cross-border lending in euros to banks in Sweden
Sources: BIS effective exchange rate statistics; BIS locational banking statistics by residence.

will adequately serve in describing more realistic outcomes with banks. This is especially true when central bank policy rates are negative.

Second, having soundly capitalised banks is a public good, but the interests of some bank stakeholders and the broader public may diverge. Soundly capitalised banks should be a central concern of central banks in fulfilment of their mandates for both monetary policy and financial stability.

Appendix: The Ninety Banks Used in the Sample for Figures 6.1 and 6.2

Abanca Corporación Bancaria SA, ABN AMRO Group NV, Allied Irish Banks plc, Alpha Bank AE, Banca IMI SpA, Banca Monte dei Paschi di Siena SpA, Banca Nazionale del Lavoro SpA, Banca Popolare dell'Emilia Romagna Società Cooperativa, Banco Bilbao Vizcaya Argentaria SA, Banco Comercial Português SA, Banco de Sabadell SA, Banco Popolare Societa Cooperativa Scarl, Banco Popular Espanol SA, Banco Santander SA, Bankia SA, Bankinter SA, Banque Fédérative du Crédit Mutuel SA, Bausparkasse Schwäbisch Hall AG, Bayerische Landesbank, Belfius Banque SA/NV, BNP Paribas Fortis SA/NV, BNP Paribas Personal Finance SA, BNP Paribas SA, BNP Paribas Securities Services SCA, BRED Banque Populaire SA, Caisse des Dépôts et Consignations, Caisse Française de Financement Local SA, CaixaBank SA, Cassa di Risparmio di Parma e Piacenza SpA, Catalunya Banc SA, Commerzbank AG, Confédération Nationale du Crédit Mutuel, Coöperatieve Rabobank UA, Crédit Agricole Corporate and Investment Bank SA, Credit Agricole SA, Crédit du Nord Société Anonyme, Crédit Foncier de France, Crédit Industriel et Commercial, Crédit Mutuel Arkéa, Dekabank Deutsche Girozentrale, Deutsche Bank AG, Deutsche Boerse AG, Deutsche Kreditbank AG, Deutsche Pfandbriefbank AG, Deutsche Postbank AG, Dexia Crédit Local Société Anonyme, Dexia SA, DZ Bank AG, Erste Group Bank AG, Eurobank Ergasias SA, HSBC France SA, HSH Nordbank AG, Hypo Real Estate Holding AG, Hypothekenbank Frankfurt Aktiengesellschaft, Ibercaja Banco SA, Iccrea Holding SpA, ING Bank NV, ING Belgium SA/NV, INGDiBa AG, Instituto de Crédito Oficial, Intesa Sanpaolo SpA, KfW, Kutxabank SA, Landesbank Baden-Württemberg, Landesbank Berlin AG, Landesbank Hessen-Thüringen Girozentrale, Landeskreditbank Baden-Württemberg – Förderbank, Landwirtschaftliche Rentenbank, LCL, Mediobanca Banca di Credito Finanziario SpA, NV Bank Nederlandse Gemeenten, National Bank of Greece SA, Natixis, Nederlandse Waterschapsbank NV, Norddeutsche Landesbank Girozentrale, NRW.BANK, Piraeus Bank SA, Pohjola Bank plc,

Raiffeisen Bank International AG, Raiffeisen Zentralbank Österreich Aktiengesellschaft, Santander Consumer Finance SA, SNS Bank NV, Societe Generale Group, The Governor and Company of the Bank of Ireland, UniCredit Bank AG, UniCredit Bank Austria AG, UniCredit SpA, Unione di Banche Italiane SpA, WGZ BANK AG Westdeutsche Genossenschafts-Zentralbank, Wüstenrot & Württembergische AG.

References

Adamati, A., P. DeMarzo, M. Hellwig and P. Pfleiderer (2010), 'Fallacies, Irrelevant Facts and Myths in the Discussion of Capital Regulation: Why Bank Equity is Not Expensive', *Stanford GSB Research Paper*, No. 2065.

Adamati, A. and M. Hellwig (2010), *The Bankers' New Clothes: What's Wrong with Banking and What to Do about It*, Princeton, NJ: Princeton University Press.

Adrian, T. and H.S. Shin (2014), 'Procyclical Leverage and Value-at-Risk', *Review of Financial Studies*, 27(2), pp. 373–403.

Borio, C., L. Gambacorta and B. Hofmann (2015), 'The Influence of Monetary Policy on Bank Profitability', *BIS Working Papers*, No. 514, October.

Gambacorta, L. and H.S. Shin (2016), 'Why Bank Capital Matters for Monetary Policy', *BIS Working Papers*, No. 558, April (forthcoming in the *Journal of Financial Intermediation*).

Goodhart, C. (1989), *Money, Information and Uncertainty*, 2nd edition, Cambridge, MA: MIT Press.

Hilander, I. (2014), 'Short-term Funding in Foreign Currency by Major Swedish Banks and Their Use of the Short-term Currency Swap Market', *Sveriges Riksbank Economic Review*, 1, pp. 1–23.

Shin, H.S. (2014), 'Bank Capital Regulation and Monetary Policy Transmission', ECB Forum on Central Banking conference Proceedings, Sintra, 25–7 May.

(2016), 'Bank Capital and Monetary Policy Transmission', ECB and its Watchers XVII Conference, Frankfurt, 7 April, www.bis.org/speeches/sp160407.htm.

7 | When Are Central Banks More Likely to Target Asset Prices?

HAIZHOU HUANG

7.1 Introduction

This chapter investigates when central banks target asset prices in practice in their monetary policy operations. There is a large body of literature on whether central banks should target asset prices, and ongoing debate in the policy circle on these important issues (see Monetary Policy Committee, 1999; Cecchetti et al., 2000; for four different views, Bernanke and Gertler, 2001 and Goodhart and Hofmann, 2000; among others). Since the 2008 global financial crisis, many central banks have used policy measures ranging from policy rate cuts to Quantitative Easing (QE), to even some unconventional policy tools to support asset prices and economic recovery.

While we can continue to discuss and debate on this important issue, we should seriously look at the empirical evidence and investigate when central banks do target asset prices in practice in their monetary policy operations. We want to understand the facts and regularity on when central banks may or may not target asset prices, if such decisions depend on whether the economy is in a boom or bust, whether an economy is advanced or still developing, and whether the financial system is bank-based or market-based.

In a normal economic environment, the short-term interest rate is often the main operational target for central banks and it is well approximated by a simple Taylor Rule (Taylor, 1993). Based on empirical analysis, Taylor models the Federal Funds Rate (FFR) as a

This chapter draws from my joint CF40 project with Jieyun Wu, 'A Study on Monetary Policy Transmission'. I would like to thank Charles Goodhart for the many lessons he taught me over the last two decades on monetary economics and central banking, through joint research and teaching as well as many discussions. I also would like to thank Adam Posen, Martin Weale, Dirk Schoenmaker and participants at the CF40-PIIE joint conference in Beijing and the conference in honour of Charles Goodhart at LSE for comments, Jieyun Wu for collaboration and help, and CF40 for financial assistance.

simple and elegant linear function of inflation and output gap. Clark, Goodhart and Huang (1999) derive a Taylor rule in a rational expectations model of the Phillips curve. To adjust the policy rate, central banks conduct open-market operation by purchasing or selling government securities, such as Treasury notes and bonds.

In a Taylor environment, targeting asset prices would make a lot of sense if and when changing asset prices affects inflation. Goodhart (2001) asks 'what weights should be given to asset prices in the measurement of inflation'. He finds that 'the links between equity prices (and exchange rates) and subsequent movements in output and (goods and services) inflation are weak', but 'the relationship between housing price movements and subsequent output and inflation is much stronger'.

Inspired by Goodhart's insights and the debate on whether central banks should target asset prices, we conduct an empirical investigation on when central banks target asset prices in practice. The main mechanism of the asset price channel is the wealth effect on consumption and aggregate demand. In addition to the asset prices channel, there are three major channels of monetary transmission: the interest rate channel, the foreign exchange rate channel, and the credit channel.

These channels work differently, depending on whether the economy is in a boom or bust, whether an economy is developed or still developing, and whether the financial system is bank-based or market-based. In Huang and Wu (2016), we find that if the economy is booming, the central banks of developed countries tend to adopt neutral to tight monetary policy with relatively higher tolerance for asset inflation, since interest rate and exchange rate channels could help neutralise the positive impact on domestic consumer inflation. For emerging market countries the monetary policy stance is also neutral to tight but with relatively lower tolerance for asset price inflation (the reason being that since interest rate is the main channel that could help neutralise the positive impact on domestic consumer inflation, leaving asset prices unattended might cause a severe inflation problem).

If the economy is in a recession or crisis, central banks of developed countries tend to adopt accommodative monetary policy. Asset inflation is favoured as both interest rate and credit channels are clogged with a low appetite for business expansion and especially with the zero lower bound. For emerging market economies, central banks also adopt accommodative monetary policy and need to keep either the credit or wealth channel open to avoid deflationary pressure.

On the specific question of when central banks target asset prices in practice in their monetary policy operations, we find that for developed and developing economies alike the asset price channel is effective, through the standard wealth effect, in affecting the real sector, and central banks in developing or bank-based economies are more likely to target asset prices, especially after a crisis.

7.2 Empirical Analysis on the Asset Price Channel

In our sample, covering the USA, select countries in the euro area, Japan and China, asset price channels are among the first to react to monetary policy. However, the effect of monetary policy via the asset price channel is existent only if increased wealth does affect real economic activity, for example consumption. We first test wealth effect on consumption for the USA, Japan, China, Germany, France and Italy; then we compare the respective effectiveness of housing and equity prices for these nations.

Similar to Catte et al. (2004), we construct econometric models of real private consumption, real household income (subtracting capital gains in housing and financial assets), total market capitalisation of stock exchanges, housing price, unemployment rate, short-term real interest rate and inflation. Quarterly data from 1980Q1 to 2015Q4 are considered (depending on data availability, sampling period differs for different countries). For France we use the CAC40 Index as a proxy for market capitalisation; for China and the euro area countries, data on capital gains are not available, so we use real disposable income. We perform unit root tests on all time series and then find cointegrating relationships for each country. Suppose for a particular country, $\ln(c_t)$ and $x_{1t}, \ldots, x_{1t}$ are cointegrated, we use Ordinary Least Squares (OLS) to directly estimate the long-run relationship:

$$\ln(c_t) = c_1 + b_1 x_{1t} + \cdots + b_n x_{nt} + ecm_t \tag{7.1}$$

Then, we estimate the error-correction form, augmented by other stationary explanatory variables:

$$\Delta\ln(c_t) = C_1 + \beta_0 ecm_{t-1} + \beta_1 \Delta x_{1t} + \cdots + \beta_n \Delta x_{nt}$$
$$+ \gamma_1 \Delta y_{1t} + \cdots + \gamma_m \Delta y_{1m} + \epsilon_t \tag{7.2}$$

Cointegrating relationships and long-run relationships are shown in Table 7.1. Take the USA as an example. $\ln(c_t)$, $\ln(\text{INCOME}_t)$,

Table 7.1. *Long-run wealth effect on consumption expenditure*

Variables	USA (1) $\ln(c_t)$	Japan (2) $\ln(c_t)$	France (3) $\ln(c_t)$	Germany (4) $\ln(c_t)$	Italy (5) $\ln(c_t)$	China (6) $\ln(c_t)$	Shanghai (7) $\ln(c_t)$
$\ln(\text{INCOME}_t)$	0.886***	1.684***	0.837***	—	0.159***	0.896***	1.053***
	(0.015)	(0.044)	(0.082)	—	(0.047)	(0.014)	(0.118)
$\ln(\text{STOCK}_t)$	0.0265***	0.0453***	-0.0172***	0.0361***	0.0107***	-0.00418	0.00569
	(0.005)	(0.009)	(0.006)	(0.008)	(0.002)	(0.004)	(0.032)
$\ln(\text{HOUSE}_t)$	0.0990***	-0.471***	0.0578***	0.0362	0.0417***	-0.0264	-0.124
	(0.008)	(0.027)	(0.022)	(0.067)	(0.009)	(0.038)	(0.082)
INFLATION_t	—	—	-0.0182***	-0.0107***	-0.00464***	-0.00673**	-0.0106
	—	—	(0.003)	(0.003)	(0.001)	(0.003)	(0.013)
UNEMPLOYMENT_t	—	0.00244	-0.00665***	-0.00919***	-0.0116***	—	—
	—	(0.004)	(0.002)	(0.002)	(0.001)	—	—
INTEREST_t	—	—	-0.0136***	-0.00846**	-0.00519***	-0.00732**	-0.0139
	—	—	(0.002)	(0.003)	(0.002)	(0.003)	(0.018)
Constant	0.410***	-4.855***	1.939*	5.632***	10.20***	0.403***	0.430
	(0.080)	(0.359)	(0.992)	(0.312)	(0.604)	(0.100)	(0.411)
Observations	144	140	52	52	51	42	39
R^2	0.998	0.975	0.988	0.921	0.977	0.998	0.953

Robust standard errors in parentheses.
*** $p < 0.01$, ** $p < 0.05$, * $p < 0.1$.

ln(STOCK$_t$) and ln(HOUSE$_t$) are cointegrated. The estimate of their long-run equilibrium relation is hardly surprising, as income, stock market value and housing price are all positively correlated with consumption. The cointegrating relationship differs for different countries. Three notable surprises arise in Table 7.1. First, consumption negatively correlates with housing price for Japan, which is probably due to the housing price bust post 1990. Second, the long-run relationship between housing price and consumption for Germany is low, probably due to stagnation in housing price between 1995 and 2010. Third, the correlation between China's asset price and consumption appears to be weak statistically (both housing and equity price).

The short-run dynamics are reported in Table 7.2. We augment the error–correction representation with other explanatory variables that are stationary or difference-stationary. Lagged values are included whenever needed to make the error term a white noise process.

The wealth effect of equity and housing prices differs in applicability and magnitude. The short-run wealth effect of housing price differs across countries. In the USA, a 1 per cent increase in the housing price leads to a 0.08 per cent increase in consumption. The number is statistically significant, but is not large economically. In Japan, although the long-run correlation between housing price and consumption is negative, housing price recovery has a large effect on consumption in the short run. As a result of long-time depression in the housing market, when it does recover (even briefly), people respond by consuming more: a 1 per cent recovery of housing price leads to a 0.25 per cent increase in consumption. The housing wealth effect in France is on the same order as in the USA. For Italy and China (as well as one of its main cities, Shanghai), the estimates are statistically insignificant.[1] The housing wealth effect in Germany is significantly negative in the statistical sense. The surprising result is nevertheless

---

[1] The literature on the housing wealth effect in China has yielded mixed results due to differences in data, sampling period and estimation procedure. Theoretical arguments can be made to rationalise the mixed evidence. A housing price increase boosts consumption for (long-time) owners, but crowds out consumption for new or potential buyers. The urbanisation process and the extremely high price-to-rent ratio of the housing market imply that the crowding-out effect could be dominating. See Chen, Guo and Zhu (2009) for the positive housing wealth effect, but Gao and Zhou (2007) and Li and Chen (2014) for the weak or negative effect.

Table 7.2. *Short-run wealth effect on consumption expenditure*

Variables	USA (1) $\Delta\ln(c_t)$	Japan (2) $\Delta\ln(c_t)$	France (3) $\Delta\ln(c_t)$	Germany (4) $\Delta\ln(c_t)$	Italy (5) $\Delta\ln(c_t)$	China (6) $\Delta\ln(c_t)$	Shanghai (7) $\Delta\ln(c_t)$
Error correction	−0.116*** (0.040)	−0.0370 (0.031)	−0.000591 (0.018)	−0.245*** (0.081)	−0.681*** (0.146)	−0.531*** (0.191)	−0.745*** (0.225)
$\Delta\ln(c_{t-1})$	—	−0.357*** (0.094)	—	—	—	—	—
$\Delta\ln(c_{t-2})$	—	−0.213*** (0.071)	—	—	—	—	—
$\Delta\ln(INCOME_t)$	0.234*** (0.053)	0.303** (0.146)	0.0574 (0.081)	0.442*** (0.109)	0.108*** (0.031)	0.874*** (0.142)	1.023 (0.638)
$\Delta\ln(INCOME_{t-1})$	—	0.455*** (0.112)	—	—	—	—	—
$\Delta\ln(INCOME_{t-2})$	—	0.222* (0.133)	—	—	—	—	—
$\Delta\ln(STOCK_t)$	0.00504 (0.006)	0.00145 (0.006)	0.00173 (0.006)	−0.00551 (0.005)	0.00331*** (0.001)	0.00954 (0.008)	0.00255 (0.039)

	(1)	(2)	(3)	(4)	(5)	(6)	(7)
$\Delta\ln(\text{HOUSE}_t)$	0.0767***	0.254***	0.0931*	-0.0752***	0.0462	0.0490	-0.284
	(0.027)	(0.078)	(0.048)	(0.024)	(0.029)	(0.076)	(0.179)
$\Delta\text{UNEMPLOYMENT}_t$	-0.00819***	-0.000451	-0.00293	0.000288	-0.00992***	—	—
	(0.002)	(0.007)	(0.003)	(0.002)	(0.002)	—	—
$\Delta\text{INTEREST}_t$	-0.000747	0.00383**	-0.00498	0.00315	-0.00688**	-0.00729***	-0.0126
	(0.001)	(0.002)	(0.004)	(0.003)	(0.003)	(0.003)	(0.018)
INFLATION_t	-0.000451	-0.00187***	—	—	—	—	—
	(0.000)	(0.001)	—	—	—	—	—
$\Delta\text{INFLATION}_t$	—	—	-0.00652	-0.00105	-0.00330	-0.00509**	0.000467
	—	—	(0.005)	(0.003)	(0.003)	(0.002)	(0.018)
Constant	0.00606***	0.00688***	0.000371	0.00163***	0.000104	-0.000844	0.00471
	(0.001)	(0.001)	(0.038)	(0.001)	(0.000)	(0.003)	(0.016)
Observations	143	137	51	51	50	41	38
R^2	0.422	0.405	0.235	0.563	0.684	0.737	0.459

Robust standard errors in parentheses.
*** $p < 0.01$, ** $p < 0.05$, * $p < 0.1$.

compatible with a number of studies.[2] The equity wealth effect is small and statistically insignificant for most countries, except for Italy where the estimate is reliable but still small in magnitude. The finding here – that the housing wealth effect is generally more important than equity – is consistent with Goodhart (2001) and Claessens, Ayhan Kose and Terrones (2011).

7.3 Empirical Estimation of a More General Taylor Rule

In this section we test whether central banks of various countries react to asset price (particularly equity price) fluctuations. We compare central banks' attitudes towards asset prices before and after the 2008 financial crisis. Based on Clarida, Gali and Gertler (1998), Fourçans and Vranceanu (2004) and Botzen and Marey (2010), we use the following extended Taylor Rule to estimate the effect of stock prices on the setting of the policy rate:

$$IR_t = \alpha + \beta_1 IR_{t-1} + \beta_2 OUTPUT_t + \beta_3 INFLATION_t$$
$$+ \beta_4 STOCK\_DEV_t + \epsilon_t, \tag{7.3}$$

where IR_t is the policy rate, $OUTPUT_t$ is output gap, defined as the difference between current industrial production and its long-run potential level. $INFLATION_t$ is the year-on-year increase in CPI, $STOCK\_DEV_t$ is the deviation of the stock market from its long-term average.

Our sample covers forty-five countries (including nineteen countries in the euro area), where developed economies include the USA, the UK, the euro area, Japan, Canada, Switzerland, Norway, Denmark and Sweden; developing economies include China, India, Brazil, Russia, South Africa, Mexico, Turkey, Bulgaria, Czech Republic, Lithuania, Hungary, Romania, Poland, Korea, Malaysia and Indonesia. For all countries, sampling frequency is monthly.

We adopt the General Method of Moments (GMM) to estimate the extended Taylor Rule for developed and developing economies. Furthermore, we individually estimate the Taylor rule for the USA, the euro area, Japan and China. All regressions are run for different periods, i.e. before versus after the 2008 financial crisis. Results are shown in Tables 7.3–7.8.

---

[2] For example, Felix Geiger et al. (2016), 'The housing market, household portfolios and the German consumer', *ECB Working Paper Series*, 1904.

Table 7.3. *Taylor Rule in developed countries*

Developed economies	1982–2016 (1)	1982–2006 (2)	2007–2016 (3)
IR_{t-1}	0.998***	0.991***	1.002***
	(0.002)	(0.004)	(0.004)
$OUTPUT_t$	0.006***	0.014***	0.003***
	(0.001)	(0.002)	(0.001)
$INFLATION_t$	–8.93E–04	0.007	–1.89E–03
	(0.003)	(0.003)	(0.003)
$STOCK\_DEV_t$	–4.63E–06	–1.30E–05**	2.94E–06
	(0.000)	(0.000)	(0.000)
Constant	0.008	0.014	–0.003
	(0.006)	(0.012)	(0.005)
R^2	0.994	0.994	0.986

Robust standard errors in parentheses.
***$p < 0.01$, **$p < 0.05$, *$p < 0.1$.

Table 7.4. *Taylor Rule in developing countries*

Developing economies	1989–2016 (1)	1989–2006 (2)	2007–2016 (3)
IR_{t-1}	0.992***	1.001***	0.988***
	(0.003)	(0.003)	(0.002)
$OUTPUT_t$	0.008***	0.008***	0.008***
	(0.001)	(0.001)	(0.001)
$INFLATION_t$	0.007***	0.003	0.008***
	(0.003)	(0.004)	(0.002)
$STOCK\_DEV_t$	4.21E–06***	1.00E–05	3.58E–06***
	(0.000)	(0.000)	(0.000)
Constant	–0.015**	–0.043**	–0.000**
	(0.008)	(0.022)	(0.000)
R^2	0.983	0.980	0.989

Robust standard errors in parentheses.
***$p < 0.01$, **$p < 0.05$, *$p < 0.1$.

For both developed (Table 7.3) and developing economies (Table 7.4), the current policy rate depends on its one-period-ahead counterpart, showing persistence in monetary policy. The current rate also positively correlates with the contemporary output gap, which is

Table 7.5. *Taylor Rule in the USA*

USA	1982–2016 (1)	1982–2006 (2)	2007–2016 (3)
IR_{t-1}	0.991***	0.980***	0.980***
	(0.004)	(0.006)	(0.008)
$OUTPUT_t$	0.012***	0.031***	0.001
	(0.002)	(0.004)	(0.001)
$INFLATION_t$	−0.006	0.034**	−0.006
	(0.008)	(0.014)	(0.003)
$STOCK\_DEV_t$	−4.55E−06	3.85E−05	−3.42E−06
	(0.000)	(0.000)	(0.000)
Constant	0.042***	−0.015	0.017
	(0.023)	(0.034)	(0.008)
R^2	0.994	0.991	0.987

Robust standard errors in parentheses.
***$p < 0.01$, **$p < 0.05$, *$p < 0.1$.

Table 7.6. *Taylor Rule in the euro area*

Euro area	1999–2016 (1)	1999–2006 (2)	2007–2016 (3)
IR_{t-1}	0.990***	0.965***	0.961***
	(0.007)	(0.013)	(0.008)
$OUTPUT_t$	0.007***	0.012*	0.004***
	(0.002)	(0.007)	(0.001)
$INFLATION_t$	0.018*	−0.025	0.046***
	(0.010)	(0.030)	(0.030)
$STOCK\_DEV_t$	2.88E−04**	6.37E−04**	7.10E−04***
	(0.000)	(0.000)	(0.000)
Constant	−0.018*	0.139**	−0.038***
	(0.009)	(0.070)	(0.007)
R^2	0.991	0.977	0.993

Robust standard errors in parentheses.
***$p < 0.01$, **$p < 0.05$, *$p < 0.1$.

expected. However, the coefficient on STOCK_DEV, β_4, is statistically insignificant for developed economies, while significant for developing countries. Namely, compared with central banks in developed economies, central banks in developing economies tend to target

Table 7.7. *Taylor Rule in Japan*

Japan	1986–2013 (1)	1986–2006 (2)	2007–2013 (3)
IR_{t-1}	0.976***	0.968***	0.735***
	(0.009)	(0.010)	(0.057)
$OUTPUT_t$	−2.18E−04	−7.90E−04	−3.49E−04**
	(0.002)	(0.000)	(0.000)
$INFLATION_t$	0.005	0.012	0.008**
	(0.010)	(0.016)	(0.000)
$STOCK\_DEV_t$	8.87E−06***	1.20E−05***	1.59E−05***
	(0.000)	(0.000)	(0.000)
Constant	0.039***	0.041***	0.141***
	(0.011)	(0.011)	(0.033)
R^2	0.982	0.980	0.925

Robust standard errors in parentheses.
***$p < 0.01$, **$p < 0.05$, *$p < 0.1$.

Table 7.8. *Taylor Rule in China*

China	1997–2016 (1)	1997–2006 (2)	2007–2016 (3)
IR_{t-1}	0.993***	0.987***	0.976***
	(0.010)	(0.010)	(0.019)
$OUTPUT_t$	0.006***	−7.85E−04	0.011***
	(0.002)	(0.001)	(0.001)
$INFLATION_t$	0.005**	0.003	0.004
	(0.004)	(0.002)	(0.006)
$STOCK\_DEV_t$	−2.30E−06	−4.29E−06	−1.43E−05
	(0.000)	(0.000)	(0.000)
Constant	0.032***	0.069***	0.142
	(0.056)	(0.039)	(0.105)
R^2	0.977	0.980	0.969

Robust standard errors in parentheses.
***$p < 0.01$, **$p < 0.05$, *$p < 0.1$.

stock price. When share value is higher than long-run average, the policy rate tends to be higher.

Dividing the sample into pre- and post-crisis periods, we find that monetary policy in developed countries does not consider asset price after the 2008 crisis; but before 2008, rates are lower whenever stock prices are higher. Central bank behaviour is vastly different in developing countries: before 2008, their policy does not target asset prices; but after 2008, they worry about the asset bubble.

US monetary policy does not target asset price before or after the financial crisis (Table 7.5). β_4 is not statistically significant in all three regressions, suggesting there is no evidence for the Federal Reserve to target asset prices. This also implies that central banks in market-based economies have a *laissez faire* attitude towards the asset market.

In comparison, central banks in bank-based economies (Japan, Table 7.6; the euro area, Table 7.7) care about asset prices: β_4 in all regressions are statistically significant and positive. Moreover, monetary policy in Japan and the euro area target asset prices both before and after the financial crisis. Finally, there is no evidence that Chinese monetary policy takes asset prices into account before or after the financial crisis (Table 7.8).

Note that some of the regressions in this section yield statistically weak β_4 coefficients (especially for China and the euro area). This might be due to the short sampling period. Hence the more appropriate interpretation would probably be 'there is no evidence that central banks target asset prices'.

7.4 Concluding Remarks

In summary, our multi-dimensional comparison of all regression results in the previous sections offers three empirical findings. First up is the wealth effect. The wealth effect of stock prices is either small or without evidence in general; the wealth effect of housing price is relatively larger in most countries, as shown in Goodhart (2001).

Secondly, in our estimation of the Taylor Rule including stock price, we find a systematic difference between advanced and developing economies. Monetary policy in advanced economies accommodates a stock price hike before 2008 but does not take stock price into account after 2008. Developing countries tend to do the opposite: they do not target asset price before the 2008 crisis but display an aversion to the asset price bubble after the crisis.

Thirdly, advanced economies (Japan, the euro area) with bank-based financial systems target asset price before and after the financial crisis. An advanced economy with a market-based financial system (the USA) does not seem to care much about asset price in setting its monetary policy, as argued by Bernanke and Gertler (2001). For China, there is no evidence that monetary policy considers asset price.

References

Bernanke, Ben S. and Mark Gertler (2001), 'Should Central Banks Respond to Movements in Asset Prices?', *The American Economic Review*, 91(2), pp. 253–7.

Botzen, W.J. Wouter and Philip S Marey (2010), 'Did the ECB Respond to the Stock Market Before the Crisis?', *Journal of Policy Modeling*, 32(3), pp. 303–22.

Catte, Pietro, Nathalie Girouard, Robert W.R. Price and Christophe André (2004), 'Housing Markets, Wealth and the Business Cycle', *IECD Economics Department Working Papers*.

Cecchetti, Stephen, Hans Genberg, John Lipsky and Sushil Wadhwani (2000), *Asset Prices and Central Bank Policy*. Centre for Economic Policy Research. Report Prepared for the Conference 'Central Banks and Asset Prices', Organized by the International Center for Monetary and Banking Studies and CEPR in Geneva on May 5.

Chen, Jie, Feng Guo and Aiyong Zhu (2009), 'Housing Wealth, Financial Wealth and Consumption in China', *China & World Economy*, 17(3), pp. 57–74.

Claessens, Stijn, M. Ayhan Kose and Marco E. Terrones (2011), 'Financial Cycles: What? How? When?', *NBER International Seminar on Macroeconomics*, 7(1), pp. 303–44.

Clarida, Richard, Jordi Galı and Mark Gertler (1998), 'Monetary Policy Rules in Practice: Some International Evidence', *European Economic Review*, 42(6), pp. 1033–67.

Clark, Peter B., Charles A.E. Goodhart and Haizhou Huang (1999), 'Optimal Monetary Policy Rules in a Rational Expectations Model of the Phillips Curve', *Journal of Monetary Economics*, 43(2), pp. 497–520.

Fourçans, André and Radu Vranceanu (2004), 'The ECB Interest Rate Rule under the Duisenberg Presidency', *European Journal of Political Economy*, 20(3), pp. 579–95.

Gao, Xiaoyan and Chunliang Zhou (2007), 'House Wealth Effect of 34 Cities: An Empirical Analysis Based on Panel Data', *Nankai Economic Studies*, 1, pp. 36–44.

Goodhart, Charles (2001), 'What Weight Should be Given to Asset Prices in the Measurement of Inflation?', *The Economic Journal*, 111, pp. 335–56.

Goodhart, Charles and Boris Hofmann (2000), 'Do Asset Prices Help to Predict Consumer Price Inflation?', *The Manchester School Supplement*, 68(s1), pp. 122–40.

Huang, Haizhou and Jieyun Wu (2016), 'A Study on Monetary Policy Transmission', Submitted to China Finance 40 Forum Working Paper Series.

Li, Tao and Binkai Chen (2014), 'Real Assets, Wealth Effect and Household Consumption: Analysis Based on China Household Survey Data', *Economic Research Journal*, 3, pp. 62–75.

Monetary Policy Committee (1999), 'The Transmission Mechanism of Monetary Policy', Bank of England. www.bankofengland.co.uk/publications/Documents/other/monetary/montrans.pdf.

Taylor, John B. (1993), 'Discretion versus Policy Rules in Practice', *Carnegie-Rochester Conference Series on Public Policy*, 39, pp. 195–214.

PART II

Financial Stability and Regulatory Policy

8 | *The Macroprudential Toolkit*

RICHARD BERNER

8.1 Introduction

Six years ago, Charles Goodhart, Anil Kashyap and I coauthored a paper called 'The Macroprudential Toolkit' (Kashyap, Berner and Goodhart, 2011). Having contributed to the development and assessment of that toolkit since then, I want to reuse the title to appraise how far we have come and where we need to go.

The punchline is not surprising. We have significantly improved financial system resilience and the tools needed to promote it but we still have more work to do.

To focus my review, I will discuss three topics: (1) improving the framework for financial stability analysis and policy decisions; (2) improving the scope, accessibility and quality of financial data; and (3) mitigating procyclicality and risks in securities financing transactions.

8.2 Background

Financial stability is about resilience. It occurs when the financial system can provide its basic functions, even under stress.

Threats to financial stability arise from vulnerabilities in the financial system – failures in these functions that are exposed by shocks. Resilience has two aspects:

1. Does the system have enough shock-absorbing capacity to continue to function?
2. Are incentives, such as market discipline or transparent pricing of risk, aligned to limit excessive risk-taking?

Shock absorbers buffer hits, while what I call guardrails – incentives that affect behaviour – are designed to constrain the risk-taking that

The views expressed here are my own and do not necessarily reflect the views of the US Department of the Treasury.

117

can create financial vulnerabilities. An effective toolkit requires both shock absorbers and guardrails.

The financial crisis exposed critical gaps in our analysis and understanding of the financial system, in the data and metrics used to measure and monitor financial activities, and in the policy tools available to mitigate potential threats to financial stability. These gaps in analysis, data and policy tools contributed to the crisis and hampered official efforts to contain it.

In the years since the crisis, US federal financial regulators have taken needed, important and well-known steps to fill those gaps and to make the US financial system more resilient. Capital and liquidity regulation, stress testing, orderly liquidation authority, and derivatives reforms are the pillars of those initiatives.

However, we don't yet have a coherent, operational set of tools to match our rhetoric and we face critical challenges in developing the toolkit. Changes that have made the banking system stronger are likely to promote a migration of financial activity to more opaque and potentially less resilient parts of the financial system. In this review, I will discuss some of our other challenges.

8.3 Improving the Framework for Financial Stability Analysis and Policy Decisions

8.3.1 A Framework

A financial stability policy framework requires clear objectives and coherent institutional roles and responsibilities. It requires an ongoing assessment and monitoring of potential threats. That assessment must consider: macroeconomic and market risks; credit conditions; default risk; funding, liquidity and run risk; and spillovers and contagion. It must also use high-quality, comprehensive and detailed data. Goodhart, Sunirand and Tsomocos (2006) and Goodhart, Tsomocos and Shubik (2013) have developed frameworks and models including default. In addition, Kiley (2016) provides a brief survey of efforts to model the effects of losses on leveraged institutions' capacity or willingness to lend or on leveraged households' capacity to borrow.

We have done a lot. We have defined resilience as the goal. We have new coordinating institutions. We have better data. We regularly assess threats. We have improved our analytical frameworks but we have work to do on governance, financial data, the cross-border nature of many vulnerabilities, and risk assessment – including operational and cybersecurity risks.

The framework also needs a comprehensive and targeted array of policy tools. It requires ways to calibrate them, criteria for choosing the right tools for the job and methods to assess their effectiveness.

We have done a lot here too. We are beginning to use some important tools in the kit but are only starting to assess unintended consequences or conflicts. Picking the right tool, calibrating and assessing effectiveness are all works in progress.

Achieving those goals is hard. The framework must be dynamic and adaptable because structural changes appear to be underway in financial intermediation and because new technology and financial innovation make our goals moving targets. Progress on those ingredients has come slowly. We need to speed it up.

Another challenge is that risks of fragmentation are emerging just when cross-border coordination is needed to level the playing field. Finally, the obstacles to policy coordination stymie adoption of best practices.

8.3.2 Governance Best Practices

Meeting those challenges by implementing the toolkit – however well-equipped – requires effective governance and clear assignment of roles and responsibilities. To start, I agree with Paul Tucker (2016) that elected officials, not unelected technocrats, must choose just how resilient to make the financial system.[1]

I believe that additional best practices for policy governance are those from the International Monetary Fund, the Financial Stability Board and the Bank for International Settlements (2016):

1. A clear mandate that forms the basis for assigning responsibility for making macroprudential policy decisions.
2. Adequate institutional foundations for macroprudential policy frameworks, for example, giving the main mandate to an influential body with a broad view of the entire financial system.

---

[1] For a comparison of US and UK institutional frameworks, see Kohn (2014).

3. Well-defined objectives and powers that can foster the ability and willingness to act.
4. Transparency and accountability mechanisms to establish legitimacy and create commitment to take action.
5. Measures to promote cooperation and information sharing between domestic authorities.

8.3.3 Toolkit Best Practices

Best practices for macroprudential policy dictate that a tool is needed to counter each source of financial instability. For example, if policymakers want to combat excessive leverage, insufficient liquidity, and procyclicality, a satisfactory toolkit must contain tools to address each one, such as capital, liquidity and margin regulations (Kashyap, Berner and Goodhart, 2011; Hanson, Kashyap, and Stein 2011). Policymakers should also assign to each target the right tool for the job – the one that has the biggest influence on the policy objective.

Although macroprudential tools should be the first line of defence against threats to financial stability and financial imbalances, many tools are untested, some of the tools have yet to be implemented, and others may lead to unintended consequences (Uluc and Wieladek, 2015). I will discuss approaches to these issues below.

Meanwhile, recognition of these issues has promoted a deeper look at the complementarity of macroprudential and other policies, and at using monetary policy to address financial imbalances (Gourio, Kashyap, and Sim, 2016).

Complementarity takes several forms. Macroprudential policy may have macroeconomic consequences. For example, if a financial crisis impairs traditional policy transmission mechanisms, macroprudential tools may be needed to restore their functioning and achieve macroeconomic goals.

In addition, the microprudential and macroprudential policy toolkits overlap and complement each other. Examples include firms' risk management, resolution tools that promote market discipline, firm-specific stress tests, and microprudential supervision and regulation. Firm-specific shock absorbers that enhance financial stability include standards for capital and liquidity.

Likewise, macroprudential tools can influence firms' safety-and-soundness or market functioning; these include common or system-wide stress tests, living wills for certain financial institutions, an orderly liquidation authority, central clearing for swaps and derivatives, minimum floors for haircuts in securities financing transactions, and liquidity regulation. Tools such as deposit insurance and emergency liquidity provision by the central bank are system-wide shock absorbers.

These overlapping toolkits throw into sharp relief the need for clear governance, defined roles and responsibilities, and coordination across authorities.

I will now turn to evaluating some key tools: stress tests, time-varying tools, crisis-fighting tools and tabletop exercises. I will also look at some unintended consequences of tools to promote resilience and ways to evaluate the toolkit.

8.3.4 Stress Tests: Microprudential and Macroprudential

Supervisory stress testing, which assesses losses under future stress scenarios, has become an essential tool for evaluating potential vulnerabilities in large, complex banking firms and for calibrating microprudential requirements, such as for capital based on firms' idiosyncratic risks.

Stress testing also has enormous potential as part of the macroprudential toolkit to assess and measure vulnerabilities, help calibrate macroprudential tools and expose any unintended consequences of using them.

Stress testing methodology has consistently improved since the crisis, especially for the Federal Reserve's complementary Comprehensive Capital Analysis and Review (CCAR) and Dodd-Frank Act stress testing procedures. The Federal Reserve is making significant progress by proposing steps towards integrating the new, risk-based bank capital standards with the CCAR's required minimums.

In addition, the Federal Reserve is proposing a new stress capital buffer that will align capital requirements with a bank's risk under stress (Tarullo, 2016). Finally, the Federal Reserve will investigate how to add three important types of shocks to stress tests: funding, liquidity and fire sale shocks; common counterparty defaults; and reactions of central counterparties.

Advances in the scope of stress testing are also notable. Supervisory stress testing has been extended to central-clearing counterparties

(CCPs), including across multiple CCPs, and to other types of financial firms.[2]

In my view, five key items are on the agenda for improving stress tests and enhancing their use:

1. Continue to improve scenario design. Reverse stress tests might help to identify hidden risks and scenarios that might cause 'material financial distress or failure of the company' for living wills.
2. Add more macroprudential elements to models and supervisory stress testing frameworks.
3. Use stress tests to calibrate and evaluate macroprudential tools.
4. Make more progress on system-wide stress testing. More regulatory data sharing is essential to achieving this goal.
5. In non-bank stress testing, balance the need to tailor stress tests to reflect risks in specific activities with the need for standardisation to make comparisons. Stress testing has already become a requirement for US money market funds, and officials are working on stress test regimes for non-bank financial institutions and mutual funds.

8.3.5 Through-the-Cycle or Time-Varying Tools

Should we develop and employ structural 'through-the-cycle' or time-varying tools – or both?

Structural tools are aimed at building resilience to shocks and creating incentives to limit risk-taking, for example, by limiting leverage and increasing the cost of risky activities. Requiring institutions to 'self-insure' with capital and liquidity buffers promotes market discipline and limits leverage and liquidity transformation. We clearly need these.

Counter-cyclical or time-varying tools are aimed at moderating financial cycles (Brunnermeier et al. 2009). We may need these too.

---

[2] The European Securities and Markets Authority (ESMA) in 2016 conducted the first EU-wide stress exercise that assessed the resilience of seventeen CCPs in the face of multiple clearing member defaults and simultaneous market price shocks. Also in 2016, the US Commodity Futures Trading Commission (CFTC, 2016) conducted stress tests of five derivatives clearing organisations registered with the CFTC in order 'to assess the impact of this set of stressed market conditions across multiple clearinghouses'.

To be sure, the same prudential tools can be used structurally and countercyclically. As risks rise, increasing capital buffers can build resilience, reduce leverage and lending activity, and 'lean against the wind' (Adrian et al. 2016). Many central bankers believe macroprudential policy is complementary to monetary policy, so central banks must have responsibilities in both areas (Constâncio, 2016a).

Nonetheless, I'm sceptical about the time-varying approach. We and our tools aren't yet capable of detecting early the difference between a healthy credit recovery and a dangerous credit boom. I'm also not sure we yet have the knowledge, experience and right institutional framework to calibrate our policy tools. Lastly, once a decision is made to use such tools, implementing them may take time, at least in the USA. Given such obstacles, the USA has a 'relative lack of measures in the ... toolkit to address a cyclical buildup of financial stability risks' (Fischer, 2015a).

However, we should not discard such tools. Tools to limit housing booms, such as variable loan-to-value ceilings, are used effectively in the UK. More analysis and experimentation are needed to help officials decide whether, when and how to use them (Claessens, 2014).

8.3.6 Crisis-Fighting Tools

So far, I have limited this discussion to pre-crisis tools. I think the steps taken to increase resilience have reduced the likelihood of a crisis and the likely consequences of a given shock for the financial system and the economy.

Those are powerful benefits but no cause for complacency. Shocks will recur and crises will happen. We should thus consider what an emergency toolkit should contain. During the 2007–8 crisis, officials stopped the panic and helped set the stage for recovery by deploying a wide variety of crisis-fighting tools. We should not let concerns about misuse require us to recreate that crisis-fighting toolkit from scratch. In his 2016 Per Jacobsson Lecture, former US Treasury Secretary Geithner (2016) noted that:

In the financial stability arena, the cool stuff these days is about prevention ... We neglect the craft of crisis management not just because it is a dirty, loathsome job, but because many fear that in financial policy planning for disaster makes disaster more likely. It is as if, in finance, it is the fire station that causes fires.

He also said that a credible emergency regime has to include:

- the ability to provide funding across the financial system, wherever there are runnable liabilities on a scale that matters;
- the ability to guarantee the liabilities of the core of the financial system;
- the ability to recapitalise the financial system, including with public resources, if necessary;
- the ability to resolve, or to liquidate in an orderly manner, large complex financial institutions; and
- the ability to provide dollars to the world's central banks and to lend to foreign financial firms with large dollar liabilities.

We have some but not all of those tools, so we should consider how to fill the gaps in this emergency toolkit. Although planning for disaster doesn't make it more likely, we need clear governance, mandates, responsibilities and accountability to implement the right emergency toolkit in the right way; otherwise, we may again reward the behaviour that led to the crisis.

8.3.7 Tabletop Exercises

We cannot easily operationalise best practices, for example, by deploying one tool for every policy goal. The task is complex and requires not just picking the right tool for the job, but assessing the interactions among the tools. Tabletop exercises can unpack that complexity by focusing on a particular scenario and a particular set of tools.

A group of Federal Reserve banks conducted a tabletop exercise in June 2015 to illustrate and better understand the complexity of policy choice (Adrian et al. 2016).

The group considered a hypothetical scenario of overheating financial markets that included leveraged lending and commercial property markets funded by increased short-term wholesale funding. They were asked to pick the right tools to address the risks in the scenario, including capital, liquidity and credit tools, as well as stress testing and supervisory guidance.

The group concluded that many prudential tools had limited applicability and could not be implemented quickly. Stress testing and margins on repo funding were the exceptions. Given those limitations, the group judged monetary policy tools to be an attractive alternative means of promoting financial stability.

Further use of such exercises will shed light on these interactions and help develop scenarios for stress testing.

8.3.8 Unintended Consequences

Financial regulation and financial stability policies can have unintended consequences. For example, in bank capital regulation, there is a trade-off between the leverage ratio and the various risk-based capital ratios. The leverage ratio requires capital against all exposures, while risk-based capital ratios better reflect the actual risk in banks' portfolios.

Leverage ratios create incentives to hold high-return, high-risk assets that carry no extra capital charge.[3] They thus discourage repo activity with potential consequences for market liquidity. For example, members of the Office of Financial Research (OFR) staff have analysed developments in the triparty repo market that appear to be influenced by responses by broker-dealer affiliates of bank holding companies to the introduction of the enhanced supplemental leverage ratio (Office of Financial Research, 2015).

According to the OFR (2014, p. 50), '[a]lso, in a stressed environment, the leverage ratio may create an incentive to sell securities rather than finance them, potentially promoting asset fire sales'. In addition, leverage ratios may promote a dispersion of money-market rates and reduce 'pass-through' efficiency from central bank policy rates to the rates at which loans are transacted (Duffie and Krishnamurthy, 2016).

Such potential unintended consequences may still be outweighed by the extra resilience from the tool. To quote Federal Reserve Vice-Chair Stanley Fischer (2016): 'Regulatory changes, even those that may have reduced market liquidity, likely have increased financial stability on balance.'

---

[3] To offset the increased capital required by the leverage ratio in the UK against central bank reserves, the Bank of England decided to 'exclude central bank reserves from the exposure measure of the leverage ratio framework. This change was a good example of close co-ordination between macroprudential and monetary policy – without it a loosening of monetary policy through the creation of reserves by the MPC (Monetary Policy Committee) to purchase assets would have led to a deterioration in banks' leverage ratios at precisely the time we would like them to support credit growth in the economy' (Shafik, 2016).

8.3.9 *Guardrails and Incentives*

Recognition is growing that guardrails and the incentives they create are important macroprudential tools. For example, a credible resolution authority is essential to reduce the expectation that a large, complex, distressed financial institution is too big to fail. Another example is that liquidity regulation should not only require liquidity buffers, but also 'provide incentives for banks or other financial firms to choose to hold the proper amount of liquidity, in excess of the required amount' to deter and survive runs (Diamond and Kashyap, 2016; Goodhart, 2008). Finally, flawed incentive-based compensation packages contributed to excessive risk-taking prior to the financial crisis. The Dodd-Frank Act requires, and regulators have recently proposed, rules to prohibit incentive-based pay that encourages inappropriate risk-taking in financial institutions.[4]

8.3.10 *Evaluation of Tools*

Macroprudential tools are hard to implement and even harder to evaluate. They are new and, in some cases, have not yet been used, let alone tested.

Three considerations are important in deciding whether the tools are having the intended effect:

1. Are the goals for using the tools clear? Are they intended as shock absorbers or are they guardrails to set incentives or controls for the activities of financial institutions and to help promote market discipline?
2. Are the tools targeting the ultimate cause of the problem rather than its symptoms? For example, the use of gates to limit redemptions after shocks hit may have the perverse effect of increasing first-to-exit incentives; clear ex-ante governance could limit such incentives.
3. Do the tools yield good bang for the buck? Targeted policies with clear, direct effects on a financial stability threat (such as minimum haircuts for securities financing transactions) are preferable to general policies with diffuse effects (such as activating a countercyclical capital buffer).

---

[4] The agencies include the Federal Deposit Insurance Corporation, the Federal Housing Finance Agency, the Federal Reserve Board of Governors, the National Credit Union Administration, the Office of the Comptroller of the Currency and the Securities and Exchange Commission (SEC 2016).

The OFR does not make policy; we inform it. We have statutory requirements to evaluate stress tests and similar tools, conduct policy studies and provide advice on the impact of policies related to financial stability. We have obtained access to the data used to conduct stress tests and we are suggesting ways to improve the tests as well as the data, including for non-bank institutions and system-wide risk assessment. For example, a recent OFR working paper found that the indirect effects transmitted through the financial system of a counterparty failure may exceed the direct impact (Cetina, Paddrik, and Rajan, 2016).

8.4 Improving the Scope, Accessibility, and Quality of Financial Data

Good data are essential for good policymaking. In recognition of that, our data work at the OFR is aimed at improving the quality, scope and accessibility of financial data (Office of Financial Research, 2016, Section 2.7). I will focus on one signature project to illustrate this.

Data gaps persist in securities financing transactions, including repurchase agreements (repo) and securities lending. The Federal Reserve collects good data on so-called triparty repo transactions. In these transactions, a third party, known as a clearing bank, manages collateral, handles administrative details and assures payment.

However, comprehensive data are scant for about half of the US repo market, in so-called bilateral repo transactions. We have mapped the sources and uses of such funds and of collateral to better understand these markets, assess risks, and identify gaps in available data. We have also launched pilot projects with the Federal Reserve and Securities and Exchange Commission to understand how to fill the gaps in data for bilateral repo and securities lending transactions with permanent collections (Baklanova, Cipriani et al., 2016); for securities lending, see Baklanova, Keane et al., 2016).

Again quoting Federal Reserve Vice-Chair Fischer (2015b):

An illustration of the possible interaction between better data and better policies is the potential role of margins in securities financing transactions. ... Improved data collection ... would allow a better view of changes in conditions and potentially contribute to the deployment of countercyclical margins, thereby further decreasing the chances of a dynamic that culminates in adverse fire sales.

High-quality repo data are critical for assessing risk in securities financing transactions, and for implementing tools to limit risk in them – my final topic.

8.5 Mitigating Procyclicality and Risks in Securities Financing Transactions

Securities financing transactions (SFTs), including repo and securities lending, play a critical role in financial markets. Assuring vibrant and resilient SFT markets should be a key policy goal. However, SFTs involve 'runnable' liabilities, and funding and liquidity shocks in them may contribute to procyclical fire sales of assets.

I think we should address such vulnerabilities with tools aimed at the activities that generate them, rather than at the institutions engaging in them. In this case, setting minimum floors on haircuts, which was a tool proposed in the earlier 'Macroprudential Toolkit' paper, has several attractive features:

- This approach addresses the vulnerability directly rather than its symptoms.
- The approach operates through strong incentives – in this case, to limit the use of short-term funding by increasing its relative cost.
- A big-enough static floor might constrain maturity transformation and procyclicality.
- The addition of a proactive variable countercyclical floor could increase stability more – at least in principle.[5,6]

In practice, designing and implementing haircut floors will be challenging. Market practices are diverse. Collateral types, clearing arrangements, intermediary varieties, and institutional frameworks differ across jurisdictions and affect the terms and conditions of individual transactions (Baklanova, Copeland and McCaughrin, 2015). Legal

---

[5] Some evidence for the power of using haircuts through central bank lending facilities is in Ashcraft, Garleanu, and Pedersen (2010). Evidence for the power of the countercyclical use of haircuts is found in Haldane (2011), in Gai, Haldane and Kapadia (2011), in Battistini et al. (2016), and in Constâncio (2016b).

[6] Dirk Schoenmaker and Peter Wierts (2016) propose an interesting extension of the concept in the form of a common 'leverage' ratio/haircut across the financial system, based on macro considerations. The resulting equity buffer/haircut can then absorb losses.

frameworks, particularly for collateral, also vary significantly. Even within jurisdictions, diversity reigns. In the USA, the US bilateral repo and securities lending have starkly different margining practices than triparty markets, including general collateral (GC) and general collateral finance (GCF) repo (Copeland and Martin, 2012; Baklanova, Cipriani et al., 2016).

Consequently, a system of minimum haircut floors is likely to be complex. The Financial Stability Board proposal for minimum haircuts on non-centrally cleared transactions includes ten different minimum haircut floors and it applies unevenly to different types of financial firms (Financial Stability Board, 2015).

Another challenge is that we are still learning about the dynamics of SFT market behaviour and thus are guessing at how to calibrate the floors. In the USA we expect different responses in triparty and bilateral repo, and we need to fill big data and analytical gaps.

Four steps should help address those challenges:

1. Understand the markets as they work today and where they may be going.
   a. Map out the sources and uses of funding and exchanges of securities for cash and other securities.[7] Consider key processes, mechanisms, and institutions to understand how market components interact. For example, broker-dealers are typically at the centre of funding flows, while CCPs are typically at the centre of collateral flows.
   b. Assess how each component might behave under stress. The durability of funding flows is a key aspect of their resilience, while the quality of collateral is a key attribute for risk assessment.
2. Close the data gaps.
   a. There is good news. The OFR,[8] the Bank of Japan[9] and the Bank of England[10] have all completed pilot data collections on bilateral SFT data. In Europe, ESMA has issued technical guidance on collecting SFT data. Joint ventures in industry for pooling collateral may prove to be useful sources for data.

---

[7] Aguiar, Bookstaber and Wipf (2014), Agostino et al. (2015), Aguiar et al. (2016).
[8] Baklanova, Cipriani et al. (2016). For securities lending, see Baklanova, Keane et al. (2016).
[9] Sato (2015).
[10] Bank of England, November 2015.

    b. Aggregation may hide double counting. When we aggregate data across jurisdictions in the future, how will we avoid double or triple counting collateral reuse?

3. Design, calibrate, and implement the policy regime. Almost every policy design decision raises empirical questions. For a time-varying regime:

    a. Can we find leading indicators to use to trigger minimum margin changes that are sufficiently robust and timely?

    b. If market behaviour is variable, non-linear, and uncertain, where should policy thresholds be set?

    c. How much change will be needed to 'lean against the wind' effectively?

    d. Should a variable regime be discretionary or automatic?

    e. Does the Federal Reserve's 1930's experience with margin floors and ceilings under Regulation T offer any guidance or insight into such questions?

    f. With different laws, market practices and cycle stages to contend with, how should we coordinate a variable regime globally?

4. Look for potential complementarities and conflicts. The effects of minimum floors for haircuts on SFT resilience likely will depend on other tools. For example, SFT markets likely will be less prone to runs – and the need to adjust haircuts would correspondingly be diminished – if institutions engaged in them have predictable 'lender of last resort' access accompanied by prudential oversight (Dudley, 2016).

In my view, minimum floors on haircuts are clearly an idea whose time has come. They can help mitigate excessive risk-taking and procyclical behaviour under stress. But I am mindful of the challenges we face in creating a through-the-cycle regime, and frankly, I am daunted by the hurdles to operationalising a countercyclical one.

These considerations underscore some major themes in this review. First, whether through the cycle or countercyclical, any system of haircut floors must be considered in the context of the overall toolkit, so we can understand potential conflicts and unintended consequences. Second, we should agree on the governance and best practices for this framework before procyclical storm clouds threaten. Last, getting the facts right is essential for understanding where SFT markets are and are likely to evolve, and in turn, critical for good policymaking. Completing our data collection on plan and consistent with Financial Stability Board guidelines is thus our top priority.

References

Adrian, T., P. de Fontnouvelle, E. Yang, and A. Zlate (2016), 'Macroprudential Policy: A Case Study from a Tabletop Exercise', *Economic Policy Review*, 23(1), pp. 1–30, Federal Reserve Bank of New York.

Agostino, C., W. Allen Cheng, and S. Rajan (2015), 'Systemic Risk: The Dynamics under Central Clearing', *OFR Working Paper* No. 15-08, Office of Financial Research.

Aguiar, A., R. Bookstaber, and T. Wipf (2014), 'A Map of Funding Durability and Risk', *OFR Working Paper* No. 14-03, Office of Financial Research.

Aguiar, A., D. Kenett, R. Bookstaber, and T. Wipf (2016), 'A Map of Collateral Uses and Flows', *OFR Working Paper* No. 16-06, Office of Financial Research.

Ashcraft, A., N. Gârleanu, and L.H. Pedersen (2010), 'Two Monetary Tools: Interest Rates and Haircuts', *NBER Working Paper* No. 16337, National Bureau of Economic Research.

Baklanova, V., A. Copeland, and R. McCaughrin (2015), 'Reference Guide to U.S. Repo and Securities Lending Markets', *OFR Working Paper* No. 15–17, Office of Financial Research.

Baklanova, V., C. Caglio, M. Cipriani, and A. Copeland (2016), 'The U.S. Bilateral Repo Market: Lessons from a New Survey', *OFR Brief* 16-01, Office of Financial Research.

Baklanova, V., C. Caglio, F. Keane, and B. Porter (2016), 'A Pilot Survey of Agent Securities Lending Activity', *OFR Working Paper* No. 16-08, Office of Financial Research.

Bank of England (2015), 'A New Sterling Money Market Data Collection and the Reform of SONIA: Summary of Consultation Feedback and the Bank's Response', November 2015.

Bank for International Settlements, Financial Stability Board, International Monetary Fund (2016), 'Elements of Effective Macroprudential Policies: Lessons from International Experience', August 2016.

Battistini, N., M. Grill, P. Marmara and K. van der Veer (2016), 'A Case for Macroprudential Margins and Haircuts', *Financial Stability Review*, May, pp. 110–19.

Brunnermeier, M., A. Crocket, C. Goodhart, A. Persaud and H. Shin (2009), 'The Fundamental Principles of Financial Regulation', Geneva Reports on the World Economy, ICMB and CEPR.

Cetina, J., M. Paddrik and S. Rajan (2016), 'Stressed to the Core: Counterparty Concentrations and Systemic Losses in CDS Markets', *OFR Working Paper* No. 16-01, Office of Financial Research.

Claessens, S. (2014), 'An Overview of Macroprudential Policy Tools', *IMF Working Paper* No. 14/214, International Monetary Fund.

Commodity Futures Trading Commission (2016), 'Supervisory Stress Test of Clearinghouses: A Report by the Staff of the U.S. Commodity Futures Trading Commission', November 2016.

Constâncio, V. (2016a), 'Principles of Macroprudential Policy', the ECB-IMF Conference on Macroprudential Policy, Frankfurt am Main, April 2016.

    (2016b), 'Margins and Haircuts as a Macroprudential Tool', the ESRB International Conference on the Macroprudential Use of Margins and Haircuts, June 2016.

Copeland, A. and A. Martin (2012), 'The Odd Behavior of Repo Haircuts during the Financial Crisis', Liberty Street Economics, Federal Reserve Bank of New York.

Diamond, D.W. and A.K. Kashyap (2016), 'Liquidity Requirements, Liquidity Choice and Financial Stability', *NBER Working Paper* No. 22053, National Bureau of Economic Research.

Dudley, W.C. (2016), 'Market Funding and Liquidity: An Overview', Federal Reserve Bank of Atlanta 2016 Financial Markets Conference, May 2016.

Duffie, D. and A. Krishnamurthy (2016), 'Pass-through Efficiency in the Fed's New Monetary Policy Setting', the Federal Reserve Bank of Kansas City Economic Symposium, 'Designing Resilient Monetary Policy Frameworks for the Future', Jackson Hole, Wyoming, August 2016.

European Securities and Markets Authority (2016), 'EU-wide CCP Stress Test 2015', Report 2016/258.

Federal Deposit Insurance Corporation, Federal Housing Finance Agency, Federal Reserve Board of Governors, National Credit Union Administration, Office of the Controller of the Currency, [and Securities and Exchange Commission] (2016), 'Agencies Invite Comment on Proposed Rule to Prohibit Incentive-Based Pay that Encourages Inappropriate Risk-Taking in Financial Institutions,'. Joint Press Release, Washington, May 16, 2016.

Financial Stability Board (2015), 'Transforming Shadow Banking into Resilient Market-based Finance: Regulatory Framework for Haircuts on Non-centrally Cleared Securities Financing Transactions', November 2015.

Fischer, S. (2015a), 'Macroprudential Policy in the U.S. Economy', the 59th Economic Conference of the Federal Reserve Bank of Boston, 'Macroprudential Monetary Policy', Boston, MA, October 2015.

(2015b), 'Financial Stability and Shadow Banks: What We Don't Know Could Hurt Us', the Federal Reserve Bank of Cleveland and the Office of Financial Research 2015 Financial Stability Conference, 'Financial Stability: Policy Analysis and Data Needs', Washington, DC, December 2015.

(2016), 'Is There a Liquidity Problem Post-Crisis?' Initiative on Business and Public Policy at the Brookings Institution Conference, 'Do We Have a Liquidity Problem Post-Crisis?' Washington, DC, November 2016.

Gai, P., A. Haldane and S. Kapadia (2011), 'Complexity, Concentration and Contagion', *Journal of Monetary Economics*, 58(5), pp. 453–70.

Geithner, T.F. (2016), 'Are We Safer? The Case for Strengthening the Bagehot Arsenal', Per Jacobsson Lecture at the 2016 Annual Meetings of the International Monetary Fund and World Bank Group, Washington, DC.

Goodhart, C.A.E. (2008), 'Liquidity Risk Management', *Banque de France Financial Stability Review*, 12, pp. 39–44.

Goodhart, C.A.E., P. Sunirand and D.P. Tsomocos (2006), 'A Model to Analyze Financial Fragility', *Economic Theory*, 27(1), pp. 107–42.

Goodhart, C.A.E., D. Tsomocos and M. Shubik (2013), 'Macro-Modelling, Default and Money', LSE Financial Markets Group Special Paper Series, Special Paper 224, June 2013.

Gourio, F., A. Kashyap and J. Sim (2016), 'The Tradeoffs in Leaning against the Wind', the IMF 17th Annual Research Conference, November 2016.

Haldane, A.G. (2011), 'Haircuts', Bank of England, August 2011.

Hanson, S.G., A.K. Kashyap and J.C. Stein (2011), 'A Macroprudential Approach to Financial Regulation', *Journal of Economic Perspectives*, 25(1), pp. 3–28.

Kashyap, A., R. Berner and C. Goodhart (2011), 'The Macroprudential Toolkit', *IMF Review*, 59(2), pp. 145–61.

Kiley, M.T. (2016), 'Macroeconomic Modeling of Financial Frictions for Macroprudential Policymaking: A Review of Pressing Challenges', *FEDS Notes*, May 2016.

Kohn, D. (2014), 'Institutions for Macroprudential Regulation: The UK and the U.S.', *Off the Record*, Brookings Institution, April 2014.

Office of Financial Research (2014), *2014 Annual Report*, pp. 50.

(2015), *2015 Financial Stability Report*.

(2016), *2016 Financial Stability Report*.

Sato, T. (2015), 'Toward Further Development of the Tokyo Financial Market: Issues on Repo Market Reform', Bank of Japan, May 2015.

Schoenmaker, D. and P. Wierts (2016), 'Macroprudential Supervision: From Theory to Policy', *National Institute Economic Review*, 235(1), pp. R50–R62.

Shafik, M. (2016), 'Pass-through Efficiency in the Fed's New Monetary Policy Setting', the Federal Reserve Bank of Kansas City Economic Symposium, 'Designing Resilient Monetary Policy Frameworks for the Future', Jackson Hole, Wyo., August 2016.

Tarullo, D.K. (2016), 'Next Steps in the Evolution of Stress Testing', Yale University School of Management Leaders Forum, Yale University, New Haven, CT, September 2016.

Tucker, P. (2016), 'The Design and Governance of Financial Stability Regimes', CIGI, September 2016.

Uluc, A. and T. Wieladek (2015), 'Capital Requirements, Risk Shifting and the Mortgage Market', *Bank of England Staff Working Paper* No. 572, December 2015.

9 | *Three Cooks or Three Wise Men?*

The Interplay between Monetary, Macroprudential and Microprudential Policies in Supporting Financial Stability

JOSÉ VIÑALS, TOMMASO MANCINI-GRIFFOLI AND ERLEND NIER

9.1 Introduction

At the time of writing, in 2017, we are still living in the shadows of the global financial crisis that began in 2007. Economic recoveries have been lukewarm at best, and public and private balance sheets remain weak. Clearly, costs of large-scale financial crises are enormous; as is the volume of suggestions to bolster financial stability. This chapter takes a higher-level view and asks which policies should be responsible for financial stability.

Monetary, macroprudential and microprudential policies all affect financial stability. But effects vary, and are not independent of one another. In practice, will each policy get in the way of the others, like too many cooks in a kitchen, or complement each other to deliver an outcome that is better than the sum of individual parts, as would three wise men?

We answer this question in three broad steps. The first sets the backdrop by discussing how monetary policy and macroprudential policy affect financial stability directly, if carried out alone. The second step, corresponding to the following sections, examines the interplay between monetary, macroprudential and microprudential policies in achieving financial stability. The last step considers which institutional settings are most conducive to attaining this goal while maximising synergies between the various policies.

The chapter concludes that a clear assignment of objectives to each policy is optimal. When monetary policy focuses on price and output stability, macroprudential policy on limiting systemic risks, and microprudential policy on ensuring the resilience of individual firms, each policy can complement the other. The broader institutional design can harness complementarities and elicit coordination where necessary. Three cooks, each with specific tools and instructions, working in separate parts of the kitchen though aware of one another, can work together to prepare a healthy meal.

9.2 Monetary Policy and Financial Stability

The view among policymakers regarding the effects of monetary policy on financial stability was drastically questioned by the crisis. Pre-crisis, most policymakers thought monetary policy should take financial stability into account, but only insofar as it affected output and inflation. Cleaning up after a crisis with aggressive easing was thought to be relatively cheap and effective. The crisis proved just the contrary, and led policymakers to ask whether monetary policy had a role in reducing risks of crises.

However, weighing this possibility has proven especially complex. The approach can be divided into three parts, all of which entail covering new terrain. First, what does the transmission mechanism look like? In other words, what is the sign and what is the magnitude of the link between policy interest rates and key financial variables, and – ultimately – the probability of crisis? The second question is about trade-offs. How much and how often do the goals of financial stability, and price and output stability conflict? If rarely, monetary policy may not have to be altered at all to support financial stability. And third, are the benefits of using monetary policy to support financial stability greater than the costs of doing so?

Recent work[1] has tried to address these questions amid a healthy and particularly active debate. Our view is that in general monetary policy should not deviate from its price and output stability objective in order to support financial stability (IMF, 2015). Although monetary policy does affect financial risks, and there are times when trade-offs between price and output stability, and financial stability, are stark, deviating from the traditional mandate is – in most circumstances – just too costly.[2]

---

[1] See, for instance, Ajello et al. (2016), Svensson (2016), Adrian and Lang (2016) and Goodhart, Sunirand and Tsomocos (2011).

[2] While agreement over this view has strengthened in policy circles (see, for instance, Yellen, 2014), some have taken an opposite view. BIS (2016), for instance, argues that monetary policy should respond to financial stability risks, even at the cost of lower inflation and output, and higher unemployment.

Transmission of monetary policy to financial stability is complex. In part, this is because short-term effects differ from longer-term effects. A rise in interest rates usually undermines financial stability upon impact. Lower aggregate demand, household earnings, asset values and firm profits contribute to making borrowers – and banks – riskier. Evidence shows that delinquencies and defaults increase following interest rate hikes, real debt to gross domestic product (GDP) rises as nominal income drops faster than nominal debt, financial sector leverage increases and banks become more likely to default (see references listed in IMF, 2015).

In the longer term, however, the picture improves as balance sheets adapt. In particular, household real debt levels generally decrease (in the order of 0.3–2 per cent after 4–16 quarters following a temporary one hundred basis point hike in interest rates, depending on the model), financial sector leverage decreases, real estate prices drop and credit spreads increase (see references listed in IMF, 2015).

These longer-term effects are positive for financial stability. The above results, together with the important work of Schularick and Taylor (2012) on the relationship between the growth rates of real debt and the risk of crises, suggest that a one hundred basis points rise in policy rates reduces the probability of crisis in a country by between 0.04 and 0.3 percentage points after 3–5 years. Although the effect may seem small at first glance, even a slight decrease in the probability of a very costly event implies a large gain in welfare.

So how does monetary policy affect these probabilities while following its traditional course? The question comes down to trade-offs between price and output stability, and financial stability objectives. It turns out that in advanced economies trade-offs are not always so stark. Financial stability risks build up in periods of growth, during which tightening monetary policy for price and output stability purposes alone is also warranted. However, trade-offs may appear starker in real time. It is only with hindsight that pre-crisis estimates of potential output appear too optimistic. Indeed, were there no trade-offs, the loose monetary policy stance in the pre-crisis period should have stemmed risks to financial stability.

But even with perfect information on the exact transmission mechanism and trade-offs, it will generally not pay off to deviate from price and output stability in pursuit of financial stability. In most scenarios, the costs of doing so would be larger than the benefits. This is because hiking interest rates beyond what is required for price and output stability significantly worsens the outlook for output, employment and inflation. The costs of higher unemployment alone far outweigh the benefits of reducing risks of much higher unemployment in the event of a crisis.

The welfare calculation should ideally be made in a fully fledged model. An open commitment to financial stability could modify behaviour, dissuading households, firms and banks to take on excessive risk. But this channel can only be taken into account with a detailed model of market imperfections, the development of risk, non-linear dynamics, and dual equilibria: one good, and one bad corresponding to a crisis. These models are still in their infancy, though they suggest there could be some gains from responding systemically to financial stability risks. However, the same models suggest that using targeted and effective macroprudential and microprudential policies is much preferred (see IMF (2015) for a survey, as well as Goodhart, Osorio and Tsomocos (2009) for one such model).[3]

For now, a simple cost-benefit analysis seems to be the best stake in the ground to inform policy action. Country specifics can then sway the benchmark analysis. For instance, a small open emerging market economy might conclude that targeting financial stability with monetary policy is even less attractive. Raising interest rates could encourage further capital inflows potentially damaging to financial stability. And the ensuing appreciation of the domestic currency could encourage risky borrowing in foreign currency.

While monetary policy has unquestionable effects on financial stability, deviations from the price and output stability objective seem overly costly in most circumstances. The baton is thus passed on to

---

[3] Others (see Greenwood, Hanson and Stein, 2016) have recently suggested that monetary policy can pursue price and output stability by setting interest rates on reserves, while using the size of the central bank's balance sheet to affect financial stability. In brief, the intuition is that ample short-term central bank liabilities – such as reverse repos, central bank paper, or interest-bearing reserves (the counterparts to large government bond holdings) – will increase the cost of privately issued short-term paper, thereby reducing its issuance, and in turn the degree of maturity transformation and reliance on runnable short-term liabilities. While this proposal is certainly worth pursuing further, there is more to ensuring financial stability than reducing liquidity mismatches on the balance sheets of financial institutions.

macroprudential and microprudential policy to ensure that the financial system remains resilient.

9.3 Macroprudential Policy and Financial Stability

Macroprudential policy has been defined as the use of primarily prudential tools to contain systemic risk (IMF 2013a). Macroprudential policy can be explicitly tasked to pursue three interlocking intermediate objectives (IMF, 2013a; IMF-FSB-BIS, 2016). First it seeks to increase the resilience of the financial system to aggregate shocks, by building and releasing buffers that help maintain the ability of the financial system to provide credit to the economy under adverse conditions. Second, it seeks to contain the build-up of systemic vulnerabilities over time, by reducing procyclical feedback between asset prices and credit, and containing unsustainable increases in leverage and volatile funding. Third, it seeks to control structural vulnerabilities within the financial system that arise through interlinkages and the critical role of individual intermediaries in key markets that can render individual institutions 'too important to fail'.

Macroprudential policy is better suited than monetary policy to achieve these financial stability objectives for at least three reasons. First, macroprudential policy interventions will tend to *entail relatively smaller costs on output*, relative to the tightening of monetary policy, thereby offering a more favourable policy trade-off. While the impact on output of some tools can be measurable, the short-run cost to output of increasing capital and liquidity requirements have generally been assessed as small, and outweighed by longer-run benefits from a reduction of the frequency and depth of financial crises (BIS, 2010; IMF-FSB-BIS, 2016).

Second, macroprudential policy intervention can be *more closely targeted* at specific sources of risk prevailing at a given point in time. For instance, where systemic risks arise from increases in bank lending in foreign currency (FX), increases in sectoral capital requirements or a cap on such lending can attenuate this risk fairly directly (see IMF, 2014b). By contrast, it is difficult to see how a shading of interest policy could achieve the same effect. Indeed, if anything, a tightening of domestic policy rates will strengthen, rather than weaken, incentives for corporates and households to borrow in FX.

Third, and most important, macroprudential policy will tend to have a much *more direct effect on resilience* than is achievable through monetary policy. This observation applies most obviously to policies in the structural dimension that are seeking to bolster loss absorbency of institutions that are too important to fail (such as capital surcharges for the largest institutions). But it will also tend to hold true for policies in the time dimension, where policies will generally work both by 'leaning against' the build-up of imbalances, and by increasing resilience of banks or borrowers to shocks. For example, a loan-to-value (LTV) limit has both these benefits: it will tend to slow mortgage credit as well as increase borrowers' resilience to asset price shocks. Indeed, a resilience effect is part of the transmission of most, if not all, macroprudential tools that work in the time dimension, including tools that work on intermediary balance sheets (capital- and liquidity-based tools) as well as those that apply to borrowers (such as LTV-type tools).

While these are strong advantages, we should not expect macroprudential policy to work perfectly since its limitations are increasingly well understood. For instance, macroprudential policy is subject to 'leakage' (IMF, 2014a) or, as Charles Goodhart has termed it, the 'boundary problem', where activity has the tendency to move outside of the scope of regulation, whenever it is binding (Goodhart, 2008). Macroprudential policy therefore requires a strong operational framework that enables policymakers to monitor and close regulatory gaps, and a sufficiently broad set of tools to contain systemic risks across the financial system (IMF 2013a, IMF-FSB-BIS, 2016).[4]

9.4 Monetary and Macroprudential Policy: Interactions and Complementarities

While monetary policy and macroprudential policy pursue different primary objectives – price (and output) stability for monetary policy, and financial stability for macroprudential policy – the conduct of each policy can have 'side effects' on the objectives of the other. We

---

[4] By contrast, a well-known argument has it that monetary policy more easily 'gets into all the cracks' (Stein, 2013). But the problem there is the reverse: because it gets into 'all' cracks, i.e. affects everything, using it will incur collateral damage for the economy. And it may even do more harm than good for financial stability when increases in policy rates lead to a crystallisation, rather than a reduction, of risks. Despite its limitations, macroprudential policy may then simply be 'the best we can do' in order to preserve financial stability.

argue that, in the presence of such side effects, effective monetary and macroprudential policies complement each other, yielding superior outcomes to a world where monetary policy – or macroprudential policy – is pursued on its own and in the absence of the other policy (see also Nier and Kang, 2016).

First, monetary policy can have a range of 'side effects' on financial stability. However, macroprudential policy can attenuate these side effects, providing more room for manoeuvre for monetary policy to pursue its primary objective.

Second, macroprudential policy can build buffers that can be relaxed in periods of financial stress. Such a policy can help keep open the transmission of monetary policy, preserving the effectiveness of monetary policy in the event of such stress.

Third, the tightening of macroprudential policy tools can have dampening 'side effects' on output. However, monetary policy can counter these effects, by adding accommodation at the margin, as long as monetary policy is effective.

9.4.1 *Use of Macroprudential Policy to Attenuate Side Effects of Monetary Policy*

Macroprudential policies that are well targeted at the sources of distortions have the potential to contain the undesirable side effects of monetary policy, creating additional 'room for manoeuvre' for monetary policy. For instance, in a number of countries, low interest rates, in combination with limited elasticity of housing supply have contributed to increases in house prices and a run-up in household debt and leverage. Targeted macroprudential policies (such as the tightening of caps on loan-to-value and debt-to-income ratios) can help contain these dynamics and increase the system's resilience to shocks to asset prices or household incomes. Similarly, higher capital requirements, or tighter leverage ratios can help maintain banks' resilience to shocks when accommodative monetary policy leads to increases in credit and leverage. By containing financial stability risks that may arise as a result of the monetary stance, active use of macroprudential policy can then create additional room for manoeuvre for monetary policy, thereby allowing monetary policymakers to more vigorously pursue their price stability objective (IMF, 2013a; Nier and Kang, 2016).

Importantly, this logic works not only for advanced economies. In small open and emerging economies, a common concern of central bankers is that positive policy rate differentials to advanced economy rates lead the banking system to pull in foreign currency denominated wholesale funding, and also create incentives for corporate and household borrowers to borrow in foreign currency. These effects can be particularly strong when higher domestic interest rates lead to expectations of exchange rate appreciation that will come to bolster domestic balance sheets (Bruno and Shin, 2013). Well-designed use of macroprudential policy can then again be used to address the resulting risks. Useful measures can include constraints on banks' wholesale funding, such as a net stable funding ratio and a liquidity coverage ratio, potentially calibrated by currency (as in Sweden or Iceland), as well as increases in capital requirements for banks' foreign currency exposures, or caps on the share of such exposures on banks' balance sheets. By containing the potential side effects of the appropriate monetary policy stance, macroprudential policy can then create greater room for manoeuvre to vary policy rates away from advanced country rates, thereby bolstering the effective monetary policy autonomy of small open economies.

9.4.2 Complementary Use of Macroprudential Policy in the Event of Financial Shocks

A second set of complementarities arises in the event of financial shocks. In the absence of macroprudential policies, monetary policymakers have often had to cut policy rates deeply and aggressively in order to bolster the financial system and maintain the provision of credit to the economy. Macroprudential policy affords a second set of policy tools under such conditions, by providing buffers against unexpected financial shocks that help keep open monetary policy transmission. Moreover, releasing macroprudential buffers in periods of financial stress may cushion the effect of such financial shocks on the provision of credit to the economy. Where macroprudential buffers have been built up, their use can then make it less likely that monetary policy runs into the effective lower bound on interest rates (Nier and Kang, 2016).

For instance, in times of financial stress, monetary easing may not transmit to increased bank lending when banks are weighed down by non-performing loans that deplete voluntary capital buffers over and above the microprudential minimum. Banks may then be reluctant to expand their balance sheets in response to monetary accommodation since this will further reduce capital ratios, potentially leading banks to hit the microprudential minimum ratios that trigger supervisory corrective action. By contrast, where macroprudential capital buffers have been built up, they can be released in periods of stress, and thereby made available to absorb losses from increases in non-performing loans. This makes it less likely that banks will pull back on credit, and can lend greater potency to the transmission of monetary policy accommodation that seeks to stimulate the provision of credit in order to boost output.

Similarly, after a fall in house prices, high-LTV borrowers may be unable to refinance their loans since the principal loan amount exceeds their property value. These borrowers can then not take advantage of lower mortgage rates that an easing of monetary policy may help bring about (Geanakoplos, 2010). A more stringent LTV constraint prior to going into the bust may mitigate this and help strengthen the transmission of monetary policy after prices correct. The transmission of accommodative monetary policy to housing markets can be further enhanced when macroprudential policy-makers relax LTV constraints for new loans and refinancing by removing the tightening that occurred ahead of the bust, since this means that a greater share of potential borrowers is able to take advantage of the low mortgage rates that monetary policy easing may bring about.

By helping monetary policy transmission, such active use of macroprudential policy can reduce the need for monetary policy to respond aggressively to adverse financial shocks. Policy synergies may then lessen the risk that monetary policy will again run into the effective lower bound on interest rates and have to resort to unconventional policy measures such as quantitative easing or negative policy rates.

9.4.3 Use of Monetary Policy to Counter Macroprudential Side Effects on Output

Complementarities also run the other way. In particular, the tightening of macroprudential policy tools can have dampening 'side effects' on output. However, as long as monetary policy is effective, monetary policy can counter these effects by adding accommodation at the margin.

Existing research suggests that tools that work on intermediary balance sheets, such as tighter capital and provisioning requirements, increase resilience but will often have only weak effects on loan rates and the volume of credit (IMF, 2013b; BIS, 2010). On the other hand, there is evidence that constraints on borrowers, such as caps on LTV ratios, do affect both the composition of output and the overall output growth in a measurable way (IMF, 2013b; Nier and Kang, 2016). However, in principle, and as long as monetary policy is effective, any undesirable effect on output can be offset by more accommodative monetary policy to reach the price stability objective.

Complications may arise, however, when monetary policy is constrained and unable to counter the effects on output. This can happen when capital requirements are tightened in financial downturns – that is, when the imposition of the macroprudential measures is ill-timed – or when monetary policy has already reached its lower bound, and thus may be unable to counter effectively the deleveraging effects set off by increases in capital requirements. Trade-offs can also arise in currency unions and under pegs, where, more generally, monetary policy is unable to respond to the imposition of macroprudential policy tools in a manner that would cushion their effects on output. In these cases of constraints on monetary policy, it will be particularly important for tools such as loan-to-value (LTV), loan-to-income (LTI), and debt service-to-income (DSTI) constraints to be tightened gradually, and in a manner that tries to avoid large effects on output (IMF, 2014a; Nier and Kang, 2016).

9.5 Macroprudential and Microprudential Policies: Complementarities and Conflicts

In principle, there are also strong complementarities between macroprudential regulation and microprudential supervision. Indeed, strong supervision is essential to ensure that the macroprudential policy stance adopted is effectively enforced across institutions. Moreover, cooperation by supervisory departments or agencies is key to ensure that macroprudential policymakers can draw on supervisory information and expertise in risk assessment and for the design of the appropriate policy response. Complementarities are particularly strong in reducing the risk of failure of individual systemic institutions, which must rely on an integrated approach, consisting of higher loss absorbency (such as capital surcharges for global or domestic systemically important banks), intensified supervision and enhanced resolvability.

Tensions between microprudential and macroprudential perspectives may also arise, both in buoyant times and in times of stress (Osiński, Seal and Hoogduin, 2013). Microprudential and macroprudential capital or liquidity requirements work through similar transmission mechanisms and it is their joint effects that will determine the outcome.

When credit growth is strong and financial imbalances build up, the microprudential supervisor may not see the need to build up buffers, since such buoyant times tend to be associated with ample profits for the financial industry and small or decreasing non-performing loans. Supervisors are then likely to take their eyes off the ball.

As the credit cycle turns, tensions can be even stronger, since the macroprudential perspective may call for a relaxation of regulatory requirements that impede the provision of credit to the economy or contribute to fire-sale effects, while the microprudential perspective may seek to retain or tighten these requirements to protect the interest of depositors of individual banks. Indeed, there is a risk that microprudential policymakers 'undo' the relaxation sought by the macroprudential policymakers, such as by increasing Pillar 2 capital charges at times when the macroprudential policymaker wants to relax the countercyclical capital buffer (Osiński, Seal and Hoogduin, 2013).

When microprudential supervisors are in charge of macroprudential policy, this can thus contribute to inaction biases that are well known to plague macroprudential policy (Nier, 2011). Indeed, since microprudential supervisors are in close contact with the financial firms, they can also develop a tendency to pay too close attention to arguments advanced by financial firms, who will invariably complain that macroprudential policy action imposes undue costs on them.

Therefore, even if the supervisory perspective is important to consider, and supervisory information can be useful, macroprudential policy is arguably best conducted by an authority which is more at arm's length to the financial industry, and more likely to adopt a macro view. This is a key reason why there is a growing consensus that macroprudential policy, if not microprudential policy (see Goodhart and Schoenmaker, 1995), should involve a leading role for the central bank – as we will discuss further next.

9.6 Institutional Considerations

A basic challenge for the design of an effective macroprudential framework is that the benefits of specific macroprudential policies – reduction in the probability and severity of financial crises – are long term and not easily measured. At the same time, macroprudential policies will almost always have an immediate and highly visible adverse effect on the profitability of financial intermediaries and may also sometimes have an effect on the availability and price of financial services to households and firms.

This can cause a bias towards insufficiently strong action, for three related reasons (Nier, 2011). The first is the basic asymmetry of the policy problem faced by the macroprudential authority. When the costs of macroprudential policies are more certain and visible than the benefits, this makes it hard for the policymaker to develop the resolve to take actions. The second is that macroprudential policies are conducted under intense lobbying pressure on the part of the financial industry since macroprudential policies will inevitably hurt industry profits. The third is that macroprudential policies are exposed to strong political economy challenges. When electoral cycles cause short-term horizons on the part of elected politicians, the macroprudential policymaker may face political interference when its policies cause a reduction in the availability and an increase in the price of financial services to parts of the electorate. Taken together, these problems create strong biases in favour of inaction or insufficiently forceful intervention.

These biases in turn put a premium on governance arrangements that increase *the willingness to act* on the part of the macroprudential policymaker, by assigning a clear mandate and creating strong accountability. They also need to foster the *ability to act* in the face of evolving systemic threats, by assigning influence over a sufficiently broad set of macroprudential instruments. And they should finally promote *effective cooperation* in risk assessments and mitigation, in a manner that preserves the autonomy of separate policy functions (Nier et al., 2011; IMF, 2013a).

An important emerging principle is that macroprudential policy is best served by assigning the main mandate to a clearly identified lead agency, which can be held accountable for achieving its objectives (IMF, 2013a). Many of the observed institutional designs provide the main mandate to an influential central body with substantial convening power and the ability to take a broad view of the entire financial system (IMF-FSB-BIS, 2016). Such a mandate can be assigned to an existing authority, a policymaking committee within the central bank or an inter-agency council that functions as the lead agency.

A second important principle is that the central bank should play a strong role in all arrangements (Viñals, 2011; Nier, 2011; IMF, 2013a). This can harness the expertise of the central bank in systemic risk identification and its incentives to ensure macroprudential policy is pursued effectively. It can foster policy coordination between macroprudential and monetary policy in a manner that preserves the independent pursuit of the latter. It can finally help shield macroprudential policymaking from political interference that can slow the deployment of tools or bias their use towards other objectives.

A third principle is that the macroprudential decision-making process should also involve the main microprudential agency (if outside the central bank structure) or the supervision department (if this is inside the central bank). This allows an integrated approach to prudential policy, where policy trade-offs can be discussed and internalised. It can create ownership of any policy action taken by the macroprudential authority when this needs to be implemented by the prudential agency. Finally, inclusion of the prudential authority is important to make full use of all available information that can be brought to bear in identifying risks and designing the appropriate policy response.

A culture of sharing information, joint analysis of risks and strong dialogue can reinforce the complementarities between microprudential supervision and macroprudential policy. Indeed, revisions made in the wake of the crisis to the Basel Core Principles now place a much stronger emphasis on the need for a macroprudential perspective in supervision.[5] Supervisory agencies should be tasked not only to ensure the safety and soundness of individual institutions, but also to contribute to the stability of the system as a whole.

This should in principle extend to all supervisory and regulatory agencies, including also securities regulators, whose cooperation is increasingly needed to contain risks in the non-bank financial system.

---

[5] In addition, the work of international standard setters, such as the Basel Committee on Banking Supervision (BCBS), is increasingly guided by the need for a macroprudential perspective in financial regulation. A key example is the establishment of the countercyclical capital buffer as part of Basel III.

To foster such cooperation, it is important that financial stability objectives be enshrined in their legal mandates, as is already the case in the UK and France, and recommended by the IMF also for the USA (in the Financial Sector Assessment Program (FSAP) for the USA).

While there can be no 'one size fits all' approach, in practice there has been an increasing prevalence of three models that each assign the main macroprudential mandate to a well-identified authority, committee, or inter-agency body, generally with an important role of the central bank (Table 9.1), and allowing the supervisory agency to participate.

Across these models, a strong role of the central bank can be achieved in a variety of ways, such as making the central bank board (or governor) the decision-making body (as in Ireland and New Zealand), having the governor chair the policymaking committee (as in Malaysia, South Africa and the UK), providing the central bank with a clearly defined role to provide its analysis of systemic risk and proposals for policy action to the attention of the decision-making body (as in France and Germany), or assigning it a leading role in the regulation and supervision of designated systemically important financial institutions (SIFIs) (as in the USA).

Importantly, a strong role of the central bank should not – and need not – come to compromise the independent pursuit of price stability through monetary policy. In particular, the introduction of a financial stability objective to guide the central bank in the pursuit of macroprudential policy need not imply the introduction of additional objectives in the field of monetary policy. Instead, the arrangements should – and can – recognise that monetary and macroprudential policy are different policy functions, which are best served by distinct mandates, as well as separate decision-making and accountability arrangements (Nier, 2011; Jácome, Nier and Imam 2012).

In particular, where macroprudential policy functions are assigned to the central bank, it is useful for the central bank law to map the macroprudential policy functions to the financial stability objective, and the monetary policy function to a price stability objective. More generally, to address the risk of dual objectives, it is useful to establish separate decision-making and accountability arrangements for monetary and macroprudential policy (IMF, 2013a), and to establish clarity ex ante on which tools are being assigned to each of these. A good example of this are the new arrangements in the UK, where the monetary policy committee is charged with achieving price stability,

Table 9.1. *Three macroprudential policy models*

	Selected country examples		
	Central bank model		Separate committee model
	Model 1 (board or governor)[1]	Model 2 (internal committee)	Model 3 (committee outside the central bank)[3]
Countries	Argentina, Belgium, Brazil,* Cyprus, Czech Republic, Estonia,* Hong Kong SAR,* Hungary, Indonesia, Ireland, Israel, Italy,* Lebanon, Lithuania, Netherlands,* New Zealand, Norway,[2] Portugal,* Russia, Singapore, Slovakia and Switzerland[2]	Algeria, Malaysia,* Morocco,* Saudi Arabia,* South Africa, Thailand and the UK	Austria (M), Chile (M), Denmark (C), France (M), Germany (M), Iceland (M), India (M), Korea (M), Malta (C), Mexico (M), Poland (C), Romania (C), Turkey (M) and the USA (M)

[1] Jurisdictions with an '*' have an additional council, including other supervisors (e.g. insurance supervisory authorities and financial market authorities), that plays a coordinating role.

[2] In Norway and Switzerland, the central bank is mandated to issue recommendations on the countercyclical capital buffer (CCyB), with ultimate decisions on the buffer rate made by the Ministry of Finance and the Swiss Federal Council, respectively.

[3] '(C)' or '(M)' indicates whether the council is chaired by the central bank or by a government minister (usually the Minister of Finance), respectively.

and the financial policy committee takes macroprudential policy decisions to achieve financial stability objectives, with a clear understanding of which policy tools are under the control of each committee, and separate accountability mechanisms underpinning the delivery of the two policy functions.

In the context of separate policy functions that each has side effects on the other, it is important nonetheless to discuss and address these side effects. For instance, the macroprudential policy authority can take account of the financial stability risks connected with a given monetary policy stance in formulating its policies. Similarly, the monetary policymaker can take account of action or inaction on the part of the macroprudential authority when calibrating its policy stance. Overlapping membership between the monetary and macroprudential decision-making bodies and the provision of common analysis to both committees (as in the UK) can foster such coordination, in a manner that avoids an erosion of monetary policy independence.

In sum, the appropriate allocation of policy objectives across all three policy functions (monetary policy, macroprudential policy and microprudential policy), as well as the broader design of institutional arrangements can help ensure that each policy plays its part in achieving both price and output stability, as well as financial stability. Ultimately, overall welfare will benefit.

Three wise men? We hope so!

References

Adrian, T. and N. Lang (2016), 'Monetary Policy, Financial Conditions, and Financial Stability', Federal Reserve Bank of New York, Staff Report No. 690, July.

Ajello, A., T. Laubach, D. López-Salido and T. Nakata (2016), 'Financial Stability and Optimal Interest-Rate Policy', FEDS Working Paper No. 2016-067, August.

Bank for International Settlements – BIS (2010), 'Macroeconomic Assessment Group, Final Report, Assessing the Macroeconomic Impact of the Transition to Stronger Capital and Liquidity Requirements', December 2010.

    (2016), *Annual Report*, June. Available at: www.bis.org/publ/arpdf/ar2016e_ov.htm.

Bruno, V. and H. Song Shin (2013) 'Capital Flows and the Risk-Taking Channel of Monetary Policy', *NBER Working Paper Series 18942*, Cambridge, MA: National Bureau of Economic Research, April.

Geanakoplos, J. (2010), 'Solving the Present Crisis and Managing the Leverage Cycle', *Federal Reserve Bank of New York Economic Policy Review*, 16(1), pp. 101–31.

Goodhart, C.A.E. (2008), 'The Boundary Problem in Financial Regulation', *National Institute Economic Review*, 266(1), pp. 48–55.

Goodhart, C.A.E. and D. Schoenmaker (1995), 'Should the Functions of Monetary Policy and Banking Supervision Be Separated?' *Oxford Economic Papers*, 47(4), pp. 539–60.

Goodhart, C.A.E., C. Osorio and D.P. Tsomocos (2009), 'Analysis of Monetary Policy and Financial Stability: A New Paradigm', CESifo Working Paper Series 2885, CESifo Group Munich.

Goodhart, C.A.E., P. Sunirand and D.P. Tsomocos (2011), 'The Optimal Monetary Instrument for Prudential Purposes', *Journal of Financial Stability*, 7(2), pp. 70–7.

Greenwood, R., S.G. Hanson and J.C. Stein (2016), 'The Federal Reserve's Balance Sheet as a Financial-Stability Tool', Paper presented at the Kansas City Federal Reserve Bank's Jackson Hole Conference, August.

International Monetary Fund (2013a), 'Key Aspects of Macroprudential Policy', IMF Policy Paper, June 2013.

(2013b), 'The Interaction of Monetary and Macroprudential Policies', IMF Policy Paper, January 2013.

(2014a), 'Staff Guidance Note on Macroprudential Policy', IMF Policy Paper, November 2014.

(2014b), 'Staff Guidance Note on Macroprudential Policy – Detailed Guidance on Instruments', IMF Policy Paper, November 2014.

(2015). 'Monetary Policy and Financial Stability', IMF Policy Paper, September 2015.

International Monetary Fund, Financial Stability Board and Bank for International Settlements (2016), 'Elements of Effective Macroprudential Policies – Lessons from International Experience'.

Jácome, L., E. Nier and P. Imam (2012), 'Building Blocks for Effective Macroprudential Policies in Latin America: Institutional Considerations', IMF Working Paper 12/183.

Nier, E. (2011), 'Macroprudential Policy – Taxonomy and Challenges', *National Institute Economic Review*, April. Available at: http://papers .ssrn.com/sol3/papers.cfm?abstract_id=1904627.

Nier, E.W., J. Osiński, L.I. Jácome and P. Madrid (2011), 'Institutional Models for Macroprudential Policy', IMF Staff Discussion Note 11/18.

Nier, E. and H. Kang (2016), 'Monetary and Macroprudential Policies – Exploring Interactions', in 'Macroprudential Policy', BIS Papers No. 86.

Osiński, J., K. Seal and L. Hoogduin (2013), 'Macroprudential and Microprudential Policies: Towards Cohabitation', IMF Staff Discussion Note 13/05.

Schularick, M. and A.M. Taylor (2012), 'Credit Booms Gone Bust: Monetary Policy, Leverage Cycles, and Financial Crises, 1870–2008',

American Economic Review, American Economic Association, 102(2), pp. 1029–61.

Stein, J. (2013), 'Overheating in Credit Markets: Origins, Measurement, and Policy Responses', speech at the research symposium sponsored by the Federal Reserve Bank of St. Louis, St. Louis, Missouri on 'Restoring Household Financial Stability after the Great Recession: Why Household Balance Sheets Matter'.

Svensson, L. (2016), 'Cost-Benefit Analysis of Leaning Against the Wind: Are Costs Larger Also with Less Effective Macroprudential Policy?', IMF Working Paper WP/16/3, January 2016; NBER Working Paper No. 21902, January.

Viñals, J. (2011), 'The Do's and Don'ts of Macroprudential Policy', Speech at the European Commission and ECB Conference on Financial Integration and Stability, Brussels, 2 May 2011.

Yellen, J.L. (2014), 'Monetary Policy and Financial Stability', Speech given at the 2014 Michel Camdessus Central Banking Lecture, International Monetary Fund, Washington, DC, 2 July 2014.

10 Liquidity, Default and the Interaction of Financial Stability and Monetary Policy

UDARA PEIRIS, DIMITRIOS TSOMOCOS
AND ALEXANDROS VARDOULAKIS

10.1 Introduction

Liquidity and default have frequently been regarded as two separable concepts. Our view, instead, is that for the most interesting and important aspects of financial stability issues, they are inherently intertwined. Credit risk affects the ease with which economic agents/institutions can raise funds to meet their liquidity needs, and market illiquidity can exacerbate solvency concerns. Indeed, the interplay of liquidity and default can justify fiat money, based on the (tax) power of government, as the stipulated means of exchange. The mere presence of a monetary sector without the possibility of endogenous default or any other friction in equilibrium will become a veil without affecting real trade and, eventually, final equilibrium allocations. Our work with Charles Goodhart has focused on the importance of default in macroeconomic analysis, which has not been until recently fully appreciated as much as other frictions, such as sticky prices or search frictions (see for example, Bhattacharya et al., 2015; Goodhart, Sunirand and Tsomocos, 2004, 2006; Goodhart et al., 2012, 2013; Goodhart, Peiris and Tsomocos, 2013, 2016; Goodhart et al., 2010; and Goodhart, Tsomocos and Vardoulakis, 2010).

The views expressed in this chapter are those of the authors and do not necessarily represent those of Federal Reserve Board of Governors or anyone in the Federal Reserve System. We would also like to thank Charles Goodhart, Philipp Hartmann, Haizhou Huang, Nuwat Nookhwun, Theofanis Papamichalis, Dirk Schoenmaker, Xuan Wang, Geoffrey Wood, Ji Yan, and seminar participants at the LSE conference in honour of Charles Goodhart, 'The Life of a Central Banker', for helpful comments. However, all remaining errors are ours. Udara Peiris was funded within the framework of the Basic Research Programme at the National Research University Higher School of Economics (HSE) and by the Russian Academic Excellence Project '5-100'.

Inevitably, concerns about liquidity and default interact. The original idea that the start of the financial crisis in August 2007 was just a liquidity problem – a widely shared view at the time – was simplistic. The initial economic shock arising from the US housing market raised the prospect of a higher probability of default, but most importantly led to a vicious spiral where default concern led to a fall in asset prices. This fall in asset prices then reinforced concerns about banks' and other financial intermediaries' solvency, and this further reduced liquidity in a range of asset markets, with a variety of self-amplifying spirals then bringing the whole financial system to its knees. Lack of liquidity dries up key financial markets, thus preventing institutions from restructuring their portfolios, adapting their strategies and steering away from potential dangers caused by exogenous economic shocks. In turn, defaults start accumulating, and the domino effect leads to further reductions in liquidity and ultimately causes financial institutions, corporations and other non-financial bodies to fail to meet their contractual obligations.

Under the presence of multiple externalities and the evolving nature of markets, in particular for short-term funding, the forthcoming regulatory architecture should recognise that there are markets that are 'too important to fail' and not only banks that are 'too big to fail'. Hence, regulation, and policy more generally, should also be focused on 'systemic markets' as well as 'systemic institutions'.

The ability to adjust monetary policy appropriately to economic conditions requires measurement of inflation and output growth. Likewise, maintenance of financial stability requires equivalent measures of financial fragility. Such measures could be used as a yardstick to assess the success of regulatory policy.

This chapter provides a summary of our work with Charles Goodhart on bringing financial stability and banking institutions into macroeconomic analysis to answer a variety of questions. Section 10.2 describes some basic modelling elements that make the interaction of default and liquidity interesting, while maintaining the General Equilibrium spirit of the analysis. Section 10.3 summarises our efforts to introduce these interactions in mainstream Dynamic Stochastic General Equilibrium Models (DSGE) that can be easily calibrated and used closely for policy analysis. In Section 10.4 we describe attempts to incorporate more elaborate banking sectors in General Equilibrium, which have a number of important real economic functions generating multiple externalities. The ability of macroprudential regulation to tackle these market failures is also discussed. Finally, Section 10.5 concludes.

10.2 A Model to Analyse Financial Fragility

The key components when building a model to analyse financial stability should include:

1. Inter-temporal decisions (as banks facilitate consumption smoothing the demands of customers).
2. Uncertainty in the future (as banks face the risk of maturity mismatches and uncertainty in loan portfolio value over time).
3. Liquid wealth or money (as the scarcity of liquidity generates costs in financial intermediation).
4. Endogenous default (as the actions of households and banks jointly determine aggregate financial stability conditions and, consequently, financial distress).
5. Incomplete risk sharing (as financial stability conditions affect welfare).

The suite of models that we have been working on over the last twenty years have attempted to combine these elements within a single coherent framework and have used it to address several issues: procyclicality of the Basel Accord (Catarineu-Rabell, Jackson and Tsomocos, 2005), collateral, money and default (Goodhart, Tsomocos and Vardoulakis, 2010; Peiris and Vardoulakis, 2015; Lin, Tsomocos and Vardoulakis, 2015), Minsky's financial instability hypothesis, risk-taking and excessive leverage (Bhattacharya et al., 2015), international capital flows (Goodhart, Peiris and Tsomocos, 2013; Peiris and Tsomocos, 2015), dividend restrictions and financial regulation (Goodhart et al., 2010; Goodhart et al., 2013), precautionary savings and default (Peiris and Vardoulakis, 2013), monetary policy and debt renegotiation (Goodhart, Peiris and Tsomocos, 2016).

10.2.1 Basic Economic Environment

There are multiple household-types that differ, at least, in their non-financial income stream and desire to smooth consumption. Households conduct financial transactions through a banking system composed of multiple bank types that differ, at least, in the balance sheet characteristics they accrue. Surplus households make deposits at banks that, in turn, extend funds to deficit households in the form of commercial or consumer loans and mortgages. There also exists an interbank market where banks with excess liquidity extend credit to deficit banks. When loans and deposits become due, fundamental uncertainty in the economy generates incentives for debtors to default. Households may suffer income or wealth losses which increase the marginal cost of repayment. This is then contrasted with the marginal costs of default, modelled as non-pecuniary (e.g. reputation) costs incurred by defaulting on the volume of debt. Individual optimality results in an endogenous default rate. Alternatively, if debt is secured by collateral such as housing, fluctuations in the price level or the relative value of the collateralised goods may result in default. Banks face similar incentives for the loans obtained from the interbank market. As a consequence, default from one sector is transmitted through the banking sector to the entire economy.

All transactions require fiat money, the creation of which is a monopoly of the central bank. Liquid fiat money is obtained by exchanging illiquid debt with the central bank, at a cost. Expanding the amount of money in the economy reduces the cost of liquidity, or equivalently, increases the liquidity of private assets and household endowments, and increases the efficiency of all transactions. Importantly, infinite liquidity may not be optimal as the limiting economy itself is inefficient due to market incompleteness and agent heterogeneity.

The model is summarised by three key equations:

1. The Quantity Theory of Money (which summarises the intratemporal relationship between liquidity, the nominal price level and real trade);
2. The Term Structure of Interest Rates (which summarises the intertemporal transmission of shocks);
3. The On the Verge condition (which summarises the marginal propensities of households and banks to default).

We will now sketch a version of the Tsomocos (2003) and Goodhart, Sunirand and Tsomocos (2006) models.

10.2.2 *The Model*

It is an exchange economy with multiple commodities. There are two periods, where there is certainty in the first and uncertainty in the second. There are both real (commodity) and financial trades in the first period, while in the second there are real trades and intertemporal financial trades are settled. Households borrow and deposit with the banking system, while banks also conduct financial trade among themselves to obtain an optimal portfolio. The central bank participates in the interbank market by injecting money and affecting the interbank rate. Banks are subject to Capital Adequacy Requirements (CARs) set by a regulator and penalties are imposed upon violations of CARs. Banks are owned by households and are liquidated at the end of the second period with profits and assets distributed to shareholders. Households and banks incur private (nonpecuniary) costs of defaulting on their financial obligations. We model the incentive for avoiding default by penalising agents and banks proportionately to the size of default. Both banks and households are allowed to default on their financial obligations but not on commodity deliveries.

In the first period, households and banks observe current prices and form correct (rational) expectations of prices in the (uncertain) second period. Households are heterogeneous with respect to their endowment/income stream and risk attitudes and hence in their propensities for default. There are also several bank types, heterogeneous with respect to risk/return preferences and initial capital, and having a captive or unique relationship with particular household types. In other words, we introduce limited access to consumer credit markets, with each household assigned (by history and custom) to borrow from a predetermined bank. This feature results in a distribution of interest rates offered to depositors and debtors in the economy.

10.2.3 *Definition of Financial Stability*

The model offers a model-based definition of financial fragility that is characterised by substantial default of a 'number' of households and banks (i.e., a liquidity 'crisis'), without necessarily becoming bankrupt, and a significant decline in the aggregate profitability of the banking sector (i.e., a banking 'crisis'). A natural question is why either one of the conditions is not sufficient by itself to constitute a financially fragile regime. Increased default without reduced profitability might be an indicator of increased volatility and risk-taking without necessarily leading to financial instability. For example, both the mean and the variance of return might have risen. On the other hand, lower bank profitability without increased default might be an indicator of a recession in the real economy and not of financial vulnerability. It is the combination of both conditions that destabilises the financial system and may produce financial crises. This definition is sufficiently flexible to encompass most of the recent episodes of financial fragility. For example, the Japanese crisis may be thought of as an example of the Keynesian liquidity trap. The Mexican crisis of the early 1990s is a classic example of liquidity and banking crisis. The late 1990s East Asian crisis was characterised by a banking crisis and economic recession as well as extensive default. Finally, the Russian crisis, the Texas Banking crisis, and the US Stock Market crash of 1987 conformed to the characterisation of a financially fragile regime generated by liquidity shortages, extensive default and declines in bank profitability.

10.2.4 Results

In this model, both regulatory and monetary policies are non-neutral and arise from the presence of incomplete financial markets and liquidity constraints (since all trade is mediated with liquid assets, i.e., money). Monetary and regulatory policies influence the distribution of income and wealth among heterogeneous agents and hence have real effects. Some other main results are:

- The central bank controls the overall liquidity of the economy and such liquidity, as well as endogenous default risks, determines interest rates.
- Nominal changes (i.e., changes in monetary aggregates) affect both prices and quantities.
- The nominal interest rate is equal to the real interest rate plus the expected rate of inflation (Fisher effect).

From an analysis of a set of comparative statics exercises, using the model, a number of implications arise.

First, in an economic environment in which capital constraints are binding, more expansionary monetary policy may lead banks in some cases to adopt riskier strategies.[1] The liquidity injected by the

---

[1] This does not imply that a deflationary bias is optimal. Inflation targeting is not considered and such a regime can be approximated by fixing money supply.

central bank can be used by some banks to expand their loans to the non-financial private sector. This can lead to a rise in the size of their assets, relative to their capital base, thus worsening their capital position. It is a well-known stylised fact that financial crises are often caused by excessive, and unwise, lending in the upswing of the cycle,[2] which then leads to non-performing loans and failures in a subsequent downturn, should an adverse shock occur. Thus, expansionary policies causing 'excessive' loan expansion can lead to financial fragility.

Second, agents who have more investment opportunities can deal with negative shocks more effectively by restructuring their investment portfolios expeditiously. Such restructuring may put even more pressure on other agents with a more restricted set of investment opportunities. For example, banks which can move into security investments when there is an adverse shock to customer borrowing may make market conditions even worse for banks which cannot so diversify. Put differently, banks with more degrees of freedom may transfer various externalities to smaller ones that have fewer alternatives in their choice sets. This result has various implications. Among them, banks with asset portfolios that are not well diversified tend to follow a countercyclical credit extension policy in the face of a tightening of regulatory standards in the loan market (e.g. tighter loan risk weights) during an economic downturn. In contrast, banks that can quickly restructure their portfolio tend to reallocate their investments away from the loan market, thus following a procyclical credit extension policy.

Third, an improvement such as a positive productivity shock, which is concentrated in one part of the economy, does not necessarily improve the overall welfare and profitability of the economy.

The last two insights relate to the innovative feature of the model of incorporating heterogeneous agents; banks and bank borrowers are not all alike. This some, fairly obvious, implications. The result of a shock depends on the particular sector of the economy which is affected and it can often shift the distribution of income, and welfare, between agents in a complex way, which is hard to predict in advance.

---

[2] See, for example, Borio and Lowe (2002).

10.3 Default and DSGE Models

Martin Shubik described money as an 'institutionalised symbol of trust' (Shubik, 1999), and Kiyotaki and Moore (2002, p. 62) coined a nice phrase, 'Evil is the root of all money'. And they are correct in this. If everyone always repaid all their debts with certainty, then there would be no need for money, most financial instruments and intermediaries like banks. All that would be needed to complete a transaction would be a handshake and the acknowledgement that the buyer is indebted to the seller. Of course, the goods that the seller would like to receive at some future date would not necessarily be what the buyer could offer, but that discrepancy could easily be resolved in complete financial markets.

This proposition already indicates one problem with the assumption that no one defaults, which is that it must imply, as a corollary, a complete set of financial markets. But, as is already well known, a complete set of financial markets not only does not exist but would allow for an Arrow–Debreu Walrasian General Equilibrium in which all transactions could be established at time zero. That would prevent default arising as a result of future bad outcomes, since all such potential outcomes could be hedged in the complete financial markets.

Perhaps even more importantly, a no default assumption, or equivalently the transversality condition in infinite horizon models,[3] would require all agents to be completely and perfectly moral, in the sense that they would never abrogate their contractual obligations. Thus, if you were to take a taxi, even though you would certainly never meet that taxi driver again, you would always pay her. If the ordinary person could get out of repaying her due debt with impunity, then she would!

The upshot of our analysis is that liquidity and default are endogenous variables that are co-determined in equilibrium. Hence, it is an oxymoron to conduct monetary and financial stability analysis when we are treating them as exogenous in the form, for example, of exogenously set credit spreads!

Incorporating default into the DSGE framework would also have the side benefit of restoring a union between macro theory and finance, since the probability of default is a prime element within

---

[3] With debt due infinitely in the future, or rolled over indefinitely at face value.

finance. While we in finance are not wedded to DSGE models, such DSGE models represent a useful discipline and framework and are also the workhorse of most macro modelling. So, our priority ought to be to embed an analytical approach to default within an otherwise standard DSGE model. Doing so has the great advantage that it provides a rationale for the use of money. If you think that the buyer of your product may not meet his resultant debt, you will ask him to pay on the nail, i.e. it provides a rationale for the cash or liquidity-in-advance[4] requirement. Similarly, the main role for banks is to be able to assess probabilities of default better than you or I. Thus, we need them in order to be able to reduce risk-premia and lower the spread between bid and ask rates. Hence, banks become an essential element of any model incorporating default and incomplete asset markets.

Nevertheless, incorporating default into a DSGE model makes the analytical exercise significantly more complex. In particular, one can no longer use the representative agent model, because only a (small) proportion of agents default at any time. The inclusion of heterogeneous agents, banks, liquidity and default greatly increases the scale of parameterisation and the dimension of such models. Nevertheless, such an extended model would at least be micro-founded, whereas a lot of frictions in most DSGE models are *not*. Moreover, it would have the benefit of having a proper foundation for the inclusion of money and financial intermediaries within the system. Consequently, a non-trivial quantity theory of money would obtain whereby when nominal changes occur both prices and quantities would adjust. Of course, during normal times when default is low and constant, one can ignore money as an inessential veil; but that would not help under those circumstances when default probability becomes prominent.

A DSGE model with default and money (Goodhart, Peiris and Tsomocos, 2016; Martinez and Tsomocos, 2016) has been constructed with default and liquidity as key features.[5] We can show how the working of the system changes, first just to take account of heterogeneous agents, and then to take account of the existence of potential default. Heterogeneous agents affect outcomes because of much more extensive distributional as well as *wealth* effects. In many

---

[4] Martinez and Tsomocos (2016).
[5] See also Clerc et al. (2015) for a DSGE model with household, entrepreneur and bank defaults, albeit in a real economy.

simulations, some agents gain and others lose, and that makes it much more difficult to assess the welfare implications of various economic developments. When we incorporate the effect of default on our system, it has significant effects on how the economy responds to various stimuli, with some notable differences from the results of models, especially in the short and medium term, in which default is assumed away, e.g. by the transversality condition. Moreover, default enables the proper assessment of the importance of collateral and the emergence of leverage cycles. Finally, incomplete financial markets allow for an active role for policy whereby welfare-improving policies can be implemented.

Of course, such a model is quite complex and cannot be reduced to the three-equation-reduced form guise in which most of the current DSGE models are now presented. Moreover, we do realise that the addition of a credit risk premium into the output equation enables the three-equation-reduced form to remain in disturbed times. However, such a stratagem completely undermines the assertion that such a model has proper theoretical micro-foundations. If one wants to understand what has been happening to our economies over the last few years, we do not think that there is any alternative to a modelling strategy in which both default and money are essential attributes of the working of the macroeconomy. Such a new paradigm would offer an integrated framework to address both monetary and regulatory policy.

10.4 Making Macroprudential Regulation Operational[6]

In Goodhart et al. (2012) and Kashyap, Tsomocos and Vardoulakis (2014b) we expand on the economic function that financial intermediaries play in the economy, study in detail the externalities associated with their behaviour and suggest regulation to tackle the inefficiencies. In particular, prior work suggests three theoretical channels through which intermediaries can improve welfare. One strand of thinking emphasises the role that they play in extending credit to certain types of borrowers (e.g. Diamond, 1984). A second views them as vehicles for improving risk-sharing. They can do this

---

[6] This section borrows material from Kashyap, Tsomocos and Vardoulakis (2014a).

through the liability side of their balance sheet by creating safe and risky claims (e.g. deposits and equity) against the assets that they hold (Benston and Smith, 1976; Allen and Gale, 1997). And the third perspective supposes that they specialise in creating liquid claims that are backed by illiquid assets (Diamond and Dybvig, 1983). We focus on two principles of financial regulation:

- Our first principle is that it is imperative to start with a general model where the financial system plays all three of these roles.

This is not true of most of the new literature on macroprudential regulation. For instance, Benes, Kumhof and Laxton (2014) have no role for liquidity provision in their set-up – to be fair, very few macro models do. Without this contribution to the financial system, certain forms of instability are ruled out; for instance, funding runs can only happen if we suppose that there is a maturity mismatch between assets and liabilities.

Likewise, regulation to fix potential runs, such as proposals for narrow banking (e.g. Cochrane, 2014), also appears to be especially appealing. But if the fragility that creates the possibility of runs is not valuable on its own, of course eliminating it would be desirable! The more challenging question is what happens if there is a fundamental underlying reason why maturity mismatches create value for some parties. In that case, regulation that stops runs for certain organisational forms may simply move activity to other unregulated entities because of the underlying legitimate demand for liquidity creation (Goodhart, 2008). Or, if the regulation is fully effective at preventing runs, then the social value of the liquidity provision is lost. A suitable model should be capable of assessing these trade-offs.

- Our second principle is that intermediaries should operate in an environment where the savers who use them are forward-looking, and the prices the intermediaries face adjust (endogenously) to the regulatory environment.

For example, much of the Basel Committee's regulatory agenda has focused on raising capital requirements for banks. The consequences of such regulations are very different when the banks have to offer attractive enough returns to entice savers to buy equity, than when the price of equity is unrelated to the size of a bank's balance sheet and/or the risks on that balance sheet.

We are unaware of any existing models that satisfy these two prin-ciples. So, in Kashyap, Tsomocos and Vardoulakis (2014b), we have constructed one by modifying the classic Diamond and Dybvig's (1983) framework. In their original model, banks only provide liquid-ity insurance to savers (by allowing depositors the option of with-drawing early), so there is no other risk-sharing or additional lending that takes place because of banks. Our modifications are designed so that banks also provide these services.

There are four specific changes that we make:

- First, savers can buy equity in a banking sector and save via deposits.
- Second, the banks choose to invest in safe assets or to fund entre-preneurs who have risky projects.

Together, these changes make banks' asset and liability structure interesting, and create a situation where there is some fundamental risk that cannot be diversified away.

- Third, the banks and the entrepreneurs face limited liability.
- Finally, there is a probability of a run, but unlike in Diamond and Dybvig, the decision whether to run is governed by the banks' leverage and mix of safe and risky assets.

In particular, when the banking system has more loans relative to safe assets, or more deposits relative to equity, a run is more likely. The possibility of the run reduces the incentive to lend and take risk, while limited liability pushes for excessive lending and risk-taking. So, the baseline economy suffers from two problems: the destructive aspects of runs (where savers can lose money, banks can fail, and borrowers have their loans pulled) and the moral hazard problems that come from limited liability.

The banks in this world not only offer liquidity insurance with their deposits but offer savers a better alternative to making direct loans to entrepreneurs. This occurs because the banks start with some initial equity, which serves as a buffer in the case where the entrepre-neurs' projects fail; so, banks are pooling and trenching risks, and by doing this they can attract more funds to lend than the savers would be willing to risk if they could not access the banks.

The bulk of our chapter explores the portfolio choices that savers and banks make in this kind of environment. One nice feature of this model is that it can be used to explore how capital regulation, liquidity regulation, deposit insurance, loan-to-value limits, and dividend taxes alter allocations and change the degree of run-risk and total risk-taking. Rather than focusing on very specific findings about how these interventions can matter, we mention here a few findings that seem likely to carry over to other models that respect our two principles.

10.4.1 Some General Findings of the Model

First, as a benchmark, we compute the portfolio allocations that a central planner would make. We find that approximating the planner's allocations with just one regulation is impossible. In this model, it takes at least two tools to overcome the two distortions. Second, the ways in which the various regulations change behaviour are very different, and combining some of them leads to very little improvement. Put differently, it is not correct to conclude that combining any two tools is necessarily enough to correct the two externalities in the model. Third, the interactions among the regulations are sufficiently subtle that it would be hard to guess which combinations prove to be optimal in this model.

We do not want to claim that our model is sufficiently general that the findings necessarily apply in all other models. But, attempting to assess different regulations (and to calibrate how they should be set) would be very difficult to do without consulting a range of models. Intuition helps, but at some point it runs out.

Finally, coming up with regulations that simultaneously eliminate runs and shrink total lending (and risk-taking) is hard. This happens because the usual interventions that make runs less likely either create opportunities for banks to raise more funds or take more risk, or so severely restrict the savers, banks or borrowers that one of them is made much worse off.

We hope that these ideas will lead others to move away from small perturbations of existing DSGE models and instead consider much more fundamental changes.

10.5 Concluding Remarks

In reality, the economic system is both complex and heterogeneous. In order to model it in a way that is mathematically tractable, rigorous and yet simple enough to be illuminating, economists have often tended to assume homogeneity among agents in the sectors involved. Unfortunately, that prevents analysis of certain key features of financial fragility, especially those relating to interbank interactions.

Some minimum structural characteristics should be present in any model attempting to capture fundamental aspects of financial instability and correcting for multiple externalities. First, it should be multiperiod, with aggregate uncertainty and agent heterogeneity. Different actions and policy recommendations are necessary for crisis resolution, depending on the structure of economic uncertainty and the impact on various economic sectors. Second, default and missing financial markets should be part of the model so that not every eventuality can be hedged; thus making regulation and policy relevant. Third, money and liquidity constraints should be explicit, since financial crises evolve from the nominal sector and subsequently spread to the real economy. Fourth, since the performance of banks is critical for the study of financial fragility and contagion, a banking sector well integrated in the model is indispensable to any modelling attempt. Finally, the regulatory framework should be clearly defined for policy and sensitivity analysis of various regulatory regimes and the associated distributional and welfare consequences.

References

Allen, F. and D. Gale (1997), 'Financial Markets, Intermediaries, and Intertemporal Smoothing', *Journal of Political Economy* 105(3), pp. 523–46.

Benes, J., M. Kumhof and D. Laxton (2014), 'Financial Crises in DSGE Models: A Prototype Model', IMF Working Paper No. 14/57, International Monetary Fund.

Benston, G.J. and C. W. Smith (1976), 'A Transactions Cost Approach to the Theory of Financial Intermediation', *Journal of Finance* 31(2), pp. 215–31.

Bhattacharya, S., C.A.E. Goodhart, D. Tsomocos and A.P. Vardoulakis (2015), 'A Reconsideration of Minsky's Financial Instability Hypothesis', *Journal of Money, Credit and Banking* 47(5), pp. 931–73.

Borio, C. and P. Lowe (2002), Asset Prices, Financial and Monetary Stability: Exploring the Nexus, Bank for International Settlements, Basel, Switzerland, BIS Working Paper No. 114.

Catarineu-Rabell, E., P. Jackson and D.P. Tsomocos (2005), 'Procyclicality and the new Basel Accord: Banks' Choice of Loan Rating System', *Economic Theory* 26, pp. 537–57.

Clerc, L., A. Derviz, C. Mendicino et al. (2015), 'Capital Regulation in a Macroeconomic Model with Three Layers of Default', *International Journal of Central Banking* 11(3), pp. 9–63.

Cochrane, J.H. (2014), 'Towards a Run-Free Financial System', in M. Baily and J. Taylor (eds), *Across the Divide: New Perspectives on the Financial Crisis*, Stanford, CA: Hoover Institution Press, pp. 197–250.

Diamond, D.W. (1984), 'Financial Intermediation and Delegated Monitoring', *Review of Economic Studies* 51, pp. 393–414.

Diamond, D.W. and P.H. Dybvig (1983), 'Bank Runs, Deposit Insurance and Liquidity', *Journal of Political Economy* 91(3), pp. 401–19.

Goodhart, C.A.E. (2008), 'The Boundary Problem in Financial Regulation', *National Institute Economic Review* 206, pp. 48–55.

Goodhart, C.A.E., A.K. Kashyap, D.P. Tsomocos and A.P. Vardoulakis (2012), 'Financial Regulation in General Equilibrium', NBER Working Paper No. 17909.

(2013), 'An Integrated Framework for Multiple Financial Regulations', *International Journal of Central Banking* 9(1), pp. 109–43.

Goodhart, C.A.E., M.U. Peiris, D.P. Tsomocos and A.P. Vardoulakis (2010), 'On Dividend Restrictions and the Collapse of the Interbank Market', *Annals of Finance* 6(4), pp. 455–73.

Goodhart, C.A.E., M.U. Peiris and D.P. Tsomocos (2013), 'Global Capital Imbalances and Taxing Capital Flows', *International Journal of Central Banking* 9(2), pp. 13–45.

(2016), 'Monetary Policy vs Debt Renegotiation: A Counterfactual Analysis on Greece', Working Paper.

Goodhart, C.A.E., P. Sunirand and D.P. Tsomocos (2004), 'A Model to Analyse Financial Fragility: Applications', *Journal of Financial Stability* 27(1), pp. 1–35.

(2006), 'A Model to Analyse Financial Fragility', *Economic Theory* 27, pp. 107–42.

Goodhart, C.A.E., D.P. Tsomocos and A.P. Vardoulakis (2010), 'Modelling a Housing and Mortgage Crisis', in Rodrigo A. Alfaro (ed), *Financial Stability, Monetary Policy and Central Banking*. Series in on Central Banking, Analysis and Economic Policies. Santiago: Central Bank of Chile.

Kashyap, A.K., D.P. Tsomocos and A.P. Vardoulakis (2014a), 'Principles for Macroprudential Regulation', *Banque de France Financial Stability Review* 18, pp. 173–82.

(2014b), 'How Does Macroprudential Regulation Change Bank Credit Supply?', NBER Working Paper No. 20165.

Kiyotaki, N. and J. Moore (2002), 'Evil is the Root of All Money', *American Economic Review* 92(2), pp. 62–6.

Lin, L., D.P. Tsomocos and A.P. Vardoulakis (2015), 'Debt Deflation Effects of Monetary Policy', *Journal of Financial Stability* 21, pp. 81–94.

Martinez, S.J.-F. and D.P. Tsomocos (2016), 'Liquidity and Default in an Exchange Economy', *Journal of Financial Stability*, forthcoming.

Peiris, M.U. and D.P. Tsomocos (2015), 'International Monetary Equilibrium with Default', *Journal of Mathematical Economics* 56, pp. 47–57.

Peiris, M.U. and A.P. Vardoulakis (2013), 'Savings and Default', *Economic Theory* 54(1), pp. 153–80.

(2015), 'Collateral and the Efficiency of Monetary Policy', *Economic Theory* 59(3), pp. 579–603.

Shubik, M. (1999), *The Theory of Money and Financial Institutions*, Cambridge, MA: M.I.T. Press.

Tsomocos, D.P. (2003), 'Equilibrium Analysis, Banking, and Financial Instability', *Journal of Mathematical Economics* 39(5–6), pp. 619–55.

11 | Systemic Risk Measurement and Quantification of Systemic Risk Amplification

MIGUEL SEGOVIANO AND RAPHAEL ESPINOZA

11.1 Introduction

In his treatise *Money, Information and Uncertainty*, first written in 1973, Charles Goodhart notes that:

[C]ertain analytical approaches involve agents operating on the basis of information which is less complete than theoretically possible ... The main constraints on the acquisition of information in these models is the time involved in that exercise; if time were unlimited and costless, then there would be no reason for agents to fail to gather, and act on the basis of, all available information. (Goodhart, 1975, p. 2)

Policymakers face these information and time constraints frequently, but it is in crisis times, when volatility is high and past information (history) becomes a poor guide, that the constraints hurt the most. The literature on financial stability must recognise these issues so that the models which will be developed incorporate changes in information in a timely fashion and become readily available to provide a valuable assessment of risk, *especially* in crisis times, and thus contribute to decision making.

This requirement raises many challenges to modellers seeking to capture systemic risk, but let us focus here on two of the challenges we think are most important. First, models must be designed to provide information conditional on a crisis occurring even though crises are infrequent and thus contribute little to the statistical relationships obtained looking at historical data. Quantification of systemic risk is

We are grateful to Zineddine Alla, Jon Danielsson, Charles Goodhart, Alfred Lehar, Dimitrios Tsomocos and conference participants at the LSE conference in honour of Charles Goodhart for their comments on early versions of this work. The last section of this chapter borrows heavily from work done jointly with Zineddine Alla and Qiaouluan Li (Alla et al., 2018), to whom we are grateful for letting us use some of the material for this chapter. The views expressed in this chapter are those of the authors solely and do not represent those of the International Monetary Fund or IMF policy.

also made difficult because of non-linearities observed during financial crises and because data is incomplete. In particular, regulatory data is slow to update and might not capture various exposures, e.g. off-balance sheet and complex relationships through markets, and the changing nature of these when volatility is high.

Second, models must provide an evaluation of systemic risk that is interpretable by the policymaker, and thus related to the policymakers' policy reaction to systemic risk. But different policymakers may have different policy reactions, depending not only on the government agencies they belong to and thus the objective functions they represent but also on their priors on the sources of risk. Systemic risk can thus refer to generalised shocks that affect several regions of the financial system; or it can refer to a 'falling domino' view of direct contagion; or it can refer to indirect contagion, in particular via a market-institutions nexus. In addition, systemic risk may relate to a specific stress scenario that the policymaker is considering.

In our research,[1] which includes various papers co-authored with Charles Goodhart, we have proposed a statistical method, described in Section 11.2, to update multivariate distributions, which characterise asset returns of entities in financial systems (banks and non-banks), using market data on the entities' probabilities of distress (PoD). When updating the multivariate density, the methodology allows us to infer the distress dependence structure across the entities in the system. As the PoDs change, the distress dependence structure inferred by the method updates consistently with the updated PoDs; i.e. it is a time-consistent structure.

Because market data is updated at high frequency and market prices incorporate market views of risk spillovers due to direct contagion (through contractual obligations across entities) or indirect contagion (through market price channels, including asset fire-sales triggered by stressed entities, or asset sell-offs due to information asymmetries), the method allows the incorporation in a *timely* manner of *updates* (which can reflect non-linear increases in periods of high volatility) in systems' distress dependence structures that incorporate market perceptions of *direct and indirect contagion* across

---

[1] Segoviano (2006), Segoviano and Goodhart (2009), Goodhart and Segoviano (2015), Cortes et al. (2018) and Segoviano and Espinoza (2017).

financial entities. We hope that these features of the methodology, which is the backbone of our proposed frameworks for systemic risk assessment and quantification of systemic risk amplification losses (SRAs), make our frameworks 'crisis-conditional', rising to the first challenge identified above.

Since multivariate distributions inferred by our method characterise implied asset values of entities making up financial systems and distress dependence structures across them, we are able to quantify complementary measures of systemic risk that provide supportive information to various systemic risk policy objectives; hence, we also hope to respond to the second challenge. We present these measures in Section 11.3.

Finally, in Section 11.4, we propose an extension to our framework that also allows us to quantify SRAs, i.e. contagion losses incurred by each financial firm, conditional on the distress of different sets of firms in the financial system. This allows us to describe the amplification mechanism due to the dependence structure in the system. We propose to use SRAs to complement the microprudential stress test (MiST) that focus on individual entities in order to make them macroprudential stress tests (MaPSTs) – that is, in addition to assessing losses incurred by individual entities under given macro financial scenarios, the proposed framework would allow us to quantify losses due to contagion across the entities in the system and identify the set of entities that would fall into distress given the amplification mechanisms triggered by specific entities falling into distress.

Importantly, our framework would estimate SRAs based on readily available market information without the need of highly detailed and granular supervisory information, which is not available in many countries or to arm-length institutions like the International Monetary Fund (IMF). Moreover, as discussed above, since the SRAs are based on market perceptions of direct and indirect contagion; they can be quantified without the need to assume ex ante market structures and agents' behaviours, which can change in unknown manners in periods of distress. Furthermore, our proposal would also make use of MiST frameworks that might already be implemented (either in 'bottom-up' or 'top-down' frameworks) with supervisory data that focus on individual entities (which in many cases is more developed, detailed and granular than supervisory data that attempts to capture contagion). Hence, we propose a framework that aims to optimise in a pragmatic manner the combined features of microprudential frameworks and data with market-based information to assess contagion losses. In other words, we aim to develop a robust and implementable MaPST framework, a subject of much interest in the macro-financial literature to which this chapter intends to contribute.

11.2 Consistent Information Multivariate Density Optimisation

A financial system, like any economic system, can be represented in a variety of ways. In many macroeconomic models, a 'representative bank' is constructed as the 'average' bank of the system. Although this abstraction may be useful to discuss, in a simplified way, certain macro-financial linkages, it also conceals the interactions among financial entities and assumes that the system is only affected by external forces; internal forces are irrelevant in such a representation of the financial sector.

With systemic risk modelling, it is on the contrary those internal forces and interactions that one wants to describe. Balance sheet data on bilateral exposures can be used, for instance, to represent a network of banks (Eisenberg and Noe, 2001). When the structure of interactions is essential, it is also useful to think about the firms in the financial system as constituent parts in a multivariate distribution of the 'state' of the system, where different states represent different valuations of the financial system, and thus different valuation of the assets of individual financial firms in that system. Microprudential surveillance is then interested in the marginals of this multivariate distribution, i.e. in identifying the risk that individual firms default; in the structural approach of Merton (1974) this is the risk that the value of the asset of the firm falls below a certain threshold, closely related to the capital buffer of the firm. Macroprudential surveillance, on the other hand, is interested in the multivariate distribution itself, but especially in the dependence structure at the tail, since the objective is to assess the risk that the asset valuation of several financial firms falls into a zone of distress.

As alluded to in Section 11.1, the difficulty in constructing such a multivariate distribution is that information on the tail is very limited. Although information on co-movement is available in many cases, the weight given by these moments to the centre of the distribution is much higher than the weight given to dependence at the tail.[2] Data on the PoDs of individual institutions is also often available, either from market data on Credit Default Swaps (CDS) or from Merton Model estimates, but this is information on the tail of each marginal, not on the dependence structure at the tail.

The objective of Consistent Multivariate Density Optimisation (CIMDO) is to construct a multivariate density that characterises the asset values for a system of firms, taking into account this information on PoDs and thus inferring a dependence structure at the tail that is consistent with the marginal information at the tail.[3] CIMDO, whose technical details are presented in the Appendix, is a general procedure which constructs multivariate densities from a prior distribution and a reduced set of information, and which ensures that the posterior distribution is the closest distribution to the prior that is also consistent with the information set – in the application described here, the information is the PoD of the different firms in the system.

The CIMDO procedure can be applied to any system of financial firms to infer a multivariate distribution of asset values for the system, from which a variety of indicators can be obtained, including the financial stability and systemic loss indicators introduced in Segoviano and Goodhart (2009) for the banking system and the SRAs introduced in this chapter and in Alla et al. (2018) – see Figure 11.1.

CIMDO is based on the Kullback (1959) cross-entropy approach. Instead of assuming parametric probabilities to characterise the information contained in the data, the entropy approach uses the data information to infer values for the unknown probability density. The advantage of this approach compared to parametric distributions relates again to the lack of data, which makes it impossible to adequately calibrate a parametric distribution.[4]

In addition, starting from a prior distribution, CIMDO distributions can be obtained from *any* information available, however

---

[2] To answer this criticism, Adrian and Brunnermeier (2016) and Chan-Lau et al. (2009) have proposed quantile regression methods, where the slope of the relationship between two variables can be different at different quantiles of the explanatory variable.

[3] CIMDO was first introduced in Segoviano (2006).

[4] Segoviano (2006) shows that, given a prior and restricted information on PoDs, CIMDO distributions are better at recovering an unknown density than a range of parametric densities (multivariate normal, multivariate t, or mixtures of normals).

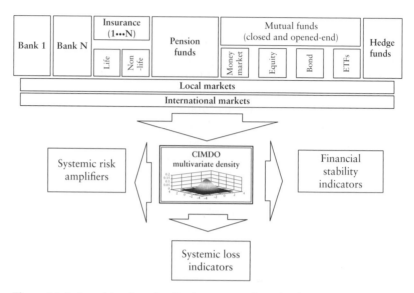

Figure 11.1 A multivariate distribution approach to the financial sector
Note: The framework considers the financial system as a financial portfolio
made of individual entities or representative sectors, whose multivariate
density of returns is estimated using the CIMDO method. When the
multivariate density is constructed, it is possible to obtain a range of systemic
risk indicators.

limited. This allows the modeller to construct multivariate distributions using only the latest information available, if this is what is needed. In that case, CIMDO distributions can be updated daily, and capture at any time the current state of the economy or of the financial system.

To summarise the CIMDO procedure (see again the Appendix for more details), the information provided by the probabilities of default of each firm is incorporated, using Merton's (1974) structural approach to the definition of PoDs as constraints on the marginal of the multivariate distribution that modify the shape of the posterior multivariate distribution. Imposing these constraints on an optimisation problem (that searches for the posterior density closest[5] to the prior density) guarantees that the posterior multivariate distribution

---

[5] Under the Kullback (1959) cross-entropy criterion. However, note that this is not a 'distance' or 'metric' in the topologic sense.

contains marginal densities that in the region of default are equalised to each of the firms' observed probabilities of default. The posterior distribution now embeds the linear and non-linear dependence, including at the tail of the distribution, which is needed to assess the risk of *joint* distress. As PoDs change daily, the distress dependence structure inferred by the method updates consistently with the new PoDs. The method thus allows a timely updating of dependence.

We show in particular in the Appendix how the CIMDO multivariate distribution is a function on the Lagrange multipliers associated with the different moment-consistency constraints, and how these Lagrange multipliers depend on the (daily) observed information on the PoD of each individual financial entity.

11.3 Financial Stability Measures

Given a multivariate density of asset returns for a system of firms, it is possible to propose a variety of financial stability measures. In this section we present different *views* of what systemic risk can mean, highlighting that different public agencies will have an in interest in systemic risk for different reasons, and we relate these reasons to different possible measures. These include four measures presented in our earlier work and two new measures that we introduce in this chapter. Although we suggest that some measures are particularly suited to certain views of systemic risk, such links are not unique as the same measure can have different applications. Finally, we contend that the central bank sits at the intersection of all these different understandings of systemic risk.

11.3.1 A Monetary Economics View of Systemic Risk

Until recently, financial stability as an academic field lived at the margin between the monetary economics literature and the finance literature. The financial crisis has now clearly highlighted the importance of financial stability for monetary policy. Even if financial stability were not an independent objective (and we will argue below that it should be), an inflation-targeting central bank would need to care about financial stability because of its impact on output and inflation. Then, as Woodford (2012) notes, 'the question of greatest concern is ... the probability of a bad *joint* outcome', and not so much the mean of the

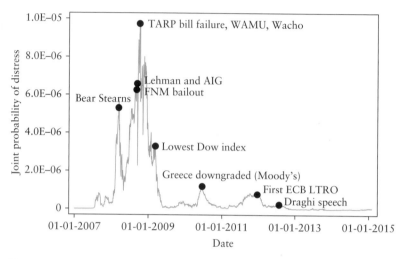

Figure 11.2 Joint probability of distress
Note: The joint probability of distress is the probability that all of the entities or sectors included in the system modelled (see footnote 6) are in distress at the same time. This is computed using CIMDO, which is re-estimated daily. The probability is small but its sharp movements allow a clear identification of stress events.

distribution of possible future net worths or the size of the lower tail of outcomes for individual institutions.

This view leads to a first proposed measure of systemic risk, the probability that all the financial institutions in a given system be in distress at the same time. The Joint Probability of Distress (JPoD), estimated over the period 2007–15 for a group of fifteen US banks and non-bank institutions and seven types of funds,[6] is presented in Figure 11.2. Although the JPoD remains very small in the whole sample, this measure strongly captures the changes in the health of the financial system. Since the JPoD assesses the probability of *all* the

---

[6] JP Morgan (JPM), Bank of America (BAC), Citi (C), Wells Fargo (WFC), Goldman Sachs (GS), Morgan Stanley (MS), Capital One Financial (COF), AIG, Berkshire Hathaway (BRK), Hartford Financial (HIG), Allstate (ALL), MetLife (MET), Prudential Financial (PRU), Lincoln Financial Group (LNC), Travelers Companies (TRV), Equity Funds, Bond Funds, High Yield Funds (USHY), Investment Grade Funds (USIG), Pension Funds, Money Market Funds (MMF), Hedge Funds.

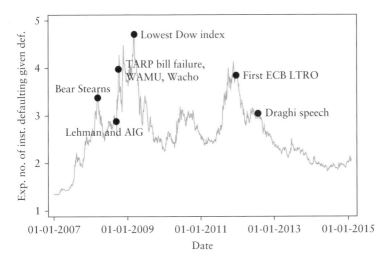

Figure 11.3 Expected number of institutions falling into distress if one falls into distress
Note: This figure shows the expected number of institutions in the system (as defined in footnote 6) falling into distress if at least one of them falls into distress (this institution is included in the tally, which is why the indicator is always higher than 1). This is computed from the CIMDO density, which is re-estimated daily.

institutions collapsing – an extremely unlikely event – it does not provide information on the risk that smaller shocks would lead to several banks (if not all) falling into distress. The JPoD can thus be complemented by another measure that assesses the expected number of banks falling into distress in a tail scenario where one bank initially failed (see Figure 11.3 and Segoviano and Goodhart [2009] for a technical definition).

11.3.2 A Regulatory View of Systemic Risk

Even if systemic risk were not affecting the path of output and inflation, the distortions and market imperfections due to financial intermediation could require corrective regulation. This is usually the realm of microprudential policy, whose role is in particular to support an appropriate valuation of risk and to limit the moral hazard consequences of limited liability and deposit insurance. But market imperfections can also be due to the structure of the banking system. In particular, because financial institutions are not 'atomistic' entities, the network structure of a financial system means that externalities are prevalent: Eisenberg and Noe (2001) modelled direct contagion risk due to bilateral exposures in a network of banks; Freixas, Parigi and Rochet (2000) showed how the withdrawal of funding at one bank can affect the entire banking system; Cifuentes, Ferrucci and Shin (2005) take into account the effect of banks' fire-sales on asset valuation and thus capture indirect contagion.

A regulator's need to assess such externalities can be answered using a measure of each firm's inward and outward contagion links. The Distress Dependence Matrix derived from CIMDO (Table 11.1) shows the probability of the institution in the row falling into distress when the institution in the column falls into distress. The estimation of this matrix for March 2015 highlights the risks coming from one bank (WFC), but also from a few non-bank financial institutions (TRV, ALL) and from the shadow banking system (Equity Funds, Pensions Funds).

The Distress Dependence Matrix is, however, only a partial measure of the contagion links of every bank; in particular it is one only focused on the 'first round' of contagion. The Shapley value, proposed in the context of systemic risk by Tarashev, Borio and Tsatsaronis (2010) and Drehmann and Tarashev (2013), can also be estimated using CIMDO distribution. In Figure 11.4, the ninety-ninth percentile systemic expected shortfall (i.e. the dollar losses of the financial system, conditional on the worst ninety-ninth percentile) is decomposed by the contribution of the different entities in the system. In line with the regulatory view suggested above, the Shapley value, interpreted as the contribution to risk of different institutions, is often proposed as a way to design corrective regulation or taxation; for instance the capital surcharge.

11.3.3 A Public Finance View of Systemic Risk

One of the most salient consequences of systemic risk is the cost to taxpayers that financial support policies can require if a crisis materialises. In their study of banking crises, Laeven and Valencia (2012) find that over the period 1970–2011, the direct fiscal costs of such

Table 11.1. *Distress dependence matrix, March 2015*

	JPM	BAC	Citi	WFC	GS	MS	COF	AIG	TRV	BRK	HIG	ALL	MET	PRU	LNC	Equity	Bond	US high yields	US inv grade	Pension	MMFs	Hedge funds	Row average
JPM	1.00	0.54	0.40	0.67	0.40	0.32	0.46	0.17	0.83	0.30	0.21	0.48	0.32	0.34	0.26	0.57	0.06	0.04	0.04	0.43	0.21	0.13	0.37
BAC	0.53	1.00	0.45	0.62	0.34	0.30	0.43	0.19	0.72	0.26	0.22	0.43	0.31	0.35	0.24	0.48	0.06	0.05	0.04	0.37	0.16	0.12	0.35
Citi	0.47	0.53	1.00	0.51	0.34	0.31	0.37	0.23	0.65	0.24	0.25	0.39	0.32	0.34	0.26	0.48	0.06	0.06	0.05	0.37	0.17	0.14	0.34
WFC	0.48	0.45	0.32	1.00	0.27	0.22	0.40	0.13	0.73	0.21	0.19	0.40	0.26	0.30	0.20	0.43	0.05	0.03	0.03	0.31	0.16	0.09	0.30
GS	0.51	0.44	0.38	0.48	1.00	0.52	0.38	0.17	0.79	0.30	0.27	0.48	0.31	0.35	0.27	0.61	0.07	0.07	0.05	0.50	0.19	0.19	0.38
MS	0.36	0.34	0.30	0.35	0.46	1.00	0.30	0.17	0.67	0.24	0.22	0.43	0.27	0.32	0.22	0.55	0.06	0.06	0.05	0.44	0.14	0.16	0.32
COF	0.30	0.28	0.21	0.36	0.19	0.17	1.00	0.10	0.57	0.16	0.15	0.34	0.21	0.26	0.18	0.38	0.04	0.03	0.02	0.27	0.11	0.08	0.25
AIG	0.12	0.14	0.14	0.13	0.09	0.11	0.11	1.00	0.25	0.08	0.08	0.13	0.10	0.10	0.08	0.17	0.03	0.03	0.03	0.14	0.06	0.06	0.14
TRV	0.01	0.01	0.00	0.01	0.01	0.01	0.01	0.00	1.00	0.01	0.00	0.02	0.01	0.01	0.00	0.02	0.00	0.00	0.00	0.01	0.01	0.00	0.05
BRK	0.24	0.22	0.17	0.24	0.19	0.17	0.20	0.09	0.58	1.00	0.15	0.34	0.17	0.20	0.18	0.39	0.06	0.04	0.04	0.31	0.16	0.12	0.24
HIG	0.19	0.20	0.19	0.24	0.19	0.18	0.21	0.10	0.44	0.16	1.00	0.34	0.25	0.35	0.28	0.28	0.05	0.04	0.04	0.22	0.11	0.10	0.24
ALL	0.14	0.13	0.10	0.17	0.11	0.11	0.16	0.06	0.69	0.13	0.11	1.00	0.15	0.17	0.12	0.27	0.03	0.02	0.02	0.19	0.08	0.05	0.18
MET	0.32	0.31	0.28	0.36	0.25	0.24	0.32	0.14	0.66	0.20	0.27	0.50	1.00	0.44	0.29	0.47	0.05	0.04	0.03	0.36	0.12	0.12	0.31
PRU	0.27	0.28	0.24	0.33	0.22	0.23	0.32	0.11	0.58	0.20	0.31	0.45	0.35	1.00	0.32	0.42	0.04	0.04	0.03	0.31	0.10	0.10	0.29
LNC	0.29	0.26	0.24	0.30	0.23	0.22	0.30	0.12	0.53	0.24	0.33	0.44	0.31	0.44	1.00	0.41	0.05	0.05	0.04	0.31	0.11	0.12	0.29
Equity	0.19	0.16	0.14	0.20	0.16	0.16	0.19	0.08	0.66	0.16	0.10	0.30	0.15	0.17	0.12	1.00	0.01	0.02	0.01	0.58	0.08	0.10	0.22
Bond	0.05	0.05	0.04	0.06	0.04	0.04	0.04	0.03	0.23	0.06	0.05	0.08	0.04	0.04	0.03	0.03	1.00	0.03	0.36	0.06	0.18	0.06	0.12
US high yields	0.29	0.34	0.36	0.30	0.38	0.40	0.32	0.31	0.44	0.37	0.34	0.37	0.32	0.34	0.34	0.52	0.31	1.00	0.37	0.56	0.33	0.59	0.40
US inv grade	0.08	0.09	0.08	0.10	0.09	0.09	0.08	0.09	0.24	0.10	0.10	0.13	0.07	0.08	0.07	0.07	0.95	0.10	1.00	0.13	0.25	0.13	0.19
Pension	0.24	0.21	0.18	0.24	0.21	0.22	0.23	0.11	0.70	0.21	0.13	0.35	0.20	0.21	0.16	0.96	0.05	0.04	0.03	1.00	0.11	0.16	0.27
MMFs	0.02	0.01	0.01	0.02	0.01	0.01	0.01	0.01	0.10	0.01	0.01	0.02	0.01	0.01	0.01	0.02	0.02	0.00	0.01	0.02	1.00	0.01	0.06
Hedge funds	0.30	0.29	0.28	0.28	0.36	0.35	0.29	0.22	0.74	0.35	0.25	0.39	0.28	0.29	0.25	0.70	0.17	0.19	0.15	0.71	0.35	1.00	0.37
Column average	0.29	0.25	0.32	0.25	0.24	0.28	0.17	0.58	0.23	0.21	0.36	0.25	0.28	0.22	0.42	0.15	0.09	0.11	0.35	0.19	0.16		0.26

Note: The table is read as follows: The probability that the Bank of America is in distress if JP Morgan is in distress is 0.53. Light shading is for cells where the conditional probability is greater than 0.33.

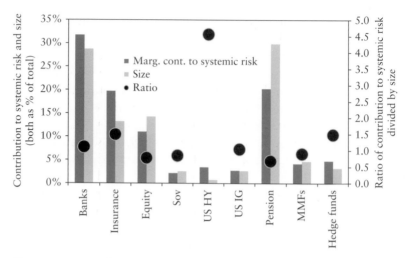

Figure 11.4 Contribution of individual institutions/sectors to systemic expected shortfall in the USA, January 2015

Note: The contribution to systemic risk is the share of the systemic expected shortfall (which is the conditional expected value of losses in the worst first quantile) that can be attributed to the sector. The shares are computed using the Shapley value (Tarashev, Borio and Tsatsaronis, 2010). The insurance sector contributes 20 per cent to systemic risk. Size is the share of the sector, measured by the size of balance sheets. Insurances represent 13 per cent of the system when measured by assets. Because the ratio for the insurance sector is 1.5, the contribution of the insurance sector to systemic risk appears to be higher than what could be expected if estimated using size only.

support policies averaged 7 per cent of gross domestic product (GDP), and reached more than 40 per cent of GDP on several occasions.[7] The indirect fiscal costs of systemic risk, which originate from the growth slowdown post-crisis, are often twice or thrice larger. When government agencies face a banking crisis, the issue of whether to intervene to stop a contagion involves a trade-off between the

---

[7] The direct costs of financial support exceed 40 per cent in Ireland in 2008, Chile in 1981, Thailand in 1997, Jamaica in 1996, Iceland in 2008, Argentina in 1980, and Indonesia in 1997.

immediate costs of support policy and the potential future costs if contagion is not halted.[8]

We propose here a new indicator of systemic risk that tailors to the need to assess such costs: the matrix $L_{i,j}$ of expected losses of an institution i, conditional on the expected loss of another institution j. The expected value of an institution is assumed to be the expected value of equity (which is distributed according to the CIMDO distribution) and the expected value of its debt liabilities (which is calculated by splitting the conditional expectation between states of nature: in the states where the institution is healthy, the value of debt is the discounted value of the notional liability; in the case where institution is in distress, the expected value of debt is adjusted by a recovery rate of 60 per cent).[9] The conditional loss is then the difference between the expected value of the firm and the value of the firm conditional on the distress of the other firm.

This matrix of contagion losses takes into account the direct and indirect channels of contagion across banks. In particular, contagion from bank Y to bank X may have only occurred because of the distress of bank Z caused by bank Y's distress. To analyse such channels of contagion, it is useful to decompose the losses of X, conditional on whether both Y and Z are in distress versus whether only Y is in distress (what we call an 'adjacent' loss). The matrix of adjacent losses for a group of five US banks is presented as a network in Figure 11.5, along the individual (i.e. marginal) PoD of each institution (the shading of each vertex).

Although a network is an incomplete presentation of dependence, since it highlights bilateral linkages whereas multivariate distributions

---

[8] In addition there are long-term costs of moral hazard, but these go beyond the scope of this chapter.

[9] We give here the exact formula in an example with two banks. Let us note eq_0 the current value of equity of X, D_t the notional value of debt of X, and p the CIMDO posterior distribution. The conditional expected value of bank X, given that bank Y is in distress, is $E_0[V_{X,t}|Y \text{ in distress}] = 1/P(Y \text{ in distress})$ $[\iint eq_0 e^{-x} p(x,y) I[y > X_d^y] dxdy + \iint D_t(x,y) p(x,y)) I[y > X_d^y] dxdy]$.

The value of debt depends on whether X is in distress. Thus, the second integral is spilt in two:

$$\iint D_t(x,y) p(x,y) I[y > X_d^y] dxdy] = \text{RR } D_t \iint p(x,y) I[x > X_d^x] I[y > X_d^y] dxdy$$
$$+ D_t \iint p(x,y) I[x < X_d^x] I[y > X_d^y] dxdy$$

where RR is the recovery rate if X is in distress.

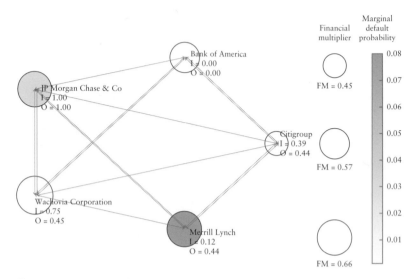

Figure 11.5 Matrix of adjacent losses for five US banks, March 2016
Note: The arrows represent the conditional losses of the destination bank given distress in the source bank, and assuming no other bank defaults (an 'adjacent loss'). The shading represents the marginal (individual) probability of default of each bank. The size of the circle is the expected losses of the financial system conditional on the bank being in distress (the 'financial multiplier').

embed more complex structures of dependence (see Section 11.4), it is a useful graphical representation of the matrix of conditional losses, which also builds a bridge with the network literature on financial stability (e.g. Eisenberg and Noe, 2001; Cifuentes, Ferrucci and Shin, 2005; Alessandri et al., 2009; Aikman et al., 2011).

11.3.4 The Role of the Central Banker

We would argue that since the central banker's role lies at the intersection of the three functions presented above, the measures we propose in this chapter are all necessary to good central banking. Indeed, the central bank is the monetary authority and thus worries about the growth and inflation consequences of systemic risk. But the central bank is also a potential creditor to the Treasury and a lender of last resort, and it thus often bears the direct financial costs of financial support policies. Finally, in many countries, the central bank is also the banking sector regulator or the macroprudential regulator.

11.4 Systemic Risk Amplification

The consequences of the Lehman Brothers failure in September 2008 underlined that understanding the mechanisms of contagion among financial institutions (FIs) is essential to design macroprudential stress tests and implement effective financial support policies. We propose here (Figure 11.6) a framework for a macroprudential stress test that can build upon the results of the standard stress test but can also take into account interconnectedness (deduced from multivariate distributions) to augment the losses estimated by the stress test with contagion losses, as measured by the conditional loss proposed in Section 11.3.

We clarify in this section how the framework should be applied and interpreted. In a Venn diagram representation of the simplest example possible, where the rectangle of Figure 11.7 identifies the states of nature corresponding to a macro-financial stress scenario, the expected loss of bank A over the whole area (i.e. the expected loss of A in the macro-financial stress scenario, which we call 'total systemic' loss and denote $Loss_{TS}$), is the sum of the expected loss of A under a micro stress test scenario ($Loss_{micro}(A)$, computed over the rectangle excluding the disc), and the excepted loss for A if the macro scenario is amplified by financial sector distress denoted S, i.e. by a systemic risk amplification (SRA), represented by the disc area. The formula is:

$$Loss_{TS}(A|S) = Loss_{micro}(A) + Loss_{SRA}(A|S) = E(V_A) - E(V_A|adv \cap S)$$

where

- the microprudential stress-test loss of bank A is the difference between the value of bank A in normal times, and its value under the adverse macroeconomic scenario:

$$Loss_{micro}(A) = E(V_A) - E(V_A|adv);$$

- the SRA loss of bank A, assuming the realisation of a given financial stress event S, is the difference between the value of bank A under the adverse macroeconomic scenario and its value, assuming the realisation of the financial event S *and* the adverse macroeconomic scenario:

$$Loss_{SRA}(A|S) = E(V_A|adv) - E(V_A|adv \cap S)$$

Since micro stress tests do not assume specific contagion losses, this equation makes the link between micro stress test valuations, which will be better estimated using granular, balance sheet data, and

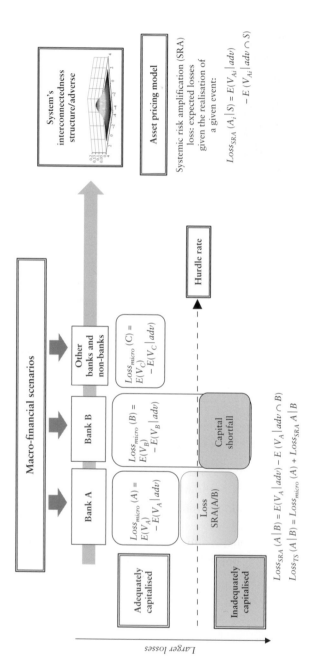

Figure 11.6 Macroprudential stress test framework

Note: This figure summarises the approach for the portfolio of banks and non-banks under analysis. For a macro scenario, an already developed MiST framework estimates losses for each individual entity. The scenario and risk factors are also employed to estimate the system's multivariate density (distress dependence structure) from which we quantify the SRA losses. SRA losses are valuable to 'explore' the impact of specific 'events'; i.e. defaults of specific entities on other financial entities in the system. Obvious events to check are the cases where specific entities fail the MiST but the impact of the default of any entity on the system (SRA losses) can also be analysed.

184

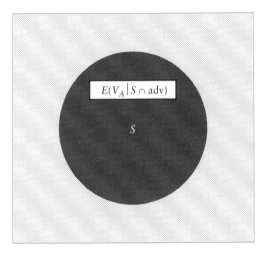

Figure 11.7 Conditional loss in a stress scenario: example with two banks
Note: The expected value of bank A's assets under an adverse scenario ('adv', computed over all the states of nature in the square) is the sum of the expected value under the adverse scenario and event 'S' (states of nature in the dark circle) and of the expected value under the adverse scenario and event 'non S' (states of nature in the remaining area).

contagion losses, which require multivariate modelling and the calculation of conditional losses. We think this decomposition is a pragmatic and robust way to develop implementable macro stress tests frameworks when data is scarce and imperfect.

From a policy perspective, it would also be of much interest to go beyond such an aggregate measure, and to decompose the conditional losses in order to identify the connecting links between the different banks. Decomposing the conditional loss permits identifying the most likely contagion events, assessing the intensity of the contagion events and thus interpreting the conditional losses provided by the multivariate density.

Our proposed decomposition aims at highlighting the respective contribution of the possible additional bank defaults that could occur assuming the realisation of an initial default.[10] We propose here an example with four banks: A, B, C and D. As before, the rectangle in

---

[10] To provide a description that can be easily interpreted, these events should represent a scenario in which the state (defaulting or surviving) of each bank is clearly defined.

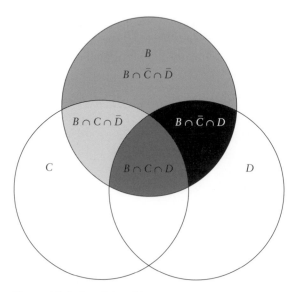

Figure 11.8 Conditional loss in a stress scenario: example with four banks
Note: The expected value of bank A's assets under an adverse scenario and assuming the default of B (i.e. the expected value computed over the states of nature in the disc labelled by B) is the sum of the expected values under events 'B, non C, D', 'B, C, non D', 'B, non C, non D' and 'B, C, D'.

Figure 11.8 represents the conditional loss for bank A in the states of nature corresponding to the macro stress scenario, and inside each circle are the states of nature for which the bank labelling the circle is also in distress.

To decompose the impact of the default of bank B on bank A, we partition the set in which the bank B is defaulting as follows:

$$\{B\} = \{B \cap C \cap D, B \cap \bar{C} \cap D, B \cap C \cap \bar{D}, B \cap \bar{C} \cap \bar{D}\}$$

In each subset of the partition, each bank (except bank A since we are assessing its losses) is either defaulting or surviving (bank B is always defaulting). This decomposition highlights and weighs the respective contribution of each possible defaulting set. The systemic risk amplifier can thus be decomposed as:

$$
\begin{aligned}
Loss_{SRA}(A|B) = {} & P(B \cap C \cap D|B)Loss_{SRA}(A|B \cap C \cap D) \\
& + P(B \cap \bar{C} \cap D|B)Loss_{SRA}(A|B \cap \bar{C} \cap D) \\
& + P(B \cap C \cap \bar{D}|B)Loss_{SRA}(A|B \cap C \cap \bar{D}) \\
& + P(B \cap \bar{C} \cap \bar{D}|B)Loss_{SRA}(A|B \cap \bar{C} \cap \bar{D})
\end{aligned}
$$

This decomposition highlights and weighs the respective contribution of each possible defaulting set, assuming the realisation of the default of bank B. The contribution of each bank to the contagion between B and A can be large either because:

- The default of the bank is likely, given the initial default of bank B. This property can be assessed using conditional probabilities of default (similar to those presented in the Distress Dependence Matrix, see Table 11.1).
- The default of the bank inflicts large losses to bank A. This can be assessed using the conditional loss measures similar to those presented in Figure 11.5.

We present in Alla et al. (2018) an application of this approach to a simplified banking system, estimated on four US banks with data for two days before Lehman Brothers defaulted. We find in this paper that contagion losses are significant and that they originate, in almost equal measure, from both the small possibility that three banks default (an unlikely event, but with very high impact) and the more probable case where only Lehman Brothers defaults (an event with low impact, but with high probability).

11.5 Conclusion

We propose a framework for systemic risk assessment and extend it to quantify contagion losses due to systemic risk amplifying forces. The framework incorporates in a timely manner updates in market perceptions of direct and indirect contagion across banks and non-banks in a financial system. This is germane, especially in periods of high volatility when historical information becomes less relevant to produce forecast assessments of risk.

We then suggest complementing micro stress tests with SRAs as a pragmatic and robust way to develop implementable macro stress test frameworks when data is scarce and imperfect.

Appendix: Consistent Information Multivariate Density Optimisation

The detailed formulation of CIMDO was first presented in Segoviano (2006). The objective of CIMDO, which is based on the Kullback (1959) minimum cross-entropy approach, is to construct a multivariate density q that characterises the asset values for a system of firms, taking into account a prior distribution p and information on PoDs and thus inferring a dependence structure at the tail that is consistent with the marginal information at the tail.

For illustration purposes, we focus on a portfolio containing two firms, whose asset returns are distributed by the random variables x and y. The objective function of CIMDO is to search for a distribution q closest to the prior p, according to the criteria

$$C[p,q] = \iint p(x,y)\ln\left[\frac{p(x,y)}{q(x,y)}\right]dxdy$$

and consistent with the observed information on marginal PoDs, which are represented by the moment-consistency constraints

$$\iint p(x,y)\chi_{(x_d^x,\infty)}dxdy = PoD_t^x, \quad \iint p(x,y)\chi_{(x_d^y,\infty)}dydx = PoD_t^y$$

PoD_t^x and PoD_t^y are the empirically observed probabilities of default (PoDs) for each firm in the portfolio and $\chi_{(x_d^x,\infty)}$, $\chi_{(x_d^y,\infty)}$ are the indicating functions defined with the default thresholds for each borrower in the portfolio. In order to ensure that $p(x,y)$ represents a valid density, the conditions that $p(x,y) \geq 0$ and the probability additivity constraint, $\iint p(x,y)dxdy = 1$, also need to be satisfied. The CIMDO density is recovered by minimising the functional

$$L[p,q] = \iint p(x,y)\ln p(x,y)dxdy - \iint p(x,y)\ln q(x,y)dxdy$$
$$+ \lambda_1\left[\iint p(x,y)\chi_{[x_d^x,\infty)}dxdy - PoD_t^x\right]$$
$$+ \lambda_2\left[\iint p(x,y)\chi_{[x_d^y,\infty)}dydx - PoD_t^y\right]$$
$$+ \mu\left[\iint p(x,y)dxdy - 1\right]$$

where $\lambda_1\lambda_2$ represent the Lagrange multipliers of the moment-consistency constraints and represents the Lagrange multiplier of the probability additivity constraint. By using the calculus of variations, the optimisation procedure is performed. The optimal solution is represented by the following posterior multivariate density as

$$\hat{p}(x,y) = q(x,y)\exp(-[1 + \mu + \lambda_1\chi_{[X_d^x,\infty]} + \lambda_2\chi_{[X_d^y,\infty]}])$$

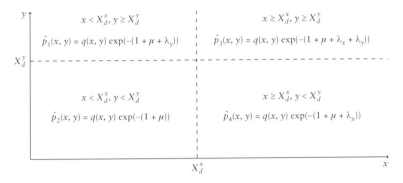

Figure 11.A1 CIMDO distribution, by default zone

Figure 11.A1 shows how the posterior distribution differs from the prior distribution in the four different zones defined by whether x and y are in the zone of default. For instance, in the zone where x defaults but not y (bottom right quadrant), the posterior density is the prior density adjusted for a coefficient which is a function of λ_x, the Lagrange multiplier for the restriction that the posterior is consistent with the observed PoD_x, and a function of μ, the Lagrange multiplier for the restriction that the posterior distribution sums to 1.

A Taylor approximation of the Lagrange multipliers gives some intuition of how the observed data on $PoDs$ and the calibration of the prior affect the Lagrange multipliers and thus the posterior (see proof in Segoviano and Espinoza, 2017). For a prior calibrated as a centred t-distribution with ν degrees of freedom and a correlation coefficient σ, the Taylor approximation yields:

$$\lambda_x = -\ln(POD_x) - 1 - \mu + \ln(\tilde{Q}_{xy}e^{-\lambda_y} + \tilde{Q}_{x\bar{y}} + (e^{-\lambda_y} - 1)J\sigma + \vartheta(\sigma^2))$$

$$\lambda_y = -\ln(POD_y) - 1 - \mu + \ln(\tilde{Q}_{xy}e^{-\lambda_x} + \tilde{Q}_{\bar{x}y} + (e^{-\lambda_x} - 1)J\sigma + \vartheta(\sigma^2))$$

$$\mu = -1 + \ln(\tilde{Q}_{xy}e^{-\lambda_x}e^{-\lambda_y} + \tilde{Q}_{\bar{x}y}e^{-\lambda_y} + \tilde{Q}_{x\bar{y}}e^{-\lambda_x}$$

$$+ \tilde{Q}_{\bar{x}\bar{y}}(e^{-\lambda_x}e^{-\lambda_y} - e^{-\lambda_y} - e^{-\lambda_x} + 1)J\sigma + \vartheta(\sigma^2))$$

where $J = \frac{t_{\frac{\nu}{2}}}{2\pi}(\nu + X_d^{x\,2} + X_d^{y\,2})^{-\nu/2}$

The approximation shows that Lagrange multipliers depend on the prior correlation coefficient but when λ_x and λ_y are small or when the default zones are small (i.e. $X_d^x \to \infty, X_d^y \to \infty$ and thus $J \to 0$, the adjustment between prior and posterior is insensitive to σ).

References

Adrian, T. and M. Brunnermeier (2016), CoVaR. *American Economic Review*, 106(7), pp. 1705–41.

Aikman, D., P. Alessandri, B. Eklund et al. (2011), Funding Liquidity Risk in a Quantitative Model of Systemic Stability. *Central Banking, Analysis, and Economic Policies Book Series*, 15, pp. 371–410.

Alessandri, P., P. Gai, S. Kapadia, N. Mora and C. Puhr (2009), A Framework for Quantifying Systemic Stability. *International Journal of Central Banking*, 5(3), pp. 47–81.

Alla, Z., R. Espinoza, Q. Li and M. Segoviano (2018), Macroprudential Stress Tests: A Reduced-Form Approach to Quantifying Systemic Risk Losses, IMF Working Paper, forthcoming. Washington, DC: International Monetary Fund.

Chan-Lau, J.A., M. Espinosa, K. Giesecke and J.A. Solé (2009), Assessing the Systemic Implications of Financial Linkages. *IMF Global Financial Stability Report, Chapter 2*. Washington, DC: International Monetary Fund.

Cifuentes, R., G. Ferrucci and H.S. Shin (2005), Liquidity Risk and Contagion. *Journal of the European Economic Association*, 3(2–3), pp. 556–66.

Cortes, P., P. Lindner, S. Malik, and M. Segoviano (2018), A Comprehensive Multi-Sector Framework for Surveillance of Systemic Risk and Interconnectedness (SyRIN), IMF Working Paper, forthcoming. Washington, DC: International Monetary Fund.

Drehmann, M. and N. Tarashev (2013), Measuring the Systemic Importance of Interconnected Banks. *Journal of Financial Intermediation*, 22(4), pp. 586–607.

Eisenberg, L. and T.H. Noe (2001), Systemic Risk in Financial Systems. *Management Science*, 47(2), pp. 236–49.

Freixas, X., B.M. Parigi and J.C. Rochet (2000), Systemic Risk, Interbank Relations, and Liquidity Provision by the Central Bank. *Journal of Money, Credit and Banking*, 32, pp. 611–38.

Goodhart, C.A.E. (1975), *Money, Information and Uncertainty*. London: Macmillan.

Goodhart, C.A.E. and M. Segoviano (2015), Optimal Bank Recovery, IMF Working Paper No. 15/217. Washington, DC: International Monetary Fund.

Kullback, S. (1959), *Information and Statistics*, New York, NJ: John Wiley & Sons.

Laeven, L. and F. Valencia (2012), Systemic Banking Crises Database: An Update. IMF Working Paper No. 12/163. Washington, DC: International Monetary Fund.

Merton, R.C. (1974), On the Pricing of Corporate Debt: The Risk Structure of Interest Rates. *The Journal of Finance*, 29(2), pp. 449–70.

Segoviano, M.A. (2006), *Consistent Information Multivariate Density Optimizing Methodology*. London School of Economics.

Segoviano, M. and R. Espinoza (2017), Consistent Measures of Systemic Risk, SRC Discussion Paper No. 74, London: Systemic Risk Centre, The London School of Economics and Political Science.

Segoviano, M. and C.A.E. Goodhart (2009), Banking Stability Measures. IMF Working Paper No. 09/4. Washington, DC: International Monetary Fund.

Tarashev, N.A., C.E. Borio and K. Tsatsaronis (2010), Attributing Systemic Risk to Individual Institutions. BIS Working Paper No. 308. Basel: Bank of International Settlements.

Woodford, M. (2012), *Inflation Targeting and Financial Stability. NBER Working Paper 17967*. Cambridge, MA: National Bureau of Economic Research.

12 What Binds? Interactions between Bank Capital and Liquidity Regulations

STEPHEN CECCHETTI AND ANIL KASHYAP

12.1 Introduction

The regulatory framework embodied in Basel III constrains the composition of banks' balance sheets. It has four parts. Two are related to capital and two to liquidity. The capital regulations include a risk-weighted requirement that forces banks that have riskier assets to hold more capital, as well as an unweighted leverage requirement that ties the level of capital to the overall size of the bank (including off-balance sheet items). These rules, which are designed to ensure sufficient buffers should banks face losses, are the outgrowth of decades of experience dating back to the original agreements in 1975.[1]

In describing the early days of the Basel Committee, Goodhart (2011) notes that the original intent was to have a liquidity requirement to complement the capital requirement. But international agreement proved elusive until the completion of Basel III in 2010. Current standards include two liquidity regulations, the liquidity coverage ratio and the net stable funding ratio.[2] These rules are intended to ensure that banks can withstand funding reductions such as deposit withdrawals or liquidity demands arising from off-balance sheet activities.

We thank Charles Goodhart for the many lessons he has taught us about central banking and financial regulation. We also acknowledge comments from the editors and valuable feedback from several senior private sector bankers who prefer not to have their names or firms identified. The views here are purely our own and should not be associated with any institutions with which we are affiliated. Any mistakes are entirely our responsibility. This research was supported in part by a Senior Houblon Norman George Fellowship at the Bank of England and by a grant from the National Science Foundation administered by the National Bureau of Economic Research.

[1] See the Basel Committee on Banking Supervision (2011).
[2] See the Basel Committee on Banking Supervision (2013, 2014).

The development and calibration of the four capital and liquidity regulations has largely proceeded independently. While the officials understand the interactions – for example, that higher capital levels reduce liquidity needs – there has been little attempt to study the full interactions among all four. The purpose of this short chapter is to provide a stylised framework for examining the overall impact of the regulatory system. The main contribution is to describe how the requirements interact so that we can study why and when which of them is likely to bind. These observations can be helpful to understanding both how bank business models may evolve and how different types of banks will perform in different stress scenarios.

Before getting to the details of our stylised model, it is useful to review the rationale for the structure of the rules. To understand this, we need to think about the fundamental functions of a bank. Following Pozsar et al. (2012), these are credit transformation, liquidity transformation, maturity transformation and access to the payments system. Each transformation function generates returns by divorcing the characteristics of the assets from those of the liabilities: credit transformation produces assets that are riskier than liabilities; liquidity transformation creates liabilities that are more liquid than the assets; and maturity transformation generates assets that are longer-term than liabilities. And access to the payments system comes from providing liabilities that are accepted as payment.

A traditional bank performs all of these intermediation functions – funding long-term, illiquid, risky assets with short-term, liquid, safe liabilities. A combination of limited liability and the government safety net (in the form of deposit insurance and other implicit guarantees), can mean that a bank's owners and managers reap the benefits of their success but may not bear the full costs of their failures, so this creates incentives to engage in too much credit transformation, too much liquidity transformation and too much maturity transformation; too much relative to what society ideally needs.

Conversely, if information problems hamper the ability of a bank to issue equity, then the scale of intermediation could be lower than society would prefer. Mandating higher capital ratios in this situation could allow the bank to issue equity that would be free of adverse selection and increase the amount of intermediation. So regardless of whether decentralised allocations lead to too little or too much intermediation, one can imagine a role for regulation.

The liquidity requirements attend to concerns with the levels of liquidity and maturity transformation, with the liquidity coverage ratio (LCR) aimed at the former and the net stable funding ratio (NSFR) at the latter. The capital requirements simply say that equity must be greater than a fraction of the sum of assets, weighted or unweighted by their riskiness. The liquidity requirements are different. The LCR says that a weighted sum of assets must be greater than a weighted sum of liabilities. And NSFR reverses this, stating that a weighted sum of liabilities must be greater than a weighted sum of assets. As we will see, the fact that the LCR and NSFR effectively reverse the inequality between assets and liabilities creates some complications.

12.2 A Stylised Bank Balance Sheet

To start, consider a bank that has a variety of assets on and off the balance sheet, some liabilities and capital. It is useful at the outset to divide the assets into three types: relatively safe, high-quality liquid assets; on-balance sheet risky assets; and off-balance sheet assets. Since the safe assets include reserves, we label them as R. We take there to be n risky assets, which we label A_i. And the q off-balance sheet assets (converted to the same units as those on the balance sheet) are labelled $OBSA_j$. We assume there are three types of liabilities: deposits D_s, bonds B_k and equity E. The division of liabilities between deposits and bonds is a shorthand. Deposits are those liabilities that are runnable, so they that are subject to the LCR. And bonds are long-term liabilities that are the primary source of available stable funding in the computation of the NSFR – so 'core deposits' would be bonds in our nomenclature. Using this notation, a bank's balance sheet looks like this:

To simplify the balance sheet, we define the following aggregates:

$D = \sum_s D_s$, the simple sum of all deposits;

$B = \sum_k B_k$, the sum of long-term liabilities;

$A = \sum_i A_i$, the simple sum of on-balance sheet risky assets.

$L = \sum_i r_i^A A_i$, the level of on-balance sheet risk-weighted assets; and

$OBSA = \sum_j OBSA_j$, the total of off-balance sheet assets.

Table 12.1. *A general bank balance sheet*

Assets	Liabilities
R	D_1
A_1	D_2
A_2	$\vdots$
$\vdots$	D_p
A_n	B_1
$OBSA_1$	B_2
$OBSA_2$	$\vdots$
$\vdots$	B_m
$OBSA_q$	E

Table 12.2. *A stylised bank balance sheet*

Assets	Liabilities
Reserves/HQLA (R)	Deposits (D)
On-balance sheet risk-weighted assets (L)	Long-term liabilities (B)
Other assets $(OA = A-L)$	—
Off-balance sheet assets $(OBSA)$	Equity (E)

Combining these, we can rewrite the balance sheet in Table 12.1 in the stylised form in Table 12.2.

Other assets (OA), is the difference between total on-balance sheet risky assets (A) and risk-weighted assets (L). Keep in mind that the overall accounting identity is that $R + A = D + B + E$, but the balance sheet in Table 12.2 allows us to keep track of all the variables that enter the various regulations that we will consider.

12.3 Regulatory Requirements

We now turn to the capital and liquidity regulations. It is straight-forward to write each of the four regulations in terms of the general balance sheet, so we start there. For capital, the risk-weighted requirement says that equity must be equal to or greater than a weighted average of the on-balance sheet risky assets (A_i) and off-balance sheet assets $(OBSA_j)$, where the weights reflect the riskiness of each item.

Taking r_i^A and r_j^O to be the risk weights, the risk-weighted capital requirement takes the form:

$$E \geq \gamma \left[\sum_i r_i^A A_i + \sum_j r_j^O OBSA_j \right], \tag{12.1}$$

where γ is the required ratio, a number like 10 per cent.

Using the same notation, since the leverage ratio applies to all assets – the safe, risky and off-balance sheet – we can write it as

$$E \geq \delta[R + A + OBSA], \tag{12.2}$$

where δ is the unweighted leverage ratio requirement, a number like 5 per cent.

Turning to the liquidity requirements, the LCR states that a bank must hold high-quality liquid assets (which are labelled as R) to cover outflows in a thirty-day stress scenario measured.[3] It applies both to runnable deposit liabilities and to contingent assets such as committed lines of credit and liquidity needed for derivatives transactions. Defining the l_s's and l_j's as the LCR run-off rates on liabilities and off-balance sheet assets, we can write this as:[4]

$$R \geq \sum_s l_s^d D_s + \sum_j l_j^o OBSA_j. \tag{12.3}$$

Finally, the NSFR states that available stable funding (a weighted average of long-term liabilities) must be at least equal to required stable funding (a weighted average of long-term assets). We can write this as:[5]

$$\sum_k a_k^B B_k + \sum_s a_s^D D_s + E \geq \sum_i f_i A_i, \tag{12.4}$$

---

[3] The debate on how to ensure that the liquidity required under the LCR is usable in crisis continues. Goodhart (2008) discusses the problem by analogy with a law that there always has to be one taxi at the train station, so the final taxi in the queue can never be used. As Diamond and Kashyap (2016) note, if the idea of the regulation is to ensure banks can withstand withdrawals, the buffer has to be made usable. If, by contrast, the purpose of the liquidity requirement is to dissuade withdrawals, then usability is less of an issue.

[4] A summary of the LCR run-off rates is in Annex 4 of the Basel Committee on Banking Supervision (2013).

[5] A summary of the NSFR weights used to compute required and available stable funding is in Tables 1 and 2 of the Basel Committee on Banking Supervision (2014).

where the f_i's are the weights used to compute required stable funding, and the a_k^B's and the a_s^D's are the weights used to compute available stable funding for the two classes of liabilities.

Each of these, equations (12.1) to (12.4), can be expressed using the simplified balance sheet in Table 12.2. For the capital requirements, this is straightforward:

(i) $E \geq \gamma(L + \psi OBSA)$ risk – weighted capital

where

$$\sum_j r_j^O OBSA_j \approx \psi OBSA;$$

and

(ii) $E \geq \delta(R + A + OBSA)$ leverage ratio requirement.

The liquidity requirements are a bit more complicated to write simply. To do it, we make the following approximations:

$$\sum_s l_s^d D_s \approx \alpha D \quad \text{and} \quad \sum_j l_j^o OBSA_j \approx \omega OBSA,$$

where the parameter α is the average of the LCR run-off rates on runnable liabilities and ω is the average of the run-off rate on off-balance sheet items.

Using these approximations, we can write the liquidity requirements as

(iii) $R \geq \alpha D + \omega OBSA$ liquidity coverage ratio.

For the NSFR, we need three more approximations,

$$\sum_k a_k^B B_k \approx \eta^B B, \quad \sum_s a_s^D D_s \approx \eta^D D \quad \text{and} \quad \sum_i f_i A_i \approx \beta A.$$

The parameters η^B, η^D and β are averages of the NSFR's available and required stable funding factors, respectively. This allows us to write

(iv) $\eta^B B + \eta^D D + E \geq \beta A$ net stable funding ratio.

Finally, we have the balance sheet identity:

(v) $R + A = B + D + E$.

At this point, there are four asset categories (R, L, A and $OBSA$) and three liability categories (D, B and E), for a total of seven variables. To reduce the dimensionality of the problem, we further assume that risk-weighted assets (L) and off-balance sheet assets ($OBSA$) are proportional to the level of on-balance sheet risky assets (A):

(vi) $L = \phi A$ and $OBSA = \theta A$.

We suppose that for any given bank ϕ and θ would be stable over time, though across banks they might differ, perhaps substantially. For example, a broker-dealer bank will have very large off-balance sheet positions, while a more traditional commercial bank may not.

This allows us to rewrite the four regulatory requirements as:

$$E \geq \gamma(\phi + \psi\theta)A \quad \text{risk} - \text{weighted capital,} \tag{i'}$$

$$E \geq \delta[R + (1 + \theta)A] \quad \text{leverage ratio requirement,} \tag{ii'}$$

$$R \geq \alpha D + \omega\theta A \quad \text{liquidity coverage ratio,} \tag{iii'}$$

$$\eta^B B + \eta^D D + E \geq \beta A \quad \text{net stable funding ratio and} \tag{iv'}$$

$$R + A = B + D + E \quad \text{balance sheet identity.} \tag{v'}$$

To examine the joint properties of these, we first normalise equity ($E = 1$). This means that all of our quantities – reserves, risk-weighted assets, deposits and long-term financing, are measured relative to equity.

Next, to reduce the dimensionality of the problem further, we use the balance sheet identity to eliminate B, the quantity of available stable funding. This allows us to rewrite (i') to (iv') as:

$$A \leq \frac{1}{\gamma(\phi + \psi\theta)} \tag{i''}$$

$$R + (1 + \theta)A \leq \frac{1}{\delta} \tag{ii''}$$

$$D \leq \frac{1}{\alpha}R - \frac{\omega\theta}{\alpha}A \tag{iii''}$$

$$D \leq R + \left(\frac{\beta - \eta^B}{\eta^D - \eta^B}\right)A - \left(\frac{1 - \eta^B}{\eta^D - \eta^B}\right) \tag{iv''}$$

All bold characters (A, D and R) represent quantities that are measured relative to equity.

12.4 Implications

The primary point of this short chapter is to recognise that based purely on the algebraic manipulations and simple approximations that we have made it is possible to express the four central regulations of the post-crisis international bank regulations in terms of three transformed variables. This representation of the regulations delivers several implications that are perhaps surprising.

First, and most obviously, we have four inequalities that restrict three variables. This means one must be redundant. By simply inspecting the final two expressions, it is clear that they are very unlikely to hold at the same time. That is, deposits (D) are bound either by the LCR (iii″) or by the expression that comes from the NSFR (iv″). The conclusion is that it is impossible to construct a balance sheet where all four requirements bind simultaneously.

At first this may seem like a feature of the system rather than a flaw. Different banks have different balance sheet composition, so some will naturally be bound by one set of regulations, while others will be bound by a different set. The existence of overlapping and potentially redundant rules ensures that all institutions will have sufficient capital and liquidity buffers regardless of the structure of their business. But is this really the case?

It is often said that the LCR and the NSFR should be thought of as complementary regulations, where the LCR provides short-term stability that safeguards an institution against a run and the NSFR buys time that could facilitate a resolution (or recapitalisation) of a distress institution. The algebra that we have presented suggests this is not quite right. Instead, one of them may be a binding constraint, while the other will be slack.

Second, looking across all four regulations, it seems likely that the tightness of the different regulations will vary according to banks' business models. For instance, it is well understood that banks with large off-balance sheet positions or large amounts of high-quality liquid assets are more likely to be constrained by the leverage ratio than by the risk-weighted capital ratio. In some sense, the whole purpose of the leverage ratio is to make sure that banks must hold some capital even if they have relatively few assets that are subject to credit risk. It also forces banks to hold capital against assets with risk weights that are too low.

The perhaps unintended consequence of this is that there is a spill-over whereby the relative tightness of the capital regulations can influence which of the two liquidity regulations is likely to be more onerous. Put differently, it is at least possible that because a bank is tightly bound by the leverage requirement, it might find itself facing very slack constraints on liquidity (or vice versa). If this were to be true, that would create incentives for a bank to begin expanding into businesses that were liquidity intensive precisely because the costs to doing so would be especially low. So qualitatively this creates a force for banks to become more homogeneous. On the one hand, pushing banks to have similar, correlated exposures would raise systemic risk.[6] On the other hand, clamping down on extreme strategies might promote financial stability.

Finally, the interdependencies in the regulations can become relevant during the kind of stress tests that have been an important part of the macroprudential policy toolkit. In many jurisdictions, banks are required to undergo assessments of the impact of macroeconomic scenarios on their level of capital. Typically, the scenarios are intended to simulate tail events where large dislocations are presumed in either financial markets or the aggregate economy (or both). If all banks can survive a simultaneous, common, severe adverse macroeconomic event and still meet regulatory requirements, the presumption is that the system as a whole is safe.

In principle, this surely makes sense. But in practice, we wonder whether the existence of overlapping requirements makes it very difficult for banks to do business. To see what we have in mind, consider a case in which the stress-test scenarios create severe ratings downgrades for municipal and corporate credits. To give some sense of what can happen, note that under the standardised approach for assigning risk weights a downgrade of a corporate credit from AA− to BBB+ results in an increase in the risk weight from 20 per cent to 100 per cent.[7] That is, a four-notch downgrade increases the capital charge on a corporate bond by a factor of five!

---

[6] See Wagner (2009) for more on this consideration.

[7] Exhibit 29 in Moody's Investor Services (2016) reports that, over the 1983 to 2016 period, the one-year migration of a corporate bond from Aa3 to Baa1 (their equivalent of a shift from AA− to BBB+) averaged 0.251 per cent. That is, roughly 1 in 400 bonds experiences such a downgrade in a given year.

The adverse scenarios in the stress tests typically include quite deep recessions – gross domestic product (GDP) drops, unemployment rate increases, a decline in house price, falling equity markets and rising corporate bond rates. Such scenarios would often imply a large rating downgrade for some securities. Because the ratio of the risk-weighted capital ratio is roughly twice the leverage ratio, it is fairly easy to see how, if the capital charge on some assets quintuples, a bank that is constrained by the latter at the start of the stress test could end up constrained by the former. Is this the intent of the regulation that banks be constrained by one requirement in normal times and a different requirement under stress?

12.5 Conclusion

Starting with Basel I, economists have been questioning the efficacy and incentive properties of the regulations promulgated by Basel Committee on Bank Supervision (e.g. Goodhart, 2010). To our knowledge, however, there have been very few attempts to comprehensively study all the regulations that are about to take effect as part of Basel III. This chapter makes a very modest attempt in that direction. We were surprised by the ways in which the regulations seem to interact and believe that more analysis of this sort could be quite productive.

References

Basel Committee on Banking Supervisions (2011), *Basel III: A Global Regulatory Framework for More Resilient Banks and Banking Systems*. Revised Version June 2011.

(2013), *Basel III: The Liquidity Coverage Ratio and Liquidity Risk Monitoring Tools*. January 2013.

(2014), *Basel III: The Net Stable Funding Ratio*. October 2014.

Diamond, D.W. and A.K. Kashyap (2016), 'Liquidity Requirements, Liquidity Choice and Financial Stability'. NBER Working Paper No. 22053, March 2016.

Goodhart, C.A.E. (2008), 'Liquidity Risk Management', *Banque de France Financial Stability Review*, 12, pp. 39–44.

(2010), 'How Should We Regulate Bank Capital and Financial Products? What Role for "Living Wills"? (Cómo Deberíamos Regular el Capital

Bancario y los Productos Financieros? Cuál es el Papel de los "Testamentos en Vida?")'. *Revista de Economia Institucional*, 12(23), pp. 85–109. ISSN 0124-5996.

(2011), *The Basel Committee on Banking Supervision: A History of the Early Years, 1974–1997*, Cambridge, UK: Cambridge University Press.

Moody's Investor Services (2016), *Annual Default Study: Corporate Default and Recovery Rates, 1920–2015*. 29 February 2016.

Pozsar, Z., T. Adrian, A. Ashcraft and H. Boesky (2012), 'Shadow Banking', Federal Reserve Bank of New York Staff Paper No. 458, revised February 2012.

Wagner, W.B. (2009), 'Efficient Asset Allocations in the Banking Sector and Financial Regulation', *International Journal of Central Banking*, 5(1), pp. 75–95.

13 | Is Burden Sharing Needed for International Financial Stability?

DIRK SCHOENMAKER

13.1 Introduction

The Great Financial Crisis of 2007/2008 highlighted that 'financial institutions may be global in life, but they are national in death' (Huertas, 2009, p. 6). National authorities were thus on their own to deal with the respective national parts of those global banks that were failing or under severe pressure. While there have been several reforms to strengthen the international banking system, no one has succeeded in addressing this coordination failure between national authorities.

The first major reform is the imposition of higher capital requirements under Basel III, together with a capital surcharge for the so-called global systemically important banks (G-SIBs). Higher capital reduces but does not eliminate the possibility of problems at these global banks. The second reform concerns the introduction of key principles for the resolution of international banks by the Financial Stability Board (FSB, 2014). Although these principles encourage cooperation between national resolution authorities, they are non–binding (Riles, 2014; Davies, 2015). As we witnessed during the Great Financial Crisis, as well as in earlier crises, authorities put non-binding agreements (like Memoranda of Understanding) aside in the heat of the moment when large sums are at stake. The third, and most recent, reform is the requirement to bail-in debt before a possible bail-out of a failing bank can take place. While bail-in might work for (small) idiosyncratic bank failures, the application of bail-in to large complex banks is uncertain and has so far not been tested.

The maintained hypothesis is that there remains a need for a fiscal backstop for (large) banks, including the large international banks. In

The author would like to thank Thomas Huertas, Roger Laeven, Carlos Mavarall-Rodriguez, Andrew Sheng, Peter Wierts and seminar participants at the Single Resolution Board, the University of Amsterdam, and the LSE conference in honour of Charles Goodhart, 'The Life of a Central Banker', for useful comments.

joint work with Charles Goodhart, we argue that only *ex ante* binding burden sharing agreements between governments can technically solve the coordination failure in providing such a backstop for international banks (Goodhart and Schoenmaker, 2009). But burden sharing, which is also labelled loss allocation, is politically controversial. The presence of large international banks is taken as given. The chapter does not analyse the (dis)advantages of large banks or financial globalisation (see Kose et al., 2009, on the latter).

The chapter is organised as follows. Section 13.2 discusses the need for a fiscal backstop and provides some estimates for the required size of the backstop. Section 13.3 analyses the (in)stability of international banking and derives three equilibrium outcomes for international coordination. We argue that the burden sharing equilibrium is the most stable, albeit politically the most difficult, outcome. Next, Section 13.4 provides empirical evidence on these different equilibria. Finally, Section 13.5 discusses policy implications and concludes.

13.2 The Need for a Fiscal Backstop[1]

The aim of the new bail-in regime is to reduce the costs of bank bail-outs for taxpayers, which we fully support. While bail-in is appropriate for individual idiosyncratic failures, it might not be possible in cases of the failures of a systemically important bank or large parts of the banking system. Several academics (e.g. Avgouleas and Goodhart, 2015; Chan and van Wijnbergen, 2015) and policymakers (e.g. Dewatripont, 2014) warn that the bail-in of large banks might be adding to, instead of dampening, financial panic. The European bail-in regime allows for a financial stability exception for government support under certain conditions (Articles 32, 44 and 56, Bank Recovery and Resolution Directive, 2014/59/EU).

Even with bail-in (which might be applied or not), in the case of a full-blown systemic crisis, there is thus still a need for a fiscal backstop by the government, either directly to recapitalise ailing banks, or indirectly as a backstop for the central bank, the resolution fund and the deposit insurance fund, as we have argued elsewhere.[2]

---

[1] This section draws on joint work with Pia Hüttl (Hüttl and Schoenmaker, 2016).

[2] In an earlier paper, we provide the arguments for a fiscal backstop (Schoenmaker, 2015).

The standing of a banking system depends on the strength and credibility of the fiscal backstop (Goodhart, 1998).

Fiscal capacity refers to the ability of the state to extract revenues to provide public goods. Applying this concept to banking, Pauly (2014) defines fiscal capacity of a country as the budget capacity to provide a credible fiscal backstop to its banking system and the political capacity to activate the budget. An example of the lack of political capacity is the dithering approach of the Japanese Ministry of Finance in its dealing with severe banking problems during the 1990s. The Japanese parliament did not approve any recapitalisation of the ailing Japanese banks beyond the bare minimum, which prolonged the crisis, culminating in the infamous lost decade of growth.

Moving to budget capacity, we can approximate the potential budgetary needs for recapitalising a country's large banks based on earlier episodes. Laeven and Valencia (2013) provide a global overview of the fiscal outlays during past crises. The direct fiscal costs of banking crises during the 1970–2011 period are on average 4 per cent of gross domestic product (GDP) for advanced countries. More importantly, the subsequent increase in debt (21 per cent of GDP) and output loss (33 per cent of GDP) are a multiple of the direct fiscal costs.

Hüttl and Schoenmaker (2016) provide a more granular overview with exact recapitalisation amounts of European banks during the Great Financial Crisis and the subsequent euro sovereign crisis. Figure 13.1 shows that the direct fiscal costs are distributed unevenly across countries, related mainly to the depth of the crisis and the size of the banking system in the single countries. The Irish banking recapitalisation costs represent 40.0 per cent of GDP, while the French government banking assistance did not exceed 1.4 per cent of GDP. Belgium and Spain with direct recapitalisations costs of about 8 per cent are borderline cases with respect to external assistance. While Belgium could support the recapitalisation of its banking system without outside help, Spain needed the European Stability Mechanism (ESM) and International Monetary Fund (IMF) financial assistance for the recapitalisation and restructuring of its banking system. This was also due to far worse macroeconomic conditions in Spain in 2012. The experience from the recent financial crises suggest that the hurdle rate for the credibility of the fiscal backstop hovers around 8 per cent of GDP, but this is not a hard and fast rule.

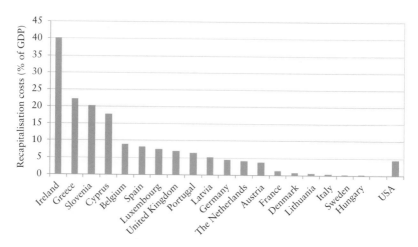

Figure 13.1 Recapitalisation costs of EU and US banking systems 2008–2014
Source: Hüttl and Schoenmaker (2016).

As this chapter examines global banks, we are interested in the recapitalisation costs of large (inter)national banks, with assets over €150 billion (or USD 165 billion). Table 13.1 illustrates that the fiscal costs of recapitalisation and asset relief of Europe's twenty-two large banks were on average 2.7 per cent of these banks' total assets; and of the thirteen large US banks, on average 2.5 per cent of total bank assets. Applying a 99 per cent confidence interval, we find a range from 0.8 to 4.3 per cent of total bank assets.

13.2.1 Fiscal Capacity for Bank Bail-Outs

Building on our analysis of earlier episodes, we can estimate the potential fiscal costs of a systemic bank bail-out. The first step is to look at the potential costs for one bank. The results from Table 13.1 indicate that equity is a more precise measure for potential rescue costs (Dermine and Schoenmaker, 2010) than the often-used measure of total assets or total liabilities (e.g. Liikanen, 2012; Langfield and Pagano, 2016). Taking the upper limit for the recapitalisation of EU and US banks as a conservative estimate (see Table 13.1), we standardise equity at 4.5 per cent of total assets. This is also close to the average capital ratio (i.e. leverage ratio) of the large European banks found by Schoenmaker and Véron (2016).

Table 13.1. *Direct recapitalisation of large EU and US banks*

#	Bank name	Total assets (EUR bn)	State aid (EUR bn)	State aid in % of total assets
	Panel A: Direct recapitalisation of EU banks (2008–2013)			
1	BNP Paribas (FR)	2,070.0	5.1	0.2
2	Royal Bank of Scotland (UK)	2,050.0	81.1	4.0
3	Crédit Agricole (FR)	1,740.0	6.0	0.3
4	Société Générale (FR)	1,075.0	3.4	0.3
5	Groupe BPCE (FR)	1,030.0	0.5	0.05
6	ING (NL)	960.0	15.0	1.6
7	Commerzbank (DE)	735.0	18.2	2.5
8	Lloyds Banking Group (UK)	715.0	28.3	4.0
9	Crédit Mutuel (FR)	580.0	2.4	0.4
10	BNP Paribas Fortis (BE)	530.0	10.8	2.0
11	Dexia (BE)	520.0	17.4	3.4
12	Nordea Bank (SE)	510.0	0.5	0.1
13	Landesbank Baden-Württemberg (DE)	410.0	14.0	3.4
14	ABN AMRO (NL)	380.0	16.9	4.4
15	Bayerische Landesbank (DE)	380.0	10.0	2.6
16	Hypo Real Estate Holding (DE)	345.0	10.7	3.1
17	KBC Group (BE)	340.0	10.8	3.2
18	NORD/LB (DE)	225.0	3.1	1.4
19	Banca Monte dei Paschi di Siena (IT)	215.0	5.8	2.7
20	HSH Nordbank (DE)	175.0	3.0	1.7
21	Bank of Ireland (IE)	170.0	7.1	4.2
22	Allied Irish Banks (IE)	150.0	21.4	14.1
	Average EU banks			**2.7**
	Lower and upper bound*			**1.1–4.3**
	Panel B: Direct recapitalisation of US banks (2008–2012)			
1	JPMorgan Chase	2,175.0	25.0	1.1
2	Citigroup	1,940.0	45.0	2.3
3	Bank of America	1,820.0	45.0	2.5
4	Wells Fargo	1,310.0	25.0	1.9
5	Goldman Sachs	850.0	10.0	1.2
6	Morgan Stanley	770.0	10.0	1.3

Table 13.1. (*cont.*)

#	Bank name	Total assets (EUR bn)	State aid (EUR bn)	State aid in % of total assets
7	PNC Financial Services Group	290.0	7.6	2.6
8	US Bancorp	270.0	6.6	2.5
9	Bank of New York Mellon	240.0	3.0	1.3
10	SunTrust Banks	190.0	4.9	2.6
11	State Street	175.0	2.0	1.1
12	Ally Financial	170.0	17.5	10.2
13	Capital One Financial	165.0	3.6	2.1
	Average US banks			2.5
	Lower and upper bound*			0.8–4.2

Note: Direct recapitalisation costs for the government are based on state aid figures for direct recapitalisation and asset relief. Large banks are defined as banks with assets above EUR 150 bn /USD 165 bn. * the lower and upper bound are based on a 99 per cent confidence interval.
Source: Hüttl and Schoenmaker (2016).

The second step is to look at the range for bail-out costs during a severe systemic crisis. Assuming that up to three of the largest banks might need to be recapitalised, we can establish a country's total potential costs. Table 13.2 shows that these costs range from 2 to 4 per cent of GDP for large countries like China, the USA and the Euro area. Japan follows closely with slightly less than 7 per cent of GDP. These figures are sufficiently low to make the fiscal backstop of these countries for their large banks credible. Table 13.2 also illustrates that the potential costs for Germany and Italy are within the 4 to 5 per cent range, but these countries are not home to global banks with USD 2–3 trillion in assets, except for Deutsche Bank.

The other euro area countries (with large banks) as well as the UK and Switzerland face potential fiscal costs for bailing out the largest banks, ranging from 8 to 13 per cent. The credibility of the fiscal backstop for these countries can be questioned – both the budgetary capacity (exceeding the indicative hurdle rate of 8 per cent of GDP) and the political willingness to spend such large amounts. We should note that these calculations do not take into account (partial) bail-in, which would lower the potential costs for the government, or the

Table 13.2. *Potential fiscal costs for major countries, 2015*

Countries	Assets in USD billion	Recapitalisation in USD billion	Fiscal costs % of GDP
Top three banks, China	8,991	405	3.7
Top three banks, USA	6,287	283	1.6
Top three banks, Japan	6,023	271	6.6
Top three banks, euro area	5,785	260	2.3
Top three banks, France*	5,465	246	10.2
Top three banks, Germany*	2,794	126	3.7
Top three banks, Spain*	2,646	119	9.9
Top three banks, Netherlands*	2,064	93	12.3
Top three banks, Italy*	1,854	83	4.6
Top three banks, UK	5,288	238	8.4
Top three banks, Switzerland	1,989	90	13.5

Note: The largest three home country banks (i.e. headquartered in the home country) are chosen for each jurisdiction. Recapitalisation is standardised at 4.5 per cent of total assets. The fiscal costs represent the potential fiscal costs of recapitalising the largest three banks as a percentage of GDP. The countries indicated with an asterisk* are members of the European Banking Union.
Source: 'Assets from Top 1000 World Banks', *The Banker* (July 2016), and GDP from Worldbank.

fiscal space of individual countries (see Demirgüç-Kunt and Huizinga (2013) on the latter).

13.3 Stability of International Banking

The provision of a credible fiscal backstop to international banks is challenging. The involved countries do not take into account any foreign externalities of a potential bank failure, and are only prepared (and politically authorised) to backstop their respective domestic part. More formally, the financial trilemma states that the objectives of (1) financial stability, (2) international banking, and (3) national financial policies for supervision and resolution[3] are incompatible

---

[3] A broad definition of the governance framework for financial supervision and resolution is used: rulemaking, supervision, lender of last resort (i.e. emergency liquidity assistance), deposit insurance, resolution and the fiscal backstop (Schoenmaker, 2013).

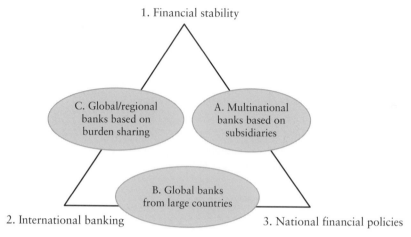

Figure 13.2 Equilibria of the financial trilemma
Source: Adapted from Schoenmaker (2011).

(Schoenmaker, 2011). Any two of the three policy objectives can be combined, but not all three; one has to give. The choice of policy-makers produces three equilibrium outcomes for the structure of the international banking system, which differ in viability and stability. Figure 13.2 illustrates the equilibria of the financial trilemma. In a similar vein, Eatwell, Gossé and Alexander (2014) develop similar, though slightly different, scenarios.

The purpose of this section is to analyse the ultimate consequences of countries' policy choice within the financial trilemma framework for the structure of the international banking system. Our analysis fits in a new literature on resolution models for cross-border banks (e.g. Bolton and Oehmke, 2016; Faia and Weder di Mauro, 2016).

13.3.1 Equilibrium A: Multinational Banks, Based on National Subsidiaries

The first equilibrium outcome is that of multinational banks, based on a string of national standalone subsidiaries.[4] This outcome results from combing the policy objectives of financial stability and national

---

[4] See Chapter 3 of Schoenmaker (2013) for a full description of bank business models. The multinational bank is a decentralised international bank. By contrast, we regard the global bank as a centralised international bank.

financial policies. The principle idea is that the national financial authorities require that the subsidiaries are separately capitalised and managed.[5] If one of the subsidiaries or the parent bank fails, the other parts of the multinational bank can continue. The national authorities can deal with each part separately and financial stability is contained at the national level without further (international) contagion. The resolution strategy is based on multiple point of entry (MPE), and deposit insurance, if any, is arranged by the respective host countries.

But is this equilibrium outcome viable and realistic? Banks still want to exploit synergies, for example, from centralised risk management and one brand name. Next, foreign subsidiaries often use a parent guarantee to enhance their creditworthiness, which reduces funding costs and makes the subsidiary a stronger counterparty in derivative transactions. Freshfields Bruckhaus Deringer (2003), an international law firm, examines to what extent legal firewalls (separate legal personality and limited liability of subsidiaries) can help to reduce or prevent contagion risk within a financial group. They find that legal firewalls can help to protect from direct contagion (credit exposures arising from intragroup transactions or operational risk from sharing of services) but are less effective in limiting indirect contagion (reputation risk and funding risk). This is because indirect contagion arises from perceptions and behaviour of (potential) counterparties and other market participants. The strategy of most major banks of developing and maintaining a global brand reinforces contagion risk.

A good example of indirect contagion is the Drexel Burnham Lambert collapse in 1990. While the Drexel Burnham Lambert Group experienced difficulties in the USA, the London subsidiary was solvent. Nevertheless, the Bank of England had to intervene as facilitator because the counterparties did not want to deal directly with the solvent London subsidiary.

In an empirical study, Anginer et al. (2017) examine the association between default risk of foreign bank subsidiaries and their parents. After controlling for common factors, they find a positive correlation of default of 0.2–0.3. Although the correlation is lower for subsidiaries

---

[5] The host country applies both capital and bail-in requirements to national subsidiaries (but not branches). The FSB proposes that each material sub-group maintains an internal Total Loss-Absorbing Capacity (TLAC) of 75–90 per cent of the external TLAC requirement that would apply to the material sub-group if it were a resolution group (Principle 18 of TLAC Termsheet, FSB, 2015).

operating in countries that impose higher capital and disclosure requirements and tougher restrictions on bank activities, host country policies
cannot break the link between the default risk of the foreign bank subsidiary and that of its parent bank located in the home country.

From these legal and empirical studies, we conclude that externalities between national subsidiaries of a multinational bank and its
parent bank cannot be eliminated completely. Supervisors and resolution authorities from the home and host countries will need to cooperate when these banks experience problems, if they want to prevent
disorderly outcomes and maintain financial stability. But where are
the incentives and/or binding arrangements for cooperation in this
MPE approach? The financial trilemma suggests that financial stability can only be managed at the national level in the case of truly standalone national banks, without further connections. So, the long run
equilibrium A is a multinational banking system, whereby the
national authorities impose increasingly high ring-fencing requirements on national subsidiaries to limit contagion.

13.3.2 Equilibrium B: Global Banks, Headquartered in Large Countries

The next two equilibrium outcomes concern centralised global
banks. We first deal with global banks headquartered in large countries. As analysed in Section 13.2, small and medium-sized countries
have less fiscal capacity to support large global banks. The equilibrium outcome B aims to achieve the policy objectives of international banking and national financial policies. While having the
headquarters in a large country solves the fiscal capacity problem, it
does not address the issue of incorporating foreign externalities
(see also Herring, 2007, and Riles, 2014, on incentive problems in
international banking). Large countries are preoccupied with the
domestic externalities of a possible failure and do not take into
account cross-border externalities.

This raises questions about the credibility of foreign retail branches
and the application of deposit insurance (from the home or host
country?). In times of crisis, the home authorities might save the
entire institution (e.g. the case of AIG with many foreign counterparties) or not. The basis for resolution, single point of entry (SPE) or
multi-point of entry (MPE), is not clear. Even if the global bank states

in its resolution plan that it will apply SPE, this is subject to time inconsistency. There are severe scenarios possible, whereby the home resolution authority and global bank jointly decide to rescue the home country part and to let the other parts go (e.g. the Federal Reserve provided bridge financing for the US part of Lehman Brothers). Faia and Weder di Mauro (2016) label this model outcome as the uncooperative SPE approach.

Given the inherent uncertainty about home country support, host countries might want to ring-fence the host country operations (e.g. by demanding a separately licensed and capitalised subsidiary) and provide host country deposit insurance. We are then back in equilibrium A, with multinational banks. Equilibrium B, with global banks from large countries, is thus not very stable for host countries. Eatwell, Gossé and Alexander (2014) call equilibrium B a USA–China hegemony. The USA and China are the largest economies, which can still afford to have large banks and also have the geopolitical power to impose their preferred model. Nevertheless, host countries may in the long run not accept the unilateral approach of these large countries.

13.3.3 Equilibrium C: Global or Regional Banks, Based on Burden Sharing

The third equilibrium outcome is global or regional banks, based on burden sharing between the countries in which the banks operate. This outcome aims to preserve financial stability and international banking. It gives up on national financial policies, as governments work together in supervision and resolution based on hard law. As countries cooperate and review these banks on a consolidated basis, the resolution strategy is structured on SPE, and all externalities (both domestic and cross-border) are taken into account. The cooperation has to be hardwired in a legally binding agreement for burden sharing. In earlier work (Goodhart and Schoenmaker, 2009), we sketch the various schemes for burden sharing, ranging from general burden sharing based on the relative size of participating countries (e.g. GDP or population) to specific burden sharing based on the relative presence of the failing bank (e.g. geographic segmentation of its assets). Faia and Weder di Mauro (2016) designate this model outcome as the cooperative SPE approach.

The technical solution of burden sharing addresses the problems of fiscal capacity and foreign externalities and is thus a stable equilibrium. The challenge is political. Are countries prepared to join forces in financial policies and thus give up part of their sovereignty in this field? Such a decision has to be put to democratic vote in the relevant parliaments. In a more general context, Rodrik (2011) doubts whether countries are prepared to give up their sovereignty in economic policy-making. But Pauly (2014) argues that the political capacity to deal with the risks from global finance is increasing. Unless, or until, fiscal authority moves to the level implied by globalising markets, effective policy capacity and durable political legitimation will remain in tension. Experimentalism and institutional innovations like the Basel process for banking supervision standards may help us live with such tensions. Similarly, public insurance systems can facilitate an expansion in transnational risk pools. Although straightforward *ex ante* burden sharing agreements remain elusive, Pauly (2014) argues that repeated *ad hoc* arrangements during and after crises do certainly give rise to reasonable expectations of future regulatory, monetary, and fiscal coordination.

Eatwell, Gossé and Alexander (2014) distinguish between regional and global banks based on cooperation. Regional cooperation is possible at the level of the European Union, the North American Free Trade Agreement (NAFTA) extended to Central American and the Caribbean countries, and a Far-East group centred on China and including Japan, Korea and the Association of Southeast Asian Nations (ASEAN) countries. In the case of global banks, multipolar collaboration is conceivable at the level of the G-20, with the necessary supranational institutions to enforce the commonly agreed rules.

Summing up, each equilibrium outcome has its own challenges. Equilibrium B is the least stable, as host countries will recognise that the home country authorities of global banks will not deal with the cross-border fall-out of a bank failure. They will thus take precautions by requiring separately capitalised subsidiaries and ring-fencing the assets in these subsidiaries. This brings us to equilibrium A, with multinational banks, where national authorities try to contain the respective fall-out in their jurisdiction, but without any authority taking care of international contagion. Equilibrium C, with burden sharing between countries, solves the coordination problem but is politically difficult to achieve.

13.4 International Banking in Practice

Can we assign the present-day international banks to these three equilibria? This section makes an attempt to do so.

13.4.1 Equililbrium A: Multinational Banks

An early example of multinational banking comes from the Antipodes. Prior to the Great Financial Crisis, New Zealand had already adopted the policy of requiring subsidiaries when the retail operations of Australian banks in New Zealand become large. The four New Zealand subsidiaries (1) ANZ Bank New Zealand – owned by Australia and New Zealand Banking Group (ANZ), (2) ASB Bank – owned by the Commonwealth Bank, (3) the Bank of New Zealand (BNZ) – owned by the National Australia bank and (4) Westpac New Zealand – owned by Westpac Banking Corporation) hold over 80 per cent of New Zealand banking assets. The idea is that these standalone subsidiaries can continue to serve New-Zealand clients and depositors, even if the Australian parent gets into difficulties. In turn, if the New Zealand subsidiaries were to experience problems, the New Zealand authorities would want to apply bail-in instead of having to rely on uncertain support from the Australian parent banks or Australian government (see Mayes (2014) for a full description of bank resolution in New Zealand).

More recently, the USA has required an intermediate US holding company for foreign banks with more than USD 50 billion of assets in the USA. In that way, the Federal Reserve can exercise full control over the US operations of foreign banks. In return, the EU has announced proposals to require an intermediate EU holding for foreign banks with more than €30 billion of assets in the EU. The USA and the EU thus seem to choose the (non-cooperative) multinational bank equilibrium for international banks entering their jurisdiction.

HSBC, Santander and BBVA are examples of large multinational banks that have a decentralised structure with national subsidiaries and openly adopt the MPE approach. HSBC is a truly international bank, spanning the three main continents: the Americas, Europe and Asia. At the global level, HSBC adopts an MPE approach, with three main resolution hubs in the UK, the USA and Hong Kong (see the US Resolution Plan, 2015 of HSBC filed at the Federal Reserve Board).

Within the USA, HSBC follows an SPE approach for the nine material entities, headed by the intermediate holding company in the USA. This mix of global MPE and regional SPE is an appealing model, respecting geopolitical realities.

The Spanish banks, Santander and BBVA, have major foreign operations in the UK (only Santander), the USA and Latin America. By getting local funding for their subsidiaries and adopting an MPE approach, they aim to compartment the risks. The Chief Economist for Financial Regulation at BBVA proposes that an SPE approach might be suitable for the euro area, as that should be regarded as a single jurisdiction, combined with an MPE approach for third countries (Fernández de Lis, 2015). This is an interesting proposal, given the foray of Spanish banks into Portugal (Schoenmaker and Véron, 2016).

13.4.2 Global Banks

The vast majority of international banks adopt the 'global bank' model. Global banks operate on a centralised business model and adopt an SPE resolution strategy (at least on paper).[6] For analytical purposes, we distinguish three broad groups of global banks:

- global banks from large countries, like the USA, China and possibly Japan;
- global banks from the euro area, which has adopted Banking Union with some – albeit limited – forms of burden sharing;
- global banks from medium-sized countries, like the UK and Switzerland, which are currently downsizing.

Our hypothesis from Sections 13.2 and 13.3 is that large countries can still afford to support global banks, but that (the credibility of)

---

[6] The USA and the UK, for example, indicate that their preferred strategy is to resolve their large cross-border banks, with a presence in both countries, on an SPE basis at the holding company level (FDIC and Bank of England, 2012). Goodhart (2014, p. 106) dryly notes: 'It is hard for me to see how such national preference [*focus on domestic retail banking in Vickers Report*] would be compatible with the more global SPE proposal emanating from the Bank of England/FDIC for the resolution of cross-border universal banks. Indeed, recent US proposals for mandatory incorporation of US-based foreign banking activities into a US subsidiary hardly presents a note of resounding confidence in the efficacy of an SPE approach.'

the fiscal capacity of medium-sized countries to support their large banks has come under pressure after the Great Financial Crisis. While ups and downs of a country's banking system are largely cyclical, we aim to examine the structural trend (corrected for GDP growth) in the aftermath of the Great Financial Crisis. Table 13.3 shows that the largest Chinese and US banks have still been growing largely in line with GDP at an annualised net rate of +1 and −1 per cent, respectively, over the 2007–15 period. Surprisingly, the Japanese banks have grown faster than the economy at an annualised net rate of +5 per cent over the same period. By contrast, the largest UK and Swiss banks have contracted at −5 and −11 per cent, respectively. The euro area banking system has, like in the USA, grown at a net rate of −1 per cent.

What can we learn from these results? The large countries seem to be able to 'maintain' their banking systems. The medium-sized countries have enacted major reforms (both higher capital charges and structural reforms), with the official aim to increase the resilience of their banking system, and with the intended side effect of downsizing their large banks including reducing these banks' foreign activities at the same time. In the aftermath of the Iceland experience with the failure of its banks in 2008, whereby Iceland was not able to support its banks' outsized foreign activities, the UK and Switzerland want to reduce their 'foreign exposures'. The major euro area countries have implemented some lighter 'Liikanen' reforms than the UK and Switzerland. An open issue is whether policymakers will shift the fiscal backstop for the euro area banking system from the country to the euro area level (see Section 13.4.4 below).

13.4.3 Equililbrium B: Global Banks from Large Countries

The first group of global banks is from large countries. This is an equilibrium insofar as these large countries can provide a credible fiscal backstop to their banking system. Table 13.3 confirms the trend that the leading global banks are based in large countries. Looking at the top twenty banks in 2015, China, the USA, the euro area and Japan are home to these banks, with still one major bank from the UK, namely HSBC, in fifth position (the position of the other UK banks is swiftly declining, with Barclays tumbling from fourth spot in 2007 to fifteenth in 2015 and RBS from first to twentieth). The Swiss

Table 13.3. *Development of global banks for major countries, 2007–15*

Banking groups	2007 Assets in USD billion	2007 Asset rank	2015 Assets in USD billion	2015 Asset rank	Change 2007–2015 Assets (%)	Change 2007–2015 GDP (%)	Change 2007–2015 Net (%)
Top five Chinese banks	3,928	—	12,684	—	16	15	1
ICBC	1,189	20	3,422	1	14	—	—
China Construction Bank	903	23	2,827	2	15	—	—
Agricultural Bank of China	726	27	2,741	3	18	—	—
Bank of China	820	25	2,591	5	15	—	—
Bank of Communications	289	—	1,103	23	18	—	—
Top five US banks	7,943	—	8,879	—	1	3	−1
JPMorgan Chase	1,562	12	2,352	7	5	—	—
Bank of America	1,716	10	2,147	9	3	—	—
Wells Fargo[a]	1,358	29/41	1,788	11	3	—	—
Citigroup	2,187	7	1,731	13	−3	—	—
Goldman Sachs	1,120	21	861	28	−3	—	—
Top eight euro area banks	14,578	—	11,807	—	−3	−1	−1
BNP Paribas	2,477	3	2,168	8	−2	—	—
Crédit Agricole	2,253	6	1,847	10	−2	—	—
Deutsche Bank	2,814	2	1,771	12	−6	—	—
Banco Santander	1,335	17	1,457	17	1	—	—
Société Générale	1,567	11	1,450	18	−1	—	—

Groupe BPCE[b]	1,184	24/44	1,268	19	1	—	—
UniCredit	1,494	15	935	25	-6	—	—
ING Bank	1,453	16	911	26	-6	—	—
Top four UK banks	10,600		6,492		-6	-1	-5
HSBC Holdings	2,354	5	2,410	6	0	—	—
Barclays	2,443	4	1,672	15	-5	—	—
RBS	3,771	1	1,207	20	-13	—	—
Lloyds Banking Group[c]	2,031	18/33	1,204	21	-6	—	—
Top three Japanese banks	4,344		6,023		4	-1	5
Mitsubushi UFJ	1,939	9	2,649	4	4	—	—
Mizuho	1,551	13	1,718	14	1	—	—
Sumitomo Mitsui	854	24	1,657	16	9	—	—
Top two Swiss banks	3,211		1,781		-7	4	-11
UBS	2,009	8	952	24	-9	—	—
Credit Suisse	1,202	19	829	31	-5	—	—
Total twenty-seven banking groups	44,604		47,667		1	3	-2

Note: Total assets and assets rank are provided for the major banks in the top twenty for both 2007 and 2015.

Mergers:

[a] Wells Fargo reports the combined assets of Wachovia and Wells Fargo in 2007;

[b] Groupe BPCE reports the combined assets of Groupe Caisse d'Epargne and Groupe Banques Populaires in 2007;

[c] Lloyds Banking Group reports the combined assets of HBOS and Lloyds TSB Group in 2007.

The change is calculated as an average annualised rate over the 2007–15 period; the net change is annualised asset growth minus annualised GDP growth.

Sources: 'Assets from Top 1000 World Banks', *The Banker* (July 2008; July 2016) and GDP from Worldbank.

banks dropped out altogether from the top twenty. The same trend is visible in investment banking. The US investment banks are about to surpass European investment banks in the European market. The Chinese investment banks are growing fast and have already overtaken the US and European investment banks in the Asian-Pacific market (Goodhart and Schoenmaker, 2016).

13.4.4 Equililbrium C: Global/Regional Banks and Burden Sharing

The second group of global banks is based in the European Banking Union, with banks like BNP Paribas, Deutsche Bank, ING and UniCredit. Table 13.2 shows that the potential fiscal costs can be large at the country level, from 10 to 12 per cent of GDP for France, the Netherlands and Spain. The credibility of the fiscal backstop to their banking system can be questioned for these countries. If the fiscal backstop were moved to the euro area level, the costs would drop to 2 per cent of GDP. The fiscal backstop will then be as credible as that of the USA and China.

The Banking Union countries thus face a political choice, which is important not only from a financial stability perspective, but also from a geopolitical perspective. If they want to stay at par with the other two world powers, these countries must organise the fiscal backstop at the euro area level.

The ESM is enshrined in an intergovernmental treaty (hard law) and based on a general form of burden sharing, with the burden sharing key based on an arithmetic average of countries' shares in population and GDP (Goodhart and Schoenmaker, 2009). The ESM was created as a fiscal backstop to member countries. Under the current arrangements, it provides a very partial backstop to the Banking Union banking system. A member country can receive an ESM loan to recapitalise its banks (the indirect recapitalisation of Article 15 ESM Treaty). Only when a member's fiscal sustainability is in danger (ESM, 2014), the ESM can directly recapitalise banks from that member country under certain conditions (e.g. an own contribution of the member country and a bail-in of 8 per cent of a bank's total liabilities) and with unanimity of votes, which might lead to protracted negotiations with an uncertain outcome. The current ESM Direct

Recapitalisation Instrument thus falls short of an *ex ante* credible fiscal backstop at the euro area level.

A first step to complete the ESM as fiscal backstop to the banking system would be to enable direct bank recapitalisation from the ESM, without first waiting for the country to go bankrupt and subsequently meeting prohibitive conditions and voting procedures (e.g. Goyal et al., 2013; Gros and Schoenmaker, 2014; Véron, 2015). A second step is to establish a Single Resolution and Deposit Insurance Fund, with a credit line from the ESM, similar to the Federal Deposit Insurance Corporation (FDIC), which has a US Treasury credit line (Gros and Schoenmaker, 2014).

In risk-sharing terms, the ESM would then be behind the bank risk-sharing, both directly by providing direct bank recapitalisation and indirectly by providing a credit line to the Resolution and Deposit Insurance Fund. The European arrangements would then match the US arrangements for bank risk-sharing (Gros and Belke, 2015).[7]

13.4.5 Global Banks without a Credible Fiscal Backstop

Our analysis suggests that the third group of banks from medium-sized countries can no longer operate as integrated global banks, based on an SPE resolution strategy. As the fiscal backstop to these banks is less credible, equilibrium B of the global banks is not sustainable for them. These banks end up by inclination in equilibrium A of the multinational banks with MPE resolution.

HSBC, the largest UK bank, already operates on an MPE resolution strategy, as discussed above. Credit Suisse, one of the two large Swiss banks, has an SPE approach at the global level with bail-in debt at the group holding company. But below that Credit Suisse is in the process of implementing separate country subsidiaries for its major operations and two subsidiaries (one at the global level and one in the USA) for shared services functions. The main country subsidiaries are planned in Switzerland for its Swiss business, in the USA

---

[7] More broadly, burden sharing for international banks, as part of a wider package of supervision and resolution of these banks by a world authority, could be organised at the global level (e.g. Schoenmaker, 2013; Eatwell, Gossé and Alexander, 2014), but that is currently not on the horizon of policymakers.

for all US activities, and in the UK as a hub for its European investment banking business (Credit Suisse, 2013).[8] This approach illustrates that while SPE is the preferred strategy, the planned legal
structure allows for MPE resolution at country level if needed. This
new legal structure thus reflects the political reality of international
banking.

It should be noted that the MPE approach with a segmented banking system is more expensive than the cooperative SPE approach with
an integrated banking system (see also Bolton and Oehmke, 2016;
Faia and Weder di Mauro, 2016). On the funding front, capital
and liquidity are trapped at the national level and cannot be freely
used within the group, which leads to higher overall holdings of
capital and liquidity (Cerutti et al., 2010). TLAC also needs to be
pre-positioned for 75–90 per cent at the national subsidiaries (see
Section 13.3). On the resolution front, SPE allows for the less costly
cooperation approach in resolution, whereby potential bail-out costs
for capital shortfalls are shared among the countries according to the
burden sharing key. By contrast, MPE forces separate resolutions. On
the operational front, a bank with an MPE resolution strategy needs
to establish a separate subsidiary for shared services to guarantee
continued services to the surviving subsidiaries.

13.5 Policy Implications and Conclusions

Much has been done to strengthen the stability of the banking system.
Nevertheless, international financial stability remains elusive. National
authorities have a natural tendency to focus on their national self-
interest, which makes it difficult to supervise and resolve international
banks in a joint spirit. Cooperation based on soft law may break
down at times of crisis, as witnessed during the Great Financial Crisis.
Nevertheless, this is still the prevailing governance approach (e.g.
Crisis Management Groups based on Memoranda of Understanding)
adopted by the Financial Stability Board (Riles, 2014; Davies, 2015).

---

[8] Credit Suisse opened a Dublin branch of Credit Suisse AG in 2016 (Credit Suisse
Annual Report 2016). It is not clear yet what the impact of Brexit is on the UK
passport and where Credit Suisse will move its European passport business; the
Asia Pacific business of Credit Suisse is relocated from the UK entity (Credit
Suisse International) to a new Singapore branch of Credit Suisse AG.

Hard law, underpinned by a binding burden sharing agreement, is needed to ensure cooperation between national authorities and can thus provide a stable basis for international banking. The euro area is in the process of building a fiscal backstop for the Banking Union. The ESM, which is based on burden sharing, would then become available for direct recapitalisation of banks and function as a backstop to a Single Resolution and Deposit Insurance Fund.

If the euro area were to establish such a fiscal backstop, it would be able to absorb banking shocks at the euro area level and thus enhance financial stability. The euro area would also come to par with the USA, China and Japan, which are the only countries left with the fiscal capacity to support large global banks (operating on an SPE resolution model). The cooperative SPE model with an integrated banking system is more cost-efficient than the MPE model with a segmented banking system. We would thus move to a multipolar system with three to four key centres. The remaining medium-sized countries, such as the UK and Switzerland, would then play a secondary role in international banking (with multinational banks operating on an MPE model).

References

Anginer, A., E. Cerutti and M. Martinez Peria (2017), 'Foreign Bank Subsidiaries Default Risk during the Global Crisis: What Factors Help Insulate Affiliates from their Parents?', *Journal of Financial Intermediation*, 29(C), pp. 19–31.

Avgouleas, E. and C. Goodhart (2015), 'Critical Reflections on Bank Bail-ins', *Journal of Financial Regulation*, 1, pp. 3–29.

Bolton, P. and M. Oehmke (2016), *Bank Resolution and the Structure of Global Banks*, Working Paper, Princeton, NJ: Princeton University.

Cerutti, E., A. Ilyina, Y. Makarova and C. Schmieder (2010), 'Bankers without Borders? Implications of Ring-Fencing for European Cross-Border Banks', in P. Backé, E. Gnan and P. Hartmann (eds.), *Contagion and Spillovers: New Insights from the Crisis*, SUERF Study 2010/5, Vienna.

Chan, S. and S. van Wijnbergen (2015), 'Cocos, Contagion and Systemic Risk', CEPR Discussion Paper No. 10960.

Credit Suisse (2013), 'Credit Suisse Group Announces Plan to Evolve Its Legal Entity Structure', Press Release, 23 November, Zurich.

Davies, P. (2015), 'Resolution of Cross-Border Groups', in M. Haentjes and B. Wessels (eds.), *Research Handbook on Crisis Management in the Banking Sector*. Edward Elgar, Cheltenham, pp. 261–82.

Demirgüç-Kunt, A. and H. Huizinga (2013), 'Are Banks Too Big to Fail or Too Big to Save? International Evidence from Equity Prices and CDS spreads', *Journal of Banking & Finance*, 37, pp. 875–94.

Dermine, J. and D. Schoenmaker (2010), 'In Banking, Is Small Beautiful?', *Financial Markets, Institutions & Instruments*, 19, pp. 1–19.

Dewatripont, M. (2014), 'European Banking: Bailout, Bail-in and State Aid Control', *International Journal of Industrial Organization*, 34, pp. 37–43.

Eatwell, J., J.B. Gossé and K. Alexander (2014), 'Financial Markets and International Regulation', in J. Eatwell, T. McKinley and P. Petit (eds.), *Challenges for Europe in the World, 2030*, Abingdon: Routledge, pp. 105–37.

ESM (2014), 'FAQ on the ESM Direct Recapitalisation Instrument', Luxembourg: European Stability Mechanism, December.

Faia, E. and B. Weder di Mauro (2016), 'Cross-Border Resolution of Global Banks: Bail in under Single Point of Entry versus Multiple Points of Entry', CEPR Discussion Paper No. 11171.

Federal Deposit Insurance Corporation and the Bank of England (2012), 'Resolving Globally Active, Systemically Important, Financial Institutions: A joint paper by the Federal Deposit Insurance Corporation and the Bank of England', Washington, DC and London.

Fernández de Lis, S. (2015), 'The Multiple-Point-of-Entry Resolution Strategy for Global Banks', blog, International Banker, 25 February.

Financial Stability Board (2014), Key Attributes of Effective Resolution Regimes for Financial Institutions, Basel.

(2015), Principles on Loss-absorbing and Recapitalisation Capacity of G-SIBs in Resolution: Total Loss-absorbing Capacity (TLAC) Term Sheet, Basel.

Freshfields Bruckhaus Deringer (2003), *Study on Financial Conglomerates and Legal Firewalls*, London: Freshfields Bruckhaus Deringer.

Goodhart, C. (1998), 'The Two Concepts of Money: Implications for the Analysis of Optimal Currency Areas', *European Journal of Political Economy*, 14, 407–32.

(2014), 'Bank Resolution in Comparative Perspective: What Lessons for Euorpe?', in C. Goodhart, D. Gabor, J. Vestergaard and I. Ertürk (eds.), *Central Banking at a Crossroads: Europe and Beyond*, London: Anthem Press, pp. 97–107.

Goodhart, C. and D. Schoenmaker (2009), 'Fiscal Burden Sharing in Cross-Border Banking Crises', *International Journal of Central Banking*, 5, pp. 141–65.

(2016), 'The Global Investment Banks Are Now All Becoming American: Does that Matter for Europeans?', *Journal of Financial Regulation*, 2, pp. 163–81.

Goyal, R., P. Koeva-Brooks, M. Pradhan et al. (2013), 'A Banking Union for the Euro Area', IMF Staff Discussion Note 13/01, Washington, DC.

Gros, D. and A. Belke (2015), *Banking Union as a Shock Absorber: Lessons for the Eurozone from the US*, Centre for European Policy Studies (CEPS), Brussels.

Gros, D. and D. Schoenmaker (2014), 'European Deposit Insurance and Resolution in the Banking Union', *Journal of Common Market Studies*, 52, pp. 529–46.

Herring, R. (2007), 'Conflicts between Home and Host Country Prudential Supervisors', in D. Evanoff, J.R. LaBrosse and G. Kaufman (eds.), *International Financial Instability: Global Banking and National Regulation*, Singapore: World Scientific, 201–20.

Huertas, T. (2009), 'The Rationale for and Limits of Bank Supervision', Paper presented at the Financial Markets Group conference 'Regulatory Response to the Financial Crisis' at the London School of Economics on 19 January 2009, London.

Hüttl, P. and D. Schoenmaker (2016), 'Fiscal Capacity to Support Large Banks', Policy Contribution 2016/17, Bruegel.

Kose, A., E. Prasad, K. Rogoff and S.J. Wei (2009), Financial Globalization: A Reappraisal, *IMF Staff Papers*, 56, pp. 8–62.

Laeven, L. and F. Valencia (2013), 'Systemic Banking Crises Database', *IMF Economic Review*, 61, pp. 225–70.

Langfield, S. and M. Pagano (2016), 'Bank Bias in Europe: Effects on Systemic Risk and Growth', *Economic Policy*, 31, pp. 51–106.

Liikanen Report (2012), High-level Expert Group on Reforming the Structure of the EU Banking Sector, Final Report, Brussels.

Mayes, D. (2014), 'Bank Resolution in New Zealand', in C. Goodhart, D. Gabor, J. Vestergaard and I. Ertürk (eds.), *Central Banking at a Crossroads: Europe and Beyond*, London: Anthem Press, pp. 123–39.

Pauly, L. (2014), 'Governing Global Risks: The Evolution of Policy Capacity in the Financial Sector', *WZB Discussion Paper*, Berlin: Wissenschaftszentrum Berlin.

Riles, A. (2014), 'Is New Governance the Ideal Architecture for Global Financial Regulation?', in C. Goodhart, D. Gabor, J. Vestergaard and I. Ertürk (eds.), *Central Banking at a Crossroads: Europe and Beyond*, London: Anthem Press, pp. 245–63.

Rodrik, D. (2011), *The Globalization Paradox: Democracy and the Future of the World Economy*, New York, NY: Norton.

Schoenmaker, D. (2011), 'The Financial Trilemma', *Economics Letters*,
     111, pp. 57–9.
     (2013), *Governance of International Banking: The Financial Trilemma*,
     New York, NY: Oxford University Press.
     (2015), 'On the Need for a Fiscal Backstop to the Banking System', in
     M. Haentjes and B. Wessels (eds.), *Research Handbook on Crisis
     Management in the Banking Sector*, Cheltenham: Edward Elgar,
     pp. 42–54.
Schoenmaker, D. and N. Véron (2016), *European Banking Supervision:
     The First Eighteen Months*, Blueprint 25, Brussels: Bruegel.
Véron, N. (2015), *Europe's Radical Banking Union*, Essay & Lecture
     Series, Bruegel.

PART III

Foreign Exchanges and International Architecture

14 | *The Case for (and Requirements of) Monetary Unions*

CHARLES WYPLOSZ

14.1 Introduction

The euro has always been seen as a bold experiment. Its creation went against the view, largely backed by history, that money and statehood are the two sides of the same coin. To that effect, much thought has gone into preparing the rules of the game. More than a decade and a half later, the same old doubts keep creeping in. The massive sovereign debt crisis can be seen as showing that the euro experiment is failing. This view notes that there should not have been a debt crisis in the first place – no other advanced country has seen one – and that it has been mismanaged. Another view is that the euro has survived and that corrective measures have been promptly adopted. Even if these measures are insufficient and incomplete, possibly even misguided in some instances, there is no indication that the experiment is fatally flawed.

These debates are not about to disappear any time soon. While all the relevant arguments have been presented in countless contributions, it may be interesting to confront them with fundamental principles. This chapter goes back to basics, monetary theory, with a twist inspired by Goodhart (1998). This all too often forgotten contribution reminds us that the fundamental characteristics of money remain unsettled. Its focus on the relationship between money, in all its forms, and statehood has direct implications for the eurozone architecture. In order to explore these implications, the chapter starts with the various interpretations of the eurozone crisis. It then examines what monetary theories tell us about monetary unions. A message is that the common currency cannot just consist of sharing a central bank. For the currency to safely operate, a great many requirements need to be fulfilled. After a reminder that there is a strong case for the euro, the chapter goes on to ask whether these requirements can be met without moving to a complete federal state in Europe, which is currently ruled out. The message is that it is possible to do so, but that political opposition is formidable.

14.2 Why Did the Eurozone Crisis Occur? Four Interpretations

Long in the making, the European monetary union had been thought through rather carefully. Its crisis is one of these rare tests that economists dare to wish for. Many interpretations, not mutually exclusive, have surfaced.

First is the observation that the Eurozone is not an Optimum Currency Area (OCA). The criteria set for admission to the eurozone essentially ignored the OCA principles. Some, like Chancellor Merkel,[1] have argued that Greece should never have been let in, while others claim that adequate instruments could and should have been built in to buttress the non-OCA eurozone.

Second, Greece and others have indulged in never-ending – in fact, increasing – budget deficits, which translated into external deficits. Both were unsustainable and eventually could not be sustained. Fiscal discipline had been recognised as a necessary condition of a successful monetary union but, for a variety of mostly controversial reasons, the Stability and Growth Pact has repeatedly failed to deliver.

Third, a common currency requires what has come to be called a banking union. Shunning this necessary condition laid the ground for a major crisis which saw some banks fail. This was more likely to happen in the absence of a common regulator, a common supervisor and a common resolution authority. Once it happened, there would be a scramble to bottle in the costs of bank rescue within the country of origin. With individual countries unable to print money, this would create a 'doom-loop' between banks and government that would transform bank crisis into a debt crisis. In order to break the loop, a monetary union needs a bank resolution fund, or an agreement for lending in the last resort by the central bank, or both. None of that was available and doom-loops developed.

---

[1] *Independent*, 28 August 2013, available at www.independent.co.uk/news/business/news/angela-merkel-says-greece-should-never-have-been-allowed-to-join-the-euro-8788435.html.

Finally, many critics noted that a monetary union cannot last for long without a fiscal union.[2] In the absence of national monetary policies, a monetary union that is not an OCA exposes member countries to heavy adjustment costs in the presence of asymmetric shocks. With rigid prices, inter-country transfers are the only way of avoiding these costs. One way or another, transfers call for a collective budget financed by collective taxes.

Following the eurozone crisis, the Stability and Growth Pact was reinforced and a banking union, so far incomplete, was set up. The eurozone has also proved to be less of a non-OCA with quite some wage and price flexibility – under duress – and labour mobility has been more extensive than hitherto believed. The need for a fiscal union remains hotly debated.

14.3 What Does Monetary Theory Tell Us?

Many of the ongoing debates, including the need for a fiscal union, invoke monetary theory principles. This is the case of the four interpretations outlined above. The OCA theory is based on the link between money and the price level. A common central bank determines the evolution of the relevant monetary aggregates. The money supply, in turn, determines the aggregate, or average price level in the monetary union. Because price stability is the first objective of a well-behaved central bank, its independence is an essential requirement. This independence must be guaranteed by the national governments of member countries. In particular, the central bank must be free of any pressure to finance national public deficits and debts. Conversely, beyond establishing the common currency as the legal tender of the union, national governments must not be called upon to support its functioning. This separation of governments and the central bank is possible because a fiat currency can exist on the basis of its own merits – chiefly price stability – and its convenience as a medium of exchange, a unit of account and and store of value.

---

[2] For instance, Bordo (2010, p. 4) states that 'if the member states are unwilling to give up fiscal authority to the central EU government and to accept the inevitability that membership in an effective monetary/fiscal union requires adherence to credible eurozone wide fiscal rules such as no bailouts and budget balance over the business cycle, then the euro experiment is doomed to failure'.

Separation could be an illusion, however. Reviving an ancient controversy, Goodhart (1998) contrasts the M-form theory of money (M for metallists) with a C-form (C for cartalists). The M-theory lies behind the reasoning above. It asserts that the value of money lies in its value, intrinsic when it is metallic, backed by the assets of the central bank when it is of the fiat variety, and in its ready adoption by the market as an efficient way of carrying out transactions. The C-theory considers instead that the value of money comes from an act of government that coerces people to use its money, in particular to pay taxes, by declaring it the sole legal tender. At the risk of oversimplification, the crucial point is that the M-theory can easily envision a stateless currency while the C-theory insists that a state is needed.

If, as Goodhart (1998) argues, the C-theory is the correct one because it is the only one that can account for the very long history of money, then those who claim that the euro cannot exist without a fiscal union are right. Indeed, from the vantage point of the C-theory, under current arrangements the euro's fate is precarious because it is a federal arrangement operating in a non-federal space. True, member states have agreed to make it the sole tender, and therefore to collect taxes in euros. In addition, the European Central Bank (ECB) management is subject to oversight by the (federal) European Parliament. But these are weak attributes. Taxes are collected at the national level and the arrangements can be called into question by member states.[3] The European Parliament has little power over the ECB because it has no instrument to bring it to yield on anything of substance. The central bank's independence, which is necessary as noted above, effectively breaks the link with its governments, but at the cost of making it vulnerable to political winds.

Furthermore, OCA theory is incompatible with C-theory. The OCA theory is entirely predicated on the M-theory, according to which a currency exists because it is useful and it survives because its central bank is committed to ensuring its usefulness (stable prices, seamless transfer payments, nearly impossible forfeiting, etc.).

---

[3] The standard counterargument is that the governments are tied by an international treaty most unlikely to be changed to please any member country. This argument has been considerably weakened recently. One needs hardly mention the very real threat of a Grexit, Brexit and the challenges to the federal ECB posed by recurrent recourse to the German Constitutional Court, to see that.

How far should this reasoning be pushed? Although the array of historical evidence presented by Goodhart is compelling, formally testing M-theory versus C-theory remains to be done and could well be impossible. In addition, it is unclear whether these are incompatible views. The M-theory rightly emphasises that the demand for money rests on its acceptability by users, while the C-theory invokes the institutions that underpin and encourage its adoption. Indeed, it is well understood – and has been for a long time – that the OCA theory misses out on institutional characteristics.[4]

14.4 The Daunting Requirements of a Monetary Union

The eurozone crisis has shown the limits of its construction.[5] It was carefully crafted as far as the M-theory is concerned: It rests on an independent central bank with a precise mandate (aggregate price stability), a powerful clearing system and the explicit recognition that fiscal discipline is necessary. It missed out on the institutions, and the reasons are those emphasised by the C-theory:

- The Stability and Growth Pact did not deliver fiscal discipline because it failed to square the circle of imposing fiscal rules on fiscally sovereign states.
- The need for a Banking Union was purposefully ignored because it would have required pooling risks across member states and therefore across national taxpayers. This need remains unfulfilled.
- The ECB is not as independent as intended because it remains *de facto* controlled by national representatives who care about domestic issues and do not share a common understanding of central banking.
- It carefully segments money and public indebtedness, because money is federal and debts are national. This rules out lending in the last resort and effective debt relief.
- More generally, it has no crisis management procedure. When banking systems tanked and sovereigns lost market access, solutions had to be imagined on the go under improvised management.

---

[4] This is why, in a textbook presentation, Baldwin and Wyplosz (2004) augment the three classic OCA economic criteria with three additional political/institutional criteria: fiscal transfers, homogeneous preferences and commonality of destiny.

[5] A presentation of the eurozone's flaws is in Wyplosz (2016).

The accompanying tensions are perfectly in line with the following quote:

It can be optimal for a sovereign country to pre-commit to a regime which will ensure price stability but only if it retains its ability to utilize its independent money creation powers in a crisis.

Footnote: One useful and illuminating way of thinking about EMU is to regard this as the monetary symbol of a political pact between the two largest countries of Northern Europe, Germany and France, that there cannot and must not ever in the future be a serious crisis, let alone a war, in their bilateral relationship. (Goodhart, 1998, p. 422)

Although the euro has survived intact (so far) following its first massive challenge, this does not mean that there will be no further challenges, or that the construction is robust enough to meet all possible challenges. It took less than ten years for the hidden cracks to be revealed and, eight years later, controversies still rage while most cracks are unattended to. It is true that the list of flaws is daunting. They all revolve around the delimitation of national sovereignty, including determining what taxpayers of a given country should be liable for.

14.5 The Case for the Euro

At this stage, it may be tempting to conclude, as many do, that the euro is a failure (Feldstein, 2012). Looking at the costs and requirements of a monetary union is indeed intimidating. A key methodological merit of OCA theory is to put the issue in the framework of costs and benefits. The costs are plain to see, but the benefits are often just mentioned in passing, like an oratory precaution, if only because they are diffuse. Yet, they are very real and significant.

First, exchange rate stability matters when countries are deeply integrated in trade. How much it matters for trade is a matter of some dispute. The initial results of Rose (2000) have been scaled back somehow (Rose, 2016) but even critics have found that the single currency has made it possible for new firms, mostly medium and small ones, to engage in trade (Baldwin and Di Nino, 2006).

Second, exchange rate stability matters when countries are deeply integrated in finance. Much of the literature of the last decade on international macroeconomics has focused on capital flow instability and exchange rate volatility. The Washington Consensus asserted that countries should either let their currencies float freely or rigidly fix them. However, Rey (2013) has shown that free floats do not provide the expected monetary policy independence. Giving up its currency is not the sacrifice that it is supposed to be.

Third and following on from the previous point, giving up the exchange rate can be helpful when financial crises occur. Indeed, a lesson of the euro crisis is that the contagion did not provoke the kind of dislocation that deep exchange rate fluctuations create, as comparisons with South East Asia or Latin American readily suggest. What did not happen matters a lot.

Fourth, inflation has been tamed. Since 1945, it has never been so low in the eurozone countries, even in Germany. Inflation has been tamed in all developed countries and many emerging market countries as well, largely because central banks have been made independent and monetary policy has been redesigned. Yet, given how national politics and institutions operate in some eurozone countries (as shown by fiscal indiscipline), it is unlikely that the record would have been as impressive without the common currency.

Fifth, for all its imperfections, the Stability and Growth Pact is acting as a counterweight to many countries' tendency to treat fiscal discipline as an issue for tomorrow. The post-2009 austerity policies have been procyclical and they are largely responsible for the eurozone's lost decade, but the message that fiscal discipline matters is slowly percolating everywhere.

14.6 A Federal State or Better Institutions?

The key assertion of the C-theory of money and of critics of the Eurozone – most of whom are M-theorists – is that a common currency cannot work without a fiscal union. The C-theory argues that money must be underpinned by the power of the state and its institutions. The Eurozone is not a state and its institutions are weak. The C-theory also holds that history has shown that currencies come and go as states do. The critics rely on the same argument: that it has never been the case that independent states have successfully established a common currency.[6] Holding that something that did not exist previously cannot exist in the future cannot be generally true, however.

---

[6] As Rose (2000) notes, this is untrue. He provides a long list of lasting currency unions. Most of them bring together small, often very small, states. The African monetary unions do not fit well that description.

While it is undoubtedly the case that a fiscal union would immensely help the eurozone, the fact is that it is not going to happen any time soon. The question must be approached differently. In the spirit that choices are made under constraints, the question is whether it is possible to make the eurozone sturdy enough without going all the way to a fiscal union. Put differently, can its institutions be adjusted adequately enough to make the euro a safe and lasting currency? The answer is positive at the technical level. The requirements listed above can be met as follows.

14.6.1 Fiscal Discipline

The challenge is to ascertain that all member states lastingly achieve debt sustainability[7] while recognising that they remain sovereign in budgetary matters. The answer is to combine two measures. First, decentralise the task to the national level. This has been agreed in the 2012 Treaty on Stability, Coordination and Governance (aka the Fiscal Compact) but diversely applied in terms of obligations and monitoring. Countries that fail in this respect should be taken to the European Court of Justice (success may require tightening the admittedly vague language of the treaty). Second, reinstate the no-bail-out clause. This clause having been violated during the eurozone crisis, its restoration may be challenging. These two measures are mutually reinforcing.

14.6.2 Banking Union

The Banking Union clearly needs to be completed. All banks must be supervised by the ECB and bank resolution requires an adequate fund. Many proposals have been advanced (e.g. Goodhart and Schoenmaker, 2014).

14.6.3 Independence of the ECB

The travails of the ECB are a reminder of the early years of the US Federal Reserve when the regional governors were defending regional interests. The adopted solution is a blueprint for the eurozone. This would require a new treaty whereby member countries would give up the right to be represented on the Governing Council. Obviously, such a step is politically challenging.

---

[7] Defining debt sustainability is a complex issue which is ignored here.

Currently, the Executive Board prepares the policy decisions. Nothing requires that the Governing Council meets monthly or, as will be the case, eight times a year. Making these meetings less frequent would reinforce the Executive Board, but such a decision would have to be approved by the Governing Council, another unlikely step. In addition, the custom is that the large countries each have a seat on the Executive Board, which is the backdoor channel for national influence. Appointing Executive Board members solely on the basis of competence would go some way towards improving the situation.

14.6.4 Lending in the Last Resort

Nothing prevents the ECB from lending in the last resort to both banks and governments (in the latter case by buying bonds from the market). As noted, resistance to burden sharing has greatly hampered the ECB during the crisis, even though the Outright Monetary Transactions (OMT) programme and quantitative easing (QE) represent a step in this direction.

Regarding banks, the European Stability Mechanism (ESM) is now able to deal with failing banks, but its interventions are too severely restricted for speedy action. Transforming the ESM into a bank resolution fund, with fast-track authority, would both permit to complete the Banking Union and make it possible for the ECB to obtain a guarantee as it lends in the last resort. The fact that potential losses by the ESM are national liabilities creates the risk of a doom-loop between banks and state losses.

Regarding public debts, even though it was long in coming, the OMT programme has brought an end to the acute phase of the eurozone crisis. QE has definitely put it to rest, but temporarily so since it stands to be reversed, partially at least. The fact that the European Court of Justice has deemed both actions as legally valid is important. It remains that OMT support is conditional on a country being in an ESM programme. Removing this hurdle would go a long way towards making the ECB a 'normal' central bank that can backstop public debts.

14.6.5 Crisis Management

Germany has emerged as the *de facto* manager of the eurozone crisis. It filled a vacuum in the governance structure. This vacuum reflects the fact that there is no 'European government'. It has led to the creation of a new post, the President of the European Council, but this president is a facilitator, not a decision maker. Clearly, member states are unwilling to transfer sovereignty. Under extreme pressure, they allowed Germany to lead, but informally.

The only practical solution is to reduce the risk of crisis and to establish procedures to deal with crises. This is the aim of the proposals above. They amount to merely delegating to the ECB powers that normal central banks have, but new difficulties loom. Being powerful enough to overcome opposition from some member states, however, puts the ECB in a difficult situation. It is bound to reinforce efforts to indirectly control it through the politicisation of its management. It will also create opposition by governments that can threaten its *de jure* independence and bolster resentment towards the common currency.

14.7 Conclusion

The euro is not a currency like others. Plainly, the single currency lacks a single government. As a result, its institutions are weak and incomplete. One solution is to deepen integration on the way to the creation of a European government. A fiscal union would be a decisive step. Another solution is to opt for modest sovereignty transfers of the kind outlined above, creating limited common (explicit and implicit) liabilities. If such a more modest evolution proves to be politically impossible, its continuous survival is in doubt. More crises may lead to more steps, but they also raise the odds of a breakup of sorts.

These limits were not recognised when the euro was created. The dominating 'muddling through' approach was that overlooked problems would be recognised as they appeared and that solutions would be found. In a way, this is what happened. Most of the solutions, however, were timid and the problems are not yet fully acknowledged at the political level. For the foreseeable future, the most likely course of events is more muddling through, with the attendant difficulties:

This divorce between monetary (federal) centralisation and governmental decentralisation at the level of the nation state, especially with the main fiscal functions remaining at that lower, national level is the source of potential tensions. Goodhart (1998, p. 424)

References

Baldwin, R.E. and V. Di Nino (2006), 'Euros and Zeros', NBER Working Paper No. 12673.

Baldwin, R.E. and C. Wyplosz (2004), *The Economics of European Integration*, New York, NY: McGraw Hill.

Bordo, M.D. (2010), 'The Euro Needs a Fiscal Union: Some Lessons from History', Shadow Open Market Committee.

Feldstein, M. (2012), 'The Failure of the Euro', *Foreign Affairs*.

Goodhart, C. (1998), 'The Two Concepts of Money: Implications for the Analysis of Optimum Currency Areas', *European Journal of Political Economy*, 14, pp. 407–32.

Goodhart, C. and D. Schoenmaker (2014), 'The ECB as a Lender of Last Resort', *VoxEU*.

Rey, H. (2013), 'Dilemma Not Trilemma: The Global Financial Cycle and Monetary Policy Independence', *Jackson Hole Conference Proceedings*, Kansas City Fed.

Rose, A.K. (2000), 'One Money, One Market: Estimating the Effect of Common Currencies on Trade', *Economic Policy*, 30, pp. 7–38.

(2016), 'Why Do Estimates of the EMU Effect On Trade Vary so Much?', CEPR Discussion Paper No. 11532.

Wyplosz, C. (2016), 'The Six Flaws of the Eurozone', *Economic Policy*, 31(87), pp. 559–603.

15 | *Machines versus Humans*

Will Human Forex Dealers Become Extinct?

TAKATOSHI ITO

15.1 Introduction

The interbank foreign exchange (forex) market evolved from decentralised markets with human dealers and human brokers to a centralised market with EBS or Reuters electronic broking computers matching buy/sell orders from many human dealers. Now in the last ten years, human dealers have been overwhelmed, at least in quote volumes. Increasingly, algorithmic programs housed in the computers of banks and other financial institutions, co-located with the EBS computer, are trading by themselves.

In the old system before the electronic broking system matched large number of quotes and trades, the exchange rate could be different for different banks, for different locations and for different sizes of orders. After the interbank trades at the EBS and Reuters were established as main electronic broking systems, market transparency increased. The same price applies to a vast majority of banks which participate in the market. Banks and customers would be assured that they would be trading at the best (ask or bid) price.

When bank computers started to be directly connected, at least three kinds of changes were generally expected. First, the speed of

Research support by JSPS Grants-in-aid for Scientific Research (in Japan), No. A-25245044 and A-17H00995 is gratefully acknowledged. I am indebted to Charles Goodhart for my interest and exposure to research using high-frequency trading data. In 1992–3, Charles and I were teaching central banking in Harvard as both of us were visiting professors. He asked me to analyse together a video tape of an electronic trading screen for twenty-four hours. We did not have research assistants at Harvard. We employed our wives to transcribe the data from the video screen to paper and then to a spreadsheet. We are indebted to our families for the first high-frequency trading paper. Part of this paper was presented in my lecture at the Asia-Pacific Econophysics conference (Ito, 2016).

price discovery upon arrival of news to the market would increase. Second, the frequency and duration of anomaly, such as negative spread and violation to parity conditions, would decrease. Third, liquidity in the market would increase.

However, these predictions of the changes in market performance – transparency, price discovery, anomaly, and liquidity – are more hypotheses than certainty. Rigorous testing is needed to prove whether predictions are correct. Rigorous testing needs a good data set. Fortunately, concentration of trades to electronic broking systems meant that relevant data that were available to bank dealers in real time became available to researchers as data sets. The data include 'firm quotes', as opposed to 'indicative quotes', and actual trading prices and volumes. The frequency of data can be tick-by-tick or aggregated to one second (or less).

In the 2010s, a period when the significance of human dealers in the interbank forex market has been marginalised by algorithm trading and electronic broking systems dominate the matching services, different changes have been occurring and the past trend is now partially being reversed. Electronic broking systems are challenged by large banks creating their own matching systems for their own customers. Some of the benefits of high-frequency trading are now being questioned. A trend towards ever faster matching services with finer trading price units (sub-dividing pips) has been partially reversed. Algorithm trading can emit noises, and protecting human brokers from extinction may have social benefits.

The rest of the paper is organised as follows. Section 15.2 discusses the evolutionary changes of the forex markets from the 1980s to the present. Section 15.3 discusses the aspect of transparency. The benefits of transparency that come with electronic broking systems seem unquestionable. However, a fixing scandal of 2013 reminded us that transparency alone would not prevent collusion among large banks to exert influences on the price in their favour. Section 15.4 surveys the literature that discusses the process of price discovery and anomaly. Section 15.5 discusses issues that pose challenges to the foreign exchange markets due to proliferation of machines. Section 15.6 concludes with prospects of further changes in the market microstructure.

15.2 Evolution of the Foreign Exchange Markets

15.2.1 Emergence of Electronic Broking Systems

In the old system, say, until the end of the 1980s, human brokers were constantly announcing the bid–ask quotes to bank dealers through squawk boxes. Human dealers in banks received customer orders and added or subtracted their own positions for execution in the interbank market, trading directly with other dealers of different banks (direct dealing) or trading through human brokers. It was more art than science to judge when and how much to buy or sell. Although human dealers were asked by the management to control risk and square the position before the end of each trading day, they held proprietary positions.

In the early 1990s, computer systems were developed to perform a broker function. Bank dealers saw rates on the computer screen and played either market-makers (posting 'firm' quotes) or market-takers (hitting posted quotes). Orders were matched by the matching computer that received orders from human dealers. EBS, Reuters-2000 and MINEX were representative order-matching system. In 1996, the MINEX was merged with EBS. When these order-matching computers were in an early stage, human brokers and direct dealing (transaction between a dealer and a dealer) coexisted. It was said that electronic broking computers were used for small-lot trading, while human brokers were used for a large-lot trading as brokers provided services to break up a large-lot trade into several small-lot trades for smooth execution.

Matching computers evolved quickly. By the early 2000s, human brokers were all but extinct. The global interbank spot foreign exchange market is dominated by two matching service computer systems: EBS and Reuters-3000. The EBS has a stronger service in markets of currency pairs involving the US dollar (USD), the Japanese yen (JPY) and the euro (EUR); and Reuters is stronger in markets of currency pairs involving British pounds (GBP), the Commonwealth currencies and the central European currencies.

15.2.2 The EBS System

The EBS matching order system matches the buy and sell quotes from banks as follows. A market-making bank submits a 'firm quote' of buy (bid) or sell (ask) to the system. The firm quotes are posted on the system and screens of all participating banks in aggregate numbers for each price quote. Another bank that monitors the market can submit a market-taking order trying to 'hit' the posted quote. A seller who finds the bid to be attractive orders a sell at the posted bid-quote. If the quotes are taken by others or cancelled by the market-maker before the order gets to the matching computer, a sell order by a market-taker will not be fulfilled and will be voided as a market-taking order.

The 'firm' quote means that if they are 'hit' by the matching order, it has to be executed. One important caveat is the existence of credit lines. A market-maker and market-taker will not be matched if they do not have a credit line between them. A participating bank has to have a certain number of banks agreed to trade with it by having contracts of credit lines. Within the daily credit lines, the EBS system matches orders. Hence, a bank's monitor shows the best bid and ask for the market, and the tradable best bid and ask for that bank. This is not a constraint for the global large banks as they have sufficient credit lines among themselves.

Most of the time, the bid–ask spread remains stable, as many banks participate in the market. The ask-side quote being hit by a buyer represents a buying pressure. If the buyer's volume of orders is less than the aggregate volume of firm ask quotes at the best ask price, the best ask will not change after the transactions. One of the definitions of a liquid market is that the price would not change when a reasonable number of trades occur. When the market is liquid and the trades occur at best ask and best bids, then the transaction prices bounce between the best ask and best bid. This is known as the bid–ask bounce and is often the source of negative correlation in the transaction price series.

However, the negative correlation as a result of a bid–ask bounce should not be taken as significant evidence for the predictability of price movements, which would refute the hypothesis of the exchange rate movement as a Brownian motion (or a random walk).

If the sum of volumes of market-taker buy orders exceeds the volumes at the best ask, then some of market-taking buy orders are left unfulfilled, and the best ask price will move up. This corresponds to a casual observation that a strong buying pressure will raise the price. When the best ask or best bid starts to move, the firm quotes tend to adjust. The interaction of actual transaction and firm bid–ask quotes presents a ground for formulating various international finance hypotheses.

15.2.3 Direct Connection (Ai) and Co-location

In May 2004, EBS started to allow direction connections of trading bank computers to the EBS matching computer. This is known as 'Spot Ai' in the EBS system. The number of bank computers that are directly connected to EBS increased sharply from 2004 to the mid-2010s.

In July 2005, the EBS Spot Ai (a direct connection to the EBS matching computer) was open to the Professional Trading Community (PTC), which includes currency overlay companies and hedge funds. Almost all members of the PTC use algorithm programs.

The EBS has three matching computers in the world: in Tokyo, London and New York. The three computers are linked to each other. However, each matching computer can match orders when the posted firm quote is hit by a market-taker from any location in the world.

The direct lines from the banks' computers to the EBS matching computer made it possible for banks to develop automated programs for market-making and -taking quotes. Market data (past and current quotes and trades) are fed to bank computers and algorithm in the bank computers recalculate and react to new information. The faster the reaction, the higher the chances of executing orders at better prices. Whether market-taking orders are fulfilled or voided depends on a first-come-first-served basis at the EBS computer. Banks attempt to locate their computers closer to the EBS matching computer. A Singaporean bank would locate a computer with algorithm not in Singapore but in Tokyo. A French bank would locate the computer in London, and a San Francisco bank would locate the computer in New York – not only in the same city, but as close as possible. Hence, the banks started to put computers in a room next to the EBS matching computer. This is called 'co-location'.

15.2.4 Decimalisation

The trading price unit has been called a 'pip'. In the case of the USD/JPY market, a pip is '0.01' JPY per USD. It was a market custom for decades to quote a bid–ask using the unit of a pip. For example, the bid–ask of '101.01–.02' represents the narrowest bid–ask spread.

This tradition changed in the EBS system in 2010–11, when it introduced 'decimalisation'; that is, the minimum price unit was subdivided by ten. For USD/JPY, the decimalised pip meant the minimum price unit became '0.001' JPY per USD. The narrowest bid–ask spread, for example, is '101.010–.011' JPY per USD.

On 30 August 2010, decimalisation was introduced for currency pairs involving the Australian dollar (AUD), the New Zealand dollar (NZD) and some of GBP and Swiss franc (CHF) trades, such as GBP/CHF, GBP/JPY and CHF/JPY. On 11 October 2010, decimalisation was introduced to the US dollar/Canadian dollar (USD/CAD), GBP/USD and the euro/British pound (EUR/GBP) trades. On 7 March 2011, decimalisation was introduced to the EUR/USD, USD/JPY, USD/CHF, EUR/CHF and EUR/JPY. This completed the process of decimalisation for major currency pairs.

The purpose of introducing decimalisation was to offer trading opportunities to those who are willing to trade inside the best ask and bid. During the hours when many banks are participating (see Section 15.4.2), the bid–ask spread tends to remain on pip, suggesting that some participants may be willing to trade inside the pip. If this inference is correct, decimalisation can enhance efficiency and increase transaction volumes by increasing the number of deals. In addition, the EBS might have felt the decimalisation was a defensive move as some competing order matching systems with decimalised trading technology were emerging.

However, decimalisation was unpopular among human dealers. Rapidly changing decimalised quotes were beyond human capability. In particular, the machine is good at placing an order just inside the human's best bid–ask in order to 'steal' trades from humans. Moreover, the narrower bid–ask spread meant a lower profit per round-trip trades (for example, profits by a market-maker after a round-trip bid–ask bounce).

Following protest from human dealers, the EBS abandoned decimalised pips and modified to 'a half pip' unit. Namely, the USD/JPY price unit became '0.005' JPY per USD. For example, the minimum bid–ask spread became, for example, '101.010–.015' JPY per USD. In September 2012, all currencies except EUR/CHF were moved from the decimalised system to the half-pip basis, and EUR/CHF moved to the half-pip basis in November 2012. Thus, decimalisation lasted only for about two years.

15.2.5 *Prime Bank and Prime Customer*

As mentioned above, trades in the EBS system can be done only between banks with credit lines. This makes many smaller banks disadvantaged in executing trades. They may be able to buy and sell at prices far behind the best bid and ask. This adds significant spread costs which they may have to pass on to customers or absorb themselves.

The EBS introduced the Prime Bank (PB) and Prime Customer (PC) system in May 2004. A PB, presumably a large global bank, can sign a PC agreement with a smaller, primarily domestic bank. The PC bank can assume the name of the PB bank in the EBS system and trade at the best bid–ask. The PB bank collects a fee from PC banks for letting the credit line be used by PC banks. This significantly improved the market function for smaller banks. It predicts that the frequency of trades behind the best bid and ask will decrease, and that the frequency of anomaly, such as a negative bid–ask spread, will also decrease.

15.2.6 *Rise of the Machines*

The statistics of how much of the total quotes and deals are done by the machines are hard to obtain, since the EBS data set that is available for researchers for a fee does not have a label for humans or machines. Chaboud et al. (2014) had access to the data with the human/machine label and analysed the changes in the market microstructure from 2003 to 2007. The ratio of the total volume with at least one algorithmic counterparty rose from zero in 2003 to 80 per cent for JPY/EUR; 60 per cent for JPY/USD and 50 per cent for USD/EUR by the end of 2007 (Chaboud et al. (2014; Figure 1)). Even these data show only an early stage in the rise of the machine. As mentioned above, machines became a dominant force, both in quote activities and deal activities, after the decimalisation of 2010–11, although we do not have concrete statistics.

15.3 Transparency

15.3.1 *The Law of One Price and 'Firm' versus 'Indicative'*

In the old system without electronic broking systems, the exchange rate, say USD/JPY, at a particular moment (say GMT 00:00:00) could not be one price. Bank A might be quoting one price to Bank B, when Bank B called up Bank A for a direct dealing. Bank C might be offering another price to Bank B. A human broker, via a squawk box, might be quoting yet a different bid and ask from the direct dealing prices. The exchange rates in the Tokyo market (the inter-bank market in Tokyo among banks in Tokyo) might be different again from the exchange rates in Singapore, although a significant deviation that presented arbitrage opportunities was taken advantage of by a bank that called up another bank in another city. Remember that the direct overseas lines were still expensive.

Market conditions were transmitted as 'indicative quotes' voluntarily by banks on the Reuters FXFX screen. These quotes were for information only. Trades at the quotes are not guaranteed. These indicative quotes were the only source of high-frequency research.

One of the first papers to use 'firm quotes' (Goodhart, Ito and Payne, 1996) exploited an electronic broking system screen, Reuters D-2000-2, from one day in June 1993. The paper emphasised the value of having 'firm quotes' and 'trading volume and price', as opposed to indicative quotes.

In the mid-1990s, the EBS data set became available for an academic purpose. The advantages of the EBS data, as opposed to indicative quote data, were significant. The EBS data recorded not only firm quotes but quote volumes, cancellation (changes in the best ask and bid), and deal volumes and prices, none of which were available in the indicative quotes. Researchers were now able to see the actual market.

15.3.2 Fixing Scandal

The forex market has become very liquid and is considered to be very competitive. Large orders can be executed without much price impact most of the time. The electronic broking system has made the pricing transparent. This was conventional wisdom.

Hence, academic researchers reacted with considerable surprise when Bloomberg broke the news in June 2013 that dealers had exchanged customers' order information and had colluded to manipulate the 4 pm London fixing rate; and that the UK Financial Conduct Authority (FCA) imposed fines in November on five banks totalling GBP 1.1 billion (USD 1.7 billion) for failing to control business practices. 'Fixing' is a market practice whereby the market price at a particular time of day (4.00 pm

London; and 9:55 am in Tokyo) is applied to all customer orders accumulated prior to the fixing time. The two fixings have different regulations and institutions. The London fix is calculated as a median price during the one-minute window around 4:00 pm. We empirically examine the movement of prices around the time of fixing. Regulators in the UK and the USA have accused banks of collusive behaviours in manipulating the price around the London fixing time. It has been mentioned in the media that there was evidence of 'chats' among traders of different institutions for the purpose of collusion. But, is there evidence for this in the price behaviour? Ito and Yamada (2017, 2018) examined the price and volume behaviours around the Tokyo fixing time and the London fixing time. They found little evidence of volatile movement (or price spikes) in prices around the fixing time. In fact, liquidity provision at the fixing time is larger than at other times, which makes the price impact of any trade smaller. At the London fixing, they found a negative correlation between the price movement before the fixing window starts and the price movement after the fixing window ends. At the Tokyo fixing, however, each bank can announce its own price based on their transactions at around 9:55 am, which can be maintained for the rest of the day. Although the market provides deep liquidity at the Tokyo fixing as well, such financial institutions announced prices to be more favourable for banks up until 2008. The deviation of the bank's fixing price from the market price can be attributed to the interest rate differential. Also, the deviation of the fixing price from the market price, in favour of banks, may be related to the settlement needs of importers later in the day. Therefore, apparent puzzles in Tokyo may be largely solved, as Ito and Yamada (2017) argued.

15.4 Was Market Efficiency Improved?

15.4.1 Efficiency

The connection of the computers owned by banks and high-frequency traders to the EBS system fundamentally changed the microstructure of the foreign exchange market. First, as many dealers got connected, the market became more liquid most of the time. Second, the bid–ask spread became narrower. Third, the same price was quoted in the public domain worldwide. Fourth, with the emergence of anomaly in terms of the emergence of violation to arbitrage conditions becoming less frequent, once the violation emerged, the time to disappear became shorter. In sum, the computer connection (machines) made the forex market more efficient.

15.4.2 Intra-Day Seasonality

Ito and Hashimoto (2006) established an intra-day regularity in quote activities, the bid–ask spread and deal activities. They found that certain time windows, around the beginning of the Tokyo market, the beginning of the London market and the beginning of the New York market had surges in their quote and deal activities. Activities became significantly calmer during the Tokyo lunch hour and towards the late afternoon in the New York market. A significant surge in activities was most pronounced at 9:55 am Tokyo time and 4.00 pm London time. These particular times are known as time for 'fixing'. These findings would repeatedly be confirmed in subsequent studies.

15.4.3 Random Walk

In the literature on international finance, the foreign exchange rate is often assumed to follow a random walk, as it is difficult to empirically prove out-of-sample predictability.[1] Traditionally, most empirical work has used daily or monthly exchange rate data. However, there has been a huge disconnect between economists who believe the daily exchange rate is following a random walk and practitioners who try to predict in real time (i.e. every minute, if not every second) a trend, a turning point, a resistance level and other technical regularities in the market. One aspect of algorithm trading is to make the judgement more systematic and automatic, using tick-by-tick data, and just one step further to finding empirical regularities in a split second.

Does the foreign exchange rate follow a random walk in tick-by-tick data? One simple test is 'a run test' when deal prices move in one direction (say, a run of positive changes). How long would it tend to continue? Ohnishi et al. (2008) showed the distribution of the changes in quote and deal prices. Hashimoto et al. (2012) showed that a 'run' – continuous increases or decreases in deal prices for the past several

---

[1] The seminal and influential papers on non-predictability are Meese and Rogoff (1983a, 1983b).

ticks – do have some predictable power over the direction of the next price movement. In many cases, the conditional probability of deal prices to move in the same direction as the last several times in a row is higher than 0.5. This was not confirmed with mid-quote prices. In addition, the longer the run continues, the larger is the reversal at the end of the run. The findings are consistent with a proliferation of a momentum trading strategy in the algorithm trading.

Ito and Hashimoto (2008) showed that the order flow, defined as the number of actual deals at the ask- (or bid-) side for a specified time interval (minutes), has some predictable power over the price movement in the contemporaneous and subsequent minutes. The contemporaneous effect is strong but it cannot be used as a prediction. The forecasting equations of the exchange rate for the next one to five minutes show that coefficients are significantly different from zero.

15.4.4 Price Discovery

Surprise contents in the regularly scheduled announcements of macroeconomic statistics, such as GDP, inflation and employment, can produce changes in exchange rates. The literature on the impact of macro announcements on exchange rates is long, using less frequent data or using high-frequency indicative quotes. Hashimoto and Ito (2010) made the first contribution to investigation of Japanese macroeconomic announcement effects using EBS data. Their paper examined the impacts of Japanese macroeconomic announcements on USD/JPY. It also showed how fast the exchange rate moved to a new equilibrium. In addition, Chaboud et al. (2004) examined US macroeconomic announcements on the exchange rate, using EBS data.

Using a unique data set, Chaboud et al. (2014, p. 2045) examined how algorithm traders and human traders reacted to news. Their conclusion is 'consistent with the view that AT improves informational efficiency by speeding up price discovery, but that it may also impose higher adverse selection costs on slower traders'.

15.4.5 Anomaly

Ito et al. (2012) examined 'negative bid–ask spread' and 'triangular arbitrage opportunities' as an anomaly in the forex market. Since EBS data consist of 'firm quotes', the existence of arbitrage opportunities are not due to stale quotes or non-executable quotes. Arbitrage opportunities in data suggest real riskless profit opportunities, or 'free lunch'. It is found that risk-free arbitrage opportunities do occur rather frequently in the foreign exchange markets. However, when they occur, typically they last only a few seconds.

In the tick-by-tick data samples taken over twelve years, the number of free lunch opportunities has dramatically declined and the probability of the opportunities disappearing within one second has steadily increased. The size of expected profits has to be higher than transaction costs. In order to show they were transacted on both sides of ask and bid (or three currency trades in the case of triangular arbitrage), we (Ito et al. 2012) examined whether the arbitrage opportunities continued for more than one second. The probability of its disappearance within one second was less than 50 per cent in 1999, but increased to about 90 per cent by 2009. Less frequent occurrence and quicker disappearance after the mid-2000s is attributed to the increased use of algorithm trading and direct connection of the bank machines to the EBS computer.

Chaboud et al. (2014) also examined triangular arbitrage opportunities using their data set, which distinguishes algorithm traders and human traders. They too detected a significant decrease in the triangular arbitrage opportunities over their sample period, 2003–7.

15.5 Challenges

15.5.1 Recent Changes

The preceding section described the rise of machines in a positive sense. The market became more efficient and more transparent. However, the recent changes in market microstructure, since about 2010, point to challenges as described below.

15.5.2 Dark Pool

As described earlier, the two electronic broking systems – EBS and Reuters – replaced human brokers by the mid-1990s when they became technologically advanced enough to match large volumes of buy and sell quotes by adding liquidity. In fact, when an electronic broking system becomes liquid, more quote orders are directed to the electronic broking system and add even more liquidity to the market. Direct dealings among human dealers outside the electronic broking system lost out to the attractiveness of the machines. Bank dealers largely became an intermediary to transmit customer orders to the electronic broking systems. Banks' proprietary trading became separated from dealers. Effectively, a bank proprietary trading desk became a hedge fund in a bank.

Just when matching of buy and sell orders from customers became concentrated in electronic broking systems – EBS and Reuters – via banks, a new movement to threaten the dominance started to emerge. As broking became concentrated in two systems, banks became larger and more dominant in receiving customer orders. Banks with large liquidity and primary banks (in the EBS) attract more customer orders. Trading shares of the top large banks have increased over the years. When banks received large buy and sell orders, they realise that they themselves could match buy and sell orders from customers instead of transmitting. Thus, banks started to build their own order matching systems for their customers. The bank system corresponds to Private Trading Systems (PTSs) in the equities market. Deutsche Bank's Autobahn is an old and established one. Other large players, such as Citibank and Barclays, have similar systems.

Banks' matching systems initially introduced in the early 2000s had one distinctive advantage over EBS and Reuters. The bank system had decimalised pips. When the EBS was quoting, say, 100.00 and 100.01, a bank system can offer a subdivided price unit, 100.000, 100.001, 100.002 … 100.009 and 100.010. Thus, customers who want to save costs associated with bid–ask spreads are induced to trade in the bank system. Bank systems grew rapidly in the early 2000s.

The defence that the EBS system introduced was direct connection from automatic trading non-banks – Commodity Trading Advisors (CTAs) and hedge funds – to the EBS system (recall Section 15.2.3), and decimalisation of the price unit (recall Section 15.2.4). However, the latter was very unpopular among bank human dealers who were not accustomed to other banks' matching systems, and pushed back to the half pip. Therefore, since the mid-2010s, the EBS, Reuters D-3000 and bank matching systems have coexisted. Moreover, companies that compare bid and ask quotes of various matching systems and direct orders to a system that offers best price have emerged. They are called aggregators.

Therefore, as far as customer orders are concerned, executions have become decentralised. In addition to centralised (over global participants) systems – EBS and Reuters – they can be matched in a matching system operated by a bank. Those trading outside EBS and Reuters can be called a 'dark pool' in an analogy to the equity market.

A proliferation of bank matching systems has several implications and challenges to the foreign exchange market. First, these bank systems offer competition in the market that enhances efficiency. As long as deal prices in the bank's system are inside the best bid and ask of the EBS and Reuters, customers benefit from using the bank's service. Second, transparency with respect to prices in a bank system can be maintained when prices in different bank systems can be seen by anyone in the foreign exchange market. The existence of aggregators guarantees such transparency. Third, there is a concern over the conflict of interest for a bank by having both a proprietary trading desk and an order matching services. EBS and Reuters systems offer pure order matching platforms, and they do not take long/short positions themselves. However, the bank operating trading platforms may accept bank prop trading orders that may take advantage of order flows from customers. Given what was revealed in the fixing scandal (see Section 15.3.2), a concern over a bank's behaviour in taking advantage of information about customer order flows cannot be dismissed easily. A conflict-of-interest concern can be averted if there is a firewall between the bank's proprietary trading desk and the bank's foreign exchange trading platform. Fourth, as mentioned above, proliferation of banks' own trading platforms offers competition. However, that may reduce the volume of orders that are transmitted to the EBS and Reuters. Hence, lower liquidity may produce volatility. The fragmented market may become inefficient.

15.5.3 Flashing

Some algorithms are programmed to continuously repeat placing a limit order and cancelling the order at very high frequency, typically at 0.25 second (or 250 millisecond) frequency. Most of the orders, typically over 90 per cent, go unfulfilled. Quotes can be 'outside' the best ask and bid, for example, ask at 100.02, when the best bid–ask is 100.00–100.01; or 'inside', for example, ask at 100.009 when the best bid–ask is 100.00–100.01.

Flashing far outside the best bid–ask may not seem relevant in adding meaningful liquidity or market-making; but pure noise, unless somehow market-making outside the best bid–ask, influences the liquidity or pricing near best ask. The reason for this behaviour remains to be analysed in the future.

Flashing inside the best bid–ask seems to be more interesting. Flashing inside the best ask bid has more chance to be hit for trade. In that sense, it seems to be adding liquidity to the market. However, this is not obvious as we examine the motive for such behaviour.

If flashing is done with a minimum volume and hit by a market-taker, it may succeed in recording new deal prices that may trigger the shift in the bid–ask band in one direction. The generated momentum may be something a flasher really wanted. For example, suppose an ask-side market-making bank is hit at 100.009 when the best bid–ask is 100.00–100.01. The deal may move the bid–ask band to 100.00–100.015. If this is true, the market-making bank can sell remaining positions at higher prices. This case is to use an initial selling at an illiquid price (1/10 pip below best ask) to be followed by large selling at a much higher price.

Another possibility is that the inside-the-best flasher may be a more deceptive player. Suppose a bank with a large long position wants to sell the currency at the very best price. It would help if the bid price became a little higher before the bank hit the price. Then flashing on the ask side might help to move the bid–ask up towards the flashing point.

In the literature, it is not well understood why flashing occurs. Flashing can add liquidity to the market, if flashed bids and asks are hit more than occasionally and with moderate price movements. However, there can be noises if they are not hit most of the time. Worse yet, flashing may become an instrument of manipulating the best bid–ask in the flasher's favour. However, information necessary to analyse various hypotheses is not disclosed in the data set available to researchers.

15.5.4 Flash Crash

Algorithm traders (machines) can make quotes and cancel quotes at very high frequency. When the price suddenly moves with the arrival of news on a political event or on macro fundamentals, such as a monetary policy decision that contains a surprise component, the market has to find a new equilibrium. During the price discovery process, the market needs to have diverse participants: momentum traders, contrarians and macro modelling types. Algorithms are believed to be mostly momentum traders, that is, if the price goes up, they buy the currency because the movement tends to continue. Some of the programs also contain a feature called 'loss cut', that is, if the price becomes lower (higher), then those who have long (short) positions will sell/buy, respectively, in order to limit losses. Suppose that a large shock occurs in the price and that the price movements trigger both momentum trading and loss cut strategy; the movement will be amplified. Homogeneous algorithms may amplify the volatility of the market.

On relatively rare occasions, the price moves suddenly without corresponding news. The market participants suspect a mistake in typing orders (fat fingers) and algorithm that amplify price movements. Again, data necessary to analyse a sudden and large change in exchange rates are not available to the researchers to date.

Kirilenko et al. (2016) examined a role of high-frequency traders during a flash crash in the US equity markets on 6 May 2010, with detailed tick-by-tick data. A large amount of sell orders were executed in the E-mini S&P 500 stock index futures market. They found that high-frequency (algorithmic) traders (HFTs) did not behave any differently than they did in the previous three days.

A similar study in the foreign exchange market is needed. In the foreign exchange markets, a flash crash occurred on 7 October 2016. In the early morning of the Tokyo market, the GBP declined sharply by about 10 per cent from around USD 1.2600 to USD 1.1378 in a matter of several minutes. This occurred with the background of the pound weakness from the possibility of a hard Brexit.

15.5.5 Role of Human Dealers

Algorithm trading is increasing its shares both in market-making (submitting quotes) and in deals. During some hours of the day, it is absolutely dominating the market. One of the possible problems with the dominance of the algorithm is its lack of diversity. Algorithms may be very similar, in which case price volatility would increase upon a shock in the price, with or without the arrival of major news. Humans are commonly believed to be buyers of the last resort when the foreign exchange rate moves very quickly because of quick selling.

Whether the dominance of machines makes the market more volatile is not proved affirmatively or negatively. However, humans tend to offer a very different strategy, so they may become the last safety net before a chaotic situation. If this is the case, then it is socially good to protect human dealers.

15.5.6 *Speed Bumps and the Protection of Human Dealers*

One of the problems of flashing is that humans with slow recognition and reaction cannot hit those short-lived quotes. Minimum quote life (MQL) means that a new quote submitted to the EBS can be cancelled only after 0.25 seconds after the quote. The MQL regulation was introduced in January 2013 but was abolished in September 2016. It is said that by 2016 it became possible that too much flashing was monitored and regulated by the electronic broking firms.

In December 2010 'continuous match' was launched. This was a matching service only for human dealers. Human dealers submitted an order of sell or buy-in amount (a minimum of 10 million units) but not the price. When demand and supply could be matched, then the EBS calculated the exchange rate as the midpoint of quotes in the main EBS spot market. This was analogous to 'market orders' in the equity market. But here the market was for dealers, not for real-side customers. This market seemed to be a sanctuary for human dealers; however, it was terminated in 2014. The need for this market was partially substituted by EBS Direct, which was launched in 2013, as explained below.

A market for quotes and deals between pre-designated liquidity providers and liquidity consumers was created by EBS as 'EBS Direct' in 2013. A liquidity provider can post quotes only valid to a particular trading partner. The prices are displayed on the EBS spot screen so that liquidity consumers can compare prices posted by a relationship liquidity provider and market (anonymous) prices. The prices are fully decimalised. Since there is no threat from faster machines to steal the trade, liquidity takers (humans) can have time to decide. EBS Direct is analogous to 'direct dealing' between human bank dealers before an electronic broking system dominated the matching process.

The EBS decided to erect a 'speed bump' called 'Latency Floor'. Submitted orders are collected and bunched for a random batching window of one, two or three milliseconds and then randomly released to the matching engine (EBS Market). It was first introduced for the AUD/USD market in August 2013 and was expanded to major currency pairs by the end of 2014. However, this is a speed bump that makes a difference in a race among machines. It is not much of a speed bump that could help humans.

15.6 Concluding Remarks

The first half of this chapter described a transition of the market microstructure of the interbank foreign exchange markets. A strong trend was the dominance of computers over humans. First, human brokers became extinct as the computer matching platform was built. Second, the bank dealers became endangered as machines were allowed to be connected directly to the EBS matching machine. Trading became concentrated at electronic broking systems – EBS and Reuters. The dominance of computers made the market more concentrated, transparent and efficient.

More recently, proprietary trading platforms, or dark pools, are spreading fast and they effectively take trading volume out of EBS and Reuters. This change possibly reduces transparency. The creation of EBS Direct is also an attempt to recognise particular relationship trading that may help human dealers, as well as slow (by milliseconds) machines.

There are a few additional challenges in the market. First, the dark pool is making the forex market decentralised, again. Transparency seems to have been reduced compared to before. Second, proliferation of algorithmic traders (machines) may pose problems. They can place and cancel quotes very quickly, much more quickly than humans can recognise and react. It has been speculated without proof whether the dominance of machines makes the foreign exchange markets more volatile (with noisy 'flashing') and/or vulnerable to a flash crash due to homogeneous algorithms. Better data would prove, one way or the other, whether activities of machines, in the race for speed in milliseconds, just add noises and vulnerability. The introduction of a speed bump, such as Latency Floor, may reflect the recognition that a speed race has reached the limits of healthy competition that enhances market efficiency. Several attempts to give advantage to humans, such as Continuous Match and MQL, did not produce any meaningful protection and were discontinued.

References

Chaboud, A.P., S. Chernenko, E. Howorka et al. (2004), 'The High-Frequency Effects of U.S. Macroeconomic Data Releases on Prices and Trading Activity in the Global Interdealer Foreign Exchange Market', *International Finance Discussion Papers* 823. Board of Governors of the Federal Reserve System (US).

Chaboud, A.P., B. Chiquoine, E. Hjalmarsson and C. Vega (2014), 'Rise of the Machines: Algorithmic Trading in the Foreign Exchange Market', *Journal of Finance*, 69(5), pp. 2045–84.

Goodhart, C., T. Ito and R. Payne (1996), 'One Day in June, 1993: A Study of the Working of Reuters 2000-2 Electronic Foreign Exchange Trading System', in J. Frankel, G. Galli and A. Giovannini (eds.), *The Microstructure of Foreign Exchange Markets*, Chicago, IL: NBER University of Chicago Press, pp. 107–82.

Hashimoto, Y. and T. Ito (2010), 'Effects of Japanese Macroeconomic Announcements on the Dollar/Yen Exchange Rate: High-Resolution Picture', *Journal of the Japanese and International Economies*, 24, pp. 334–54.

Hashimoto, Y., T. Ito, T. Ohnishi et al. (2012), 'Random Walk or a Run. Market Microstructure Analysis of Foreign Exchange Rate Movements Based on Conditional Probability', *Quantitative Finance*, 12(6), pp. 893–905.

Ito, T. (2016), 'The Exchange Rate Movements with High Frequency Data', Keynote Speech, Asia-Pacific Econophysics conference 2016, at University of Tokyo, 24 August 2016.

Ito, T. and Y. Hashimoto (2006), 'Intra-day Seasonality in Activities of the Foreign Exchange Markets: Evidence from the Electronic Broking System', *Journal of the Japanese and International Economies*, 20(4), pp. 637–64.

(2008), 'Price Impacts of Deals and Predictability of the Exchange Rate Movements', in T. Ito and A. Rose (eds.), *International Financial Issues in the Pacific Rim, NBER East Asia Seminar on Economics*, vol. 17, Chicago, IL: University of Chicago Press, pp. 177–215.

Ito, T. and M. Yamada (2017) 'Puzzles in the Tokyo Fixing in the Forex Market: Order Imbalances and Bank Pricing' *Journal of International Economics* 109, November, pp. 214–34.

(2018), 'Did the Reform Fix the London Fix Problem?' *Journal of International Money and Finance*, 80, February, pp. 75–95.

Ito, T., K. Yamada, M. Takayasu and H. Takayasu (2012), 'Free Lunch! Arbitrage Opportunities in the Foreign Exchange Markets', *NBER Working Paper* No 18541, November 2012.

Kirilenko, A., S. Mehrdad, A.S. Kyle and T. Tuzun (2016) 'The Flash Crash: The Impact of High Frequency Trading in an Electronic Market', *Journal of Finance* 72(3), June, pp. 967–98.

Meese, R.A. and K. Rogoff (1983a) 'Empirical Exchange Rate Models of the Seventies: Do They Fit Out of Sample?' *Journal of International Economics*, 14, pp. 3–24.

(1983b) 'The Out-of-Sample Failure of Empirical Exchange Rate Models: Sampling Error or Misspecification?' in J.A. Frenkel (ed.), *Exchange Rates and International Macroeconomics*, Chicago, IL: Chicago University Press, pp. 67–105.

Ohnishi, T., H. Takayasu, T. Ito et al. (2008), 'Dynamics of Quote and Deal Prices in the Foreign Exchange Market', *Journal of Economic Interaction and Coordination*, 3, pp. 99–106.

16 | *The Case for Flexible Exchange Rates Revisited*

ROBERT Z. ALIBER

16.1 Introduction

The last forty years have been the most turbulent in international monetary history. There have been four waves of financial crises: The first involved Mexico, Brazil and ten other developing countries in the early 1980s. Japan, Finland and Sweden were in the second wave in the early 1990s. Norway had experienced a crisis a few years earlier. The Asian Financial Crisis that began in mid-1997 was the third in the series and initially involved Thailand, Indonesia, Malaysia and the Philippines, and subsequently South Korea. Mexico had a crisis during its presidential transition at the end of 1994. The USA, Britain, Iceland, Ireland and Spain had banking crises in the fourth wave in 2007/8. Greece and Portugal had sovereign debt crises fifteen months later.

The differences among the key features of these crises were about as significant as the differences among Poland Spring, Vichy, Pellegrino, Fiji, LaCroix, Perrier and the other brands of bottled water. Each country experienced a boom in the several years before its crisis. The price of its securities increased and the price of its currency increased in real terms and usually in nominal terms. Each country except Japan experienced an increase in its capital account surplus. Japan experienced a decline in its capital account deficit. The price of securities in each of these countries increased to ensure that there was an induced increase in its current account deficit that corresponded with an autonomous increase in its capital account surplus; otherwise the market in its currency would not have cleared. The price of real estate and securities in Japan surged in the second half of the 1980s to ensure that its current account surplus declined as its capital account deficit fell.

The frequency and severity of banking and currency crises have increased sharply since the early 1970s transition to the floating currency arrangement. The monetary constitution for the floating currency arrangement – the counterpart of the 'rules of the game' of the gold standard – is a set of articles by Friedman (1953), Friedman and Roosa (1967), Johnson (1969), Sohmen (1969) and others that appeared in the 1950s and the 1960s. One view is that a floating currency arrangement provides the low-cost approach towards the adjustments that are necessary to cope with a much larger number of goods market and money market shocks. In contrast the view in this chapter is that the surge in the number of money market shocks has occurred because central bank monetary policies are no longer constrained by anchors to parities.

Section 16.2 reviews the source of monetary turbulence in the last thirty years. The factors that have led to surges in the prices of securities in the countries in the several years before their booms morphed into crises are identified. Section 16.3 focuses on whether a banking crisis is an 'Act of God' or a predictable event. Section 16.4 develops a scorecard on the positive claims of the proponents. They assumed that the market prices of currencies would change in response to goods market shocks, while they slighted the likelihood and the impacts of money market shocks. Section 16.5 reviews the arguments about the choice of an optimal currency arrangement that minimises monetary instability.

16.2 The Source of Monetary Turbulence

As previously mentioned, every banking crisis since the early 1980s except the one in Japan was preceded by the increase in the country's capital account surplus; Japan experienced a decline in its capital account deficit. The increase in the capital account surplus in each of these countries led to an increase in the supply of credit; similarly the reduction in Japan's capital account deficit led to an increase in its domestic credit supply. The increase in the prices of securities in each of these countries was an integral part of the adjustment process to ensure that its current account deficit increased as its capital account surplus increased; a country cannot experience an increase in its capital account surplus unless at the same time its current account deficit increases by the same amount. The DNA of the banking crisis in each of these countries was embedded in the surge in cross-border investment inflows, which were too rapid to be sustained. When the inflows slowed, the prices of currencies and of securities declined.

Every country that has had a banking crisis since the early 1980s
has previously had an economic boom. Nearly every country – the
primary exception is Japan – experienced an increase in cross-border
investment inflows in the several previous years; its capital account
surplus increased and the price of its currency increased. Japan's capital account deficit declined and the price of the yen increased in the
second half of the 1980s. (The first difference of the change in
Japan's capital account balance was identical with the first differences
in the changes in the capital account balances of these other
countries.)

One of the stylised facts is that there have been long swings in the
prices of currencies since the move to flexible exchange rates, which
have led to the terms 'overshooting' and 'undershooting'; the pattern
is that the price of a country's currency increased as its capital
account surplus increased. The price of the US dollar increased during
the first half of the 1980s, and throughout most of the 1990s as the
US capital account surplus increased. Iceland's capital account surplus increased during most of the period from 2003 to mid-2008 as
its capital account surplus surged.

The pattern is symmetrical: when the investment inflows to a
country slowed, the price of the country's currency and the price of
its securities declined. Iceland's capital account surplus was nearly
20 per cent of its gross domestic product (GDP) in the summer of
2008; when the investor demand for the IOUs of the Icelandic
banks declined, the capital account surplus evaporated, the price
of the krona fell sharply, and the price of Icelandic securities
plummeted.

The variability in the ratios of capital account surplus to GDP has
been many times larger than when currencies were anchored to
parities. Between 2004 and 2006, this ratio changed by 10 per cent in
Mexico. The variability in cross-border investment inflows has been
the source of the turbulence. An increase in these inflows leads to an
increase in the price of a country's currency. The price of its securities
also increases as an integral part of the adjustment process to ensure
that the market in the country's currency clears. If a country experiences an autonomous increase in its capital account surplus, there
must be an induced increase in its current account deficit.

The transfer problem process identified by Keynes in his analysis of
post- World War I reparations illustrates that a shock that leads to

an autonomous increase in a country's capital account surplus must necessarily lead to an induced increase in its current account deficit; its capital account surplus cannot increase unless there is a counterpart increase in its current account deficit (Keynes, 1920). The increase in the country's capital account surplus leads to an increase in the supply of credit, and the price of securities increases. Consumption spending and investment spending expand in response to greater household wealth. The larger the autonomous increase in the country's capital account surplus, the larger the induced increase in household wealth necessary to ensure that the country's spending on imports increases. Japan needed a massive increase in household wealth to achieve a modest increase in its imports and a decline in its current account surplus.

The pace of the increase in the country's capital account surplus depends on the pace of the increase in its current account deficit, which depends on the increase in the market price of its currency relative to the long-run average price and on the increase in household wealth. The pace of the increase in its current account deficit depends on the pace of the increase in household wealth.

The market in currencies would not clear if the induced increase in spending on imports was smaller than the autonomous increase in the capital account surplus; instead the price of its currency and the price of securities both would continue to increase until the increase in the supply of the currency corresponded with the increase in demand.

The increase in the price of securities in response to a given increase in the capital account surplus may be significantly larger in some countries than in others, and for several different reasons. The smaller the increase in imports for a given increase in the price of the country's currency, the larger the increase in the price of securities. The smaller the increase in consumption spending and investment spending as household wealth increases, the larger the increase in the price of securities. The smaller the increase in spending on imports as consumption and investment spending increase, the larger the increase in the price of securities.

The market in currencies differs from other financial markets in that it is an intermediate market and incorporates both goods market transactions and money market transactions. The market in currencies is not efficient; the adjustment in the market price of the country's currency to new information is prolonged rather than immediate. (The prolonged adjustment partly explains why the banks and other firms that trade currencies have realised such massive rates of return – the proverbial 'shooting fish in a basket'.) The stylised fact is that the changes in the price of the currency in the forward market 'under-predict' the change in the price of the currency in the spot market during the term to maturity of the forward contract. (There have been extended periods when a country's currency has been at a discount in the forward market. If the price of the currency in the forward market is viewed as a proxy for the anticipated price in the spot market on the date that the forward contract matures, the inference is that the price of the currency would decline; but, in fact, the price of the currency has increased for an extended period).

Every country that has had a banking crisis has had an extended episode when the increase in its external indebtedness was significantly larger than the increase in its GDP. Moreover, the increase in its external indebtedness was larger than the interest payments on the indebtedness. As a result, some of the borrowers in the country relied on money from new loans to pay the interest on outstanding loans.

The inference from the increase in the ratio of the country's net external indebtedness to its GDP is that the country was on a non-sustainable trajectory for the increase in its indebtedness; at some stage it was inevitable that one or several of the lenders would become more cautious in buying more of the borrowers' IOUs. The price of the indebted country's currency would decline and perhaps abruptly, and the price of its securities also would decline sharply.

Whether the decline in investor demand for the IOUs available in a country will lead to a 'soft landing' or instead to a 'hard landing' and a banking crisis depends on a complex of factors including the scope of the decline in the price of its currency and the ratio of its indebtedness denominated in various foreign currencies to its GDP.

The fact that a country has had a banking crisis reflects market failure; the lenders failed to ask about the endgame and where the borrowers would get the cash to pay the interest if the money was no longer available from new loans (Dornbusch, 1976).

16.3 Is a Banking Crisis an 'Act of God?'

Lewis (2014) reviewed Secretary of Treasury Timothy Geithner's memoir *Stress Test* (Geithner, 2014):

> The causes of the crisis, in other words, were the same old-fashioned madness of crowds and extraordinary popular delusions responsible for every panic dating back to the Dutch mania for tulip bulbs ... The story that Geithner goes on to tell blames everyone and no one. The crisis he describes might just as well have been an act of God. (Lewis, 2014)

The memoirs of Paulson (2010) and King (2016) and others suggest that each believed that the 2007–8 crisis was a random event, a 'bolt out of the blue'. No government appears to have adopted prophylactic measures to dampen the impact of the sharp decline in the prices of securities that occurred when the investment inflows slowed in the months before the crisis climaxed.

Every banking crisis since the early 1980s was a predictable event although its timing was uncertain. The necessary condition for a banking crisis is that the increase in the external indebtedness of every country except Japan had increased at a rate that was too rapid to be sustained. Similarly, the increase in the domestic indebtedness of a large group of borrowers within each country including Japan had been too rapid to be sustained. The sufficient condition was that the external indebtedness of each country was too large relative to its GDP; the implication was that the inevitable decline in the price of the indebted country's currency would lead to a sharp increase in the domestic counterpart of the liabilities denominated in a foreign currency. The capital of the banks in the country would decline when the price of its currency and the price of its securities fell. The trigger for each crisis was an event that led the lenders to become more cautious in buying the borrowers' IOUs.

The banking crisis that occurred in Iceland in September 2008 was 99.44 per cent likely for at least two years. Iceland's external indebtedness had increased by more than 15 per cent a year after 2002; its net external indebtedness had reached 90 per cent of its GDP. The external indebtedness of the Icelandic banks was more than 200 per cent of the country's GDP.

The trigger for the crisis in Reykjavik was the failure of Lehman Brothers, which led to a freeze in the international credit market, which meant that the Icelandic banks could no longer sell their IOUs to foreign banks; hence they lacked the funds to pay the interest on their IOUs denominated in a foreign currency. The Icelandic households and business firms could no longer sell their IOUs to the Icelandic banks, and so they lacked the funds for debt service payments. Iceland's current account deficit was nearly 20 per cent of its GDP in mid-2008. When the foreign demand for the IOUs of the Icelandic banks plummeted, the price of the Icelandic krona declined by 50 per cent. Icelandic borrowers incurred large revaluation losses on their IOUs denominated in a foreign currency. Those borrowers with debt service payments to make in the next few months experienced a surge in the krona counterpart of these payments. Many of these borrowers sold krona securities to get the cash for these payments, and the price of these securities fell sharply. About 15 per cent of the assets of each of the three Icelandic banks were the stocks of various Icelandic firms, including the two other banks. Each bank incurred large revaluation losses on its holdings of these securities, its capital declined, and each bank had to shrink its assets.

It was predictable that the price of the Icelandic krona would decline sharply once the inflows stopped. Each of the other adjustments was also predictable although the scope of the adjustments could only be estimated. If the demand of foreign banks for the IOUs of the Icelandic banks had declined in September 2007, Iceland would have experienced a meltdown that would not have differed significantly from the decline that occurred a year later.

As Iceland's external indebtedness increased relative to its GDP, the likelihood increased that an event that triggered a slowdown in lenders' purchases of the IOUs of the Icelandic banks would lead to a banking crisis. If this decline in demand had occurred in 2004, Iceland might have been able to adjust to the declines in its capital account surplus and in the price of the krona without a crisis. As its external indebtedness and the price of the krona both increased, the likelihood of a crisis increased when the foreign demand for its securities slowed. The 'date of no return' after which an Icelandic banking crisis was 99.44 per cent predictable might have been no later than the Spring of 2005.

The puzzle is that the lenders failed to see that Iceland had passed the 'date of no return' for a crisis as early as 2005. The data on Iceland's external indebtedness and on the price of the krona were readily available. The lenders had a lot of 'skin in the game' even though their claims on the Icelandic banks were a trivially small part of their portfolios; the losses would be embarrassing and some careers would crater. The implication is that they had failed to analyse the source of the crisis in Mexico in the early 1980s, in Japan and in Sweden in the early 1990s, and in Thailand and Indonesia in 1997; the lenders did not have the appropriate model for the sustainability of increases in external indebtedness (Christiansen, 2011). Similarly the stewards of international banking arrangements – the bank stock analysts, the credit rating agencies, the International Monetary Fund and the Organisation for Economic Cooperation and Development did not appear to have asked the 'greater fool question': 'Where will the borrowers get the money for the debt service payments if the money is no longer available from new loans?'

Each of the countries that has experienced a banking crisis had previously crossed the threshold of its own 'date-of-no-return' months, or even a year or two, before its crisis. The USA crossed the date of no return in the summer of 2005; Japan crossed the date of no return in the late 1980s because the increase in domestic indebtedness was much too rapid to be sustained.

16.4 Why Is the Case for Flexible Exchange Rates Flawed?

The case for flexible exchange rates is intellectually bankrupt because the proponents' normative objective of monetary independence for the central bank in each country is not consistent with the implicit assumption that underlies the major positive claims that investor demand for foreign securities is constant (Aliber, 1975, 2016). If a central bank changes its discount rate or its money supply (i.e. monetary independence), investor demand for foreign securities will not be constant.

One of the normative objectives of the proponents is monetary independence. They did not want a central bank to be constrained from following a more expansive monetary policy because its holdings of international reserve assets were paltry; nor did they want it to be constrained from following a more contractive policy because it would have to buy foreign currencies to prevent the price of its currency from increasing. Their other normative objective was to minimise the deviations at national borders between domestic prices and costs and foreign prices and costs that might occur because of tariffs, currency controls, and the overvaluation and undervaluation of national currencies.

One of the most significant of their positive claims was that the deviations of the market prices of currencies from long-run average prices would be smaller if currencies were not anchored to parities. The changes in the prices of currencies would be gradual, perhaps because they would be continuous and there would be fewer currency crises. They also claimed that each country would be more fully insulated from shocks in other countries because shocks would lead to changes in the prices of currencies rather than to increases in trade and payments surpluses.

Several of their positive claims were responses to the criticisms of Nurkse who suggested that uncertainty about the prices of currencies would deter international trade (Nurkse, 1944). He also wrote that changes in cross-border investment inflows in the French franc in the first half of the 1920s had been dis-equilibrating.

The post-1970 data on the changes in the prices of currencies and cross-border investment inflows challenge the positive claims of the proponents. The deviations between the market prices of currencies and the long-run average prices have been much larger than when currencies were anchored to parities. The proponents claimed that there would be fewer currency crises; instead there have been more – and most have been twinned with a banking crisis. They claimed that each country would be more fully insulated from shocks in other countries by the changes in the prices of currencies; instead the source of each of the banking crises since the early 1980s has been the sharp variability in cross-border investment inflows. They suggested that if currencies floated freely, the demand for international reserve assets would be much smaller; instead the supply of international reserve assets has become much greater – in large part because some central banks have intervened to prevent the prices of their currencies from increasing as a way to increase employment in their manufacturing sectors.

The proponents failed to recognise that once currencies were no longer anchored to parities, the average inflation rate would be higher, and the difference in inflation rates and changes in the difference in inflation rates would be higher. Hence they failed to recognise that the difference in interest rates and changes in this difference would also be greater. Investors would have a greater incentive to change the currency composition of the securities in their portfolios as the relationship between the interest rate differential and the anticipated change in the price of the currency would change more frequently and by larger amounts.

The proponents did not recognise that the market is an intermediate market that accommodates the payments associated with cross-border trade in securities as well as cross-border trade in goods. They believed – implicitly, if not explicitly – that the market in currencies was efficient, and that the price of a currency in the forward market was an unbiased forecast of its price in the spot market on the date the forward contract matures adjusted for a risk premium (Thaler, 1992). A money market shock would lead to an immediate change in the anticipated spot price of the currency, but the current spot price would not immediately move to the anticipated spot price discounted to the present by the interest rate differential because the changes in production patterns and consumption patterns that were required for changes in the country's current account balance were prolonged rather than immediate.

The proponents ignored that the cost of hedging the uncertainty about the prices of currencies will be higher when currencies are not anchored to parities. They failed to recognise that the uncertainty about the price of currencies had been transferred to uncertainty about the cost of hedging. They did not comment on how the cost of hedging should be measured. The proponents also failed to distinguish transactional uncertainty associated with specific contracts from systemic uncertainty about changes in monetary policy and other shocks that would lead to changes in the price of a currency. An analogy is that an individual can buy flood insurance for a home in the flood plain; the cost of the insurance depends on the height of the insured property above the flood plain of the river.

The most contentious disagreement between the proponents and their critics centres on the impacts of changes in investor demand for foreign securities. When Nurkse (1944) wrote that speculative capital flows in the French franc in the 1920s had been dis-equilibrating, he was concerned about the impacts of changes in investor demand for foreign securities on the prices of currencies and the goods price level. He presented an empirical observation. The proponents did not challenge this observation and say it was wrong. Instead the response was 'if speculative capital flows were de-stabilizing, the speculators would lose money, and eventually be followed by stabilizing speculators'. This statement about the range of movement in the price of the currency is orthogonal to Nurkse's observation about the impacts of cross-border investment inflows on the prices of securities.

The claim of the proponents that the floating currency arrangement was preferable to deal with goods market shocks that would lead to declines in competitiveness cannot be challenged. The proponents ignored that there would be many more money market shocks when currencies were not attached to parities, in part because central banks could pursue independent monetary policies. Changes in investor demand for foreign securities in turn would lead to changes in the market prices of currencies. Moreover, investor demand for foreign securities might change for numerous other reasons. The assumption that is buried in the claims of the proponents is that investor demand for foreign securities would not change, despite the sharp increase in the number of money market shocks as central banks followed independent monetary policies.

The proponents never explicitly acknowledged the assumption that money market shocks would not lead to changes in investor demand for foreign securities; their positive claims about the changes in the prices of currencies depended on this assumption. The proponents had a strong commitment to monetary independence but they ignored the impact of changes in monetary policy on investor demand for foreign securities. The proponents refused to acknowledge that there was a conflict between their two normative objectives.

16.5 The Case for Flexible Exchange Rates Reviewed

Yogi Berra's quip that 'If you don't know where you are going you'll end up someplace else' applies to recent initiatives to reduce the likelihood and severity of another banking crisis like the one in 2007–8. The cause of this crisis was the sharp increase in cross-border investment inflows to the USA, which induced a boom so that there would be an increase in the US current account deficit that would correspond with the autonomous increase in the US capital account surplus. The increase in these inflows led to the increase in house prices and a boom in consumption spending. When the cross-border investment inflows slowed, some borrowers who had relied on money from new loans to pay the interest on outstanding loans defaulted on their indebtedness.

The conventional explanation is that the US banking crisis was precipitated by the reckless behaviour of the banks and other lenders. This explanation ignores that Britain, Spain and several other countries had banking crises at the same time as the one in the USA. It also ignores the similarity between the events in many other countries that had banking crises in one of the several previous waves. There were numerous villains in the credit extension activities in the several years before the crises, but they were responding to the superabundance of credit; they were the channels for the distribution of credit and not the cause of the superabundance. If the increase in the US capital account surplus between 2002 and 2006 is taken as a given, the USA would have had a banking crisis in 2008 – even if Mother Theresa had been Chair of the Federal Reserve and the Sisters of Charity had been in charge of bank regulation. Each of the banking crises since the early 1980s has resulted from the sharp variability in cross-border investment inflows. An increase in the inflows to a country leads to an increase in its capital account surplus and in the price of its currency. The price of securities in the country increase and the country has a boom. The increases in its external and domestic indebtedness are too rapid to be sustained. When the investment inflows slow, the price of its currency and the price of its securities decline.

Each of these crises was a predictable event, because the increase in indebtedness was too rapid and the level of indebtedness was too high relative to its GDP. The date of no return for the implosion had been passed many months before. The dates when the imbalances would morph into crises were uncertain, because the triggers for the crises could be a random event. The succession of crises indicates massive market failures. The lenders fail to ask – time and time again – where the borrowers will get the money to pay the interest if they can no longer obtain the money from new loans.

The succession of boom and bust cycles illustrates that the floating currency arrangement is inherently unstable because the boom induced in response to the increase in investment inflows is associated, not sustainable. The case for flexible exchange rates is intellectually bankrupt because of the implicit assumption that investor demand for foreign securities will be a constant in the short run, despite money market shocks in the form of changes in central bank discount rates and fiscal policies.

The move to a floating currency arrangement in the 1970s was inevitable, given the significant difference in national inflation rates and the incipient imbalances that had developed. The continued reliance on this arrangement has been facilitated by reliance on the set of arguments that has been costly. Neither of the proponents' normative objectives have been achieved. The distortions at national borders from the changes in the market prices of currencies relative to long-run average prices have been very large. The costs to economic growth from sequence consumption booms followed by the massive wealth losses and de-capitalisation of the banks have been massive. More than forty countries have imported major macro shocks as a result of increases in investor demand for their securities.

The proponents had two normative objectives. One was monetary independence and the other was minimal distortions at national borders between domestic costs and prices and foreign costs and prices because countries adopted tariffs or exchange controls to maintain an overvalued currency or because of episodes of overvaluation and undervaluation. One of the major positive claims of the proponents was that the deviations between the market prices of currencies and long-run average prices would be smaller than when currencies were attached to parities because the changes in the market prices of currencies would track differences in national inflation rates. Another was that the changes in the market prices of currencies would be continuous and hence gradual, and therefore sharply different from the episodic devaluations under an adjustable parity system. The proponents claimed that there would be fewer currency crises. They claimed that countries would be more fully insulated from shocks in other countries.

More than forty years of data facilitate the conclusion that there is no empirical support for any of these major claims. The deviations between the market prices of currencies and the long-run average prices have been much larger than when currencies were attached to parities. Some currencies have fallen off steep cliffs. The sharp declines in the price of the currencies of some countries have been larger than the periodic stepwise reductions under the adjustable parity system. There have been more currency crises and most have been associated with a banking crisis. The boom and bust cycles in more than forty countries have resulted from increases in their capital account surpluses (or in the case of Japan in the second half of the

1980s, from a decline in its capital account deficit). Changes in these cross-border investment inflows have been both dis-equilibrating to the national markets in securities and de-stabilising to the market in currencies. In the absence of the constraints imposed by a commitment to a parity, a large number of countries have limited the increases in the prices of their currencies as part of their export-led growth strategies.

The costs to the USA of the accumulation of these strategies has led to a sharp reversal of the US international investment position from the world's largest creditor country in 1980 to the world's largest debtor in 1990, which reflected that the US trade balance reverted from a surplus to a deficit. The USA incurred the costs of shifting productive resources from the tradable goods sector to the non-tradable goods sector.

The large changes in the market prices of currencies mean that the normative objective of the proponents that the deviations at the national borders between domestic costs and prices and foreign costs and prices has not been achieved. Although the national central banks are no longer constrained in their policy choices by the commitment to a parity, their freedom to change their policies is constrained because the price of their currency is set by market forces. As a result monetary policy may need to be directed to counter the change in the price of the currency that has resulted from changes in investor purchases of foreign securities.

The confidence that the proponents had in their claims was based on the implicit assumption that investor demand for foreign securities would not change in response to changes in monetary policy or to any other event. The logic is impeccable: If investor demand for foreign securities is a constant, then the changes in the price of a country's currency will track the difference between its inflation rate and those of its trading partners. The rationale for central bank independence is that changes in its monetary value – its discount rate or the rate of money supply growth – would lead to changes in real value. The proponents would not acknowledge that changes in the monetary value would lead to changes in the nominal and the real price of its currency.

The costs of the floating currency have been high. The rates of economic growth have been lower during the period when currencies have been floating, but obviously many factors have contributed to the decline in the growth rate. The large changes in the market prices of currencies relative to the long-run average prices have been a source of uncertainty. The waves of consumption booms followed by the massive wealth losses and de-capitalisation of the banks have been costly. The massive changes in the market prices of currencies relative to long-run average prices has led to massive changes on the profit rate in the production of tradable goods and almost certainly have deterred investment. Some countries in Asia have followed 'beggar thy neighbour' policies and underpriced their currencies, which has contributed to lower growth rates in the traditional industrial countries.

The policy objective is to return to one of the normative objectives of the proponents: to minimise distortions at the national borders between domestic prices and costs and foreign prices and costs. The changes in real exchange rates that result from monetary shocks should be minimal. A new financial instrument should be adopted to defeat or dampen the carry trade – to put in some speed bumps that will deter carry trade transactions. The carry trade transactions initially appear profitable because the market in currencies is not efficient. The social benefits of unfettered carry trade transactions have been trivial, while the social costs have been extraordinarily high.

References

Aliber, R.Z. (1975), 'Monetary Independence Under Floating Exchange Rates', *Journal of Finance*, XXX(2), pp. 365–76.

(2016), 'A Lego Approach to International Monetary Reform', *International Atlantic Economic Journal*, 44(2), pp. 139–57.

Christiansen, L. (2011), 'Iceland: Geyser Crisis', in R.Z. Aliber and G. Zoega (eds.), *Preludes to the Icelandic Banking Crisis*, London: Palgrave Macmillan.

Dornbusch, R. (1976), 'Expectations and Exchange Rate Dynamics', *Journal of Political Economy*, 84(6), pp. 1161–76.

Friedman, M. (1953), 'The Case for Flexible Exchange Rates', in *Essays in Positive Economics*, Chicago, IL: University of Chicago Press.

Friedman, M. and R.V. Roosa (1967), *The Balance of Payments: Free versus Fixed Exchange Rates*, Washington, DC: American Enterprise Institute for Public Policy Research.

Geithner, T. (2014), *Stress Test: Reflections on Financial Crises*, New York, NY: Crown Publishers.

Johnson, H.G. (1969), *The Case for Flexible Exchange Rates, 1969*, London: Institute for Economic Affairs.

Keynes, J.M. (1920), *The Economic Consequences of the Peace*, New York, NY: Harcourt, Brace, and Howe.

King, M. (2016), *The End of Alchemy; Money, Banking and the Future of the Global Economy*, New York, NY: W.W. Norton & Company.

Lewis, M. (2014), 'The Hot Seat, review of *Stress Test*', by T.F. Geithner, *New York Times, Sunday Book Review*, May 15.

Nurkse, R. (1944), *International Currency Experience: Lessons of the Inter-War Period*, Princeton, NJ: League of Nations, Princeton University Press.

Paulson, H.M., Jr. (2010), *On the Brink, Inside the Race to Stop the Collapse of the Global Financial System*, Business Plus, New York, NY: Hachette Book Group.

Sohmen, E. (1969), *Flexible Exchange Rates*, revised edition, Chicago, IL: The University of Chicago Press.

Thaler, R.H. (1992), *The Winner's Curse: Paradoxes and Anomalies of Economic Life*, Princeton, NJ: Princeton University Press.

17 Cross-Border Banking and Monetary Independence

Difficult Partners

MARCUS MILLER

17.1 Introduction

For Milton Friedman, money was a potent national symbol – a creation of the nation state with a key economic role to play. Misgoverned, money may cause crisis – witness the Great Depression. But properly managed, it can promote the welfare of the people. This, it seems, is what inspires his monumental *Monetary History of the United States*, co-written with Anna Schwartz (Friedman and Schwartz, 1963), and accounts for his lifelong fascination with monetary policy. Some countries may choose to sacrifice their monetary independence – by joining the Gold Standard, like the USA until 1934, or by pegging to an external currency, as many did after World War II. But for Friedman a floating exchange rate and well-managed money was a recipe for stability and enterprise: *honi soit qui mal y pense!*

In reality, of course, money is not the sole creation of the state. For most businesses and households the money – and near-money – they use is to be found on the balance sheets of private corporations, licensed and regulated by the state maybe, though increasingly protected by limited liability. These corporations have their own interests to pursue, both at home and, if the cap fits, outside national boundaries by cross-border banking.

In these circumstances, Friedman's perspective may prove misleading. Does it not rest on the Assumption of Triple Coincidence, to use the terminology of Avdjiev, McCauley and Shin (2016a, 2016b), where this involves assuming that the currency area, the gross domestic product (GDP) boundary and the realm of decision making all coincide? 'No doubt', they say, 'this is an elegant simplification for analytical purposes. However, the assumption of the triple coincidence can

Discussions with Gianluca Benigno and Angus Armstrong and the technical assistance of Songklod Rastapana are gratefully acknowledged.

mislead in a world of multinational firms and international currencies in which financial flows are important in their own right' (Avdjiev, McCauley and Shin, 2016b). For, with national monetary systems increasingly 'joined at the hip' by financial integration, a floating exchange rate with capital mobility is no longer a guarantee of monetary independence – a point persuasively pursued in recent papers by Helene Rey (2013, 2016) and with co-authors, e.g. Passari and Rey (2015), and with the application of these ideas to emerging markets analysed in Aoki, Benigno and Kiyotaki (2015).

While Rey focuses on the existence of a *global financial cycle* which affects countries independently of the exchange rate regime, in this chapter we examine the transmission of *financial crisis*, in particular. The focus is on international linkage via the 'risk-taking channel', using the US subprime crisis as a case in point. The effects of the US 'shadow banking' crisis reverberated around the financial world; but freely floating exchange rates provided scant protection for trans-Atlantic neighbours in the UK and the EU.

What about the regulation of banks in the home country – and hopefully elsewhere? Will that not offer the necessary insulation? As it happened, the Basel Committee on Banking Supervision (BCBS), first established in 1975, had come to see its mission as devising bank regulations – to be applied country by country – so as to ensure financial stability in the economies of the West. Concern that there might be a regulatory 'race to the bottom' had led to the Basel Accord of 1998 with an 8 per cent Capital Adequacy Requirement to be applied to Risk Weighted Assets.

There is no doubt that this marked a significant step in coordinating financial regulation among independent sovereign states. In the eyes of one observer, 'Through the Basel Accord, nations effectively pooled their sovereignty to win back from markets some of the control that was slipping away from each individually ... [it] promoted capitalist stability and the long-term transposition of liberal national democratic ideals to the changed world economy driven by stateless capital' (Solomon, 1995, p. 447). His concluding assessment was, it should be said, much less optimistic:

As competent as central bankers have been, I find it frightful the extent to which we are relying for the prosperity of the free world economy – and ultimately the stability of democratic society – on the judgement of a handful of expert technocrats who, to tell the truth, are often caught by surprise like the rest of us about the transformations occurring in the economy and the financial system. (Solomon, 1995, p. 508)

The financial crisis that started in August 2007 was later to prove how justified these doubts were. Therefore, as Charles Goodhart (2011, ch. 16, p. 581) puts it bluntly in concluding his comprehensive study of the BCSB over the years 1974–97, 'the key question is: why the apparatus of financial regulation failed to prevent a systemic failure'. The answer, he notes with regret, is in large part because those involved in devising the regulations had 'insufficient appreciation of financial economics'! For, as he points out, academics such as Kiyotaki and Moore (1997) had been stressing the 'dynamic effects of amplifying forces within the financial system' as a driver of cycles of financial booms and busts.[1] Concern with such dynamics was evidently at odds with the view of national bank regulators and the BCBS that their duty lay in 'improving the risk management practices of *individual* banks'. Nonetheless, where there are self-reinforcing dynamics at work, Goodhart (2011, p. 578) argues, 'their duty is to strengthen the stability of the financial *system* as a whole'.

The early Basel perspective suffered, one could say, from the Fallacy of Composition – the fallacy that ensuring each institution behaves well will ensure the system as a whole is safe and sound. This perspective remained in place as Basel I was upgraded to Basel II. That it put unwarranted trust in Credit Rating Agencies and ignored the role of *externalities*[2] was forcefully pointed out in Danielsson et al. (2001), an 'Academic Response to Basel II' from economists at LSE – including Charles Goodhart – which warned that Basel II would promote rather than check systemic crisis. Sadly, the warning was ignored.

The same happened when, at the Jackson Hole jamboree in honour of Mr Greenspan, Rajan (2005) famously warned the assembled

---

[1] Further discussion, with examples, is available in Miller and Zhang (2015).

[2] The externalities referred to here (sometimes called 'pecuniary externalities') are the side effects of asset price changes due to the balance sheet rules imposed in the financial sector to check moral hazard. While these balance sheet rules work well for idiosyncratic shocks to the agents concerned, they can generate significant side effects – in the form of fire-sales, for example – when shocks are correlated. See the Annex for further discussion – and the analogy of income externalities in Keynesian economics.

bankers and academics that financial innovation was making the world riskier; and Shin (2005) used the swaying of the Millenium Bridge on its opening day to illustrate the idea of dangerous internal dynamics. They were ignored; as was the dramatic warning given at the conference on *Cycles Contagion and Crises* at LSE in June 2007, when Adrian and Shin used evidence from US investment banking to show that there was an asset boom in progress which could at any moment turn to bust.[3] 'In the subprime mortgage market in the U.S., when the balance sheets are expanded fast enough, even borrowers that do not have means to repay are granted credit ... the seeds of the subsequent downturn in the credit cycle are thus sown' Adrian and Shin (2008, p. 36).

Since the financial crisis, perceptions have greatly changed – not least because of the revisionist writings of Hyun Shin and Helene Rey. In Shin (2010, Chapter 10), for instance, there is an outline of macroprudential policies needed to limit externalities. These include regulatory intervention (with leverage caps and liquidity ratios), forward-looking provisioning charges on new loans, with structural reform to shorten the intermediary chain. Likewise, Rey (2013) adopts a potentially radical approach in considering what regulatory protection will be needed to secure monetary independence. Noting that 'at the heart of the transmission mechanism is the ability of financial intermediaries, whether banks or shadow banks to leverage up quickly to very high levels when financing conditions are favour-able', she concludes that 'macroprudential policies are necessary to restore monetary policy independence for the non-central countries. They can substitute for capital controls, although if they are not suffi-cient, capital controls must also be considered'.

The idea of this chapter is to take the subprime crisis as an illustra-tion of the two themes discussed above. First that, with cross-border banking, financial crisis can spread internationally irrespective of the exchange rate regime; and second that the regulations needed to check such undesirable 'exports' must take account of externalities, particularly those operating through asset prices.

---

[3] The paper was also presented at the BIS Annual Conference in June 2007. In both cases actual publication of the conference proceedings came much later, as Adrian and Shin (2008, 2010), respectively. Crises pay scant respect to publishers' timetables!

17.2 Joined at the Hip

Mr Greenspan was proud of the way the US economy weathered the collapse of the dotcom bubble; so he was sanguine about the subsequent boom in mortgage credit and house prices in the USA. A key reason why the subprime crisis was so different – and so dangerous – was that most of the assets in question were, on this occasion, held by highly leveraged institutions. Indeed, *almost two-thirds of subprime assets were on the balance sheets of leveraged institutions* (i.e. Investment Banks, Commercial Banks, Hedge Funds and US Government Sponsored Enterprises [GSEs]), as indicated in Table 17.1.

For a total of assets worth approx. USD 1.4 trillion, this gives an exposure of not far short of USD 1 trillion for leveraged institutions. A sizable fraction of these assets were held by non-US banks; however; their exposure comes to approximately USD 0.21 trillion or USD 210 billion.

How were these holdings financed? An indication is given by the graph in Avdjiev, McCauley and Shin (2016b), shown as Figure 17.1 below, where the thickness of the arrows indicates the size of the outstanding stock of claims. As between 2002 and 2007, Europe evidently borrowed an extra USD 1.1 trillion in the USA, and invested this back again. (This will include the exposure discussed above.) So, as the authors put it, 'the dollars raised by borrowing from US money market funds flowed back to the United States through purchases of securities built on subprime mortgages'.

The effects of the ensuing financial crisis on US banking institutions were simply catastrophic.

Table 17.1. *Subprime exposure by type of institution*

	Per cent of exposure	Approx value
Total of subprime assets	100	USD 1.4 trillion
Non-leveraged institutions	35	—
Total leveraged institutions	65	USD 0.91 trillion
Of which US	50	USD 0.70 trillion
Non-US	15	USD 0.21 trillion = USD 210 billion

Source: Shin (2010, p. 153, Table 9.1).

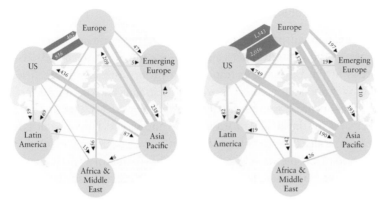

Figure 17.1 US dollar-denominated cross-border claims
Note: Arrows directed from region A to region B indicate lending from banks located in region A to borrowers located in region B.
Source: Avdjiev, McCauley and Shin (2016b).

Each of the former Big Five investment banks failed, was sold, or was converted into a bank holding company. Two mortgage giants and the world's largest insurer were placed under government control. And in early October, with the stroke of the president's pen, the Treasury – and by extension, American taxpayers – became part-owners in what were once the nation's proudest financial institutions. (Sorkin, 2009, p. 529)

Does the fact that the gross exposure of foreign banks was hedged on a currency basis (by short-term US dollar borrowing) mean that non-US banks were not exposed? Not at all: it suggests rather that non-US banks had joined the party and were behaving just like the US investment banks! So when the value of mortgage backed securities (MBS) collapsed, they too would take a hit on their balance sheets. What that would mean in terms of the euro or sterling would depend on movements in exchange rates; but floating rates would not deflect the blow. If a European bank is behaving like a US bank, then it will win or lose like a US bank. The currency exposure of European banks holding subprime assets may have been hedged, but they were exposed to serious capital losses nonetheless.[4]

---

[4] The Treasury bail-out of RBS in the UK (for £45 billion (or USD 70 billion), now worth only about £14 billion) was closely linked to its exposure to subprime assets (due in large part to hurried acquisition of a Dutch bank).

17.3 Danger: Pecuniary Externalities at Work

Ordinarily, foreign participation in US banking might not have been
a matter of much importance –just like opening commercial banking
branches in the USA, for example, with profits and losses appearing
on the parent's balance sheet. But for investment banking in 2002–7,
these were no ordinary times. It is true that considerable efforts were
being made by the BCBS to ensure that individual banks were adequately capitalised; and to ensure that there was a level playing field
internationally. But, as argued above, the regulatory analysis was
deeply flawed in that it ignored market failures and pecuniary
externalities.

Hence, as Adrian and Shin (2008, 2010) pointed out, the stage was
set for a major boom and bust in investment banking – a roller-
coaster ride that foreign banks were free to join, with the floating
exchange rate offering no path for escape.

17.3.1 *Investment Banking: The Shin Diagram*

How can we demonstrate that investment banks may be exposed to
insolvency by 'pecuniary externalities' involving asset prices?[5] What
better device than the two-sector model spelled out in Shin (2010) –
and the diagrammatic representation that goes along with it (shown
in Figure 17.2)? That is the purpose of this section. The figure shows
how the demand by 'active' or leveraged investors, together with that
of 'passive' investors, determines the price of risky assets. The amount
of risky assets is taken to be fixed in supply, with returns having a
uniform distribution, with mean return q, and downside risk of z.

The demand by passive investors, measured from the right-hand
axis, lies below the mean q with a slope reflecting their degree of risk
aversion, parameterised as τ. The demand curve for active investors is
measured from the left-hand axis, where the kink reflects the level of
their initial equity e; and the downward slope thereafter indicates, not
risk aversion, but the effect of adhering to a Value at Risk (VaR) rule
designed to ensure that the bank's equity will bear all the downside
risk. A fall in price allows for more assets to be held as there is *less
risk per asset* (specifically $p - (q - z)$) to be covered by this equity.

---

[5] Sometimes referred to as 'dynamic feedback effects'.

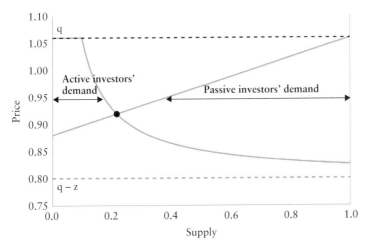

Figure 17.2 Market-clearing price of risky assets
Note: The equilibrium price lies 'within the band' between q and q − z where initial equity covers the maximum expected risk exposure on the balance sheet of the leveraged investors. So investment banks are dutifully following Basel Rules. (q = 1.06; z = 0.26; τ = 0.125; e = 0.026)

Given the parameter values indicated, market-clearing equilibrium is, where the schedules intersect.[6]

17.3.2 Pecuniary Externalities[7]

How will this equilibrium respond to unanticipated improvements in asset quality – in the expected pay-off q, for example, or in the maximum downside risk z? Each bank will respond to the parametric shift, taking the price of risky assets as given; but the concerted response will change asset prices and, assuming marking-to-market, the equity base of the banks themselves. If banks then proceed to expand their balance sheets as much as the VaR rule permits, the effect of such 'macro' shocks (i.e. those which affect every bank) will be amplified by 'pecuniary externalities'. It is the system-wide response to these price changes that gives the amplification.

---

[6] More details are available in Miller, Zhang and Rastapana (2016).
[7] See Annex for discussion of these 'externalities', with relevant references.

17.3.3 How Price Changes Amplify Common Shocks: Effect of a Quality Upgrade

The case of a perceived improvement in the mean of the distribution neatly indicates how the marking-to-market of asset prices together with VaR rules can generate 'pecuniary externalities' in the form of booms and busts. So, as in Shin (2010, p. 33), let the *mean* of the risky asset pay-off increase from q to q' without any change to the *downside risk* of the uniform distribution, which remains at z. Without marking–to-market, this will lead to an upward shift in the demand for both active and passive and investors as illustrated by the vertical shift from A to B in Figure 17.3. The price of risky assets will rise in response to the good news on quality, but the holdings of active investors will be unchanged.

Things do not end there if asset prices on the books of the leveraged institutions are marked-to-market and risk-taking is governed by VaR rules. For the rise in the equity of active investors will allow them to expand their holdings; and – assuming they fully exploit this profit opportunity – the effect will be a shift to the right of the demand by the investment banks. Allowing for the pecuniary externality, therefore, equilibrium shifts from A to C, with risky asset holdings by the active investors expanding by $y'_A - y_A$. As risk C lies

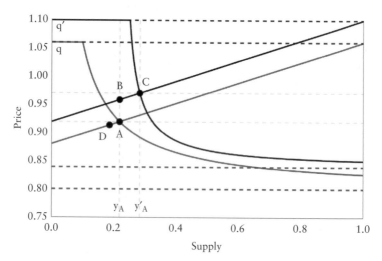

Figure 17.3 Increased market share of active investors with 'good news' on mean return

closer to the mean return than A, the risk premium will have fallen, which is why risk-averse investors move out.

17.3.4 What If the Quality Upgrade Was a Mistake?

It is widely argued that Rating Agencies were prone to assign higher ratings to subprime assets than were warranted (Akerlof and Shiller, 2014). This may not have been too evident when house prices were rising; but when they started to fall, it became clear that much of the lending to subprime borrowers would have to be written down. This was foreseen by Angelo Mozilo, the co-founder of Countrywide, a key player in marketing subprime mortgages: in an email to other Countrywide bank executives, dated 1 August 2005, he wrote: 'when the loan resets in five years there will be enormous payment shock and the borrower is not sufficiently sophisticated to truly understand the consequences, then the bank will be dealing with foreclosure in potentially a deflated real-estate market. This would be both a financial and reputational catastrophe' (Chatterjee, 2014).

Given the allegations of unprofessional behaviour made by Akerlof and Shiller – and repeated here – it is worth recording the outcome of subsequent legal actions taken by the US Department of Justice. Faced with the charge that they had handed out excessively rosy ratings for residential MBSs and collateralized debt obligations (CDOs) to try to win more business from 2004 to 2007, Standard and Poor's settled in 2015 by paying fines amounting to USD 1.4 billion. Would such a substantial sum have been paid on a charge that was unfounded? For good measure, the Department of Justice sued Moody's for the same reason, with a settlement of USD 0.9 billion in January 2017.

One way of looking at the boom/bust cycle in terms of this model is to think of the boom as driven by the (unjustifiably) 'good news' initially supplied by the Ratings Agencies; and the bust is what happens when these ratings are later reversed (when house prices have peaked, for example). The outcome is shown in Figure 17.3, where the reversal of the good news does not, however, lead to a return to A; rather to a point like D where investment banks have had to contract their holdings. Why is there an 'asymmetric' response to symmetrical news shocks? It arises because the capital gains on marking-to-market when the good news arrives are calculated on the basis of *initial* holdings at A; but the capital losses when the bad news arrives are calculated on the basis of the *expanded* holdings at C. With less equity on balance, they end up with fewer assets.

Could this asymmetry be sufficient in and of itself to trigger widespread insolvency? Not for the case shown in Figure 17.3, where the 'bad news' leads to a fall in the holdings of the leveraged sector, but the price fall (from C to D) lies well within the band of tolerable downside risk established in good times.

17.3.5 Catastrophic Outcomes

If the news shocks were larger, however, this could trigger generalised insolvency. This would occur, obviously, if the upward shift was big enough so that *the initial point A lies below the band of sustainable outcomes in the 'good news' equilibrium.* For if $q' - z$ exceeds the initial price at A, then a news reversal that takes equilibrium prices any lower will by definition wipe out the equity base of the investment banks.

Such a big shock will be sufficient for mass insolvency, but it is not strictly necessary. Take the 'intermediate' case sketched in Figure 17.4, where a symmetrical return to the initial equilibrium at A would be just manageable despite mark-to-market capital losses;

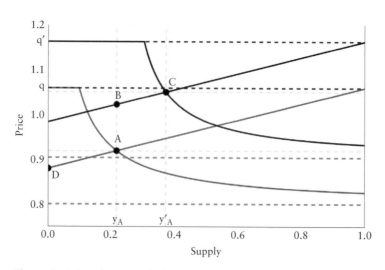

Figure 17.4 Simple reversal of 'good news' leads to insolvency

but the asymmetry leads to unsustainable losses for the investment banks (as selling assets leads to insolvency). Since any outcome below the 'band of sustainable outcomes' established in the good times implies negative equity of investments banks, the only possible equilibrium is at D where investment banks are forced to withdraw from the market, and passive holders determine the asset price.

Note that, in either the 'big shock' or 'intermediate' cases, the financial system exhibits what mathematicians such as Zeeman (1974) and Arnold (1984) refer to as 'catastrophic' behaviour – highly asymmetrical responses to symmetrical movements in exogenous forces. Good news, when rescinded, wipes out the entire equity base of investment banks!

For a careful dynamic analysis of a model much like that of Shin (2010), the reader is referred to simulations carried out by Aymanns et al. (2016, p. 263). In the Abstract, it is reported that:

A calibration of parameters to data puts the model in [a region where] there is a slowly building price bubble, resembling the period prior to the Global Financial Crisis, followed by a crash resembling the crisis, with a period of approximately 10–15 years. We dub this the Basel leverage cycle.

While this supports the view that the Basel II system was inherently unstable, we should point out that, for these authors, boom–bust behaviour is driven by cyclically varying leverage targets rather than by the activities of Rating Agencies.

So much for the technicalities. What is the broader issue that this formal analysis is designed to illustrate? It is the *fragility of equilibrium* in a context where profit-hungry, highly leveraged intermediaries are subject to a VaR mandate and mark-to-market accounting but free of any macroprudential oversight; and where regulatory oversight of subprime lending has been let slip for political reasons,[8] with credit standards left for Rating Agencies to set. If they rate a bundle of mortgages as triple A, they must be OK.

But what if, as Akerlof and Shiller (2014, Chapter 2) argue, the Rating Agencies themselves had distorted incentives? What if they were acting outside their area of proven competence – namely in rating corporate bonds – but were incentivised to give high ratings to

---

[8] Because, for example, getting low-income households onto the housing ladder is seen as a way of compensating for income inequality – as Calomiris and Haber (2014) suggest was the case in the USA.

complex products by generous fees paid by investment banks eager to expand their balance sheets? Then the stage is set for an unsustainable credit boom which will help pump up house prices, with the endogenous shifts in the lending capacity of the investment banks, induced by mark-to-market accounting, helping to accentuate the boom. Ultimately, however, as Mr Mozilo had foreseen, the end is financial disaster when house prices peak. And, willy-nilly, this will involve those hapless non-US banks who used 'the dollars raised by borrowing from US money market funds ... to finance purchases of securities built on subprime mortgages'(Avdjiev, McCauley and Shin, 2016b).

On the vexed question of why the Basel regulatory regime, designed to ensure financial stability in Western banking, should have failed so spectacularly to do so, Goodhart (2011, p. 564), in his history of the Basel Committee on Bank Supervision, offers the following fascinating observation:

From the mid-1990s there was an interesting variant of the 'capture' hypothesis, wherein the regulators come to adopt the self-interested positions of the regulated. In this variant the regulators are intellectually captured by the belief that the best versions of the models designed by banks for their own purposes should also be applied by the regulators.

But such an alignment is *not* necessarily desirable. Regulators should have different objectives from banks; the purpose of regulation – to deal with externalities and market failures in the financial system – is quite different from the purpose of banks – the maximisation of the current value of future discounted income flows of individual banks.

17.4 Conclusion

With the subprime crisis as the focus of attention, our observations closely match what Rey has argued on the basis of studying what she has dubbed the 'global financial cycle'; namely that, with cross-border banking in operation, the exchange rate regime cannot ensure monetary independence; and that macroprudential regulation is a more relevant policy option.

This look-back at recent history prompts a final reflection. Recall the famous episode in 2009 when Queen Elizabeth, on a visit to the LSE, asked why economists there had not seen the crisis coming. The answer given by Tim Besley and Peter Hennessy (2009) was that the lack of foresight on the part of their colleagues had many causes, but it was principally 'a failure of imagination'. What our account suggests is a better answer would have been: since 2001 some of our colleagues have been warning the world repeatedly that the Basel Rules were crisis-prone – but no-one was listening!

Annex Pecuniary Externalities: Macro Effects from VaR Constraints

That 'externalities' may include price increases induced by 'microprudential' rules may be unfamiliar; but the example of a Rating Agencies upgrade of mean returns on risky assets helps to illustrate this. Market-wide expectations of higher returns will, not surprisingly, lead to an increase in the market-clearing price – this is straightforward enough. But the fact that some agents, specifically highly levered Investment Banks, are subject to prudential regulation in the form of a VaR rule can lead to a subsequent series of price (and quantity) adjustments on their part – an amplification that may be referred to as a pecuniary externality.[9] For, if the initial asset price increases are marked-to-market, then the banks can – in line with VaR – purchase more risky assets; and, if this applies to all Investment Banks, their combined and synchronised purchases will push the price up further. But this will trigger a new round of marking-tomarket, more lending, etc. As this goes on for many rounds, some prefer to call the process a 'dynamic feedback' effect.

To convey the idea of such externalities to delegates at Jackson Hole, Shin (2010, p. 3) chose to draw an analogy with the dynamic effects following on from a gust of wind hitting the Millenium Bridge, which on the day it was formally opened had to be closed for restructuring. As he explained later:

The wobbling of the bridge is an example of a shock that is generated and amplified within the system. The wobble of the bridge feeds on itself. When the bridge wobbles everyone adjusts their stance, which makes the wobble even worse. So the wobble will continue and get stronger even though the

---

[9] Technically, the value of equity relevant to the demand for risky assets by any individual bank will depend on the market price of risky assets in its portfolio; but, as this reflects market demand, it will be an externality for the individual bank. (See Greenwald and Stiglitz, 1986.)

initial shock (say, a small gust of wind) has long passed. The pedestrians on the bridge are rather like modern banks that react to price changes, and the movements of the bridge itself are rather like [price] changes in the market. Shin (2010, p. 3)

The logic is reminiscent of the Keynesian notion that, when some firms and households are 'liquidity constrained' and there is insufficient aggregate demand, individual spending decisions can have a positive externality for the system as a whole. If one thinks of these liquidity constraints as the equivalent for firms and households of the VaR constraint for banks, the externality in this case is the increase in the spending power of others achieved despite these financial constraints. As Duncan Foley (2006, p. 186) expresses it:

The spender has the private advantage of purchasing the commodity she wants, but she also increases the money balances of another agent, which permits that agent to make a desired purchase that was previously impossible because of financial constraints. Because individual spenders do not take into account the external impact of their decisions, the volume of spending may be too small to employ all the resources of the economy, and there is a case for government intervention to subsidize spending (or to spend itself) to make up the difference.

Under a boom scenario, however, where Investment Bank balance sheets are over-expanding and leading to a house-price bubble, the appropriate intervention would be to *reduce* the expansion of lending – by imposing leverage caps; or imposing a provisioning charge when new loans are made; or perhaps by an explicit Pigovian tax on bank equity (which could be put in a resolution fund) (see Shin, 2010, p. 163).

References

Adrian, T. and H.S. Shin (2008), 'Liquidity and Leverage', Paper presented at LSE conference, June 2007, Chapter 1 of *Cycles, Contagion and Crises*, Special Paper Series No. 183, FMG, LSE (November), pp. 5–45.

(2010), 'Liquidity and Leverage', Paper presented at BIS Annual Conference, June 2007. *Journal of Financial Intermediation*, 19(3), pp. 418–37.

Akerlof, G.A. and R.J. Shiller (2014), *Phishing for Phools: The Economics of Manipulation and Deception*, Princeton, NJ: Princeton University Press.

Aoki, K., G. Benigno and N. Kiyotaki (2016), 'Monetary and Financial Policies in Emerging Markets', Working Paper, April.

Arnold, V.I. (1984), *Catastrophe Theory*, Berlin: Springer-Verlag.

Avdjiev, S., R. McCauley and H.S. Shin (2016a), 'Breaking Free of the Triple Coincidence', *Economic Policy*, 31, pp. 409–45.

(2016b), 'Conceptual Challenges in International Finance', *voxEU*, 28 September.

Aymanns, C., F. Caccioli, J.D. Farmer, V.W.L. Tan (2016), 'Taming the Basel Leverage Cycle', *Journal of Financial Stability*, 27, pp. 263–77, http://dx.doi.org/10.1016/j.jfs.2016.02.004.

Besley, T. and P. Hennessy (2009), *The Global Financial Crisis—Why Didn't Anybody Notice: Letter to the Queen*, London: British Academy.

Calomiris, C.W and S.H. Haber (2014), *Fragile by Design: The Political Origins of Banking Crises and Scarce Credit*, Princeton, NJ: Princeton University Press.

Chatterjee, P. (2014), 'Bank of America to Pay $16.65 Billion to Settle Mortgage Fraud Charges', *Corpwatch Blog*, August 21, www.corpwatch.org.

Danielsson, J., P. Embrechts, C. Goodhart et al. (2001), 'An Academic Response to Basel II', Financial Markets Group, Special Paper 130, LSE.

Foley, D.K. (2006), *Adam's Fallacy*, Cambridge, MA: Harvard University Press.

Friedman, M. and A.J. Schwartz (1963), *A Monetary History of the United States, 1867–1960*, Princeton, NJ: Princeton University Press.

Goodhart, C. (2011), *The Basel Committee on Banking Supervision: A History of the Early Years 1974–1997*, Cambridge: Cambridge University Press.

Greenwald, B.C. and J.E. Stiglitz (1986), 'Externalities in Economies with Imperfect Information and Incomplete Markets', *The Quarterly Journal of Economics*, 101(2), pp. 229–64.

Kiyotaki, N. and J. Moore (1997), 'Credit Cycles', *Journal of Political Economy*, 105(2), pp. 211–48.

Miller, M. and L. Zhang (2015), 'The Hedgehog and the Fox: From DSGE to Macro Pru', *Manchester School*, 483(S3), pp. 31–55.

Miller, M., L. Zhang and S. Rastapana (2016), 'A Comedy of Errors: Misguided Policy, Mis-sold Mortgages, and More', *CEPR DP* 11533.

Passari, E. and H. Rey (2015), 'Financial Flows and the International Monetary System', *Economic Journal*, 125(584), pp. 675–98.

Rajan, R. (2005), 'Has Financial Development Made the World Riskier?' in *Economic Policy Symposium Proceedings: The Greenspan Era*, Kansas City, MO: Federal Reserve Bank of Kansas City, pp. 313–69.

Rey, H. (2013), 'Dilemma, Not Trilemma: The Global Financial Cycle and Monetary Policy Independence', in *Economic Policy Symposium Proceedings: Global Dimensions of Unconventional Monetary Policy*, Kansas City, MO: Federal Reserve Bank of Kansas City, pp. 285–333.

(2016), 'International Channels of Transmission of Monetary Policy and the Mundellian Trilemma', *IMF Economic Review*, Palgrave Macmillan, 64(1), pp. 6–35.

Shin, H. (2005), 'Commentary: Has Financial Development Made the World Riskier?' in *Economic Policy Symposium Proceedings: The Greenspan Era*, Kansas City, MO: Federal Reserve Bank of Kansas City, pp. 381–86.

Shin, H.S (2010), *Risk and Liquidity*, Oxford: Oxford University Press.

Solomon, S. (1995), *The Confidence Game*, New York, NY: Simon and Schuster.

Sorkin, A.R. (2009), *Too Big to Fail*, New York, NY: Viking Penguin.

Zeeman, E.C. (1974), 'On the Unstable Behaviour of Stock Exchanges', *Journal of Mathematical Economics*, 1(1), pp. 39–49.

18 International Liquidity

PHILIPP HARTMANN

Liquidity is an important concept in economics, with high relevance for many policy issues, including for central banks. At a general level it refers to the ease with which goods and assets can be exchanged. It has proven to be a challenge, however, to develop a commonly agreed and used definition of it, partly because liquidity has a number of different facets.[1] It has microeconomic and macroeconomic, financial and monetary, as well as important international dimensions. In this chapter I want to look at international liquidity.

International liquidity problems have been a recurrent subject in modern economic history. Frequently, these have been discussed in terms of potential shortages or excesses of the main reserve asset(s) supporting an international monetary standard. For example, Cassel (1928) worried about the shortage of gold after the re-establishment of the gold standard in the inter-war period. Or Triffin (1960) warned that under the Bretton Woods system of fixed exchange

Any views expressed are only the author's own and should not be regarded as views of the ECB or the Eurosystem. I am grateful to Mario Cannella, Lavinia Franco, Philipp Hochmuth and Zohair Alam (IMF) for a lot of research assistance and to Manmohan Singh for making his data available and for answering a lot of questions on collateral markets. I would also like to thank Roland Beck, John Beirne, Johannes Breckenfelder, Michael Ehrmann, Maurizio Habib, Tobias Helmersson, Peter Hoffmann, Catherine Koch (BIS), Ludovit Kutnik, Livio Stracca, Georg Strasser, Oreste Tristani, Mika Tujula, Julian von Landsbergen and Bernhard Winkler for literature suggestions and advice.
[1] For example, the *New Palgrave Dictionary of Economics* (www.dictionary ofeconomics.com/dictionary, Durlauf and Blume, 2008) has entries for liquidity constraints, thin markets, money or the liquidity trap but no entry on liquidity more generally.

293

rates the supply of US dollars that would be needed for financing imbalances of international payments could become larger than the stock of gold that the USA had available for redeeming dollars at the agreed parity. It was also discussed whether an international lender of last resort was needed for providing liquidity to support international banks or countries in crises (e.g. Kindleberger, 1978; Fischer, 1999).

Recently, international liquidity issues have moved to centre stage again. Particularly, major international organisations developed surveillance frameworks for 'global liquidity' (see CGFS [2011], IMF [2014b] and BIS [2015] for the Bank for International Settlements [BIS] Global Liquidity Indicators website[2]). This surveillance activity pays special attention to cross-country (and aggregate international) bank credit. The policy objective seems to be international financial stability.[3] Some academic research substantiated this particular perspective (Bruno and Shin, 2015; Claessens, Cerutti and Ratnovski, 2016). Other academic work has reconsidered the debate on the availability of sufficient reserve currency/assets in today's floating exchange rate system (e.g. Farhi, Gourinchas and Rey, 2011; Eichengreen, 2012) and discussed the roles that a lack of safe government bonds (Eichengreen, 2016) or the emergence of new international currencies, such as the Chinese renminbi (A. Taylor, 2013), may play in it. In fact, ensuring a sufficient amount of international liquidity may have to be backed up by fiscal capacity (Obstfeld, 2011).

While I include credit flows as one important dimension, and the availability of sufficient reserve assets as another, in the discussion in this chapter, I argue that an encompassing international surveillance framework for liquidity should take a broader perspective. I first distinguish six major dimensions of international liquidity. I chose those because each of them corresponds to an important dimension of liquidity and relates to major contemporaneous policy questions. Then I focus on five of them, review their evolution before, during and after the recent financial crisis and briefly sketch some major policy issues they raise at present, including with respect to the roles of central banks. I end with some concluding remarks.

[2] www.bis.org/statistics/gli.htm.
[3] For further discussions of global liquidity from a monetary policy or financial stability perspective, see ECB (2012) and ECB (2011), respectively.

18.1 Dimensions of International Liquidity

On the basis of the extant literature and recent practical policy debates, I can see six dimensions of international liquidity, which are summarised in Table 18.1.

The first I denote as 'international financial market liquidity'. It refers to the ease with which assets that are of key importance for the international monetary and financial system, such as government

Table 18.1. *Dimensions of international liquidity*

(1) International financial market liquidity	Ease of buying and selling key internationally traded assets
(2) International funding liquidity	Ease with which financial intermediaries or non-financial corporations can receive funding from non-residents or in international currencies
(3) Private monetary liquidity	Cross-country trends of holdings of liquid assets by financial intermediaries, non-financial corporations or households
(4) Central bank liquidity	Cross-country trends in (aggregate) provision of money/liquidity by key central banks in international currencies
(5) International payments liquidity	Availability of generally accepted means for settling international payments (or of safe assets that are easily convertible in such means)
(6) International public liquidity support (not covered in this chapter)	Funds provided by, or available from, central banks for short-term support to financial intermediaries in foreign currencies (could also be defined including short-term support of international organisations to countries for managing balance of payments or budget crises)

Source: Author.

bonds or blue chip stocks from major economies, can be traded. These assets play important roles in international investment portfolios, for example because of the size of their domestic markets, their high credit worthiness or the good legal and governance frameworks they are subject to. A vast number of investors depend on the liquidity of the markets in which they are traded.

The second dimension I call 'international funding liquidity'. It describes the ease with which financial intermediaries or non-financial corporations can receive funding from non-residents or in international currencies. This very much coincides with the global liquidity concept used by the BIS or the International Monetary Fund (IMF), as referred to in the introduction of this chapter. It can also be seen as the international dimension of what used to be called 'general financing conditions' in the literature.

The third dimension, in Table 18.1, can be described as 'private monetary liquidity'. Here I mean the cross-country trends in buffers of liquid assets that financial intermediaries, non-financial corporations or households hold. For example, firms or households in several major countries could sometimes particularly 'hoard' cash and therefore be relatively resilient to shocks, or in other times be vulnerable to shocks when their liquidity holdings are low.

Fourth, central banks provide base money as part of their monetary policies and sometimes also emergency liquidity to restore financial stability in crisis situations. Surely, cross-country trends in the total creation of money by central banks, notably those issuing major international currencies, are a salient factor in international liquidity. Since an important part of the overall creation of money is endogenous, as driven by the demand of the private economic sectors, I do not call this 'public monetary liquidity' but 'central bank liquidity'.

The fifth, and last, dimension of international liquidity that I cover in this chapter can be regarded as the contemporaneous version of the availability of reserve assets that came up regularly in economic history (see the exemplary references in the introduction). While in the various forms of fixed exchange rate systems of the past certain amounts of reserve assets at the aggregate or individual country level were necessary for the agreed parities to hold, the application to today's mostly floating exchange rate system is less direct. Still, a certain availability of generally accepted means for settling international payments will make international trade and capital account transactions easier. These means include, inter alia, the availability of widely accepted international currencies and of assets that are safe and can be easily converted into such currencies. I call this 'international payments liquidity'.

There is also a sixth dimension of international liquidity that I denote as 'international public liquidity support'. This includes, for example, the swap agreements between central banks through which they provide liquidity in foreign currencies to financial intermediaries in their jurisdictions when private markets lead to shortages in those currencies. One could also include short-term assistance of international organisations, such as the IMF, to countries for which liquidity problems lead to balance of payments or budget crises in this category. In other words, this category may also be regarded as the liquidity aspects of what is now often referred to as the 'global financial safety net'[4] and what the historical literature described as 'international lender of last resort' (see the introduction). Unfortunately, there is not enough space in this chapter to do justice to this topic in addition to the other five dimensions above.

For all these dimensions too much or too little liquidity may not be good for the global economy or single countries' economies. For most of them too much liquidity could lead, inter alia, to excessive financing (negative net present value investments being financed), financial stability risks or economic over-heating and inflation. Too little liquidity could lead to financing constraints or subdued economic activity and disinflationary pressures. Only private monetary liquidity is somewhat different in this regard, because too much of it may be associated with too little economic activity. Liquidity hoarding is more likely to be associated with low investment or low consumption.

What makes these liquidity dimensions international? I use three criteria. They need to refer to:

i. the provision or receipt of funds or assets to or from abroad;
ii. the provision or receipt of funds or assets in foreign or international currencies; or
iii. common developments among (several) major economies.

---

[4] For recent discussions of the global financial safety net, see for example ECB (2016), Denbee et al. (2016), IMF (2016) and Scheubel and Stracca (2016). Allen (2013) provides an extensive discussion of central bank swap lines.

While the six dimensions are distinct, they are by no means independent of each other. Quite important relationships, and sometimes overlaps, exist between them, which – in the interest of space – I will not discuss further.[5] Needless to say, any attempt to define international liquidity and assess it empirically is fraught with difficulty and there are certainly other valuable ways to describe the field.

18.2 International Financial Market Liquidity

Financial market liquidity is typically measured with microstructure indicators such as trading volume, bid–ask spread or price impact of trades. At the international level the liquidity of major fixed-income and equity markets of the countries issuing the main international currencies and hosting the most important financial centres are of particular relevance.

Concerning fixed-income markets, a recent cross-country study by the G-20 Committee on the Global Financial System finds that their liquidity suffered significantly during the crisis but – using standard quantitative measures – has recovered recently to levels similar to before the crisis (CGFS, 2016). Figure 18.1 provides an example of this for the transaction costs observed in the benchmark government bond markets of Germany, Italy, Japan and the USA.

The average results for many such standard measures, however, are not consistent with widespread market commentary about liquidity deteriorations in fixed-income markets (e.g. Barclays, 2015; ICMA, 2016; Hooper, Slok and Luzzetti, 2016). In fact, they seem to mask some signs of fragility and 'bifurcation' in liquidity. As regards the former, even the major benchmark bonds of AAA-rated sovereign issuers behind the two main international currencies have experienced occasional tangible market disruptions. For example, between 2014 and 2015, US Treasuries exhibited an unusual 'flash rally' event and German bunds a 'sudden reversal'.[6]

'Bifurcation' refers to the phenomenon that some market segments, in particular the ones that are traditionally less liquid, show signs of

---

[5] For example, Korniyenko and Loukoianova (2015) analyse relationships between central bank liquidity, international funding liquidity and international payments liquidity. All the dimensions also mix demand and supply factors, albeit to varying degrees.

[6] Adrian, Fleming and Vogt (2016) discuss two more recent market disruptions in US fixed-income markets.

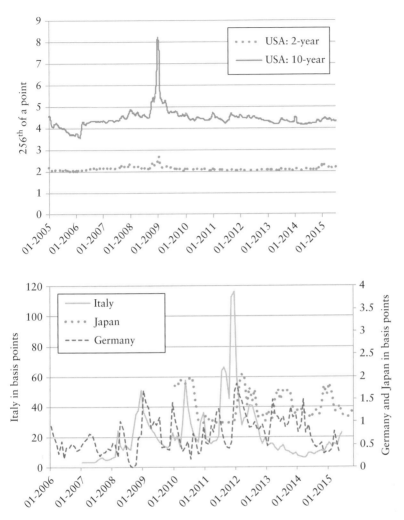

Figure 18.1 Bid–ask spreads of major benchmark government bonds
Note: Bid–ask spreads are defined as the difference between ask and bid
prices divided by the average of the two.
Sources: CGFS (2016) and Brokertec.

not sharing the normalisation of liquidity in the major segments. For
example, Bao, O'Hara and Zhou (2016) estimate that for stressed US
corporate bonds the price impact of trades has increased after the introduction of the Volcker Rule. In line with market commentary, Adrian,

Fleming and Vogt (2016) find that trade sizes in US corporate bond markets remain low after the crisis. But they argue that this could also be explained by other factors than more difficult block trading (e.g. the increased role of high-frequency trading). Duffie (2016) presents evidence of reduced market-making in the US general collateral repo market. Kurosaki et al. (2015) find that a host of less standard measures indicate a loss of liquidity in the Japanese government bond market and associated repo and futures markets since the autumn of 2014.

Equity markets seem to have received a little less attention in the recent international financial market liquidity debate compared to fixed-income markets. Aggregate turnovers in the major stock exchanges tend to be around or above their pre-crisis levels.[7] But turnover velocity, the ratio of total trading volume and total market capitalisation, tends to be around or below pre-crisis levels (except for the Tokyo Stock Exchange). This aggregate measure of equity market liquidity is shown in Figure 18.2. A more granular discussion of liquidity developments across more market segments, combining practical experience and research, is provided by PricewaterhouseCoopers (2015). It finds mixed evidence for recent developments in equity market liquidity.

One point of concern is whether the growth of high-frequency or algorithmic trading over the last decade is positive or negative for equity market quality. In what concerns the specific question that is of most interest in the context of this article, my reading of the available empirical literature is that technical progress and electronic trading led on average to a measurable improvement of liquidity and trading costs in equity markets (e.g. Hendershott, Jones and Menkveld, 2011; Boehmer, Fong and Wu, 2013; Menkveld, 2016). This notwithstanding, aggressive forms of high-frequency trading (e.g. that exploit speed differences between operators) can give rise to manipulative trading strategies (such as order anticipation or momentum ignition) that can impair market integrity (SEC, 2014; Miller and Shorter, 2016) or deteriorate liquidity through 'toxic' arbitrage opportunities (Foucault, Kozan and Tham, 2017) or 'back-running' large informed orders (Kervel and Menkveld, 2016). Moreover, in stressed market conditions automated order execution can interact with algorithmic trading in a way that leads to extreme price movements and the quick erosion of liquidity (CFTC and SEC, 2010).

---

[7] The figures are available from the author upon request.

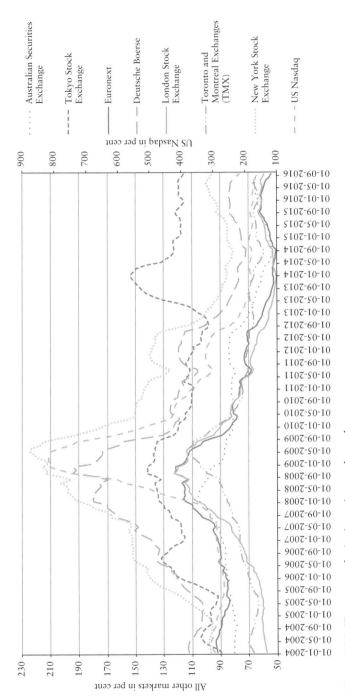

Figure 18.2 Turnover velocity in major stock markets

Note: Turnover velocity is defined as aggregate electronic order book trading volume of domestic shares divided by their aggregate market capitalisation times one hundred. It is annualised and displayed as twelve-month moving average in the figure.

Sources: World Federation of Exchanges and European Central Bank (ECB) calculations.

Another point of concern is the impact that the emergence of new trading venues is having on equity markets. The main issue is whether the competition and diversity benefits of this new 'fragmentation' exceed potential costs in terms of reduced liquidity or price discovery problems. The literature, as surveyed by SEC (2013), seems to suggest that the emergence of 'lit' venues[8] have been beneficial, without any measurable losses of liquidity, as long as the overall fragmentation does not exceed certain thresholds. For 'dark' venues,[9] however, some negative effects on market quality have been found, including for measures of market liquidity, e.g. when they are not limited to block trading or exceed relatively low shares of total trading.

All in all, three main groups of factors tend to drive recent liquidity developments in major bond and equity markets. First, post-crisis (private) de-risking and (public) re-regulation reduce banks' proprietary trading and market-making activities. For example, the enhanced risk sensitivity of major dealers seems to make them more reluctant to accept sizeable inventories so that it becomes more difficult to conduct large trades. Second, while technical progress and market transparency initiatives tend to lower trading costs in the long term (as discussed above), some forms of high-frequency trading and some 'dark' trading venues may also contribute to diverse liquidity outcomes. Third, novel unconventional monetary policies tend to have supportive short-term effects on many financial markets, but they can also add elements of fragility. First, asset valuations and liquidity may depend much more on market expectations about central bank behaviour, notably when expectations about turning points emerge (think, for example, of the US Federal Reserve's taper tantrum of 2013). Second, large amounts of assets are held on central banks' balance sheets and are not available as collateral or for trading (e.g. CGFS, 2017; Singh, 2017).

Three policy directions seem to emerge from this discussion. First, while ensuring the safety of systemic banks remains an important objective of post-crisis regulatory reforms, it is of great importance that the regulatory environment preserves incentives for resilient market-making. Second, while technical progress and electronic trading

---

[8] These are trading systems that display quotations in the consolidated quote streams.
[9] These are trading systems that are not 'lit', as defined in the previous footnote.

are overall beneficial for financial market liquidity, there need to be limits to some aggressive forms of high-frequency trading, and 'dark' trading venues should be reserved primarily to block trading. Third, central banks need to be particularly careful in communicating about their rather complex unconventional monetary policies and are well advised to adopt securities lending programmes (as many actually do) through which they give some of the assets otherwise encumbered on their balance sheets back to the markets. (I shall come back to the issue of unconventional monetary policies in Section 18.5.)

18.3 International Funding Liquidity

International funding liquidity can be measured via quantities or prices. Quantities are typically captured with the amounts of funding that financial or non-financial corporations receive from abroad or in international currencies. The costs of borrowing are captured with the associated interest rates on loans or corporate bonds and the costs of equity financing via the associated returns.

Let us look at international bank lending first, which is shown in Figure 18.3, distinguishing the parts that go to other banks (grey area) from the parts that go to non-banks (dotted area). Three observations stand out from the figure. First, there is a pronounced cycle (which seems to behave counter-cyclically to general financial market uncertainty, as captured by the Chicago Board Options Exchange VIX indicator also displayed in the figure). Total cross-border bank credit fluctuates between +20 per cent and −10 per cent per annum. Second, inter-bank lending is more volatile than retail lending. Third, since the financial crisis, the average growth rate and the volatility of this cross-border credit cycle have declined materially.

The volatile capital flows that are visible in Figure 18.3 provide a rationale for their surveillance and perhaps also for elements of the global financial safety net that can contain the potentially disruptive implications of violent credit flows in and out of countries and thereby help preserve international financial stability. Going beyond the bank credit in Figure 18.3, the Committee on the Global Financial System (2011) and the Bank for International Settlements (2015) developed a framework for assessing international funding liquidity (denoted there as 'global liquidity') with the help of a multiplicity of indicators. The IMF (2014b) developed a surveillance

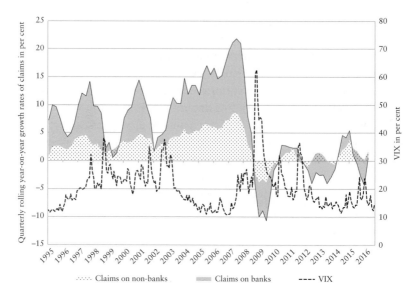

Figure 18.3 International bank lending
Note: Bank claims include all BIS reporting banks' cross-border credit plus
local credit in foreign currency. The data is quarterly but the two measures
are expressed in year-on-year growth rates. Inter-bank and retail lending are
stacked upon each other, so that the grey and dotted regions show their
relative growth contributions.
Sources: BIS (global liquidity indicators) and Chicago Board Options
Exchange.

dashboard of drivers, transmission channels and outcomes. Policy
options for containing disruptive cross-border flows or limiting their
effects include capital controls and prudential supervision and regulations (e.g. IMF, 2012c, 2013, 2015). In particular, the exposure of
emerging market economies to an international financial cycle of
capital inflows and outflows (e.g. Rajan, 2014 or Rey, 2013) may
make high-quality domestic financial supervision and a pragmatic
approach to some capital controls necessary for those countries.
Sound domestic monetary and fiscal policies, while important, will
probably not be enough (see also Section 18.5).

Let me turn from the widely debated 'global liquidity' to an aspect
of international funding liquidity that has received much less attention to date. This is the international availability and onward use of
collateral assets. Many investors (such as hedge funds, insurance

companies, pension funds or sovereign wealth funds) have assets in their portfolios which they will not wish to sell for some time. But they may have an interest in earning a further margin on them by lending them out for a while. Conversely, other financial operators that have short-term liquidity needs may desire to borrow such assets for use as collateral in secured re-financing transactions. There is a global market for reallocating these collateral assets among lenders and borrowers, which primarily ten to fifteen major banks operate.[10]

Figure 18.4, whose right-hand side displays the numbers from Singh (2016a, Table 1), describes the activity in this market before and after the financial crisis, including both public and private assets. It shows estimates of the total volume of secured transactions (solid and dashed lines), the collateral pledged for onward use at the above major dealers (solid line with triangles) and the ratio between the two, which defines the collateral reuse rate (solid line with squares). Numbers for the last two categories are not available before 2007.[11]

Whereas the available collateral appears relatively stable, secured transactions declined dramatically after 2007 and never recovered (Singh, 2016a). This implies the sharp reduction in the estimated rate at which collateral is reused. One interpretation of this decline in the international 'collateral velocity' or 'collateral multiplier' (Singh, 2011) is that the 'lubrication' of international financial markets, e.g. the ease with which secured funding can be raised, has suffered since the financial crisis. For example, the Basel III re-regulation of banks includes the requirement to hold a minimum amount of high-quality liquid assets (Basel Committee, 2013) and a limit to leverage (Basel Committee, 2014a). Both limit balance-sheet space and increase the effective costs of onward use of collateral (Singh, 2017).[12]

---

[10] See Singh (2016b) for a detailed description of this market.

[11] I am grateful to Manmohan Singh for authorising the reproduction of the figures since 2007 and for making the yet unpublished figures for the estimated volume of secured transactions before 2007 (dashed line) available. Note, however, that the latter figures (marked as 'not verified') could not be cleaned for potential reporting errors and may therefore constitute rough estimates.

[12] Duffie (2016) argues that the supplementary leverage ratio in the USA led to a reduction in trading of repurchase agreements. As many repos are backed by high-quality Treasury securities and therefore constitute low-risk, low-return business (at the individual level), he reasons that they are not attractive for dealers to intermediate when these are subject to a constraining regulatory ratio that is not weighted for risks.

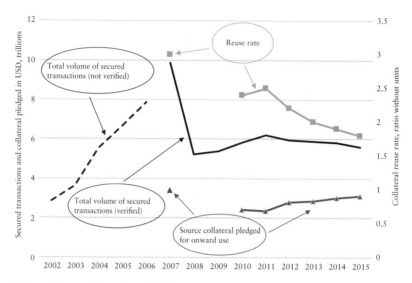

Figure 18.4 Collateral available at, and its reuse via, major international dealers

Note: The reuse rate is the ratio between the total volume of secured transactions and the collateral pledged at major dealers for potential onward use. It has no units.

Sources: Singh (2016a, Table 1) for data as of 2007 and unpublished pre-2007 data courtesy of Manmohan Singh. The total volume of secured transactions is derived from annual reports of the most important international banks intermediating collateral (Bear Stearns, Lehman Brothers [both only 2007], Citigroup, Goldman Sachs, JP Morgan, Merrill Lynch/ Bank of America, Morgan Stanley, Barclays, BNP Paribas, Credit Suisse, Deutsche Bank, HSBC, Royal Bank of Scotland, Société Générale, UBS and Nomura). The collateral pledged at these major dealers for onward use is calculated from proprietary data of hedge funds in major international financial centres and from data of the Risk Management Association (covering collateral pledged by pension funds, insurance companies, sovereign wealth funds, etc.).

Another interpretation is that collateral reuse, and therefore the markets for secured transactions, had grown out of proportion, which was corrected by the crisis and subsequent de-risking and re-regulation. Notice that the rough estimate of their size displayed in the dashed line shows a sharp upward trend between 2002 and 2006. Some observers have argued that excessive chains of collateral reuse helped build up leverage and interconnectedness and therefore turned into conduits of financial contagion during the crisis (e.g. Gorton and Metrick, 2012; FSB, 2016). Once market stress hits, the multiple uses of the same collateral assets mean that some collateral providers cannot promptly access their securities when they need them, borrowers cannot roll over their liabilities when they have to do so, and the supposed coverage of exposures in the system turns out to be partial, leading to unexpected losses.

There seems to be a trade-off here. Some reuse of collateral is required for supporting international funding liquidity. Too much reuse of collateral, however, may contribute to illusory liquidity and become a risk to financial stability. Baranova, Liu and Noss (2016) estimate the supply chain of high-quality public bond collateral for 2014 data at around four, which means that a high-quality government bond available for reuse is on average reused about four times.[13] They argue that this might constitute a 'required intermediation activity' and discuss how financial stress can lead to imbalances between collateral demand and supply and adversely affect dealers' intermediation capacity.

The few available studies on the international reuse of collateral typically rely on incomplete data (that require simplifying assumptions), many of which are not publically available. In order to gain a better understanding of the optimal level of international collateral reuse as a contributor to international liquidity and draw more firm policy conclusions, it is of great importance that better data become more readily available to research, policy and market communities. The Financial Stability Board (FSB, 2016) recently engaged in an initiative for generating such data. It deserves strong support and should ultimately lead to the dissemination of sufficiently representative and granular data in the appropriate format so that the needed research on the value and risks of collateral reuse can be conducted.

18.4 Private Monetary Liquidity

In the framework that I presented in Section 18.1, private monetary liquidity is captured by the holdings of liquid assets by households,

---

[13] This number is higher than the ones in Figure 18.4, because Singh's collateral data are broader including also below AAA and private assets such as equities.

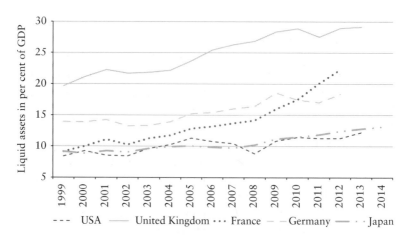

Figure 18.5 Liquidity holdings of non-financial corporations in major economies
Note: Liquidity holdings comprise currency and deposits and are expressed in per cent of GDP.
Sources: Currency and deposits: OECD Financial Accounts. Data for France and Germany only available until 2012 and for the USA and the UK until 2013. GDP: Bureau of Economic Analysis for the USA; Office for National Statistics for the UK; Institut National de la Statistique et des Etudes Economiques for France; Statistisches Bundesamt for Germany; Cabinet Office of Japan.

non-financial corporations and financial intermediaries. Liquidity holdings can be measured in a narrow or broader sense. Narrow measures incorporate cash holdings and current account balances, relative to total assets, equity or gross domestic product (GDP). Broader measures add other assets to them that can be easily converted into current account balances or cash.

For some time the literature has pointed towards a secular increase of liquidity holdings by non-financial corporations in major economies (Bates, Kahles and Stulz, 2009; IMF, 2011a, 2014a; Iskandar-Datta and Jia, 2012; Horioka and Terada-Hagiwara, 2013). This is corroborated by Figure 18.5, which shows a narrow measure of corporate liquidity holdings in the G-5 economies. The common upward trend is clearly visible in all five countries, although this data starts only in 1999.

The phenomenon is to some extent paradoxical, because one would expect that with technical progress and financial development the need to hold cash for corporations would decrease rather than increase.[14] An active corporate finance literature has discussed the factors that can explain (high) corporate liquidity holdings. They include the following: agency problems or weak corporate governance frameworks that allow managers to retain 'free cash flows' for personal motives rather than investing them or paying dividends; cash flow or general business uncertainty that strengthens precautionary motives; the needs of firms that operate in sectors that require particular flexibility in investment or hiring patterns (e.g. firms that are in the 'technology race' or rely on mobile human capital for making intangible investments); scarcity of investment and growth opportunities (including the value of waiting for better times); external financing constraints and underdeveloped or malfunctioning financial systems as well as national tax regimes and international tax loopholes that provide incentives for holding funds abroad rather than for repatriating profits. While the secular increase in corporate liquidity holdings since at least the 1990s is fairly common, the reasons for it can be quite different across countries (e.g. Iskandar-Datta and Jia, 2012) and also over time (e.g. Naoki, 2012). Therefore, depending on the country considered, most of the above factors seem to have played some role in this trend. In the crisis and post-crisis environment a number of features related to the above factors keep incentives for elevated corporate liquidity holdings high. These include, inter alia, economic uncertainties about the recovery, a host of political uncertainties and low opportunity costs of holding liquidity (e.g. related to low interest rates).

Interestingly, also households' liquidity holdings have been rising in countries like the USA, Japan or the euro area (since at least the late 1990s).[15] This phenomenon seems to be much less discussed in the literature than the corporate liquidity trend. For reasons of space

---

[14] In other words, it gives the impression that recent levels of corporate liquidity holdings are excessive, i.e. significantly higher than what would be needed if firms and markets were efficient and companies would only hold the liquidity they need for covering current expenses (paying for investments, wages, taxes or dividends).

[15] Some indicators are available from the author on request.

I do not address it further in this chapter, although it is an interesting area for future research.

Concerning financial intermediaries, the financial crisis has shown that not only capital but also liquidity buffers of banks have been too low and liquidity risk management too weak. In fact, there seems to have been a decline of liquidity holdings by banks over several decades (e.g. Banerjee and Mio, 2014; Bonner and Hilbers, 2015) and in the run-up to the crisis an over-reliance on unstable sources of short-term financing (e.g. Huang and Ratnovsky, 2011; Hahm, Shin and Shin, 2013). This reversed in the financial crisis, when banks hoarded liquidity (e.g. Berrospide, 2013; Acharya, Shin and Yorulmazer, 2011) and short-term funding markets dried up (e.g. Cassola et al. 2008; Gorton and Metrick, 2012; Heider, Hoerova and Holthausen, 2015). Following this experience, the new global liquidity standard of Basel III introduces a liquidity coverage ratio and a net stable funding ratio (Basel Committee, 2010, 2013, 2014b) in order to make banks adopt a more cautious approach to managing liquidity already in good times, so as to be more resilient to liquidity shocks when financial stress hits. The gradual phasing in of these regulatory instruments is also contributing to a re-increase of banks' liquidity holdings. (Their financial stability advantages are the flip-side of part of the balance sheet constraints for collateral reuse that I mentioned in Section 18.3.) It is interesting to see that in terms of liquidity holdings banks and non-financial corporations had been on, more or less, opposite trajectories, but the crisis and subsequent re-regulation made banks again more similar to non-financial corporations.

What are the policy implications of the corporate liquidity 'hoarding' phenomenon referred to before? First, to the extent that it reflects economic uncertainties and limited growth prospects, appropriate demand and supply-side policies that firm up the current recovery and lay the ground for an increase in potential growth are called for. Second, and related to the first point, the scarcity of investment opportunities could be alleviated through policies that foster innovation. Third, as the recovery strengthens and monetary policies normalise, the opportunity costs of holding cash should rise. Fourth, in countries where financing constraints play a role in increasing transparency through accounting reforms, restructuring of the banking system or the development of capital markets and other non-bank financing sources (e.g. Sher, 2014) could be considered. Fifth, in the countries where there is evidence of agency problems in corporate control, corporate governance reforms (such as enhancing the presence and independence of outside directors, limiting dual roles of chief executive officers [acting also as chairman of the supervisory board], introducing a corporate governance code [including fiduciary responsibilities for institutional investors] and strengthening firm audit and monitoring functions) could help (see e.g. Aoyagi and Canelli, 2014; Sher, 2014). Sixth, the international harmonisation of tax systems would be desirable. Since this does not seem to be very realistic, it would be important to further pursue international agreements that limit the exploitation of gaps and mismatches in tax rules allowing the artificial shifting of profits to low or no-tax locations, such as the Organisation of Economic Cooperation Development's (OECD) Base Erosion and Profit Shifting (BEPS) initiative.[16] From this list it becomes clear that high corporate liquidity holdings may be a symptom (or side effect) of other problems in major economies. Therefore, most policy measures that could be considered are not intended to reduce corporate liquidity holdings as such but to address the deeper underlying problems.

18.5 Central Bank Liquidity

The monetary liquidity created by central banks has traditionally been measured with various monetary aggregates, ranging from base money to M3. But in times where money aggregates are not targeted, narrow aggregates underestimate the total liquidity creation of central banks and broad aggregates are driven by many factors that cannot be influenced by central banks. Moreover, when one wants to make the stocks comparable across central banks and divide by GDP, then one may see differences in the velocity of money rather than differences in total liquidity creation. Hence, monetary aggregates may not be the best measures for capturing central banks' liquidity creation.

This is why in Figure 18.6 I look at a measure that expresses the total balance-sheet size of four major central banks in per cent of their domestic GDP. This measure is also meant to capture the total stimulus that the central banks try to provide to their respective economies in times when interest rates are at, or close to, their lower bounds, and unconventional monetary policies, such as asset purchase programmes,

---

[16] See www.oecd.org/tax/beps/.

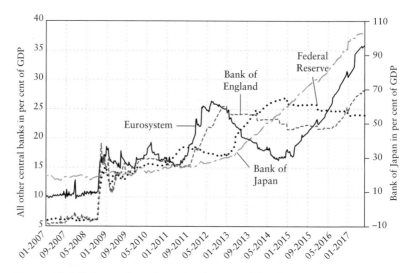

Figure 18.6 Balance-sheet sizes of major central banks
Note: Balance-sheet size is measured as total assets in per cent of domestic GDP.
Sources: Bank of England, Bank of Japan, ECB, Federal Reserve Board and ECB calculations.

are very large.[17] Due to the severity of the financial crisis (and of the subsequent European debt crisis) as well as the depth and length of the associated recessions, central bank liquidity reached unprecedented peace-time levels (e.g. Ferguson, Schaaf and Schularick, 2014).

The relative extent of these expansions depended on the relative length and severity of recessions in different constituencies, on their economic and financial structures, on the degree with which other policy branches (notably fiscal and structural policies) were also able to support the recoveries and potential growth, and on the different central bank objectives and tools. In the USA the peak level mildly exceeded 25 per cent of GDP; the euro area and the UK recently broke 35 per cent and 28 per cent, respectively (all left-hand scale in Figure 18.6). In Japan the central bank's balance sheet even exceeded 100 per cent of GDP lately (right-hand scale in Figure 18.6).

Whether the monetary policies behind them were – from a cost-benefit perspective taking into account both the achievement of

---

[17] It does not capture, however, central banks' forward guidance communication.

central bank objectives and unintended side effects – overall just right, too drastic or too timid, remains the subject of fierce debates. Supporters point to:

- large and protracted deviations from statutory central bank objectives and evidence that target variables move in the right direction in response to the policies;
- risks of deflation and stagnation comparable to the Great Depression in the 1930s; and
- the absence of (sufficiently strong) other policies moving central bank target variables in the right direction and avoiding very bad economic outcomes.

In other words, central banks just did what was needed to fulfil their objectives in very difficult times and to avoid economic disaster.[18]

Critiques argue that unconventional monetary policies (also in combination with low (and sometimes even negative) policy rates):

- stretch or even violate central bank mandates;
- are little effective, have contradictory elements and coincidental movements of target variables towards central bank objectives are largely driven by other factors (such as commodity price or exchange rate fluctuations);
- imply sizeable adverse economic side effects, such as distortions in financial markets (e.g. with respect to asset valuations, market fragilities or trading strategies; see also Section 18.2), financial stability risks (see also Section 18.3), moral hazard on the side of governments, economic uncertainty or contributions to inequality;
- make the fulfilment of other policy authorities' mandates more difficult (e.g. prudential policies with respect to various financial intermediaries at home or macroeconomic management in emerging economies); and
- cause major exit challenges (including the risk of central bank losses, which may in turn unduly delay the normalisation).

---

[18] For central bank policymakers providing the rationale for their unconventional monetary policies and defending their effectiveness see, for example, Bernanke (2012), Draghi (2015) or Kuroda (2015). For research papers supporting their effectiveness see, for example, Kapetanios et al. (2012), Gambacorta, Hofmann and Peersman (2014), Engen, Laubach and Reifschneider (2015), Andrade et al. (2016) or Ciccarelli and Osbat (2017).

In their eyes the costs of such policies exceed their benefits (or they tend to do so when being multiplied over time (QE1, QE2, etc.) or when their durations exceed certain times).[19]

It is outside the scope of this chapter to reach a conclusion about which camp is right. The judgement may also differ across constituencies.[20] Assuming that unconventional monetary policies create domestic stimuli in the countries that undertake them, the issue is how this adds up internationally. Bernanke (2013) argues that the additional aggregate demand amounts to a positive-sum game among the countries involved. Since all the major industrial countries engage in similar monetary expansions, exchange rates should not change persistently (which makes the current episode different from the early 1930s tariff war and beggar-thy-neighbour competitive devaluations). Moreover, a few recent studies (e.g. Ammer et al. 2016; Georgiadis, 2016) point out that the contractionary effects on foreign countries via exchange rate depreciations and exports may be over-compensated by expansionary effects via expenditures and imports of the source countries. So, even if unconventional policy drives the exchange rate down, still a positive-sum game may emerge among countries with similar positions in the business cycle. I am not aware of any study, however, that tries to assess analytically both the adequacy of the aggregate demand effects at the international level and the costs of potential unintended side effects. As a sub-issue of such an analysis, we do not know at this juncture whether the effects of unconventional monetary policies on aggregate central bank liquidity creation in the major international currencies are optimal or at least net welfare positive.

I see, nevertheless, a few selected conclusions from this experience, which may have implications for future monetary policies. First, central banks and academia do not yet possess proper frameworks for assessing the relative benefits and costs of monetary policies as

---

[19] See, for example, White (2012), who also discusses many of the above arguments. Other critical voices include Meltzer (2015), Goodhart and Wood (2016) and Taylor (2017). Goodhart, as cited by *The Economist* (2016), points out that trying to make negative rates effective via bank lending (which would require passing them on to deposit rates) would amount to political suicide.

[20] Blinder et al. (2017) interpret the results of a survey showing mixed results for central bank governors' views about whether quantitative easing monetary policies would remain in central banks' regular toolkit in the future as indicative for much still being unknown about their costs and benefits.

extreme as the ones that we have experienced during the last decade. On the one hand, analytical models that can compare in a consistent way the welfare benefits and welfare costs of the closer fulfilment of statutory central bank objectives with the unintended side effects mentioned above largely are still to be developed. On the other hand, and perhaps even more challenging, if some of the most important side effects severely affect non-central bank policy branches (e.g. bank, securities market, insurance or pension supervision[21] or fiscal policy and prudence), then the standard economic answer would be coordination, through a higher authority or through negotiation between central banks and the affected authorities. Both solutions, however, are inconsistent with the strong independence that has so far been regarded as a corner stone of modern central banking.[22] In other words, a redefinition of central bank independence may have to be considered if extreme unconventional monetary policies have also to be conducted in the future.[23]

Second, it has been argued that international spillovers of unconventional monetary policies can be large (e.g. Neely, 2015; Chen, Mancini-Griffoli and Sahay 2014; Chen, Filardo and Zhu 2016).[24]

---

[21] See e.g. Aldrick (2012) citing Goodhart or the European Insurance and Occupational Pensions Authority (EIOPA, 2014) on pensions. Based on a very careful analysis, Chodorow-Reich (2014) argues that the Federal Reserve's unconventional monetary policies tended to have beneficial or neutral effects on the asset prices of US bank holding companies and life insurers. Moreover, reach-for-yield behaviour of US pension and money market funds that can be identified after such policies dissipated after a few years. A close look at the results, however, reveals a large diversity of findings across policy announcements and intermediaries and a frequent absence of statistical significance for credit default swap (CDS) premium and bond yield measures. In addition, the narrow event windows that had to be used for banks and life insurers may be vulnerable to short-termism of investors. Finally, the US policy mix considered does not include negative policy rates, as in the case in the euro area, Japan, Sweden or Switzerland, and the USA also recovered more quickly from the crisis than other economies.

[22] The Deutsche Bundesbank, founded in 1957, is widely seen as the first role model of an independent central bank. For a recent discussion of the literature and merits of central bank independence, see e.g. Fischer (2015).

[23] This conclusion would not apply if research showed that the dominance of monetary policy over all other policy branches was superior to other scenarios in terms of economic welfare.

[24] They seem to be particularly pronounced for US asset purchase programmes, whereas euro area unconventional monetary policies seem to have much weaker international effects (e.g. Chen et al. 2017).

In particular, via capital inflows and outflows they can significantly disturb the domestic macroeconomic management of some emerging market economies that have different cyclical positions from the source countries and create financial stability risks for them (e.g. Rajan, 2014).[25] At this point, it does not appear likely that emerging economies could sufficiently ring-fence their economies from spillovers originating from extreme monetary policies of a country at the centre of the international monetary system by improving their domestic economic policies. For example, even if emerging economies could afford freely floating exchange rates, this would not allow a fully independent monetary policy (Rey, 2013) and the traditional domestic counter-cyclical approach to it could well amplify the problematic capital inflows and outflows. This, in turn, would make it harder to design effective macroprudential measures or capital controls leaning against them (see also Section 18.3).

There are also concerns that sizeable exchange rate effects of unconventional monetary policies could give rise to so-called 'currency wars' (a term coined by Brazil's finance minister Guido Mantega in 2010). Stimulating the domestic economy via policies that depreciate the exchange rate cannot work for all countries at the same time, as some countries' depreciations are other countries' appreciations. The extant literature is not yet clear about how important the exchange rate is as a transmission channel for unconventional monetary policy and whether it is more or less important than for the transmission of conventional monetary policy.[26] But since the extent of such policies have been rather extreme for major economies (see Figure 18.6), but not

---

[25] Fratzscher, Lo Duca and Straub (2013) find that US quantitative easing policies increased the procyclicality of portfolio investment flows to emerging economies. Moreover, for an emerging economy such as Mexico, which has significant foreign bank presence, the internal risk effects of foreign quantitative easing programmes may be larger than positive real economy effects (Morais, Peydro and Ruiz, 2015). All this is consistent with monetary policy spillovers being positive, i.e. expansionary US policies having a stimulating effect on the economies of other countries and vice versa. See also the discussion on the international financial cycle and its link to US monetary policy in Section 18.3.

[26] For recent estimates of the exchange rate channel in the transmission of conventional and unconventional monetary policies in the euro area, see for example Ciccarelli and Osbat (2017).

identical, and their timing different, exchange rate implications cannot be ignored (even if estimated elasticities were comparable to conventional monetary policy).

All in all, these observations suggest that the previous consensus that monetary policy should focus at the statutory domestic objectives[27] and that the gains from international monetary policy coordination are small, at best, may have to be revisited in a world where sizeable unconventional policies are not a rare exception (at least with respect to the effects on emerging economies and perhaps on other advanced economies that have different cyclical positions from the source countries).[28]

18.6 International Payments Liquidity

In today's floating exchange rate environment it is less straightforward how to measure the 'reserves' that are available for settling international payments than was the case in fixed-rate regimes such as the Bretton Woods system. In Figure 18.7 I follow Eichengreen (2016, Chart 8), who aggregates world gold holdings, base money created by OECD central banks and highly rated debt securities of OECD countries and supranational institutions as a measure of 'international liquidity'.[29] The idea is that these liquid and safe assets can either be used directly in settling current or capital account transactions or be easily converted into the currencies needed for this purpose. For example, if their availability was too low, then the concern is that trade in goods or assets could be hampered. I added to the figure a measure of world trade growth (black line), keeping in mind that it is highly endogenous, much like the total stock of liquid and

---

[27] Kenen et al. (2004) date the so-called OHIO doctrine, which stipulates that it is best if every country's economic policies keep its own house in order, back to the Reagan–Thatcher era of the 1980s.

[28] Borio (2014) makes a similar point in that central banks were reminded by the crisis period that they need to take their global interactions more into account. J. Taylor (2013), however, argues that the main reason for sizeable international repercussions of unconventional monetary policies was the deviations they implied from the usual central bank rules. A return of major central banks to some monetary policy rules could bring the world economy close to a cooperative equilibrium, in his view.

[29] I would like to thank Barry Eichengreen for his permission to reproduce his chart.

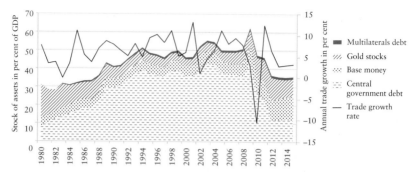

Figure 18.7 Liquid and safe assets for settling international payments
Note: Liquid and safe assets for settling international payments are measured
as the aggregate stock of central government debt, multilateral debt, base
money and gold in per cent of world GDP. Central government debt is AAA
and AA-rated sovereign debt securities of OECD countries, multilateral debt
is debt securities of supranational organisations, base money is high-powered
money created by central banks of OECD countries, and gold stocks are
global gold holdings by governments, central banks, the IMF and the private
sector.
Sources: Eichengreen (2016, Chart 8) for liquid and safe assets for settling
international payments in per cent of world GDP; OECD for trade growth
and ECB calculations.

safe assets. While a relationship between the two variables is hard to
see for yearly fluctuations, their hump-shaped development over the
whole thirty-five years covered in the figure is consistent with a mildly
positive long-term correlation.

More specifically, after a long period of an increasing stock of
liquid and safe assets, in line with quite steady trade growth,
Figure 18.7 shows a marked decline between 2009 and 2012. This
happened when the financial crisis proceeded and, in Europe, turned
into a sovereign debt crisis, i.e. precisely when the demand for safe
assets was extremely high as investors were flying to safety.
Moreover, ongoing regulatory reforms, such as the Basel global
liquidity standard (Basel Committee, 2010, 2013, 2014b) and the
transfer of over-the-counter derivatives onto central clearing counterparties (Financial Stability Board, 2010), are further adding to the
demand for high-quality liquid assets. As can be seen from the dimin-
ishing area with dashed horizontal lines, the main source of the

reduction in 'supply' comes from the reduction of highly rated OECD country sovereign debt. The subsequent base money creation of OECD central banks (although being very large by historical standards in terms of domestic GDP – see Section 18.5 above) could only partially compensate for the reduction in supply of highly rated government debt relative to world GDP (expanding the dotted area in Figure 18.7). As observed already by Caballero (2010), Credit Suisse (2011, Exhibit 174) and Garcia (2011), most of this was due to downgrades of government debt during the European sovereign debt crisis, which further reinforced the reduction of private 'safe assets' from the preceding financial crisis.

Since the resulting demand–supply mismatch may be weighing on global growth, the issue emerges of what might be done about it. The market mechanism may not be doing its regular job, because many interest rates are at, or close to, their lower bounds. On the one hand, an attempt could be made to reduce the demand for safe assets, which may be excessively high in the present context. This could be achieved through strengthening growth policies, resolving remaining financial sector fragilities and reducing potential policy uncertainties. Many of the relevant policy options, however, may take time to gain traction.[30]

On the other hand, the supply of safe assets could be (re-)increased. One avenue in this direction would be that high-quality sovereign borrowers issue further public debt. Large sovereigns that could make some difference in this regard are, for example, the USA or Germany, but they alone may not have the incentives or capacity to do so in sufficient amounts. Another avenue for expanding the spectrum of safe public assets would be to pool debt among euro area countries; be it via euro bonds (Farhi, Gourinchas and Rey, 2011), where different sovereigns stand in for each other, or via European Safe Bonds (ESBies; see Brunnermeier et al. 2011), which are the senior tranche of a securitisation of different sovereign bonds. In both ways European countries could create a significantly larger pool of

---

[30] Caballero and Farhi (2013) suggest that the government could also tax the wealth of the agents with the highest demand for safe assets and finance a fiscal expansion from the proceeds (potentially including redistributing the money to agents with a low demand for safe assets). In theory, this could be a faster approach.

liquid and relatively safe public debt.[31] So far, however, it has proven to be difficult to move in these directions, in particular for the different interests of fiscally strong and fiscally weaker European countries. A third avenue for increasing the global supply would be to have emerging economies, notably large ones such as China, undertake the necessary fiscal, regulatory and legal reforms for developing their financial systems, opening up their capital accounts and becoming issuers of internationally liquid and safe public debt (e.g. Farhi, Gourinchas and Rey, 2011). Despite the willingness of Chinese authorities to gradually develop the internationalisation of the renminbi, however, the prospect of a sizeable amount of internationally liquid and safe renminbi debt seems to be rather far off.

Both variants imply moving towards a multipolar international monetary and financial system, with less reliance on the dollar and US public debt (e.g. Eichengreen, 2009, 2011, 2016; Dailami and Masson, 2011). This may be justified for overcoming Triffin-type problems that the dominant economy at the centre of the system does not have the incentives to issue sufficient assets (Farhi, Gourinchas and Rey, 2011) or for lower growth in the centre relative to other countries and international investors' interest in diversifying their portfolios (Portes, 2012).[32] In such a multipolar system the dollar, the euro and the renminbi, or US, European and Chinese public debt would share the responsibility for providing enough international liquid and safe assets.

Increasing the issuance of the best sovereign borrowers, however, raises immediately the question of how it can be ensured that these bonds remain of high quality. In the aftermath of the crisis public

---

[31] If managed well, this could also break the adverse sovereign-bank nexus and help stabilise European Economic and Monetary Union. In a recent note, however, Standard and Poor's (2017) warned that – based on its standard methodology – it would probably rate ESBies in the lower half of the investment grade spectrum rather than AAA. The reasons for this are the limited diversification of a portfolio of euro area sovereign bonds and the high correlation of euro area sovereign default risk. Moreover, Standard and Poor's expects that ESBies would reduce the overall supply of AAA assets, as some of the current AAA sovereign bonds would be repackaged into lower-rated ESBie.

[32] Hartmann (1998) argues that the medium of exchange and store of value functions of money imply centrifugal and centripetal forces, respectively, that can lead to multiple international currencies of varying importance.

debt has reached very high levels in major economies.[33] For example, gross general government debt in advanced economies has increased from 74 per cent of GDP in 2006 to 108 per cent in 2016 (IMF, 2011b, 2017). By 2016 large high-debt countries include particularly Japan (239 per cent) and Italy (133 per cent); but also the USA reached 107 per cent of GDP. In other words, major advanced economies face a public debt overhang, which needs to be resolved over time (IMF, 2012b). Even though precise thresholds about critical public debt levels are hard to pin down, the historical experience is that excessive debt-accumulations precede sovereign defaults and make countries vulnerable to confidence and financial crises (Reinhart and Rogoff, 2009; IMF, 2012b). Therefore, the room for increasing the amount of public debt is limited for many advanced economies at present.

Hence, a more sustainable – even though probably slower – avenue for re-increasing the amount of liquid and safe assets in the international monetary system may be to consolidate public finances in the countries that lost their high creditworthiness in the crisis (see e.g. IMF, 2012a). In fact, as the economic recovery is strengthening in advanced economies, this may not be procyclical any longer, even though some central banks have already started to exit from their ultra-expansionary monetary policies. As pointed out by Caballero and Farhi (2013), healthy public finances and therefore fiscal capacity are central to the ability of escaping a 'safety trap'.[34] Only when their public finances are solid and public debt levels limited, fiscal authorities of major countries are able to issue further public debt in response to shocks that make safe asset demand exceed safe asset supply. In other words, as the world moves towards a multipolar monetary system, it is key that the main providers of liquid and safe assets (say, the USA today and the major member countries of the euro area, as well as China in the future) have sound public finances to start with.

---

[33] For example, governments had to dedicate significant fiscal resources to stabilising their banking systems and assume very expansionary fiscal stances to cushion the crisis recessions. As Turner (2016) describes it, private sector debt overhangs were transferred to public sectors but not removed.

[34] These authors start from a shock to the demand for safe assets, but the same reasoning applies to a safety trap associated with a drop in safe asset supply, such as sovereign downgrades.

18.7 Concluding Remarks

In this chapter I have divided the concept of international liquidity
into six dimensions that have a significant cross-border component,
that relate to foreign or major international currencies or that relate
to joint trends in major countries. This includes, but goes way
beyond, the 'global liquidity' dimension (which I denote as 'international funding liquidity') recently emphasised by the BIS and the IMF,
which focus particularly on international financial stability issues. I
argue that global economic and financial surveillance should take a
broad approach and cover all six dimensions.

I find that international financial market liquidity has broadly nor-
malised after the financial crisis, but it seems to have become more
fragile and some traditionally less liquid market segments seem to have
lost some liquidity. International funding liquidity is strongly cyclical,
but the growth rate and volatility of cross-border credit has declined
since the financial crisis. Private monetary liquidity, in particular liquidity holdings of firms and households, has followed a similar upward
trend in major countries for about the last two decades or more.
Central bank liquidity has reached unprecedented peace-time levels during the crisis. In contrast, international payments liquidity has declined
materially during the crisis, mainly because of downgrades of European
sovereigns that diminished the available amount of safe assets. (For reasons of space I do not particularly discuss the sixth international liquidity dimension, the one that captures public liquidity support.) Many of
these liquidity dimensions cannot be added up, but – respecting their
similarities and differences – I do not find a general shortage of international liquidity across the dimensions discussed in this chapter. In some
areas there are high levels of liquidity, in other areas there is diminished
liquidity, and yet in other areas further research is needed.

Several of these liquidity developments have similar origins. For
example, the crisis recessions, slow recoveries and (in the eyes of
some) limited growth prospects for the future contributed to major
liquidity provisions by central banks, corporate cash hoarding and a
reduction in cross-border credit cycles. The fiscal costs of financial
instabilities and the significant deficit spending programmes for cushioning the crisis recession significantly increased public debt (often
already from relatively high levels) and reduced the creditworthiness
of many sovereigns, which in turn reduced the availability of liquid

and safe assets and therefore international payments and international funding liquidity. Post-crisis de-risking and financial re-regulation contributed to reduced market-making in some markets and the reduction in the cross-border credit cycle. Very large asset purchase programmes of central banks – albeit stabilising in the short term – may over time also contribute to some liquidity fragilities in financial markets and to some encumbrance of liquid and safe assets, thereby reducing international payments liquidity.

The observations made in analysing these developments raise a number of policy considerations that have a bearing on the underlying forces influencing international liquidity. For example, financial regulation needs to be designed in a way that preserves incentives for market-making in major international assets. It may also have to discourage aggressive forms of high-frequency trading and limit 'dark' trading venues to block trading. Moreover, emerging economies need to possess sound prudential frameworks and may have to adopt a pragmatic approach towards capital controls in order to cushion the effects of the international credit cycle on their economies. Also, data need to be made available for properly analysing to what extent global collateral reuse is needed for lubricating the financial system and to what extent it risks acting as a conduit for contagion. Furthermore, ways need to be found for how soaring corporate cash hoarding can be brought back into real investment. In addition to growth policies this may also include corporate governance reforms or international tax agreements. International spillovers of unconventional monetary policies, in particular towards emerging economies, suggest revisiting the current consensus on international monetary policy coordination. It is also advisable that central banks running large asset purchase programmes use securities lending facilities (as many actually do) to avoid contributing to the encumbrance of (liquid and safe) assets. They need also to be careful about communication on these and other unconventional monetary policies, notably close to turning points. Finally, as the economic recovery in advanced economies strengthens, consolidating public finances may be a more sustainable approach to re-increasing the availability of liquid and safe assets for ensuring international payments liquidity than the further issuance of sovereign bonds by large countries that have already reached high debt levels. Needless to say, many of these policy considerations are important way beyond the optimal level of international liquidity.

References

Acharya, V., H. Shin and T. Yorulmazer (2011), 'Crisis Resolution and Bank Liquidity', *Review of Financial Studies*, 24(6), pp. 2166–205.

Adrian, T., M. Fleming and E. Vogt (2016), 'Market Liquidity after the Financial Crisis', *Federal Reserve Bank of New York Staff Reports* 796, October.

Aldrick, P. (2012), 'QE "counterproductive", Charles Goodhart warns', *The Daily Telegraph*, 2 November.

Allen, W. (2013), *International Liquidity and the Financial Crisis*, Cambridge, UK: Cambridge University Press.

Ammer, J., M. De Pooter, C. Erceg and S. Kamin (2016), 'International Spillovers of Monetary Policy', Federal Reserve Board International Finance Discussion Paper Notes, 8 February.

Andrade, P., J. Breckenfelder, F. De Fiore, P. Karadi and O. Tristani (2016), 'The ECB's Asset Purchase Programme: An Early Assessment', ECB Working Paper No. 1956, September.

Aoyagi, C. and G. Canelli (2014), 'Unstash the Cash! Corporate Governance Reform in Japan', IMF Working Paper No. WP/14/140, August.

Banerjee, R. and H. Mio (2014), 'The Impact of Liquidity Regulation on Banks', BIS Working Paper No. 470, October.

Bank for International Settlements (2015), 'Global Liquidity: Selected Indicators', Basel, 7 February.

(2016), *Quarterly Review*, Basel, March.

Bao, J., M. O'Hara and X. Zhou (2016), 'The Volcker Rule and Market-Making in Times of Stress', Federal Reserve Board Finance and Economics Discussion Series 2016-102, September.

Baranova, Y., Z. Liu and J. Noss (2016), 'The Role of Collateral in Supporting Liquidity', *Journal of Financial Market Infrastructures*, 5(1), pp. 1–26.

Barclays (2015), 'The Decline in Financial Market Liquidity', 24 February.

Basel Committee on Banking Supervision (2010), 'Basel III: International Framework for Liquidity Risk Measurement, Standards and Monitoring', December.

(2013), 'Basel III: The Liquidity Coverage Ratio and Liquidity Monitoring Tools', January.

(2014a), 'Basel III Leverage Ratio Framework and Disclosure Requirements', January.

(2014b), 'Basel III: The Net Stable Funding Ratio', October.

Bates, T., K. Kahles and R. Stulz (2009), 'Why Do U.S. Firms Hold So Much More Cash Than They Used to?', *Journal of Finance*, 64(5), pp. 1985–2021.

Bernanke, B. (2012), 'Monetary Policy since the Onset of the Crisis', speech at the Federal Reserve Bank of Kansas City Economic Symposium, Jackson Hole, 31 August.

(2013), 'Monetary Policy and the Global Economy', speech at the London School of Economics, 25 March.

Berrospide, J. (2013), 'Bank Liquidity Hoarding and the Financial Crisis: An Empirical Evaluation', *Federal Reserve Board Finance and Economics Discussion Series 2013-03*.

Blinder, A., M. Ehrmann, J. de Haan and D.-J. Jansen (2017), 'Necessity as the Mother of Invention: Monetary Policy after the Crisis', ECB Working Paper No. 2047, April.

Boehmer, E., K. Fong and J. Wu (2013), 'International Evidence on Algorithmic Trading', paper presented at the American Financial Association Annual Meetings in San Diego.

Bonner, C. and P. Hilbers (2015), 'Global Liquidity Regulation – Why Did It Take So Long?', De Nederlandsche Bank Working Paper No. 455, January.

Borio, C. (2014), 'Central Banking Post-crisis: What Compass for Uncharted Waters?', in C. Goodhart, D. Gabor, J. Vestergaard and I. Ertürk (eds.), *Central Banking at a Crossroads: Europe and Beyond*, London: Anthem Press, pp. 191–216.

Brunnermeier, M., L. Garicano, P. Lane et al. (2011), 'European Safe Bonds', Euro-nomics Group.

Bruno, V. and H. Shin (2015), 'Cross-border Banking and Global Liquidity', *Review of Financial Studies*, 82(2), pp. 535–64.

Buiter, W. (2010), 'Reversing Unconventional Monetary Policy: Technical and Political Considerations', in M. Balling, J.M. Berk and M.-O. Strauss-Kahn (eds.), *The Quest for Stability: The Macro View*, Vienna: SUERF, pp. 23–43.

Caballero, R. (2010), 'Understanding the Global Turmoil: It's the General Equilibrium Stupid', *VoxEU*, 21 May.

Caballero, R. and É. Farhi (2013), 'A Model of the Safe Asset Mechanism (SAM): Safety Traps and Economic Policy', NBER Working Paper No. 18737, January, forthcoming in Review of Economic Studies under 'The Safety Trap'.

Cassel, G. (1928), *Postwar Monetary Stabilization*. New York, NY: Columbia University Press.

Cassola, N., M. Drehmann, P. Hartmann, M. Lo Duca and M. Scheicher (2008), 'A Research Perspective on the Propagation of the Credit Market Turmoil', *ECB Research Bulletin*, 7, pp. 2–5.

Chen, Q., A. Filardo and F. Zhu (2016), 'Financial Crisis, US Unconventional Monetary Policy and International Spillovers', *Journal of International Money and Finance*, 67, pp. 62–81.

Chen, Q., M. Lombardi, A. Ross and F. Zhu (2017), 'Global Impact of US and Euro Area Unconventional Monetary Policies: A Comparison', BIS Working Papers No. 610, February.

Chen, J., T. Mancini-Griffoli and R. Sahay (2014), 'Spillovers from United States Monetary Policy on Emerging Markets: Different This Time?' IMF Working Paper No. WP/14/240, December.

Chodorow-Reich, G. (2014), 'Effects of Unconventional Monetary Policy on Financial Institutions', *Brookings Papers on Economic Activity*, Spring, pp. 155–204.

Ciccarelli, M. and C. Osbat (2017) (eds.), 'Low Inflation in the Euro Area: Causes and Consequences', ECB Occasional Paper No. 181, January.

Claessens, S., E. Cerutti and L. Ratnovski (2016), 'Global Liquidity and Cross-Border Bank Flows', paper presented at the 63rd Economic Policy Panel Meeting, Amsterdam, April.

Committee on the Global Financial System (2011), 'Global Liquidity – Concept, Measurement and Policy Implications', CGFS Paper No. 45, November.

(2014), 'Market-making and Proprietary Trading: Industry Trends, Drivers and Policy Implications', CGFS Paper No. 52, November.

(2016), 'Fixed Income Market Liquidity', CGFS Paper No. 55, January.

(2017), 'Repo Market Functioning', CGFS Paper No. 59, April.

Commodity and Futures Trading Commission and Securities and Exchange Commission (2010), 'Findings Regarding the Market Events of May 6, 2010', 30 September.

Credit Suisse (2011), '2012 Global Outlook', Fixed Income Research, 1 December.

Dailami, M. and P. Masson (2011), 'Prospects for a Multipolar International Monetary System', Danish Institute for International Studies Report 2011, 13.

Denbee, E., C. Jung and F. Paterno (2016), 'Stitching Together the Global Financial Safety Net', Bank of England Financial Stability Paper No. 36, February.

Draghi, M. (2015), 'Monetary Policy: Past, Present and Future', speech at the Frankfurt European Banking Congress, 20 November.

Duffie, D. (2016), 'Financial Regulatory Reform after the Crisis: An Assessment', in European Central Bank, *The Future of the International Monetary and Financial Architecture*, Proceedings of the Sintra Forum on Central Banking, Frankfurt am Main, pp. 142–83.

Durlauf, S. and L. Blume (eds.) (2008), *The New Palgrave Dictionary of Economics*, 2nd edn, Basingstoke and New York, NY: Palgrave Macmillan.

Eichengreen, B. (2009), 'The Dollar Dilemma: The World's Top Currency Faces Competition', *Foreign Affairs*, 88(5), pp. 53–68.

(2011), *Exorbitant Privilege: The Rise and Fall of the Dollar and the Future of the International Monetary System*, London: Oxford University Press.

(2012), 'International Liquidity in a Multipolar World', *American Economic Review Papers and Proceedings*, 102(3), pp. 207–12.

(2016), 'Global Monetary Order', in European Central Bank, *The Future of the International Monetary and Financial Architecture*, Proceedings of the Sintra Forum on Central Banking, Frankfurt am Main, pp. 21–63.

Engen, E., T. Laubach and D. Reifschneider (2015), 'The Macroeconomic Effects of the Federal Reserve's Unconventional Monetary Policies', Federal Reserve Board Finance and Economics Discussion Series 2015-005, 14 January.

European Central Bank (2011), 'Global Liquidity: Measurement and Financial Stability Implications', *Financial Stability Review*, December, pp. 140–48.

(2012), 'Global Liquidity: Concepts, Measurements and Implications from a Monetary Policy Perspective', *Monthly Bulletin*, October, pp. 55–68.

(2016), 'The Layers of the Global Financial Safety Net: Taking Stock', *Economic Bulletin*, 5(4), pp. 36–52.

European Occupational Insurance and Pensions Authority (2014), 'Low Interest Rate Environment Stock Taking Exercise', EIOPA-BoS-14/103, 28 November.

Farhi, E., P.-O. Gourinchas and H. Rey (2011), *Reforming the International Monetary System*, London: Centre for Economic Policy Research.

Ferguson, N., A. Schaaf and M. Schularick (2014), 'Central Bank Balance Sheets: Expansion and Reduction since 1900', in European Central Bank, *Monetary Policy in a Changing Financial Landscape*, Proceedings of the Sintra Forum on Central Banking, Frankfurt am Main, pp. 133–70.

Financial Stability Board (2010), 'Implementing OTC Derivatives Market Reforms', Basel, 25 October.

(2016), 'Transforming Shadow Banking into Resilient Market-based Finance – Possible Measures of Non-cash Collateral Re-use', Basel, 23 February.

Fischer, S. (1999), 'On the Need for an International Lender of Last Resort', *Journal of Economic Perspectives*, 13(4), pp. 85–104.

(2015), 'Central Bank Independence', 2015 Herbert Stein Memorial Lecture at the National Economists Club, Washington, 4 November.

Foucault, T., R. Kozan and W. Tham (2017), 'Toxic Arbitrage', *Review of Financial Studies*, 30(4), pp. 1053–94.

Fratzscher, M., M. Lo Duca and R. Straub (2013), 'On the International Spillovers of US Quantitative Easing', ECB Working Paper No. 1557, June.

Gambacorta, L., B. Hofmann and G. Peersman (2014), 'The Effectiveness of Unconventional Monetary Policy at the Zero Lower Bound: A Cross-country Analysis', *Journal of Money, Credit and Banking*, 46 (4), pp. 615–42.

Garcia, C. (2011), 'The Decline of Safe Assets', FT Alphaville, 5 December.

Georgiadis, G. (2016), 'Determinants of Global Spillovers from US Monetary Policy', *Journal of International Money and Finance*, 67, pp. 41–61.

Goodhart, C. and G. Wood (2016), 'The Internal Contradictions of QE ... or Should It Be Quite Erroneous?', *The Daily Telegraph*, 3 October.

Gorton, G. and A. Metrick (2012), 'Securitized Banking and the Run on Repo', *Journal of Financial Economics*, 104(3), pp. 425–51.

Grosse Steffen, C. (2014), 'The Safe Asset Controversy: Policy Implications after the Crisis', Deutsches Institut für Wirtschaftsforschung Roundup 3, 7 January.

Hahm, J.-H., H. Shin and K. Shin (2013), 'Noncore Bank Liabilities and Financial Vulnerability', *Journal of Money, Credit and Banking*, 45(s1), pp. 3–36.

Hartmann, P. (1998), *Currency Competition and Foreign Exchange Markets: The Dollar, the Yen and the Euro*, London: Cambridge University Press.

Heider, F., M. Hoerova and C. Holthausen (2015), 'Liquidity Hoarding and Interbank Market Rates: The Role of Counterparty Risk', *Journal of Financial Economics*, 118(2), pp. 336–54.

Hendershott, T., C. Jones and A. Menkveld (2011), 'Does Algorithmic Trading Improve Liquidity?', *Journal of Finance*, 66, pp. 1–33.

Hooper, P., T. Slok and M. Luzzetti (2016), 'Bond Market Liquidity', Deutsche Bank Market Research, August.

Horioka, C. and A. Terada-Hagiwara (2013), 'Corporate Cash Holding in Asia', ADB Economics Working Paper No. 381, October.

Huang, R. and L. Ratnovsky (2011), 'The Dark Side of Bank Wholesale Funding', *Journal of Financial Intermediation*, 20(2), pp. 248–63.

Ingves, S. (2014), 'Global Liquidity Regulation, supervision and Risk Management', keynote address to the De Nederlandsche Bank seminar 'Liquidity risk management – the LCR and beyond', Amsterdam, 15 May.

International Capital Market Association (2016), 'Remaking the Corporate Bond Market', Zurich, July.

International Monetary Fund (2011a), 'United States 2011 Article IV Consultation – Selected Issues', IMF Country Report 11/202, 7 July.

(2011b), 'Fiscal Monitor', September.

(2012a), 'Safe Assets: Financial System Cornerstone?', Chapter 3 in Global Financial Stability Report, April 81–122.

(2012b), 'World Economic Outlook', October.

(2012c), 'The Liberalization and Management of Capital Flows: An Institutional View', 14 November.

(2013), 'Key Aspects of Macroprudential Policy', 10 June.

(2014a), 'Canada – Selected Issues', IMF Country Report 14/2815 January.

(2014b), 'Global Liquidity – Isses for Surveillance', IMF Policy Paper, 11 March.

(2015), 'Measures Which Are Both Macroprudential and Capital Flow Management Measures: IMF Approach'.

(2016), 'Adequacy of the Global Financial Safety Net', IMF Policy Paper, 10 March.

(2017), 'Fiscal Monitor', April.

Iskandar-Datta, M. and Y. Jia (2012), 'Cross-country Analysis of Secular Cash Trends', *Journal of Banking and Finance*, 36(3), pp. 898–912.

Kapetanios, G., H. Mumtaz, I. Stevens and K. Theodoridis (2012), 'Assessing the Economy-Wide Effects of Quantitative Easing', *Economic Journal*, 122(564), pp. F316–F347.

Kenen, P., J. Shafer, N. Wicks and C. Wyplosz (2004), International Economic and Financial Cooperation: New Issues, New Actors, New Responses, 6th Geneva Report on the World Economy, International Center for Monetary and Banking Studies and Centre for Economic Policy Research, Geneva and London.

Kervel, V. van and A. Menkveld (2016), 'High-Frequency Trading Around Large Institutional Orders', paper presented at the Western Finance Association Meetings, 29 January.

Kindleberger, C. (1978), *Manias, Panics, and Crashes – A History of Financial Crises*, New York, NY: Basic Books.

Korniyenko, Y. and E. Loukoianova (2015), 'The Impact of Unconventional Monetary Policy Measures by the Systemic Four on Global Liquidity and Monetary Conditions', IMF Working Paper No. WP/15/287, December.

Kuroda, H. (2015), 'Quantitative and Qualitative Easing: Theory and Practice', speech at the Foreign Correspondents' Club of Japan, 20 March.

Kurosaki, T., Y. Kumano, K. Okabe and T. Nagano (2015), 'Liquidity in JGB Markets: An Evaluation from Transaction Data', Bank of Japan Working Paper Series No. 15-E-2, May.

Meltzer, A. (2015), 'The QE Trap', *Intereconomics*, 50(3), pp. 171–72.

Menkveld, A. (2016), 'The Economics of High-Frequency Trading: Taking Stock', *Annual Review of Financial Economics*, 8, pp. 1–24.

Miller, R. and G. Shorter (2016), 'High Frequency Trading: Overview of Recent Developments', Congressional Research Service Report, 4 April.

Morais, B., J.-L. Peydro and C. Ruiz (2015), 'The International Bank Lending Channel of Monetary Policy Rates and Quantitative Easing', World Bank Policy Research Working Paper No. 7216, March, *Journal of Finance*, forthcoming.

Naoki, S. (2012), 'Firms' cash holdings and performance: Evidence from Japanese corporate finance', Research Institute of Economy, Trade and Industry Discussion Paper No. 12-E-031, May.

Neely, C. (2015), 'Unconventional Monetary Policy Had Large International Effects', *Journal of Banking and Finance*, 52, pp. 101–11.

Obstfeld, M. (2011), 'International Liquidity: The Fiscal Dimension', *Bank of Japan Monetary and Economic Studies*, 29, pp. 33–48.

Portes, R. (2012), 'The Triffin Dilemma and a Multipolar International Reserve System', in R. Baldwin and D. Vines (eds.), *Rethinking Global Economic Governance in Light of the Crisis*, London: Centre for Economic Policy Research, pp. 47–55.

PricewaterhouseCoopers (2015), Global Financial Markets Liquidity Study. Report for the Global Financial Markets Association and the Institute of International Finance, August.

Rajan, R. (2014), 'Competitive Monetary Easing: Is It Yesterday Once More?', keynote address at the Bookings Institution event Global Monetary Policy: A View from Emerging Markets, Washington, 10 April.

Reinhart, C. and K. Rogoff (2009), *This Time Is Different – Eight Centuries of Financial Folly*, Princeton, NJ and Oxford: Princeton University Press.

Rey, H. (2013), 'Dilemma Not Trilemma: The Global Financial Cycle and Monetary Policy Independence', in Federal Reserve Bank of Kansas City, *Global Dimensions of Unconventional Monetary Policy*, Proceedings of the Economic Policy Symposium, Jackson Hole ,WY, pp. 285–333.

Scheubel, B. and L. Stracca (2016), 'What Do We Know about the Global Financial Safety Net? Rationale, Data and Possible Evolution', ECB Occasional Paper 177, September.

Securities and Exchange Commission (2013), 'Equity market structure literature review – part 1: Market fragmentation', 7 October.

(2014), 'Equity market structure literature review – part 2: High frequency trading', 18 March.

Sher, G. (2014), 'Cashing in for Growth: Corporate Cash Holdings as an Opportunity for Investment and Growth in Japan', IMF Working Paper No. WP/14/221, December.

Singh, M. (2011), 'Velocity of Pledged Collateral', IMF Working Paper No. WP/11/256, November.

(2016a), 'Collateral Flows and Balance Sheet(s) Space', *Journal of Financial Market Infrastructures*, 5(1), pp. 65–82.

(2016b), *Collateral and Financial Plumbing*, 2nd Impression, London: Incisive Media.

(2017), 'Collateral Reuse and Balance Sheet Space', IMF Working Paper No. WP/17/113, May.

Standard and Poor's Financial Services (2017), 'How S&P Global Ratings Would Assess European "Safe" Bonds (ESBies)', RatingsDirect, 25 April.

Taylor, A. (2013), 'The Future of International Liquidity and the Role of China', *Journal of Applied Corporate Finance*, 25(2), pp. 86–94.

Taylor, J. (2013), 'International Monetary Policy Coordination: Past, Present and Future', BIS Working Papers No. 437, December.

(2017), 'Sound monetary policy', Testimony before the Subcommittee on Monetary Policy and Trade, Committee on Financial Services, U.S. House of Representatives, 16 March.

The Economist (2016), 'Monetary Policy: Goodhart's New Law', Buttonwood's notebook, 10 May.

Triffin, R. (1960), *Gold and the Dollar Crisis: The Future of Convertibility*. New Haven, CT: Yale University Press.

Turner, A. (2016), *Between Debt and the Devil: Money, Credit and Fixing Global Finance*, Princeton, NJ: Princeton University Press.

White, W. (2012), 'Ultra Easy Monetary Policy and the Law of Unintended Consequences', Federal Reserve Bank of Dallas Globalization and Monetary Policy Institute Working Paper No. 126, September.

PART IV

The Millennium Challenges
of Central Banks

19 | *Overburdened Central Banks*
Can Independence Survive?

OTMAR ISSING

19.1 Independence: Ups and Downs

The preferences of society for stable money are the foundation for the political decision to endow the central bank with the status of independence. A recent paper by Masciandaro and Romelli (2015) shows the ups and downs of Central Bank Independence (CBI) over a period from 1972 to 2012.[1] The index for CBI remains rather low and stable until the late 1980s when it gets a boost, reaching its peak before the financial crisis. This empirical observation coincides with a slow start of research on this topic but which now fills whole libraries. For a long time there was hardly any interest in CBI. It is telling that one of the first studies on the relation between CBI and inflation by Bade and Parkin (1980) was an unpublished discussion paper. Only with a considerable time lag to the 'great inflation' a large series of papers was published on this relation. More or less in parallel, the concepts of time inconsistency (Kydland and Prescott, 1977), credibility, rules versus discretion (Barro and Gordon, 1983) or the importance of personalities (Rogoff, 1985) were developed. It took some time before these different strands of theoretical and empirical work were connected to an encompassing approach (see e.g. Cukierman, 1992).

19.2 The Example of the European Central Bank

When the statute of the future European Central Bank (ECB) was discussed in the early 1990s, a kind of consensus had emerged in academia. CBI combined with a clear mandate is at least conducive if not indispensable for guaranteeing price stability, i.e. low and stable inflation. Consistent monetary policy, corresponding communication,

---

[1] The research is based on a GMT index developed by Grilli, Masciandaro, and Tabellini (1991) which covers political and economic aspects.

and transparency can overcome time inconsistency and achieve credibility, also fostered by respected persons at the helm of the central bank. Without the track record of the Bundesbank (and the insistence of the German authorities), however, it might have been impossible to achieve a unanimous accord to endow the ECB with the status of independence – at a time when no other national central bank in Europe enjoyed this status.

Yet, this accord could hardly hide the fact that not all countries were enthusiastic about this decision. In the run-up to the French referendum in 1992, for example, President Mitterrand in a televised debate emphasised that the technocrats at the future central bank would not decide exercising their own competence but would implement the decisions taken by the Council (see Issing, 2008, p. 59).

In this context it is not without irony that the original law (on the Bank Deutscher Länder, 1948) establishing CBI after World War II in Germany goes back to a dictate by the Allies. When the law on the Deutsche Bundesbank was discussed and finally ratified in the Federal Parliament (1957), the central bank had already gained such a reputation with the public that CBI was included in the mandate although Chancellor Adenauer was opposed to this idea. In the course of time the Bundesbank enjoyed such prestige that an initiative to change the Bundesbank Law and dismiss CBI was just unthinkable, although this could have been done by a simple majority in the parliament.[2]

19.3 CBI under Pressure

As already indicated, the index for CBI showed a strong increase around the year 1990. The statute of the (future) ECB might have contributed to this global development. Overall central banks enjoyed a reputation which had been hardly observed before. The great moderation, a combination of low inflation and stable inflation accompanied by substantial growth and low unemployment, seemed

---

[2] In this context it is interesting to note that between 1979 and 1990 no fewer than 200 bills were submitted to the US Congress which contained 307 proposals on fifty-six issues that would alter the structure of the Federal Reserve System relating to its conduct of monetary policy (Akhtar and Howe, 1991).

to justify this prestige and at the same time confirm the constitutional aspect of CBI.

What seemed to be a final, optimal steady state for the institutional arrangement lasted for a much shorter period than had been expected. The financial crisis can be seen as the turning point. CBI is not anymore a kind of undisputed institutional element of central banking and has found itself under heavy pressure.

In a first phase after the collapse of financial markets, the prestige of central banks even increased. Additionally, after having managed the great moderation, central banks were now also seen as the saviours of the financial system. This perception has triggered expectations on the actions of central banks which went beyond the limits of what they can achieve (BIS, 2016).

I call this situation 'expectational overburdening', as one of the dimensions of 'institutional overburdening'. Expectations beyond what central banks can finally deliver will lead to disappointments. Underperforming against an elevated benchmark will end up in a blow to reputation and will undermine the case for independence.

What is more, the same is true for 'operational overburdening', i.e. overloading the central bank with more and more responsibilities and competencies. In this respect the ECB is a special case.

Firstly, despite strong concerns demonstrated in the de Larosière Report (2009), the ECB was mandated with banking supervision. Potential conflicts with monetary policy and interference with politics imply a high risk for the reputation of the central bank.

Secondly, the more member states fail to fulfil their responsibilities, the more the ECB comes in with expansionary monetary policy as a kind of substitute for missing structural reforms. In the end the ECB is seen as the only institution within the Economic and Monetary Union (EMU) that has the power and ability to act and disposes of the necessary instruments, which in this context means buying government bonds to prevent the emergence of high spreads. This is even more relevant in the context of the announcement of Outright Monetary Transactions (OMT) and the promise of delivering 'whatever it takes'. It is not surprising that the ECB is perceived as 'the only game in town'.

This institutional overburdening has already triggered a discussion about whether so much power should be given to an independent central bank. The attacks on the status of independence of the ECB will continue irrespectively of success. If the ECB is successful in keeping the EMU together, acting as 'the only game in town', it will be judged as an institution too powerful to be run by 'unelected technocrats'. If it fails, it will be seen as a failure of the 'unelected technocrats', for which no one can be made accountable.

A general, global threat to independence comes from responsibility for financial stability, which on the basis of a special mandate would expose the central bank to the need to interact with other public authorities. (The idea put forward, e.g. by Goodhart (2011), to separate the decision-making process into monetary policy and financial stability is intellectually interesting but hard to implement.) How can independence de jure and/or de facto survive in such an environment?

On the other hand, without a specific mandate a central bank is also not free from any responsibility for financial stability. Therefore, the question arises regarding what traditional monetary policy can contribute to meet this challenge. How can financial stability considerations be integrated into an appropriate monetary policy strategy? Price stability is not enough to ensure financial stability – this is the experience gained in the context of the financial crisis. Risks can emerge despite low and stable inflation, or might even be fostered by monetary stability (the Minsky moment). A pure inflation-targeting approach which ignores money and credit obviously cannot be the answer. The fact that this conclusion is widely ignored signals high risks for future policy mistakes. The ECB's two pillar strategy, which includes the assessment of monetary and credit developments in its decision-making process, can be seen as an approach of the central bank to foster financial stability while preserving the maintenance of price stability. The 'rest' should be delivered by macroprudential policies which still have to stand the test for their efficiency.

Finally, independence comes under pressure from cooperation or coordination with fiscal policy. For James Tobin, monetary policy should be conducted as a kind of debt management which would leave the central bank as a department of the government. Meltzer (2004, 2014a, 2014b), in his impressive work on the history of the Federal Reserve, shows that this cooperation (or whatever it might be called) with the government ended in a regime of fiscal dominance. The debate on 'de facto' and 'de jure' independence of the Federal Reserve has become relevant also for other central banks. If a central bank just gives in to political pressure and/or does not deliver on its own mandate, independence is de facto suspended. The intention to regain sovereignty on the basis of unchanged legal independence will be a demanding challenge.

19.4 Concluding Remarks

Appropriate institutions are indispensable for society. On the other hand, the preferences of society can change and lead to initiatives to adopt institutional arrangements to these changes.

CBI is not exempt from this interaction. Therefore, the trend triggered by the 'great inflation' in the 1970s, and fostered by consequent research to endow the central bank with independence, must not be seen as a final step to an institutional arrangement for the central bank which would last forever. Social preferences evolve over time and can be rather fragile. The memory of high inflation in the past might abate or even disappear. The EMU member countries, for example, have very different memories in this respect, which also creates different opinions on the CBI. It might be difficult, if not impossible, to change the legal statute of the ECB. Nevertheless, if support by the public and politics declines, it is highly uncertain whether the ECB can deliver what was intended when it was endowed with independence. However, an unchanged legal status would always oblige the ECB to legitimise a monetary policy which is not geared to maintain price stability.

As a general observation one might argue that even an independent central bank cannot lastingly defend monetary stability against a society of excessive demands (Issing, 1993, p. 36) – in other words every society ultimately gets the rate of inflation it deserves and basically wants. However, not giving independence to the central bank or – even more – taking it away, opens the door for higher inflation in the future. (This would start a new round of discussion on the pros and cons of CBI.)

References

Akhtar, M.A. and H. Howe (1991), The Political and Institutional Independence of U.S. Monetary Policy, Banca Nazionale del Lavoro, Review, September.

Bade, R. and M. Parkin (1980), *Central Bank Laws and Monetary Policy*, Unpublished Manuscript, Department of Economics, Canada: University of Western Ontario.

Bank for International Settlements (2016), *86th Annual Report*, Basel 26 June.

Barro, R.J. and D. Gordon (1983), 'Rules, Discretion and Reputation in a Model of Monetary Policy', *Journal of Monetary Economics*, 12, pp. 101–21.

Cukierman, A. (1992), *Central Bank Strategy, Credibility, and Independence: Theory and Evidence*, Cambridge, MA: MIT Press.

de Larosière, J., L. Balcerowicz, O. Issing et al. (2009), *The High-Level Group on Financial Supervision in the EU*, Report, Brussels, February.

Goodhart, C. (2011), 'The Changing Role of Central Banks', *Financial History Review*, 18(2), pp. 135–54.

Grilli, V., D. Masciandaro and G. Tabellini (1991), 'Political and Monetary Institutions and Public Financial Policies in the Industrial Countries', *Economic Policy*, 6, pp. 341–92.

Issing, O. (1993), *Central Bank Independence and Monetary Stability*, Occasional Paper 89, London: Institute of Economic Affairs.

(2008), *The Birth of the Euro*, Cambridge: Cambridge University Press.

Kydland, F.E. and E.C. Prescott (1977), 'Rules Rather than Discretion: The Inconsistency of Optimal Plans', *Journal of Political Economy*, 85.

Masciandaro, D. and D. Romelli (2015), 'Ups and Downs of Central Bank Independence from the Great Inflation to the Great Recession: Theory, Institutions and Empirics', *Financial History Review*, 22(3), pp. 259–89.

Meltzer, A.H. (2004), *A History of the Federal Reserve, Volume 1: 1913–1951*, Chicago, IL: University of Chicago Press Economics Books, University of Chicago Press.

(2014a), *A History of the Federal Reserve, Volume 2, Book 1: 1951–1969*, Chicago, IL: University of Chicago Press Economics Books, University of Chicago Press.

(2014b), *A History of the Federal Reserve, Volume 2, Book 2: 1970–1986*, Chicago, IL: University of Chicago Press Economics Books, University of Chicago Press.

Rogoff, K. (1985), 'The Optimal Commitment to an Intermediate Monetary Target', *Quarterly Journal of Economics*, 100, November.

20 | *Central Banks, National Balance Sheets and Global Balance*

ANDREW SHENG

Central banking is a lifelong calling. The subject of central banking can be narrowly or broadly defined, but anyone who has lived and worked in central banking for so long as Charles Goodhart would understand that it is broader than monetary policy, financial stability and having quasi-fiscal functions, management of the national debt, operation of the payment system and the guardian of the nation's financial conscience and moral standards (Mizen, 2003a, b).

Being a keen observer and writer on institutions, Charles has reminded us that the essence of central banking lies in its power to create liquidity, by manipulating its balance sheet (Goodhart, 2010). Institutions are the mezo (intermediary) between micro-economic behaviour and the management of macro-economic behaviour of economic participants. To understand institutional behaviour, we need to appreciate both history and meta-economics (why economists and institutions think the way they think and behave).

This chapter embarks on a study of central banks through the lens of their balance sheets within the context of national balance sheets and the interrelations with the global balance sheet. If central banks manage system liquidity manipulating their balance sheets, through affecting the balance sheet of the commercial banks, the state and other sectors, then it must not be forgotten that the line between liquidity and solvency is quite blurred. To a large extent, because central bank intervention has quasi-fiscal effects, its financial stability activities also have quasi-solvency implications. Lending to a too-big-to-fail (TBTF) financial institution is actually equity, because by holding such debt, the central bank is likely to share potential

The author is grateful to Mr Ng Chow Soon for comments and Ms Jillian Ng for research assistance in the preparation of this article. All errors and omissions are those of the author.

losses of the TBTF borrower in the event that it fails. After all, it is the rescue of such systemically important institutions that prevents contagion (or spread of both illiquidity and losses) to the system as a whole.

Put simply, the central bank provides sufficient liquidity for the economy as a whole not to seize up but in crisis situations it performs a non-elected quasi-fiscal function of absorbing losses or shocks by financing the economy through its monetary creation powers. The power to act so independently to allocate losses is a political and governance issue that has not yet been resolved satisfactorily.

Seen in that perspective, this chapter argues that if we are to look at the long-term history of the evolution of central banks and the real economy, it has become increasingly clear that central banks play an important stability role through management of either the national debt or the liquidity of the financial system. In emergency situations, however, the central bank becomes also the equity provider of last resort, because its power to create money enables its balance sheet to hold any asset (Caruana, 2012).[1] The 1997–8 Asian financial crisis demonstrated that while the central bank can create domestic money, a non-reserve currency central bank cannot create freely usable foreign exchange, so that without sufficient foreign exchange reserves or swaps with reserve currency central banks, it cannot avert a foreign exchange crisis (Filardo and Grenville, 2012).

The 2007–9 advanced country financial crisis demonstrated on the other hand that reserve currency central banks are able to create both reserve currencies to help the domestic economy as well as valuable foreign exchange swaps to assist other central banks in need of hard foreign exchange. This reminds us that reserve currency central banks have monetary operations that have global effects, but these are rarely considered from a global balance sheet perspective. Balance sheets are useful because for the system as a whole to balance, all assets and liabilities must sum up like a balanced matrix. This chapter examines three aspects of central bank balance sheet management – global effects, financial stability and exchange rates – dividing the world into net borrowers and net savers.

In reviewing the progress of central banking historically (Goodhart, 2010), we are struck by Goodhart's observation that central banks

---

[1] Note that in accounting terms, losses are also 'assets', which must be financed.

changed their roles and tools when the circumstances of the real economy and the financial sector forced a pragmatic shift. In the era prior to 2008, central banks were more reactive to change. But since 2008, central banks have begun to take very bold and unconventional measures to respond to financial and economic crises.

This chapter argues that central banks may be the only institution (however imperfect politically) that can facilitate a flow and stock transformation of the real economy. Section 20.1 examines the impact of expansion of the national central bank balance sheet through changes in the Net International Investment Position (NIIP) at the global level. Seen from the perspective of global net borrowers, it seems perfectly rational for deficit or debtor countries to impose a tax (negative interest rate) on savers. Much as negative interest rates are unfair and have distortive effects on distribution and market incentives, central banks are accountable to the greater national interest, rather than sectional or foreign interests. Negative interest rate taxation on savers means that adjustment in the current international monetary system is more symmetric than conventionally assumed, meaning that systemically important deficit countries can impose their losses (or burden share) with the surplus countries.

Section 20.2 looks briefly at the two surplus country central banks – the People's Bank of China (PBoC) and the Bank of Japan's experiences in liquidity and balance sheet transformation. It is argued that in recent times, both central banks were actually trying to manage the liquidity needs of their respective economies undergoing transformation.

Section 20.3 explores the 'meta' issue of central bank policy that has moved out of traditional management of monetary and financial stability into the more political issue of becoming 'the only game in town', as the primary policy instrument to tackle deflation. It argues that central banks have emerged by accident (or forced through crisis) to become an important quasi-fiscal institution between national savings and the allocation of resources to finance either debt or equity. Unconsciously or unwittingly, the central bank is evolving from a lender of last resort to a 'loss-holder of last resort'. If a balance sheet recession requires the rewriting of an imbalanced or impaired national balance sheet, perhaps the central bank balance sheet management should be considered positively, becoming a quasi-fiscal tool to change the national balance sheet, both sectorally and nationally (within the global context)?

20.1 Sudoku on Global Flows and Stocks

Conventional single-economy analysis suffers a common weakness by ignoring the fact that borders have become less meaningful when the world has become more interconnected, interdependent and interactive through globalisation. Hence, domestic monetary policies have very significant impact on both the exchange rate, trade and capital flows and therefore, spillovers to the rest of the world.

Consequently, we should analyse monetary policy action through their impact not only on the domestic economy, but also on the world as a whole. This is particularly relevant for G5 reserve currencies of the US dollar, euro, yen, sterling and renminbi (RMB).

In recent years, G4 central banks (the Federal Reserve, European Central Bank, Bank of Japan and Bank of England) have used their balance sheets very creatively in the exercise of unconventional monetary policy (UMP). There are essentially two aspects of UMP that are controversial, namely, moving beyond the lower bound of zero interest rates to negative interest rate policy (NIRP) and also quantitative easing (QE) through the expansion of the central bank balance sheet. There has been a growing literature on the damaging effects of the NIRP on the business model of banks and financial markets, including the quasi-fiscal taxation of savers and therefore income and wealth inequality (Goodhart, Pradhan and Pardeshi, 2015). The implications of balance sheet expansion on the rest of the national balance sheet are debated hotly in both advanced and emerging markets.

Surprisingly, the Geneva Report[2] on 'What Else Central Banks Can Do' (2016) argues that the damage from NIRP can be manageable and that rates could even go lower without much adverse consequences. Furthermore, QE could be expanded further by increasing the scale and also the range of assets that central banks can purchase, including risky assets such as equity.

It is perfectly understandable that central banks rose to the challenge of combating financial crises by using UMP, although they seemed to have violated the Bagehot Rule by freely lending, not at positive real rates but even breaching the lower boundary of zero interest rates. Nine years after the global financial crisis (GFC), the advanced country central banks are still trying to fight secular deflation, particularly the European Central Bank and the Bank of Japan,

---

[2] Ball et al. (2016), *Geneva Reports on the World Economy*, 18.

	Domestic demand	*Net trade*	*GDP*
High-saving countries	18,000	1,000	19,000
Low-saving countries	28,500	–1,000	27,500
Total	46,500	0	46,500

Figure 20.1 Global net savings balance USD billion
Source: Mervyn King (2010), data for G20 countries, rounded to nearest USD 500 billion, 2008 data.

although the Federal Reserve is debating actively when to taper (gradually raise interest rates) as the US economy appears to reach full employment and begin to recover.

Nomura Chief Economist Richard Koo has argued that the world is going through a Japan-like balance sheet recession, requiring either a rewriting of the national balance sheet flow or a stock solution (Koo, 2009). When the national system builds up excessive debt, the debt can be written off either by inflation or by debt-restructuring, which means loss allocation is done by crisis-forced bankruptcy, orderly restructuring (such as debt-equity swaps or fiscal transfers) or through higher inflation. High-growth countries can absorb debt losses also through allowing high interest rate margins, forcing losses on depositors. So far, attempts by advanced country central banks to push inflation have not succeeded, requiring more creative solutions on dealing with growing debt (Goodhart, Baker and Sleeman, 2009; Goodhart and Pradhan, 2016).

Former Bank of England Governor Mervyn King famously likened the global trade balance to a 3 × 3 table of Sudoku, where between high-saving and low-saving countries, the net trade adds up to zero (King, 2010). In essence, the high-saving (poorer countries) were financing the low-saving (rich countries) by roughly USD 1 trillion in 2008 (Figure 20.1).

In a zero-sum world, we can also create a sudoku for the NIIP for the world as a whole, since the sum owed by deficit countries (net debt to foreigners) is equal to the sum of the surplus economies' claims on the deficit countries.

Table 20.1 shows the NIIP tables for the largest deficit and surplus countries, with Germany taken out of the eurozone to a separate item in the surplus category. The NIIP position reflects the accumulated effect of trade flows, but also financial flows, including valuation effects from exchange rate changes. It should be noted that for the sum of deficits to equal the sum of surpluses, the table also includes errors and omissions, arising from slightly different national measures used in calculating their international investment position.

It is no coincidence that since 2008, the central bank balance sheets of the G4 (reserve currency status) countries have risen sharply, with the Bank of Japan rising to nearly 80 per cent of gross domestic product (GDP) (Figure 20.2). The PBoC balance sheet varied between 50 and 65 per cent of GDP, whereas the central bank assets of financial centres like Hong Kong or Singapore are in excess of 80 per cent of GDP.

Over the same period, the level of the deficit countries' NIIP has tended to grow (Table 20.1) from a manageable balance (USD 1 trillion or 3.1 per cent of world GDP in 1997) to USD 10 trillion or 13 per cent of world GDP at the end of 2014. In all three deficit countries, the level of net external liabilities has almost trebled, ranging from 1.7 per cent of GDP to as high as 40.3 per cent of GDP. The bulk of the deterioration occurred in the USA, from a net debt of USD 0.79 trillion or 9.2 per cent of GDP in 1997 to USD 7.02 trillion or 40.3 per cent of GDP by the end of 2014.

In flow terms, what is remarkable was that in the period 1997–2007, the deterioration in NIIP for the deficit countries was mainly due to the eurozone (excluding Germany). However, in the period 2007–2014, the US deficit accounted for the bulk of the growth in NIIP liabilities of the G3 deficit countries. Because of cuts in fiscal spending during the euro-debt crisis, the eurozone economies (including Germany) had by 2014 reduced their trade and financial capital deficits to near balance.

On the other hand, between 1997 and 2007, China accounted for 41 per cent of the surplus (growth in NIIP), largely due to her rising current account surpluses, whereas her share of total surplus declined to only 22 per cent in the next period. On the other hand, over the

Table 20.1. *Global net international investment positions (NIIPs): unsustainable deficits growing faster than surpluses*

Country	USD trillion			% of national GDP			% of world GDP		
	1997	2007	2014	1997	2007	2014	1997	2007	2014
Deficit countries	**−0.95**	**−4.43**	**−10.15**	**−6.5**	**−14.2**	**−33.9**	**−3.1**	**−7.8**	**−13.0**
USA	−0.79	−1.28	−7.02	−9.2	−8.8	−40.3	−2.6	−2.3	−9.0
Euro area except Germany	−0.08	−2.54	−2.60	−1.7	−18.5	−27.3	−0.3	−4.5	−3.3
UK	−0.08	−0.60	−0.53	−6.1	−21.1	−17.7	−0.3	−1.1	−0.7
Surplus countries	**0.99**	**4.19**	**6.87**	**13.3**	**37.5**	**36.5**	**3.2**	**7.4**	**8.8**
China	−0.12	1.19	1.78	−12.9	34.0	17.1	−0.4	2.1	2.3
Japan	1.03	2.12	3.46	23.8	48.8	75.3	3.3	3.7	4.4
Germany	0.08	0.88	1.63	3.9	26.5	42.1	0.3	1.6	2.1
ROW	**−0.04**	**0.23**	**3.28**	**−0.5**	**1.6**	**11.3**	**−0.1**	**0.4**	**4.2**
World GDP	30.9	56.7	77.8						

Sources: US Bureau of Economic Analysis (BEA), China State Administration of Foreign Exchange (SAFE), Japan Ministry of Finance, Eurostat, Deutsche Bundesbank, World Bank, International Monetary Fund (IMF).*Source*: Ruskin, A. (26 January 2016), 'Plan for a US-China "Plaza Accord"', Deutsche Bank, p. 2.

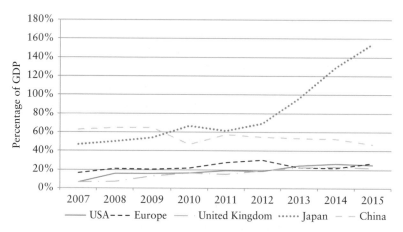

Figure 20.2 Total assets on central bank balance sheets
Sources: Statistics Canada and Bank of Canada Calculations; US Federal
Reserve, US Bureau of Economic Analysis; European Central Bank; Bank of
Japan, Cabinet Office of Japan; Bank of England, Office for National
Statistics.

second period, Japan increased her surplus position to USD 1.34 trillion or half of the increase in NIIP growth. Over this period, the rest
of the world's increase in NIIP was larger than Japan's, Germany's
and China's put together, due largely to the commodity boom.

In sudoku terms, if the world was divided into surplus and deficit
groups, with the deficit countries being the reserve currency issuer,
then the deficit group can continue to finance its deficit through the
issuance of liability to the surplus group. Thus an NIRP is a 'tax' on
the saver. In other words, a reserve currency country can use QE to
get out of trouble because it has no hard budget constraint – it can
print its way out, with the saver that is 'trapped' for lack of alternative safe haven currencies bearing not only negative yields, but also
potential losses through depreciation of the safe haven currency.

Surplus savers are willing to engage in capital flight to safe haven
currencies because of the rising level of uncertainties arising from
geo-political tensions, domestic political unrest and local civil strife.
Regional safe haven currencies such as the Swiss franc have to engage
in NIRP in order to discourage capital flows.

I draw two tentative conclusions from the above data in NIIP terms. First, the USA is truly suffering from the Triffin Dilemma, with a growing deficit as the rest of the world is willing to hold dollars, which obliges the USA to run larger NIIP positions (rather than just trade deficits). This net liability to the rest of the world can only be financed by lower interest rates. Lower interest rates have had two effects – creating domestic asset bubbles and also through the exchange rate effect, which initially had a depreciation effect on the dollar.

Second, even if the Federal Reserve begins to think about exiting QE, the fact that the European Central Bank and the Bank of Japan are willing to continue QE and NIRP means that there is a relative real interest rate differential between the US dollar and non-dollar assets, which still makes it attractive to invest in the US dollar assets. These capital inflows can be of two varieties – a hedged inflow (borrowing dollars to finance investments in US dollar assets) or an unhedged variety (true capital flight into dollars).

This continued capital inflow into the US dollar despite near zero interest rates, without the capacity of the US economy to reflate its real economy, means that the US dollar plays the same deflationary role as gold in the 1930s. Investment in gold had a deflationary impact on the real economy because liquidity is sucked into a non-productive asset.

The dilemma for the Federal Reserve appears to be a procyclical situation whereby any increases in interest rates would attract more inflows into the dollar, creating exchange rate appreciation that widens the current account deficit and also increases the NIIP deficit owing to foreigners through capital inflows. This unsustainable situation has caused some observers to ask for another round of the Plaza Accord, namely, a concerted effort to weaken the US dollar.

20.2 Surplus Country Central Bank Options in Balance Sheet Management

The policy problems of deficit countries and surplus countries are not symmetric. While it is true that it is difficult to force surplus countries to revalue or reflate, in many ways central banks facing a current account surplus would either have to allow a revaluation of the currency or have to sterilise foreign exchange reserve increases. The central banks of Japan and China both have experienced such growth in foreign exchange reserves.

The People's Bank of China had to increase its balance sheet substantially due to the growth in foreign exchange reserves, which was financed by statutory reserve requirements on the banks (Table 20.2).

Based upon the Japanese experience, if the central bank did not sterilise capital inflows or allow a major revaluation of the exchange rate, the surplus country would either face higher inflation, asset bubble or face lower interest rates. In the last decade, neither the Chinese nor Japanese experienced any inflation, but UMP clearly had an impact on upward pressure on asset prices and downward pressure on interest rates and exchange rates (Iwata and Takenaka, 2012).

However, the PBoC and the Bank of Japan both experienced complex policy issues as the real economy underwent major structural transformation (in both cases GDP slowdown). In essence there is the risk that too much liquidity provision by the central bank creates moral hazard, and under-provision of liquidity could lead to capital inflows or emergence of shadow banking that negates conventional monetary policy.

When China faced a major slowdown in exports after the 2007 shock to global trade, Chinese exporters faced substantial liquidity problems because their customers had shifted from being credit providers (through their letters of credit) to demanders of trade credit (no imports without supplier credits). Initially, the system was fairly liquid due to the high level of investments from the 2009 RMB 4 trillion stimulation programme that drove credit creation by the commercial banks. However, as the PBoC tightened monetary policy in the wake of excess liquidity and asset inflation in 2010/2011, shadow banking interest rates diverged from official interest rates, giving rise to arbitrage opportunities for the rise of shadow banking (Sheng and Ng, 2016).

China today is in the midst of major transformation from the old hardware-driven, consumer-goods export, industrial supply chain to a knowledge-and domestic consumption-driven software and services economy. This means that there is creative destruction from the loss of value from excess capacity, polluting, energy inefficient and obsolete hardware industries, which are still sucking scarce resources in their efforts to survive and maintain employment. On the other hand, the new service sector start-ups and small (including micro) and medium enterprises (SMEs) are starved of working capital and equity. In a situation where there is a high level of uncertainty arising from the transition, it is obvious that equity capital is more risk-absorbent

Table 20.2. *People's Bank of China balance sheet*

Items	Level							
	2007	2008	2009	2010	2011	2012	2013	2014
Foreign assets	12.5	16.3	18.5	21.5	23.8	24.1	27.2	27.9
Foreign exchange	11.5	15.0	17.5	20.7	23.2	23.7	26.4	27.1
Monetary gold	0.0	0.0	0.1	0.1	0.1	0.1	0.1	0.1
Other foreign assets	0.9	1.3	1.0	0.8	0.5	0.4	0.7	0.7
Claims on government	1.6	1.6	1.6	1.5	1.5	1.5	1.5	1.5
Of which: central government	1.6	1.6	1.6	1.5	1.5	1.5	1.5	1.5
Claims on other depository corporations	0.8	0.8	0.7	0.9	1.0	1.7	1.3	2.5
Claims on other financial corporations	1.3	1.2	1.2	1.1	1.1	1.0	0.9	0.8
Claims on non-financial corporations	0.0	0.0	0.0	0.0	0.0	0.0	0.0	0.0
Other assets	0.7	0.8	0.8	0.8	0.7	1.1	0.8	1.1
Total assets	**16.9**	**20.7**	**22.8**	**25.9**	**28.1**	**29.5**	**31.7**	**33.8**
Reserve money	10.2	12.9	14.4	18.5	22.5	25.2	27.1	29.4
Currency issue	3.3	3.7	4.2	4.9	5.6	6.1	6.5	6.7
Deposits of other depository corporations	6.9	9.2	10.2	13.7	16.9	19.2	20.6	22.7
Deposits of financial corporations excluded from reserve money	0.0	0.1	0.1	0.1	0.1	0.1	0.1	0.2
Bond issue	3.4	4.6	4.2	4.0	2.3	1.4	0.8	0.7
Foreign liabilities	0.1	0.1	0.1	0.1	0.3	0.1	0.2	0.2
Deposits of government	1.7	1.7	2.1	2.4	2.3	2.1	2.9	3.1

Table 20.2. (*cont.*)

Items	Level							
	2007	2008	2009	2010	2011	2012	2013	2014
Own capital	0.0	0.0	0.0	0.0	0.0	0.0	0.0	0.0
Other liabilities	1.5	1.4	1.9	0.8	0.6	0.5	0.6	0.3
Total liabilities	**16.9**	**20.7**	**22.8**	**25.9**	**28.1**	**29.5**	**31.7**	**33.8**
GDP	26.6	31.4	34.1	40.2	47.3	51.9	56.9	63.6
Foreign exchange in % of GDP	43%	48%	51%	51%	49%	46%	46%	43%
Deposits of other depository corporations as % of GDP	26%	29%	30%	34%	36%	37%	36%	36%
Total assets as % of GDP	**64%**	**66%**	**67%**	**65%**	**59%**	**57%**	**56%**	**53%**
Total fin assets	100	98	121	142	157	180	198	
PBoC total assets as % total fin assets	17%	21%	19%	18%	18%	16%	16%	
Total social financing (TSF) stock	32.1	38.0	51.2	65.0	76.7	91.4	107.5	122.9
PBoC total assets as % of TSF stock	53%	55%	44%	40%	37%	32%	30%	28%

Source: People's Bank of China.

than debt funding, which creates system fragility. Unfortunately, due to lagged development of the capital market, equity funding accounted for less than 5 per cent of the total social funding in the last decade. It was the imbalance in capital market development versus bank development that led to excessive leverage in the Chinese economy.

Like China, Japan is also a net lender to the world, with NIIP claims on the world equivalent to 75 per cent of GDP (see Table 20.1), compared with 17 per cent of GDP for China at the end of 2014. The high level of debt in Japan (gross public debt of 250 per cent of GDP, non-financial corporate debt of 234 per cent of GDP) has been manageable precisely because this is domestic debt (IMF, 2016). The public debt and large fiscal deficits have been made sustainable due to exceptionally low interest rates, but the costs have been borne by savers (households, pensioners) who are holders of long-term Japanese bonds.

As Bank of Japan Governor Kuroda mentioned, the success of Qualitative and Quantitative Easing (QQE) has been record profits by Japanese corporations, particularly from a lower yen rate, with tentative signs of some recovery in investments and wages (Kuroda, 2016). The September 2016 announcement by the Bank of Japan that it would target the yield curve could be interpreted as an innovative financial stability measure. By targeting inflation rate at 2 per cent per annum and the willingness to buy Japanese government bonds (JGBs) at a flat yield curve price implies that the central bank stands ready to take long-maturity JGBs off the books of pension and long-term funds that are subject to massive capital loss if the Bank achieves its inflation target. The Bank already owns one-third of JGBs and has the capacity to finance the holdings of such JGBs through its reserve requirements on banks or through its seigniorage power.

Put in another way, both the PBoC and the Bank of Japan are attempting to facilitate the change in the real sector through their balance sheets, including the capacity to take losses (real or potential) of the banking system and the long-term savings sector onto their books. Indeed, the Ministry of Finance can do so either through the issues of debt or imposing higher taxes to finance these transformations. But this is politically difficult. Being not subject to legislative approval of its actions, the central bank can take quasi-fiscal action, provided that the cost is not excessively high inflation. In the current

deflationary environment, the deficit countries are hoping that inflation would reappear to erode the real value of their excessive debt. In
a world dominated by reserve currency economies, the surplus countries are hostage to the UMP of the deficit economies.

As is now well known, the effectiveness of UMP would depend on
the effectiveness of the transmission mechanism to the real economy.
In an open economy, the inability of the domestic economy to absorb
new funds from UMP will cause funds to leak through the balance of
payments abroad, affecting the exchange rate. This is exactly what
happened initially, with the immediate effect of UMP affecting the
exchange rate. In a situation when surplus savers perceive that their
exchange rate may depreciate, capital outflows will be procyclical,
weakening the exchange rate and stimulating exports. Japan's trading
partners have been willing to allow the yen to depreciate in order to
help Japan reflate its economy.

Thus, in a highly interconnected and interdependent world, domestic policies have spillover effects, but central banks are answerable to
domestic politicians and not to global savers or investors.

20.3 Implications for Central Bank Policies Going Forward

The above observation that in undertaking UMP, the central bank
may have accidentally evolved into a quasi-fiscal agent to help the
real economy transit to the next order has many disturbing and unexplored implications. Detractors of UMP already consider that central
banks are violating the rules and exercising excess discretion, particularly in quasi-fiscal activity. Technically, there should be no taxation
without representation. As Governor Kuroda has quoted Ben
Bernanke, 'quantitative easing works in practice but does not work in
theory'. Where do we go from here?

The fundamental fiscal dilemma is that in democratic politics it is
almost impossible to raise taxes, but in order to please the electorate,
welfare expenditure increases, leading to larger and larger fiscal deficits. This can only be funded by lower and lower interest rates, forcing
central banks to deal with the monetary stability and bank stability
issues. Someone has to bear the losses when the economy goes
through a transition – huge creative losses or losses from obsolescence
when inefficiencies in the economy show up as non-performing loans
in a bank-dominant financial system.

Who should bear these losses? The losses of an economy are eroded through either inflation, devaluation or crises that wipes out old debt and equity. Central bank holding of such assets gives the illusion that losses have no costs.

What does excessive debt truly mean? At negative interest rates, the debt burden is passed from the borrower to the saver. The losses can be 'forced' on the saver or creditor if the saver or creditor has no alternatives to be 'taxed'. Reserve currency issuers have an extra degree of freedom. Global net savers have little alternative to the G4 reserve currencies, while the RMB is not yet a liquid alternative due to lack of opening of the capital account in China and the relative illiquidity of Chinese capital markets. Small economies may be able to devalue, but large players cannot devalue without huge spillover effects.

The Modigliani–Miller equivalence of debt and equity has a corollary that ultimately, a 'trapped' holder of debt is actually holding equity (Sheng, 2015). The TBTF debtor imposes equity-like losses on holders of its liability if it defaults. And it looks as if there are many elephants in the world that are learning to become TBTF, passing their losses to everyone else.

If governments are not willing to impose hard budget constraints or pain in the form of higher taxation or making TBTF borrowers bankrupt, then the debt problem will not go away. The logical implication of UMP is that the central bank becomes ultimately a larger and larger holder of all debt, because with its seigniorage power, it alone can hold more assets and appears to bear all losses, until the losses are wiped out by inflation, distributing it more widely (Shirakawa, 2010).

There is sufficient recent experience with central bank losses and central bank rescue of banking systems through the swap of central bank liabilities for bad assets, including injecting equity into failed banks. There are recent experiences of central banks incurring large losses from foreign exchange debt incurred on behalf of governments, central banks buying equity holdings (the Hong Kong Monetary Authority and the Bank of Japan holding exchange-traded funds), all of which are UMP or unconventional central bank measures or tools exercised under exceptional circumstances. In other words, in extraordinary circumstances, central banking has undertaken exceptional measures to restore national balance sheets by using its ability to manipulate its own balance sheet (Turner, 2015).

From a systemic point of view, the core global international financial system question is that when we have a very strong dollar with zero interest rate, and inability of the US financial system to improve the transmission mechanism to the real economy (recycle inflows into real economic activity), capital flight into the US dollar plays the same deflationary role as gold holdings in the 1930s (Goodhart, Bartsh and Ashworth, 2016). If the dominant reserve currency nation does not play a recycling role, the system as a whole will become more deflationary.

All this shows that no central bank or economy is an island in a globalised financial and trading system. Central banks cannot run away from the political economy of geopolitics, because ultimately monetary policy has quasi-fiscal implications that cannot be divorced from politics (Goodhart, 2004).

The most difficult part of the future role of central banking in an era in which it has played an interventionist role is its legitimacy and accountability (Goodhart, 2010). Central banks have evolved profoundly, because the world has become a more integrated, interconnected and interdependent system through technology, globalisation and the power of ideas. For the larger players, it is no longer possible to consider monetary policy without their global spillovers. For the smaller players, the hard budget constraints are even tougher, since capital, talent and people can move in nanoseconds (King, 2016). Central banks are therefore complex, adaptive institutions in a complex adaptive world.

This ensures that in a constantly evolving world, we need common sense in this systemic world that is no longer common.

References

Ball, L., J. Gagnon, P. Honohan and S. Krogstrup (2016), 'What Else Can Central Banks Do?', *Geneva Reports on the World Economy*, 18, London: ICMB and CEPR Press.

Caruana, J. (2012), 'Why Central Bank Balance Sheets Matter', BIS Paper No. 66, *Are Central Bank Balance Sheets in Asia Too Large?* pp. 2–9. Retrieved from www.bis.org/publ/bppdf/bispap66b.pdf (accessed 18 November 2016).

Filardo, A. and S. Grenville (2012), 'Central Bank Balance Sheets and Foreign Exchange Rate Regimes: Understanding the Nexus in Asia', in

BIS Paper No. 66, *Are Central Bank Balance Sheets in Asia Too Large?* pp. 76–110. Retrieved from www.bis.org/publ/bppdf/bispap66e_rh.pdf (accessed 18 November 2016).

Goodhart, C. (2004), *New Directions in Financial Stability*, Per Jacobsson Lecture, Bank for International Settlements, Zurich, Switzerland. Retrieved from www.perjacobsson.org/lectures/062704.pdf (accessed 18 November 2016).

(2010), *The Changing Role of Central Banks*, BIS Working Papers No. 326, Bank for International Settlements. Retrieved from www.bis.org/publ/work326.htm (accessed 18 November 2016).

Goodhart, C., M. Baker, and C. Sleeman (2009), *Quantitative Easing: Necessary, Successful and Ready to Wind Down, UK Economics*, London: Morgan Stanley Research Europe.

Goodhart, C., E. Bartsh and J. Ashworth (2016), *Transmission Matters – Musings on Money Multipliers and Credit Creation, Global Economics*, London: Morgan Stanley Research.

Goodhart, C. and M. Pradhan (2016), *Demography versus Debt*, Morgan Stanley, explanatory note to Manoj Pradhan, Charles Goodhart, Patryk Drozdzik 2016. *Life after Debt*, Global Issues. New York, NY: Morgan Stanley Research.

Goodhart, C., M. Pradhan and P. Pardeshi (2015), *Could Demographics Reverse Three Multi-Decade Trends?*, London: Global Issues, Morgan Stanley & Co. International Plc.

International Monetary Fund (2016), 'Japan: 2016 Article IV Consultation – Press Release; and Staff Report', IMF Country Report No. 16/267. Retrieved from www.imf.org/external/pubs/ft/scr/2016/cr16267.pdf (accessed 18 November 2016).

Iwata, K. and S. Takenaka (2012), *Central Bank Balance Sheet Expansion: Japan's Experience*, BIS Paper No. 66, *Are Central Bank Balance Sheets in Asia Too Large?*, pp. 132–59. Retrieved from www.bis.org/publ/bppdf/bispap66g.pdf (accessed 18 November 2016).

King, M. (2010), *Global Imbalances*, Speech by Mervyn King at the University of Exeter, Bank of England. Retrieved from www.bankofengland.co.uk/archive/Documents/historicpubs/speeches/2010/speech419.pdf (accessed 18 November 2016).

(2016), *The End of Alchemy: Banking, the Global Economy and the Future of Money*, London: Little, Brown Book Group Limited.

Koo, R. (2009), *The Holy Grail of Macroeconomics: Lessons from Japan's Great Recession*, Singapore: John Wiley & Sons.

Kuroda, H. (2016), *Moving Forward: Japan's Economy under Quantitative and Qualitative Monetary Easing*, Speech at the Japan Society in

New York, Bank of Japan. Retrieved from www.boj.or.jp/en/announce
ments/press/koen_2015/data/ko150827a1.pdf (accessed 18 November
2016).
Mizen, P. (ed.) (2003a), *Central Banking, Monetary Theory and Practice:
Essays in Honour of Charles Goodhart*, vol. 1, Cheltenham and
Northampton: Edward Elgar.
  (2003b), *Monetary History Exchange Rates and Financial Markets:
Essays in Honour of Charles Goodhart*, vol. 2, Cheltenham and
Northampton: Edward Elgar.
Sheng, A. (2015), *The New Politics of Central Banking – The Central
Bank Trap*, Institute for New Economic Thinking, 6th INET
Annual Conference, Paris, France. Retrieved from andrewsheng.net/
files/Sheng_New_Politics_of_Central_Banking_FINAL.pdf (accessed 18
November 2016).
Sheng, A. and C. S. Ng (2016), *Shadow Banking in China*, London: John
Wiley.
Shirakawa, M. (2010), 'High-level Policy Panel on Financial Stability Issues:
Unconventional Monetary Policy – How Central Banks Can Face the
Challenges and Learn the Lessons', BIS Papers No. 52, *The International
Financial Crisis and Policy Challenges in Asia and the Pacific*,
pp. 378–82. Retrieved from www.bis.org/publ/bppdf/bispap52w.pdf
(accessed 18 November 2016).
Turner, A. (2015), *Between Debt and the Devil*, New Jersey, NJ and
Oxfordshire: Princeton University Press.

21 | Recognising the Economy as a Complex, Adaptive System
Implications for Central Banks

WILLIAM WHITE

21.1 Lessons from the Past

It will be argued in this chapter that the way in which monetary policy is conducted needs to change fundamentally. Past practice, based on the assumption that the structure of the economy is both knowable and controllable, is simply wrong. A philosopher would say we have made a profound ontological error by misreading the fundamental nature of the object of our attentions. In reality, the economy is a complex and adaptive system, like many others in nature and society, and cannot be well understood or closely controlled. Recognising this fact should have profound implications for economic policy in general but monetary policy in particular. Adapting to this new analytical framework will be the principal millennium challenge for central banks, and will also raise questions about the political framework relating central banks to governments.

Recent global economic developments bear witness to the inadequacies of the analytical framework which has guided monetary policy over the last few decades. The single minded and successful pursuit of price stability by central banks has not provided the 'strong, sustainable and inclusive growth' sought by the governments of the G20. The strong, global growth seen during the years of the 'Great Moderation' came to an abrupt end with the economic crisis that erupted in the advanced market economies in 2007. Moreover, that crisis now has global reach and threatens still more serious economic problems in the future. Every geographical area has easily identifiable imbalances that threaten its future growth and prosperity, and other regions in turn. Finally, income and especially wealth inequality within nations worsened everywhere prior to the crisis, and these trends have continued since.

In short, highly expansionary monetary policy provided strong growth for a while, but it was neither sustainable nor adequately

inclusive. Indeed, it will be argued in this chapter that highly expansionary monetary policy has actually contributed materially to both
economic and financial instability (unsustainability) and to perceptions that the gains from stronger growth and from international
trade have been unfairly shared among the social classes (non-inclu-
siveness). The social and political implications of these shortcomings
are now becoming increasingly evident.[1]

A particular shortcoming of prevailing analytical models is how little emphasis they put on supply-side developments. In pursuing price
stability prior to the crisis, central banks failed to recognise that low
inflation in the 1990s, and subsequently, was not due to inadequate
demand that required monetary easing. Rather, it was due to positive
supply-side shocks associated with technological advances and the re-
entry of China and other 'command and control' economies back
into the world trading system. More recently, central banks have also
failed to see how easy monetary policies could lead to a vicious circle
of resource misallocations, lower potential growth,[2] and the apparent
'need' for still more easy money.[3]

Furthermore, on the demand side of the economy, central banks
failed to see the dangerous implications of the cumulative increase in
credit and debt also associated with easy monetary policies. Over
time, these 'headwinds' have threatened less demand, not more, con-
stituting another vicious and downward spiralling circle. All of these
analytical shortcomings attest to the need to see our domestic economies, and even more the global economy, as complex systems or even
systems of systems.[4]

The adaptive aspect of our economies also needs to be underlined.
Both the real and financial sectors have evolved under the influence of

---

[1] The rise of 'populist' political movements to confront entrenched 'elites' is a
byproduct of these shortcomings. They have arisen now because, while
distributional issues always matter, they take on increased importance when
growth is weak as is typical of a post-crisis period. There are, in fact, legitimate
sources of political concern of a more secular nature. See Acemoglu and
Robinson (2013) and Wedel (2009).

[2] For convincing documentation see Borio et al. (2015).

[3] It has become fashionable to assert this in the context of a Wicksellian model.
Lower potential growth lowers expected profits and the 'natural' rate of
interest. It is then contended that the financial rate of interest must be lowered
as well. As discussed below, this argument does not stand up when the
economy is viewed as an evolving system over time.

[4] See Haldane (2015).

new technology and the general trend towards deregulation and liberalisation. Global trade and cross-border interactions were rising until very recently, with emerging market economies becoming globally important. Initially, financial systems were national, bank-based and characterised by a high degree of cartelisation. Over the years however, this changed profoundly with a move towards globalisation, securitisation (not least the rise of 'shadow banking') and a considerable degree of consolidation. In sum, the economy provides a highly dynamic and shifting structural backdrop for monetary policy, both influencing it and being influenced by it.

Finally, we need to recognise the complex implications of simultaneous changes arising in different parts of the economy. Ultimately, changes in individual parts of the economy which seem to improve economic efficiency can actually make the system as a whole less stable. The globalisation and technical progress referred to above clearly raised our efficiency in producing global goods and services. Various developments in the financial sector also provided efficiency gains. The single-minded focus of monetary policy on price stability was also thought to be a positive innovation. Yet, put all together, these positive developments produced the serious problems that now face the economic system as a whole.

In summary, the principal lesson from the past is that the economy should be treated as a complex, adaptive system; an ecosystem rather than a machine. Suggestions of this sort can be dated back to ancient times. More recently, they have come to be associated with the work of the Santa Fe Institute,[5] and still more recently, work being carried out under the auspices of the Institute for New Economic Thinking (INET) and the Organisation for Economic Co-operation and Development (OECD)[6] among others. A recent book by Simpson (2013) draws links between the classical school of economics and

---

[5] For a fascinating account of the origins of the Santa Fe Institute, and an early meeting between physicists and economists to discuss complexity, see Waldrop (1992). It is telling that the chapter which describes this meeting is entitled 'You Guys Really Believe That?'

[6] INET has sponsored many projects, including ongoing work at the Martin School at Oxford University. The OECD, recognising its failure to predict the crisis, founded an ambitious institution-wide project called 'New Approaches to Economic Challenges'. In this context, the OECD has organised a number of conferences on how the insights of complexity economics might be applied to practical policymaking.

modern complexity economics. The latter seems to be able to address the wide range of issues that preoccupied the former. How do we achieve, not just strong growth, but sustainable and inclusive growth? In contrast, mainstream macroeconomic thinking, as practised by academics and increasingly by central banks, has had a much narrower focus. However, in spite of its limitations, the mainstream view has not yet been adapted to embrace this alternative way of looking at the economy.

21.2 Throwing Off the Old Analytical Order

The analytical frameworks (and econometric models) still used by most central banks are based on a large number of unrealistic, simplifying assumptions.[7] These are needed in order to ensure the economy is (in principle) both understandable and controllable. In almost every respect, however, they conflict sharply with the assumptions suggested by treating the economy as a complex, adaptive system. Moreover, these assumptions effectively rule out any analysis of the important issues of sustainability and inclusiveness which, as noted above, are now part of the policymaker's objective function.

Perhaps most important, it is assumed that the economy tends automatically and quickly to revert to full employment and to low inflation, supposing that the latter is the objective sought by the central bank. Otherwise put, the economy will revert to a desirable 'equilibrium'. Similarly, financial markets generate prices consistent with underlying fundamentals. Money, credit and debt generally play no role, while stocks and cumulative processes have also tended to be ignored. Single 'representative agents' stand in for the many millions of diverse households and firms. Moreover, these agents maximise their individual lifetime utility (given perfect knowledge of the future and the nature of the economy), without any recourse to emotion or the good of others. Finally, all shocks follow a Normal Distribution whose properties do not change over time.

Taken all together, these assumptions yield highly linear forecasts which rule out the unexpected consequences of policy changes, not least radical changes to monetary policy. In short, in the world described by this analytic framework, central bankers can easily

---

[7] For particularly biting criticisms, see Buiter (2009) and Romer (2016).

achieve their inflation objectives, and really bad outcomes simply cannot happen.

At the least, this conclusion might be thought curious. There is now a huge set of historical studies documenting past economic and financial crises, to say nothing of this most recent one.[8] As well, the lack of realism of many of the assumptions underlying current models has been repeatedly and convincingly demonstrated. For example, years ago Mandelbrot provided evidence that changes in stock market prices were determined by a Power Law Distribution rather than a Normal (bell curve) Distribution.[9] For a more recent example, year ahead forecasts by the International Monetary Fund (IMF) (and most others) of economic growth in the major economies have been revised down nine years in a row. Similarly, inflation has come in under the forecast value for a similar period of time. These outcomes must throw into doubt the fundamental assumption of a rapid return to 'equilibrium'.

In spite of these shortcomings, central banks appear to have generally maintained the analytic frameworks in place prior to the onset of the crisis. That is strongly suggested by the fact that monetary policy since the crisis has essentially been 'more of the same'. Why is this so? One charitable interpretation is that, while central banks have indeed experienced growing doubts about the usefulness of their analytical frameworks, they see no policy alternatives. They have become 'the only game in town'. A less charitable interpretation is that they (or at least an important subset[10] of them) do continue to believe their policies will succeed in raising nominal demand and also that these policies, in spite of their increasingly experimental and totally unprecedented nature, will have only limited, undesirable side effects.

What might have induced such analytical rigidity in the face of so much evidence to the contrary? Kuhn (1962) suggests that needed

---

[8] The classic reference for past crises is Kindelberger and Aliber (2005). See also Schularick and Taylor (2009).

[9] See the references in Mandelbrot and Hudson (2004).

[10] It should be noted that not all central banks are the same. See White (2011). The Bundesbank in particular has always been suspicious of mainstream (Anglo Saxon?) thinking, and has used a second, monetary pillar to inform its analysis of the longer-run relationship between money growth and inflation. The European Central Bank has taken over this tradition, but seems increasingly to be drawing a relationship between credit (rather than money) and the possibility of deflation (rather than inflation) via a 'boom–bust' cycle.

'paradigm' shifts in the natural sciences often take decades to achieve. Those who have taught accepted ways of thinking for a lifetime are loath to give them up. Yet, as shown in White (2013), monetary economists and central bankers have in the past repeatedly shown themselves willing to change their analytic frameworks in the face of 'stubborn facts' that indicated that a change was required. Why then is this time different? The answer might be found in the more recent reflections of Kahneman (2013). He suggests that when belief systems are suddenly and surprisingly shocked by events, the reaction is not to question the beliefs in a fundamental way but to retreat deeper into them. After all of the self-congratulatory, central bank rhetoric around the 'Great Moderation', the events following the onset of the crisis perhaps constituted just such a shock.

One can only speculate on what central bankers will do should the global economy weaken once more, perhaps in the context of further financial disorder. On the one hand, previous beliefs might be maintained, inducing central bankers to 'double down' on still more experimental policies. On the other hand, still more evidence that these policies were actually making things worse might trigger the desired paradigm shift. In the event, making this shift will be the main challenge for central banks in the coming years. Eventually reality must be recognised.

21.3 Embracing the Economy as a Complex, Adaptive System

Complex, adaptive systems can be found everywhere. Nothing in nature[11] or society[12] seems linear and stable. Thus, it seems inherently odd to assume that the economy almost uniquely possesses these characteristics. Moreover, these systems have been well studied by other disciplines and share key properties. They are made up of many agents following simple rules, constantly interacting, and responding (evolving) in response to changing circumstances. Moreover, many such systems display 'emergent properties'; that is, properties that do not

---

[11] See Buchanan (2000).

[12] For an interesting, non-technical overview, see Ball (2012). It contains chapters on predicting traffic, crowd movements, norms and decision making, how crime spreads, social webs, disease and epidemics, economic and financial systems, fostering cooperation, the development of cities and modelling modern conflict.

derive from the nature of the underlying components but the interactions between them. There is no equilibrium (except death) in such systems. Agents' actions are premised on assumptions about emergent properties, but actions change those properties in a never-ending dynamic.

The application of this way of thinking to economics would seem totally realistic. The economy is in fact made up of many different sectors (consumers, companies, financial institutions, regulators, etc.) each comprising many (perhaps millions) of diverse agents. Economic agents do seem to follow relatively simple rules (heuristic devices) to guide their economic activities, but rules which might well include concern for others as well as their own direct interests. Interactions between economic agents do create feedback effects and unexpected outcomes, often of a highly non-linear nature, as described in Section 21.1 above.

The emergent properties of the economic system would be the macroeconomic aggregates that we currently study. Moreover, explicitly identifying them as emergent phenomena would satisfy the desire for 'micro foundations' much more effectively than the fiction of the Representative Agent. Furthermore, this way of thinking puts the emphasis on dynamic efficiencies over time, the true source of rising living standards, rather than static efficiencies associated with resource allocation. Finally, the recognition of diverse agents invites an analysis of distributional issues.

Evidence from other disciplines indicates that complex, adaptive systems can behave in a stable fashion for long periods of time. Nevertheless, it seems also to be the case that they break down (fall into crisis) on a regular basis. Moreover, the magnitude of a crisis is inversely related to frequency as determined by a Power Law. Put otherwise, extreme events happen much more frequently than a Normal Distribution would imply, with cascade effects often at the heart of developments. The costs of these crises, to the extent they can be measured, can also be extremely high. The study of cybernetics was developed to help modulate such extreme events. While Wikipedia provides a long list of disciplines to which cybernetic insights have been applied, economics is notable by its absence.

Fortunately, even without recourse to the sophisticated mathematics of dynamic, non-linear systems, the simple embrace of the true nature of the economic system reveals many lessons. The extent to which they apply to governments in general, as opposed to central banks in particular, is discussed in the next section. While many lessons can be identified, they all share one insight: Complex, adaptive systems can be influenced by policy but they cannot be tightly controlled. Policymakers should therefore be much more humble in their aspirations.[13]

First, there is a trade-off between static efficiency and dynamic stability in complex adaptive systems. This trade-off is often labelled 'fitness'.[14] The lesson is that policymakers should influence the institutional structure with a view to increasing fitness.[15] Evidently, this raises issues of 'how much is enough'. More regulation might well increase financial stability, but still more regulation might well cut legitimate lending. This could eventually lead to recession, more bad loans and financial instability by another route. Moreover, too much regulation and tight controls can reduce the alertness of economic agents to both threats and opportunities. Ease of entry and exit is also crucial if evolutionary developments are to be encouraged while avoiding disruptive discontinuities. Finally, attention should be paid to how cascading effects are avoided in other complex systems, e.g. through accepting redundancy and therefore static 'inefficiency'.

The development of Agent based Computational Economics (ACE) models now provides some guidance as to which institutional reforms would increase fitness, supposing different patterns of assumed behaviour on the part of economic agents.[16] Guidance as to behaviour comes from various sources – not least laboratory experiments – with model validation coming in part from the capacity to replicate economic phenomena in the real world. Such models can also provide guidance about the effects of different policy rules on systemic stability. Advances in both computing and data collection ('big data') imply growing scope for this kind of analysis.

Specifically with respect to the fitness of the financial sector, reliance on regulation to foster stability should be complemented by

---

[13] For an important work advocating just such an approach, see Hayek's (1975) Nobel Prize lecture.

[14] See Beinhocker (2007).

[15] See Colander and Kupers (2014). For a more sceptical view of what is possible, see Kirman (2016).

[16] For a recent review of where this modelling now stands, see Bruno, Faggini and Parziale (2016).

self-discipline and market discipline.[17] The former would be encouraged by rolling back public safety nets,[18] re-establishing bankers' sense of fiduciary responsibility, changing compensation practices and making the threat of prison more compelling. The latter would be encouraged by improved auditing and accounting standards, by the re-establishment of 'relationship' banking to encourage trust building, and by getting rid of unnecessary complexity.

Second, we must recognise that complex, adaptive systems will inevitably break down in spite of efforts to increase their fitness. The lesson is that the official sector should be prepared. This has both ex ante and ex post implications. Prior to a crisis, steps should be taken to ensure the authorities – in particular central banks – have the instruments in hand needed to manage a crisis. Memoranda of Understanding between all involved parties, special bank insolvency regimes, and regular 'war games' would also be recommended. During a crisis, central banks must provide lender-of-last-resort functions, perhaps in both domestic and foreign (via swaps) currencies. Since crises can vary in significant ways, central banks should also have the legal capacity to respond flexibly.[19] While central banks should likely lead a crisis management team, Treasuries must also be involved if public money has to be spent.

Third, given the uncertainties associated with the behaviour of complex, adaptive systems, policy should focus on minimaxing rather than maximising. Otherwise put, the lesson is that the objective of policy should be to avoid truly bad outcomes. This implies a greater willingness of central banks to accept small downturns that redress imbalances in the economy. This would support the Schumpeterian notion of 'creative destruction'. Moreover, by redressing imbalances on a regular basis, much larger downturns, with potential social and even political side effects, might be avoided. Finally, a minimaxing strategy would imply that highly experimental policies should be

[17] White (2014).

[18] As noted below, central banks must continue to play a central role in the management of crises. However, what is also notable is how the scale and scope of safety net measures have altered and expanded over time. See White (2004).

[19] Some provisions of the Dodd-Frank Act in the USA are not helpful. Concerns can also be raised about the capacity of the US Congress to impede the implementation of the Federal Reserve's swap agreements with other central banks.

avoided until their potential side effects have been evaluated. This is, of course, standard practice in the pharmaceutical industry, if not yet in central banking.

A corollary of this lesson is that monetary policy should be conducted in a more symmetric way, leaning against economic upturns as vigorously as downturns. Historically, it appears that the size of the latter is closely related to the size of the former. Studies of complex, adaptive systems in other disciplines also indicate that new control instruments can sometimes play a useful role. This would indicate that the use of so-called 'macro prudential instruments', to complement monetary policy in leaning against expansionary forces deemed excessive, might well be useful. Note, however, that this is a different role than is currently envisaged for using macroprudential instruments to allow 'lower for longer' interest rates.

Fourth, the trigger for a crisis could be anything if the system as a whole is unstable. Moreover, the size of the trigger event need not bear any relation to the systemic outcome. The lesson is that policymakers should be focused less on identifying potential triggers than on identifying signs of potential instability. This implies that paying attention to macroeconomic 'imbalances' may pay bigger dividends than trying to assess financial instability through highly disaggregated 'risk maps' of the sort currently being encouraged by the G20 and the IMF. The latter are not only expensive to monitor, but potential rupture points in the financial fabric can change rapidly in real time. Perhaps more important, serious economic and financial crises can have their roots in imbalances outside the financial system, as attested to by Reinhart and Rogoff (2009), Koo (2003)[20] and many others.

Which particular macroeconomic imbalances merit attention? Traditional models, which treat domestic inflation as the only macroeconomic imbalance of interest to central banks, are surely wrong.[21] This is all the more the case as domestic inflation seems increasingly under the influence of global forces. Similarly, reversion to a Wicksellian model that focuses on the gap between the 'natural rate'

---

[20] Reinhart and Rogoff note how a weak economy can destroy credit ratings and increase non-performing loans. Thus, damage can run from the real side to the financial side as well as running the other way. Koo emphasised excessive corporate debt in Japan, the need to delever, and a decade or more of very weak investment.

[21] White (2005).

of interest (near-term expectations of profit) and the 'financial rate' of interest can also be highly misleading. Today, many economists suggest that the 'natural rate' has fallen sharply and therefore central banks should push down the financial rate as well. However, if expectations of profit have been reduced by other 'imbalances', created by easy monetary policies in the past, it is not self-evident that the answer is 'more of the same'.

If the economy is a complex, adaptive system, attention should be paid to any significant and sustained deviation of macroeconomic variables historical norms. While comforting explanations can sometimes be found, such deviations often indicate the rising probability of a crisis and/or the costs of a potential crisis. In this regard, the Bank for International Settlements has been a leader in identifying rising levels of credit and debt as harbingers of future problems. Closely related, it has also focused attention on gross capital inflows as indicators of future instability, as well as other financial sector imbalances. Evidently, real-side imbalances such as low saving rates prior to the crisis (in the USA) and high investment rates (in China) also deserve serious attention. As stressed by Turner (2016), developments in property markets should be monitored particularly closely given how often they have been at the root of subsequent problems.

Fifth, complex, adaptive systems are always changing. The lesson is that central banks must be careful not to fight the last war. For example, looking back on some of the post-war crises associated with large capital inflows, the sources and destinations of those flows commonly differed. The Latin American crisis of the 1980s involved banks lending to sovereigns. The South Asian crisis of the 1990s had banks lending to non-sovereigns. Today, recent capital flows have involved non-banks (largely asset management companies) buying non-sovereign debt. Looking back on these events, central banks generally failed to recognise that a habitual threat to financial stability (capital inflows) was re-emerging but in a slightly different form. Similarly, the expansion of 'shadow banking' and the development of new financial instruments prior to the crisis received remarkably little attention.

Viewing the economy as always changing might also throw new light on the 'rules versus discretion' debate. Haldane (2012) has suggested that increasingly complex financial systems need not be met with increasingly complex regulation. This suggests a similar question with respect to the conduct of monetary policy. On the one hand, it could also be argued that relatively simple rules for the conduct of monetary policy might provide the best framework within which to guide the evolution of the financial system. On the other hand, it could be argued that an evolving system requires an evolving policy response. This issue needs more attention, perhaps through the use of ACE models as noted above.

Sixth, in complex adaptive systems, the future is unknowable. The lesson is that near-term forecasting, on the basis of past data, is simple extrapolation and essentially useless. At the very least, central bankers (and the IMF and the OECD) should admit to the limitations of their knowledge, perhaps substituting alternative scenarios for forecasts. For the same reason, what economic agents face is not risk (where probability distributions are known) but radical uncertainty (where they are not known). This implies that the comfort given by risk management techniques may be largely illusory and that capital buffers (for unexpected losses) should be much larger than is currently demanded.[22] More generally, it suggests more prudent behaviour on the part of all economic agents, presumably including central banks as well.

Seventh, with many agents in a complex, adaptive economy, central banks should analyse the distributional implications of monetary policy more explicitly. One reason is that distributional effects might alter the transmission mechanism of monetary policy. For example, low interest rates favour debtors and disfavour creditors. If the former have a lower marginal propensity to consume than the latter, the expected expansionary effects of the policy might be muted. Moreover, if monetary policy does contribute to rising inequality (of either income or wealth), the undesirable social implications of this should be explicitly recognised. Central banks would then have the motivation to muster convincing arguments as to why their policies were still doing more good than harm. Finally, if central bank policies

---

[22] This suggestion has been made by Admati and Hellwig (2013). Indeed, there is something fundamentally odd about the risk weights underlying the Basel capital requirements. They seem to imply that regulators and bankers have some knowledge of the riskiness of each asset. However, this should guide provisioning for expected losses, not unexpected losses, which are assumed to come totally out of the blue. Perhaps this logic helps explain Admati and Hellwig's preference for a high level of capital relative to unweighted assets.

are thought to have distributional implications, this will attract political attention since distributional issues are archetypically political. Such issues are discussed further below.

21.4 Central Bank 'Independence' in a Complex, Adaptive Economy

Central bank 'independence' has been oversold, as have been the costs of that independence being lost. The history of central banking and, more generally, the evolutionary development of government attest to this. Developments around the ongoing crisis indicate a further diminution of that 'independence'. Finally, explicitly embracing the economy as a complex, adaptive system clearly implies the need for more domestic cooperation between different agencies of government, including central banks. The fundamental domestic question is how the longer-term policies needed for 'strong, sustainable and inclusive growth' can be kept free from political influences driven by near-term electoral prospects.

First, take a look back in history. Central bank 'independence' is in fact a very recent development in most advanced market economies.[23] After World War II most of the large central banks were almost totally dominated by their respective Treasuries. It took the inflationary experience of the 1970s, allied with a growing belief in 'efficient' and 'self-adjusting' markets, to foster the cult of central bank independence in the major economies.[24] Moreover, it should also be noted that many emerging market economies have never conformed to this ideal. While many of their central banks have formally adopted inflation-targeting regimes, their respective governments have often subjected this regime to the objective of controlling the exchange rate or pursuing other objectives. The influence of the Communist Party on the

---

[23] Germany and some other central European countries that suffered hyperinflation in the 1920s and immediately after World War II are notable exceptions.

[24] Simpson (2013) notes that this kind of process is consistent with the way in which government institutions have always evolved. As the needs for services change, or prevailing theories change about how best to do things (after a process of trial and error), government institutions will evolve in consequence. White (2013) traces out the almost continuous process of evolutionary change at central banks over the last fifty years.

activities of the People's Bank of China is a rather egregious example of this form of behaviour.

Closely related, the word 'independence' bears much closer scrutiny. In democratic countries, all government institutions need to be governed by three things: a mandate, a set of powers or instruments, and ways of ensuring accountability. Generally speaking, the mandate is provided by government and it is the government that tries to hold the central bank accountable. What this implies is that the term 'independence' really means the capacity to use the central bank's powers free from political influence. This implies a much narrower meaning of the word than is generally understood.[25]

Turning now to the influence of recent developments on central bank independence, there can be little doubt it has been further compromised. First, in the pursuit of quantitative easing, central banks have purchased many assets that could conceivably decline in price. Were the central bank's capital to be wiped out, it would surely pay a reputational price. Recapitalisation by governments, while not strictly necessary, would almost inevitably come with conditions attached. Second, many of the central bank's actions have had distributional implications. More narrowly, interventions in financial markets have altered prices, creating winners and losers.[26] Some financial institutions seeking liquidity support from central banks have received it and others have not. More broadly, debtors have gained and creditors have lost. It has also been alleged that the already rich (with financial assets) have benefited at the expense of the middle class. As noted above, all these distributional effects invite political oversight. Third, and perhaps most important, the failure of central banks' policies to resolve the ongoing crisis has undermined their credibility and led to calls for more direct government action. It is increasingly evident that economies do not 'self-adjust' back to a desirable equilibrium.

---

[25] Again, Europe is somewhat of an exception. Since the eurozone does not have a government, the European Central Bank has decided for itself what is meant by 'price stability'. Accountability has generally referred to ex ante accountability (explanation of policies) rather than ex post accountability (you're fired).

[26] For example, the European Central Bank's purchases of corporate bonds have had a big effect on interest rate differentials between companies. Equity purchases by the Bank of Japan have driven a wedge between the performance of the Nikkei and the Topix.

If embracing complexity means more integration between central banks and other agencies of governments, that process has already begun. In their pursuit of unconventional policies to stimulate aggregate demand, central banks have blurred the distinction between fiscal and monetary policy. Buying in longer-term government bonds and replacing them with the shortest possible government liabilities (bank reserves held at central banks) is essentially debt management, and imprudent debt management at that. Moreover, the use of macroprudential instruments implies using existing instruments of financial regulation for the purpose of stabilising the economy as a whole. This raises the issue of who is in charge? Unfortunately, under the pressure of events, these developments have occurred without adequate thought about the longer-run institutional implications.

Looking forward to more normal times, the pursuit of 'strong, sustainable and inclusive growth' immediately raises the issue of trade-offs between these objectives should they conflict.[27] Presumably only elected governments could make such value-laden decisions, albeit preferably in the context of a cross-agency committee.[28] At the same time, it remains important to agree upon institutional structures designed to minimise short-term political interference in areas that should be left to technical experts, central banks and regulatory agencies in particular. Similarly, those structures should specify mechanisms for cooperation and, where possible, a clear allocation of responsibilities and associated accountability. Accepting the notion of a complex, adaptive economy implies that the future of central banking will be less 'neat' than in the recent past. Nevertheless, if that is the reality, then central bankers and others must adapt to it.

References

Acemoglu, D. and J.A. Robinson (2013), *Why Nations Fail*, London: Profile Books.

Admati, A. and M. Hellwig (2013), *The Banker's New Clothes*, Princeton, NJ: Princeton University Press.

Ball, P. (2012), *Why Society Is a Complex Matter*, Berlin: Springer-Verlag.

---

[27] Sometimes they will not conflict. For example, more inclusive growth (say, encouraging women and older people to participate in the workforce) would encourage both stronger growth and more inclusive growth.

[28] This is a suggestion made in a recent Group of Thirty (2015) report.

Beinhocker, E.D. (2006), *The Origin of Wealth: The Radical Remaking of Economics and What It Means for Business and Society* New York, NY: Random House Business.

Borio, C., E. Kharroubi, C. Upper and F. Zampolli (2015), 'Labour Reallocation and Productivity Dynamics: Financial Causes, Real Consequences', *BIS Working Papers No. 534*, Basel, December.

Bruno, B., M. Faggini and A. Parziale (2016), 'Complexity Modelling in Economics: The State of the Art', *Economic Thoughts*, 5(2), pp. 29–43.

Buchanan, M. (2000), *Ubiquity*, New York, NY: Crown Publishers.

Buiter, W. (2009), 'The Unfortunate Uselessness of Most "State of the Art" Academic Monetary Economics' blogs.ft.com/maverecon.

Colander, D. and R. Kupers (2014), *Complexity and the Art of Public Policy: Solving Society's Problems from the Bottom Up*, Princeton, NJ: Princeton University Press.

Group of Thirty (2015), *Fundamentals of Central Banking: Lessons from the Crisis*, Washington, DC: Group of Thirty.

Haldane, A. (2012), 'The Dog and the Frisbee', in *The Changing Policy Landscape*, Symposium Sponsored by the Federal Reserve Bank of Kansas City, Jackson Hole, WY.

    (2015), 'On Microscopes and Telescopes', Speech given at the Lorentz Centre Workshop on Socio-Economic Complexity, Leiden, 27 March.

Hayek, F.A. (1975), 'The Pretence of Knowledge', in *Full Employment at Any Price*, The Institute of Economic Affairs, Occasional Paper No. 45, London.

Kahneman, D. (2013), *Thinking, Fast and Slow*, New York, NY: Farrar, Straus and Giroux.

Kindelberger, C.P. and R.J. Aliber (2005), *Manias, Panics and Crashes*, 5th edn, Basingstoke: Palgrave Macmillan.

Kirman, A. (2016), 'Complexity and Economic Policy: A Paradigm Shift or a Shift in Perspective? A Review Essay on David Colander and Ronald Kuper's Complexity and the Art of Public Policy', *Journal of Economic Literature*, 54(2), pp. 534–72.

Koo, R.C. (2003), *Balance Sheet Recession: Japan's Struggle with Unchartered Economics and Its Global Implications*, Singapore: John Wiley and Sons.

Kuhn, T.S. (1962), *The Structure of Scientific Revolutions*, Chicago, IL: University of Chicago press.

Mandelbrot, B.B. and R.L. Hudson (2004), *The Misbehaviour of Markets*, London: Profile Books.

Reinhart, C.M. and K.S. Rogoff (2009), *This Time is Different: Eight Centuries of Financial Folly*, Princeton, NJ: Princeton University Press.

Romer, P. (2016), 'The Trouble with Macroeconomics', Commons Memorial Lecture of the Omicron Epsilon Society. January 5.

Schularick, M. and A.M. Taylor (2009), 'Credit Booms Gone Bust: Monetary Policy, Leverage Cycles and Financial Crises 1980–2008', *NBER Working Paper Series No. 15512*, NBER, Cambridge, MA.

Simpson, D. (2013), *The Rediscovery of Classical Economics: Adaptation, Complexity and Growth*, Cheltenham: Edward Elgar.

Turner, A. (2016), *Between Debt and the Devil*, Princeton, NJ: Princeton University Press.

Waldrop, M.M. (1992), *Complexity: The Emerging Science at the Edge of Order and Chaos*, New York, NY: Simon and Schuster.

Wedel, J.R. (2009), *Shadow Elite*, New York, NY: Basic Books.

White, W.R. (2004), 'Are Changes in Financial Structure Expanding Safety Nets?' *BIS Working Papers No. 145*, Basel, January.

(2005), 'Is Price Stability Enough?' BIS Working Papers No. 250, Basel, March.

(2011), 'Why All Central banks Are Not the Same', in S. Gokarn (ed.), *Challenges to Central Banking in the Context of Financial Crisis*, Mumbai: Reserve Bank of India.

(2013), 'Is Monetary Policy a Science? The Interaction of Theory and Practice over the Last 50 Years', in M. Balling and E. Gnan (eds.), *50 Years of Money and Finance: Lessons and Challenges*, Vienna: Larcier (SUERF).

(2014), 'The Prudential Regulation of Financial Institutions: Why Regulatory Responses Might Not Prove Sufficient', Economics Department Working Paper No. 1108, OECD, Paris.

22 | *The Changing Fortunes of Central Banking*

CHARLES GOODHART

22.1 Introduction

This is an appropriate occasion for reflection on the changing patterns of central banking, primarily, but not only, in the UK, over the last fifty or sixty years, and 'with greater doubts' for trying to peer into the uncertain future of the next fifteen or so years. In my view, a helpful way of dividing this past into manageable and coherent segments is to use the classification that I developed in my earlier paper on the event of the Austrian Central Bank's 200th birthday (Goodhart, 2016) of periods of 'Consensus' about the role and functions of central banks, notably the Bank of England (BoE), and periods of 'Uncertainty and Disturbance'.

During the last sixty years, there have been two periods of 'Consensus': the 1950s to the early 1970s, the Bretton-Woods period; and then the early 1990s until 2008–9, the Great Moderation with Inflation Targetry. There have also been two periods of 'Uncertainty and Disturbance': the 1970s and 1980s; and now the struggles since 2008–9 to get our economies back on track and to prevent deflation. Each of these earlier periods lasted around twenty years, but I see no necessary reason for a constant periodicity, nor that we are doomed to a further ten to fifteen years of 'disturbance and uncertainty' now.

It is surely not just a coincidence that the periods of Consensus have been associated with relatively successful macroeconomic outcomes, whereas the periods of Uncertainty have been much less good. Data for the UK (and much the same would hold for the USA and the main European countries) are shown in Table 22.1.

What I shall try to do is take each historical period, one by one, outline its main characteristics from the viewpoint of a central banker, and then outline the reasons for the transition to a new regime. But in each case I shall also add some *obiter dicta*, some

Table 22.1. *UK annual average*

Period	Real growth % change	Inflation % change	Unemployment %
1945–71	2.6	4.4	1.7
1972–91	2.3	10.0	7.7
1992–2007	2.8	2.8	6.7
2008–15	0.9	2.9	7.1

personal reflections on what took place. The final forward-looking section will be, perforce, sketchier, since its main characteristics remain hidden in the mists of the future and are uncertain rather than probabilistic.

22.2 The Bretton Woods Consensus

22.2.1 Basic Characteristics

A. **External Conditions.** Under the Bretton Woods Consensus, exchange rates were pegged to the dollar but capable of adjustments. Such adjustments, however, involved severe reputational damage and were rare. The system was protected by comprehensive exchange controls, but these latter could be avoided, e.g. the dreaded 'leads and lags'.

B. **Role of Monetary Policy.** Interest rates were raised to protect the exchange rate and lowered to encourage investment. Macroeconomic stabilisation was supposedly achieved by (Keynesian) fiscal policy. There was no overt concern about monetary aggregates; but there was background concern about funding the debt and deficit, owing to a fear of a potential monetary inflationary surge.

C. **Monetary Control:** This was achieved by quantitative ceilings on bank lending and by continuous efforts to limit public sector deficits and refund maturing debt.

D. **Monetary Theory:** Multiplier theory was generally taught but transferred into liquidity (ratio) terms in the UK (Sayers, 1967 and Radcliffe, 1959). It was *not* accepted in the BoE where the

Credit Counterpart approach was adopted (Needham and Goodhart, 2018, forthcoming).

E. **Bank Supervision:** There were no capital ratios. Cash and liquidity ratios were applied, which were adjustable via Special Deposits. Some in Her Majesty's Treasury (HMT) and the BoE believed in ratio controls, but many did not. There was no on-site supervision.

F. **Central Bank within Government:** The BoE was strictly subservient to HMT. BoE played the role of agent to HMT (i.e. the Chancellor) and was the principal player in the foreign currency and gilts market, exchange control, and setting interest rates and ceilings. The main policy weapon of the BoE was specialised market knowledge rather than economic expertise.

22.2.2 What Broke the System?

Strains mounted in Bretton-Woods as the relative power and objectives of European countries rose relative to those of the USA. Such strains could be more easily exploited via growth of the euro–dollar wholesale money market, fostered by London (against occasional US attempts to halt it).

Within countries, the continuation of controls led to increasing distortions, e.g. from controlled banks to uncontrolled near-banks.[1] There was a growing belief that monetary aggregates and the banking system could be controlled better by market mechanisms such as interest rates, rather than by quantitative controls, ceilings and caps. The relative stability of econometric studies of demand for money studies both supported this view and provided a counter to Radcliffe.

22.2.3 Obiter Dicta

In these years I provided the main source of econometric expertise (such as it was!) within the BoE and this was used as supporting background to the Competition and Credit Control (Bank of England, 1971) reform, which removed both the quantitative restrictions on, and the constraints on competition among, the major UK

[1] As noted in the Fforde Christmas Eve note in 1970, see Capie (2010, pp. 486–8).

banks. In particular, the Demand for Money functions, which Goodhart and Crockett (1970) tested for broad money, were not only apparently stable but showed *no significant response* to the prior introduction or removal of bank lending ceilings (a finding that has never been challenged), whereas the interest elasticity was significant.

So why was the future (1972/73) not like the past, and why did M3 surge, relative to the then current levels of incomes, prices and interest rates after Competition and Credit Control? My own answer relates to the key role of *relative* interest rates. Prior to 1971, the London clearing banks (LCBs) interest rates, both on time deposits and loans, had for decades remained completely fixed by the cartel agreement. LCBs could not compete for deposits. Moreover, the scale of their holdings of public sector debt meant that any shift in the relativity of bank lending and deposit flows could be easily absorbed.

Post Competition and Credit Control, the LCB cartel was abolished, and they were encouraged to compete. They did so energetically, raising the rates offered, especially on Certificate of Deposits (CDs), relative to the charges made on loans. If the spread between loan rates and deposit rates vanishes to zero, as it did on occasions in 1972/73, access to liquidity for private sector borrowers becomes costless, so it is optimal for such borrowers to expand both their loans and their deposits until it drives the marginal utility of extra liquidity to zero, i.e. a huge amount. The key take-away is that the rate spread that the banks choose to set is a key determinant of the growth of the monetary aggregates.

Was this predictable at the time? Certainly not from UK historical data. Should we at the BoE have reacted quicker after the event? Perhaps, but 1972–4 was a confused and difficult period.

22.3 The Disturbed Decades: 1971–1991

22.3.1 Basic Characteristics

A. **External Conditions:** Bretton-Woods broke down and could not be repaired. Within Europe there were various attempts to maintain pegged rates, e.g. the Snake and then the Exchange Rate Mechanism (ERM). Exchange controls were increasingly abandoned. Capital flows increased, giving a greater risk of 'sudden stops'.

B. **Role of Monetary Policy:** This has to be seen against the background of conflict between Keynesian policies, with incomes policies to counter inflation, and monetarist policies, with control
over the monetary aggregates, to control inflation. In the UK,
despite genuflections towards Monetarist Targetry, Keynesian and
incomes policies were still the main drivers until 1979 but were
then widely assessed to have failed. With the arrival of the
Thatcher Conservative Government, HMT turned to Monetarist
Targetry, despite concern from the BoE that strict control of the
various monetary aggregates (Ms) was inconsistent with the structure of the UK's banking and financial systems. But inflation was
defeated, albeit painfully, and growth recovered after 1981/82,
despite patent failures to hit the monetary targets, *and* further
breakdowns of Demand for Money relationships. So Monetarist
Targetry was assessed by the end of the 1980s as also being a failure. Chancellor of the Exchequer, Lawson, moved back to an
exchange rate target.

C. **Monetary Controls:** After the blowout in 1972/73, there was a
reversion to direct controls (in a disguised form) via 'the corset'.
The removal of exchange controls made this unviable. Interest
rates had a devastating effect on the exchange rate and the manufacturing industry (1980–2); hence the 1981 Budget and subsequently 'over-funding'.

D. **Monetary Theory:** The application of the (academically taught)
multiplier theory to practical policy 'proposed by monetarists'
was resisted (successfully) by the BoE. There were sharply different growth rates of narrow money (M1) and broad money (M3)
credit. Which M was the right M? (See Niehans, 1981.)[2]

E. **Bank Supervision:** The Fringe Bank Crisis (see Reid, 2003), itself
related to the aftermath of Competition and Credit Control, and
the Mexico, Argentina and Brazil (MAB) crisis of 1980/81 led to

---

[2] Alan Walters, Mrs Thatcher's personal advisor, had brought in Niehans as an
independent expert to advise on which monetary aggregate was giving a better
indication of the overall thrust of monetary policy, since the various aggregates
were trending in different directions. Niehans advised in his paper that the
narrow aggregate (M1) should be preferred to the broad aggregate (M3). But
the latter had been the focus of Conservative Party policies since 1979, and to
admit that this had been mistaken would have been politically embarrassing.
So Niehans' paper was hushed up and put on one side.

the BoE establishing a banking supervisory department (Banking and Money Market Supervision [BAMMS]). This took the lead on banking supervision although occasional scandals blemished its reputation.

F. **Central Banks within Government:** This was the most difficult and disturbed period. In the 1970s, the clash between monetarist (lite)[3] and Keynesian (incomes) policies occurred within the BoE and HMT. Relationships between HMT and the BoE (Chancellor Healey and Governor Richardson), however, remained good. In the 1980s, failure to hit the M3 targets was blamed by Thatcher and Lawson on the BoE, and assessed as lack of zeal, even sabotage. Relationships with the Ministers in HMT were often strained.

22.3.2 What Brought Such Disturbances to an End?

When New Zealand introduced an inflation target at the end of the 1980s (I served for a time as adviser to the Reserve Bank [RBNZ] there), it soon became widely realised that this was equivalent to a monetary target after adjustment for all, foreseen and unforeseen, fluctuations in velocity. It was equally acceptable to Keynesians and monetarists, largely terminating the prior analytical disputes, and brought an end to the battles over which M should be the focus.

Meanwhile the collapse of the ERM in Europe reinforced the view that the most stable regimes were at the poles, either floating or fixed.

22.3.3 Obiter Dicta

Worldwide financial stability was more endangered by the Less Developed Country (LDC) crisis in 1981, when MAB all threatened to default, than by any other event prior to the Lehman failure in 2008. Yet the crisis was averted by a combination of permissive accounting (on a mark-to-market basis, most city-centre New York banks and several international European banks had become insolvent), forbearance and evergreening. The banks were pressurised to roll over their loans to MAB, who in turn used the money in large

---

[3] The Conservative Government at the time introduced policies that tended towards the monetarist position, but did not follow them in every respect. So their policies could be described as monetarist-lite.

part to maintain interest payments on schedule. So successful was this joint (central bank-led) operation, that 1981 does not usually appear on lists of bank crises.

This event raises several questions. First, the successful outcome was achieved by methods which are now generally condemned, at least by most academics, as wrong in principle and generally counter-productive. Second, studies of financial stability focus on those events where the authorities have *failed* to defuse an adverse shock, and ignore all those cases where the authorities *succeeded* in doing so. Does this asymmetry impact a bias – perhaps a severe bias – to our understanding of what methods work best in this field of analysis?

22.4 The Great Moderation

22.4.1 Basic Characteristics

A. **External Conditions:** Capital flow increased hugely, and the Washington Consensus (see Williamson, 2004) condemned any form of exchange controls. In this context the only stable regimes were to float, though in some cases with some degree of 'management' or rigidly fixed (currency board, dollarisation, etc.). However, the euro was introduced without the necessary preconditions for success.

B. **Role of Monetary Policy:** Inflation Targetry to achieve price stability, defined as an inflation target of (about) 2 per cent, plus or minus a margin, ruled supreme. Fiscal policy focused on non-macroeconomic issues (e.g. supply-side, structural, distributional). What is, perhaps, surprising was how successful it was before 2007/8 with non-inflationary continuous expansion (NICE). With hindsight, some of that success was due to fundamentals, e.g. the entry of China and Eastern Europe into the global trading system, and not just to the wisdom of central banks.

C. **Monetary Control:** Concerns about the growth of the monetary aggregates disappeared with remarkable rapidity. The Ms ceased to be noted or discussed. The monetary transmission mechanism was almost universally analysed as running directly from the official set short-term rate to expenditure decisions. Whereas financial intermediation was now treated as a veil (i.e. ignored), expectations (e.g. of future rates and future inflation) took centre stage.

D. **Monetary Theory:** This was relegated to a backwater. Interest rates were set by a (Taylor) reaction function and then directly affected expenditures (the three equation model). Why bother with monetary theory?

E. **Bank Supervision:** The key was requiring banks to hold enough capital, given the moral hazard of deposit insurance. Liquidity needs could, it was thought, be met via markets (asset liquidity gave way to funding liquidity). But belief in efficient markets and rational behaviour led the authorities to accept much lower ratios and 'lighter-touch' supervision than subsequently turned out to be needed. The Basel approach tried to imitate best market practice, thereby following the market and any imperfections going along with it.

F. **Central Bank within Government:** Central banks generally gained operational independence to set short rates in pursuit of the inflation target. Combined with their success in maintaining the NICE Great Moderation, these were the glory years for central bank governors.

22.4.2 *What Brought It to an End?*

The short answer is the failure of Lehman Bros. The longer answer is that during the 2000s a standard property market (residential and commercial) boom interacted with massive bank credit expansion and over-leveraging. This was focused on several countries (e.g. USA, UK, Spain and Ireland) but spread to banks in a wider range of countries via international financial markets. This bubble was largely financed by short-term wholesale funding which was uninsured, informed[4] and flighty (see the papers by Schularick and Taylor, 2012; Jordá, Schularick and Taylor, 2016), which made the collapse much more intense. The momentum of the prior boom was enhanced by the optimism engendered by the 'great moderation' that 'this time, it's different' (Reinhart and Rogoff, 2011); and, of course, it fitted the Minsky thesis that stability breeds instability. And a belief, as

---

[4] These investors knew when banks were getting into trouble, and were thus more likely to withdraw their deposits than the bulk of uninformed retail depositors.

supported by Greenspan, in rational, efficient markets dominated fears about 'irrational exuberance'.

22.4.3 Obiter Dicta

To my mind, some of the narratives that have become widely accepted have been less than helpful. Partly because Lehman Bros. was an investment bank, and US investment banks were in the eye of the storm, much of the narrative has focused on the dangers posed to traditional banking functions by investment banking and by the utilisation of 'exotic' derivative contracts (e.g. Collateralized Debt Obligation [CDO] squared). This ignored the fact that any bank (whether retail, universal or investment) that became both over-levered and swept up too far into financing real estate (whether directly or via derivatives) got into trouble.

   While the emphasis on achieving higher capital ratios was, of course, fully justified, the handling of the transition was badly botched in Europe, allowing bank chief executives to aim to protect the return on equity by delevering on route to higher ratios. Not until recently, with the application of Net Stable Funding Ratios (NSFRs), has the danger of financing illiquid mortgages with short-term wholesale money been addressed. Finally, the whole question about reforming the structure of housing finance, to avoid a recurrence of a future property market and banking boom and bust, has not been tackled, perhaps because it remains too politically sensitive.

22.5 The Great Financial Crisis: 2008 Onwards

22.5.1 Basic Characteristics

A. **External Conditions:** Few countries could protect themselves from capital flows and international pressures without exchange controls (Rey, 2013). The Washington consensus evaporated. The euro struggled from one crisis to another. Overall, it has been a non-system, but there are few ideas of how, or whether, to achieve anything better.
B. **Role of Monetary Policy:** The Inflation Targetry model remains in place, now reinforced by Unconventional Monetary Policies, such as Quantitative Easing, and forward guidance. But monetary policy

now has to achieve a second objective, i.e. financial stability. A new (set of) instruments, i.e. macroprudential measures, are proposed, but it is far from clear whether these can do the job.

C. **Monetary Control:** It used to be thought that, since a central bank can create money, it must be able to bring about higher inflation without any difficulties. Yet central banks have struggled to raise inflation rates back to target. Those who think only of direct links between interest rates and expenditures blame this on the Zero Lower Bound (ZLB) and consider ways of bypassing the ZLB. Others worry about the weaknesses in the banking system.

D. **Monetary Theory:** The role of banks and the possibility of (bank) default, both of which were not considered in the previous standard Dynamic Stochastic General Equilibrium (DSGE) models, have been shown to matter a lot. Current theory is adjusting slowly to reality, as for example in the European Central Bank's Macroprudential Research Network and often grudgingly.

E. **Bank Supervision:** This is where the action has been. Required capital ratios have been ratcheted upwards; liquidity requirements have been reintroduced for the first time since the 1970s, in the guise of Liquidity Coverage Ratios (LCRs) and NSFRs. Stress testing has become a new mechanism, and the resolution method has shifted from bail-out to bail-in, though the efficacy of the latter has yet to be fully tested. Much has been done, though there is inevitable disagreement as to whether too much, too little (or even too much in some areas and too little in others).

F. **Central Bank within Government:** This has now become less clear-cut. The unconventional measures used by central banks (Quantitative and Qualitative Easing, Credit Easing, Various Funding Schemes, etc.) have led them both into somewhat unfamiliar markets and raised the risk of potential losses. Moreover, many of the quantitative macroprudential measures, e.g. loan to value or loan to income ratios for housing, could in principle be largely mimicked by price (tax and subsidy) alternative measures. So the question of where to draw the proper boundary between the domains of fiscal and monetary policies has become more pressing, though more so in the USA than in Europe. Quite why Americans are much more concerned about this issue than Europeans is an interesting, but unexplored, issue.

22.5.2 *What Will Bring It to an End?*

Obviously we do not know, since it has not ended yet. A necessary, but perhaps not sufficient, condition is probably a stronger, generalised recovery in Europe. That would seem to depend on overcoming the travails of the single euro currency system and restoring the European banking system to greater health. Generalised fears about a secular stagnation are a core issue. If the productivity declines could be reversed, if growth in advanced economies could be re-established and the growth slowdown in emerging economies could be moderated (a new equilibrium could be found), then the current period of disturbance is likely to end.

Meanwhile political and social willingness to make the current macroeconomic structure work is under increasing strain, which implies that time alone may not ease current difficulties.

22.5.3 *Obiter Dicta*

If one's mindset has the transmission mechanism of monetary policy as running primarily and directly from official short-term interest rates to expenditures, as in most DSGE models, then the analysis is clear. Equilibrium real rates have fallen so far that the ZLB is proving a serious barrier.

If, however, one has absorbed even some small portion of the monetarist analysis of the 1960s and 1970s, one, like me, is also led to ask how the massive expansion of the monetary base (a huge blowout) failed to lead to an equivalent surge in commercial bank assets and liabilities, to an accompanying fast growth in broad money and then to a recovery in nominal incomes.

The bank money multiplier failed. Was this because banks were in a liquidity trap, or constrained by capital insufficiency, or both together? Even if the private sector demand for loans was sluggish, banks could have expanded by buying existing longer-term assets. Against such a more monetarist background, a number of questions arise:

a. If part of the problem is weak bank profitability, is the current emphasis, in the UK on encouraging banking competition misguided? In the 1930s the financial collapse was attributed to excessive competition and the proposed remedy was to encourage cartels. Are we correct to reverse the supposed lessons from history?

b. Banks undertake maturity mismatch. Quantitative Easing and forward guidance have removed the upwards slope to the yield curve, further damaging bank profitability. Quantitative Easing shortens the average duration of overall public sector debt. If rates are at an all-time low, should not the desired direction of travel be the reverse, to lock in historically low rates for as long as possible? The first experiment with Quantitative Easing (QE1) was a huge success, since it lowered risk premia, but have subsequent Quantitative Easings been increasingly counter-productive?

c. One reason that the money multiplier was supposed to work was that reserve deposits at the central banks had a lower return (zero) than earning assets. Now that interest is paid on such reserve deposits, have we built in a permanent liquidity trap into our banking structure? Should, or could, central banks sharply differentiate the rate payable on marginal reserve deposits from that paid on the average level of such deposits?

d. The need for higher bank equity, post 2008, is undeniable. But was the transition to higher ratios managed in the least damaging manner? Given the poor prospects for bank profitability, the least damaging method of raising bank equity would have been for enforced injections of public sector funds (as in Troubled Asset Relief Program [TARP]), but, after 2008, this was ruled out on political grounds. What else could have been done?

e. The shortage of bank capital has been greatly exacerbated by the massive fines for bad behaviour. From a macroeconomic viewpoint, this has been a disastrous own-goal. Bad behaviour does need to be punished, but the relevant punishment needs to fall on responsible individuals, *not* on the institution. An analogy might be that if some soldiers (or police) misbehave, the penalty should not be to strip the relevant battalions (police stations) of their armour (equipment) but to penalise the soldiers and their non-commissioned officers and officers. It would be better to build in an assumption that the chain of command *should* organise the structure so they can control their subordinates' actions; hence illegal action by such subordinates implies culpable failure by their seniors, even if there was no intention to allow it (*mens rea*).

f. Have the central banks been so focused on the direct transmission route from interest rates to expenditures that they have overlooked the effects of their various actions on the route via financial intermediaries. Once upon a time central bank governors were mostly bankers by profession; then they became economists. Perhaps what we need is a mixture of both?

22.6 Whither Now?

Almost by definition we do not know when the next period of consensus for central bank activity will come, or what its basic characteristics will be. But I do have a brief 'wish-list' about what differing characteristics I would like to see in such a braver new world. These are as follows:

1. Stop anthropomorphising banks. Strategy is set, and decisions are taken, by individuals (mainly senior bank managers, especially the chief executive), not by an institution. Bank X is incapable of action; it is Bank X's management that sets the pace. The incentive structure of people is largely, though not wholly, influenced by their remuneration package. Besides the focus on capital and liquidity ratios, the authorities should intervene much more aggressively in trying to prevent the remuneration structure from having adverse social externalities.

2. Reform housing finance. The typical financial boom and bust cycle has involved the interaction of a property price cycle with a bank lending cycle. The worst mix which we had was the finance of long-term mortgages, with a small equity buffer, on the basis of short-term, wholesale, uninsured, runnable bank funding. What is needed, since property finance is, by nature, long term, is some combination of a much larger equity buffer with finance provided by much longer-term funding, e.g. covered bonds.

3. Remove fiscal advantages for debt finance. As a generality, particularly given the present debt overhang, there is a need to shift the balance of advantage more towards equity, away from debt finance.

4. Central bankers/central bank economists need to combine macroeconomics and finance/financial expertise, and the recruitment needs of central banks require university curricula that combine the two. We should not continue with a situation where central bank policies are dominated by macroeconomists who are ignorant about the financial sector or financial transmission mechanisms.

Best wishes for the next sixty years!

References

Bank of England (1971), *Competition and Credit Control*, Green Paper, May.

Capie, F. (2010), *The Bank of England: 1950s to 1979*, Cambridge, UK: Cambridge University Press.

Goodhart, C.A.E. (2016), 'Whither Central Banking?'. Paper presented at the Conference in Honour of the 200th Anniversary of the Austrian Central Bank (Oesterreichische Nationalbank), to be published in the Proceedings of that Conference in 2017.

Goodhart, C.A.E. and A.D. Crockett (1970), 'The Importance of Money', *Bank of England Quarterly Bulletin*, 10(2), pp. 159–98, June.

Jordá, O., M. Schularick and A.M. Taylor (2016), 'The Great Mortgaging: Housing Finance, Crises and Business Cycles', *Economic Policy*, 85, January, pp. 107–40.

Needham, D.J. and C.A.E. Goodhart (2018), 'Historical Reasons for the Focus on Broad Monetary Aggregates in Post-WWII', forthcoming in *Financial History Review*.

Niehans, J. (1981), 'The Appreciation of Sterling: Causes, Effects, Policies', Money Study Group Discussion Paper, also see Center for Research in Government, Policy and Business, vol. 11, Graduate School of Management, Rochester, NY: Center Symposia Series.

Radcliffe Report (1959), *Committee on the Working of the Monetary System: Report*, London: HMSO.

Reid, M. (2003), *The Secondary Banking Crisis, 1973–75: Its Causes and Course*, 2nd new edition, London: Hindsight Books Limited.

Reinhart, C.M. and K.S. Rogoff (2011), *This Time Is Different: Eight Centuries of Financial Folly*, Princeton, NJ: Princeton University Press.

Rey, H. (2013), 'Dilemma not Trilemma: The Global Financial Cycle and Monetary Policy Independence'. Presented at the Jackson Hole Symposium, Federal Reserve Bank of Kansas City, www.kansascityfed.org/publicat/sympos/2013/2013rey.pdf.

Sayers, R.S. (1967), *Modern Banking*, 7th edition, Oxford, UK: Clarendon Press.

Schularick, M. and A.M. Taylor (2012), 'Credit Booms Gone Bust: Monetary Policy, Leverage Cycles, and Financial Crises, 1870–2008', *American Economic Review*, 102(2), pp. 1029–1061.

Williamson, J. (2004), 'The Washington Consensus as Policy Prescription for Development', Institute for International Economics, https://piie.com/publications/papers/williamson0204.pdf.

Index